Professional Reviews

'Kathy Fray really gets it. Her parenting philosophy is holistic, centred and well-grounded, and her views on nutrition and wellbeing are informative and inspired. I personally believe the motherhood experience makes everything else in life pale into insignificance, but we need mentoring and tools to be the best parents we can be, so am delighted to recommend **Oh Grow Up** to any parent of young children and indeed, to anyone who wants to live a more healthy life.'

Allison Roe MBE, world record marathoner

I finally got to read your book... WOW it is great and touches on so many areas I have been working on and has all the same philosophies I have lived with for many years!! Such a great easy, practical, humorous read that is full of learning and many reminders that you can do a better job in so many areas with a shift of mind set and behaviours.

Barbara Kendall, MBE, Olympic & World Champion WindSurfer

'I have over the years devoured many 'parenting books' – in fact my husband even gave me one last Mothers Day ... is that a man's idea of the perfect gift? But just as we encourage our children to become life-long learners, the same principles apply to parenting – and there are always new ideas and approaches that can help prepare you to face the challenges of raising children.

'This book is like a 'Bible' not to be ingested in one sitting but something to refer to many, many times as you share the different milestones with your children. It is comprehensive, covering a multitude of topics and undoubtedly a great resource to call upon. This is a modern up-to-date parenting manual that addresses many of today's issues.'

Dame Susan Devoy, DNZM CBE, *World Champion Squash Player*

'I have three energetic boys yet confess to having never read a parenting book before. Perhaps I perceived they were, as Kathy puts it, 'patronising, pious, mothercraft books, with condescending definitions of the perfect parent.' Well then, this no-nonsense guide is not how parenting books are supposed to be! It has got, as Kathy says, 'so much incredible and fascinating stuff to tell you!' that it's difficult to put it down. You can randomly flick to a page and immediately be drawn in. I wish I had read it eight years ago when we were starting our family.

Oh Grow Up is pacey, easy to read, and incredibly informative. It's as up-front, humourous and hard hitting as Muhammad Ali and punches above its weight with its non-politically correct stance on many parenting issues. And the comprehensive nutrition and health 'power to the people' sections (which can be treated as a reference tool for dealing with health issues) are compulsory reading.

So, please please please read it. Same goes for the entire Western World; someone needs to deliver a copy (or two) to Oprah!'

Rob Hamill, *Trans-Atlantic Rowing Champion*
& author of *The Naked Rower*

Not only does Fray give parenting tips that really work, but she also includes discussions about physical development, nutrition, diseases, drugs and remedies and many other topics. The chapter on personality types is a great help in tailoring your parenting style to your child's character.

Heidi Hendrikse, *Daily Post*

This is a comprehensive book with topics ranging from age-stage overviews and nutrition through to the A-Z of diseases and drugs together with their natural alternatives. It is a reference book to dip in and out of as you see fit; otherwise, you could be in serious danger of neglecting your child, as it's easy to get caught up in the next interesting chapter!

Thanks to this broad base of information there is something for everyone, from first-time parents to, as Fray rather eloquently puts it, "the gnarled, well-honed, old-hand guru grandparent".

Fray is opinionated and she makes no apologies for this. In her author's note she admits that there may be parts of the book which are "a tad too out there or new to your thinking" ... Her essential philosophy is one of holistic health and this comes across strongly in her guide. She talks about parenting the whole child - physically, emotionally and spiritually ... use it to understand and enjoy your children.

Catherine Campbell, *Nelson Mail*

Personally, I devoured the parts about ages and stages. I agreed wholeheartedly with the chapter on being environmentally aware and responsible ... Read this if you like Diane Levy [or] Nigel Latta.

Her Magazine

Employing her usual approach of insights from a parent who has done the hard yards, as opposed to those from a parenting expert, Kathy

Fray brings us excellent material outlining the physical, mental, social and emotional developmental stages of every age of childhood. Her advice is clear … and is a welcome input to those of us who are confused about the plethora of advice available. As Kathy herself describes it, **Oh Grow Up** is about 'parenting with spirit: strength, guts, soul'.

Kidspot

    As I see it there are 2 parenting styles, the salmons and the apples. The salmon-like parent chooses to swim upstream ignoring the flow of the majority. Making the tough choices, gasping for air and really LIVING life. Salmons know the direction they are going in and they set themselves determinedly (if that is a word!) to achieve their course. Apple parents are like an apple-bobbing barrel. They float around next to everyone else and don't try too hard to experience the highs and lows of parenting. Everything is average and as soon as a new idea plops in the barrel they all splosh about a bit then go back to what they were doing before. Apple parenting is easier probably, not as many hard decisions to make just a lot of doing what everyone else is doing. Apples don't have to make decisions for their children they just do what everyone else is doing. I think Kathy Fray would be a salmon in this analogy. Her book is very comprehensive. It's not just about parenting styles and getting your offspring to turn into healthy, contributing adults, it's about everything. It's a bit like having a readily accessible experienced (and opinionated) parent who has a large dose of nutritional and health background and a generous swig of hippy (and I mean this as a compliment) thrown in for good measure … I really like that she treats a child as body (lots of health, food, alternative medicines), soul (parenting with strength and love, building relationships) and spirit (values/morals, the fourth dimension, eternal). Many great parenting books are pretty much all soul, which is fine and necessary but we are people with a physical body and, most important to me, a spirit … Kathy's writing style is easy to follow and pretty relaxed, be prepared for a few expletives. The book covers toddlers to teens but the food and medical stuff is relevant to anyone ... She's not a PC 'everything you choose is okay' type, which I love. I think as parents we all need to be more salmon and less apple in order to help our children grow up to become strong, loving and whole adults who will be healthy in body, soul and spirit.

Kiwi Mummy Blogs

Her introduction cuts to the chase clearly outlining her intent and dispelling with the myth of parental perfection. Truthfully and succinctly Fray describes her latest book as 'eclectic, boundless and liberated; it's eccentric, unconventional, alternative and passionate; and once again has an undercurrent of spiritual awe for parenthood and life.' The honesty of her delivery style gives a balanced perspective that culminates in a refreshingly informative and grounding presentation. This is not a clinical prescription for those afflicted with offspring; moreover, it reads as a relaxed chat with an experienced traveller ... one with an open file of well-schooled contacts. Fray's wise work is supported throughout with quotes and avenues for further reading. This effectively positions **Oh Grow Up** as a key resource, one with depth and scope for guidance from both within and beyond its covers.

Fray has developed her gentle, funny and non-judgemental book in a way that is both thought provoking and relevant to all people spending time with children. By first covering general developmental steps the reader can familiarise with the style of her vehicle in preparation for the interesting journey ahead through sections discussing the care and nurturance of the mind body and soul.

Each chapter combines the perfect measures of humour, fact and experience to maintain the high energy nature of this book. There is something for everyone in this enlightened decoding of those parenting myths, whether you take what you need and pop back for the rest later, or read and re-read. This is a very practical book that will resonate.

Angela Patterson, *Soul Destiny Foundation*

oh grow up
toddlers to preteens
DECODED

Kathy Fray

Copyright © 2017 Kathy Fray

Kathy Fray asserts her moral right to be identified as the author of this work.

All rights reserved. No part of this publication may be produced or transmitted in any form or by any means, electronic or mechanical, including photocopying, recording or information storage and retrieval systems, without permission in writing from the copyright holder.

Published by MotherWise
Website: www.MothersWise.com

ISBN 978-0-473-66425-1 (Paperback)
ISBN 978-0-473-66426-8 (EPUB)

Contents

AUTHOR'S NOTE xv
FOREWORD xxii
INTRODUCTION xxiv

SECTION ONE AGE-STAGE OVERVIEWS 1

CHAPTER ONE 2
THE 'TODDLING' TOTS — ONE-AND TWO-YEAR-OLDS OVERVIEW

PHYSICAL DEVELOPMENT 3
COUGHS, COLDS AND GERMS 5
INTELLECTUAL DEVELOPMENT 6
SOCIAL–EMOTIONAL DEVELOPMENT 9

CHAPTER TWO 17
THE 'PLAYFUL' PRESCHOOLER — THREE- AND FOUR-YEAR-OLDS OVERVIEW

PHYSICAL DEVELOPMENT 18
INTELLECTUAL DEVELOPMENT 20
SOCIAL–EMOTIONAL DEVELOPMENT 28

CHAPTER THREE 37
THE 'EDUCATED' NEW ENTRANT — FIVE- AND SIX-YEAR-OLDS OVERVIEW

PHYSICAL DEVELOPMENT 38
INTELLECTUAL DEVELOPMENT 39
SOCIAL–EMOTIONAL DEVELOPMENT 44

CHAPTER FOUR 51
THE 'WANNABE TALENTEDS' — SEVEN- TO NINE-YEAR-OLDS OVERVIEW

PHYSICAL DEVELOPMENT 52
INTELLECTUAL DEVELOPMENT 54
SOCIAL–EMOTIONAL DEVELOPMENT 59
MORAL DEVELOPMENT 63

CHAPTER FIVE ... 67
THE PUBESCENT PRETEEN — 10- TO 12-YEAR-OLDS OVERVIEW

- PHYSICAL DEVELOPMENT ... 68
- INTELLECTUAL DEVELOPMENT ... 71
- SOCIAL–EMOTIONAL DEVELOPMENT ... 73
- MORAL DEVELOPMENT ... 77
- LOOKING TO THE FUTURE — IDENTITY VS ROLE ... 81

SECTION TWO CHILDREN'S BODIES ... 85

INTRODUCTION ... 86
LIVING IN A TOXIC WORLD

- OVERFED YET UNDERNOURISHED ... 87
- ORGANIC FOOD ... 92
- HOLISTIC HEALTH ... 95

CHAPTER SIX ... 98
'WHOLISTIC' NUTRITION FOR PHYSIOLOGICAL WELLNESS

- NUTRITION IQ ... 98
- DUMP THE JUNK — DAILY DIET STRATEGY FOR YOUR FAMILY ... 113
- A–Z OF EXTRAORDINARY FOODS ... 121
- 'FEED ME RIGHT' FOOD ADDITIVES TO AVOID ... 136

CHAPTER SEVEN ... 141
NATURAL HEALTH — REMEDIES AND THERAPIES FOR WELLNESS AND HEALTH

- TRENDY OLD NATURAL HEALING REMEDIES ... 145
- TRENDY OLD NATURAL DEPRESSION REMEDIES ... 152
- PSYCHOSOCIAL TREATMENTS ... 158
- A–Z OF NATURAL HEALING THERAPIES ... 160

CHAPTER EIGHT ... 184
DISEASES, DRUGS AND NATURAL ALTERNATIVES — THE GOOD, THE BAD AND THE UGLY

- A PILL FOR EVERY ILL, AND A BILL FOR EVERY PILL ... 185
- A–Z OF DISEASES, CONDITIONS, DRUGS AND NATURAL ALTERNATIVES ... 193

SECTION THREE CHILDREN'S MINDS 259

INTRODUCTION 260
THE MIND'S HARDWARE AND SOFTWARE
- THE MIND'S HARDWARE: THE BRAIN 261
- THE MIND'S SOFTWARE: PERSONALITY AND INTELLIGENCE 270

CHAPTER NINE 281
PERSONALITIES! PERSONALITIES! EACH SO MAGICAL AND MYSTICAL!
- PERSONALITY OVERVIEW 283
- PERSONALITY TYPING — THE BIG FOUR 289
- PERSONALITY TYPING — THE SIXTEEN 295
- NEURO-LINGUISTIC PROGRAMMING 298
- LOVE LANGUAGES 300
- BIRTH ORDER 302
- SCHOLASTIC EDUCATION STYLES 304
- DIVINE DESTINIES (ASTROLOGY & NUMEROLOGY) 314

CHAPTER TEN 351
THE FOUR NEW IQS
- ENVIRONMENTAL IQ 352
- COSMOPOLITAN IQ 359
- OLD AGE-NEW AGE IQ 363
- STREETWISE IQ 367

SECTION FOUR CHILDREN'S SPIRITS 371

INTRODUCTION 372
TEACHING SOUL

CHAPTER ELEVEN 375
PARENTING WITH SOUL
- PARENTS OF THE VOID 376
- OH GOD . . . WHAT THE HELL DO WE TELL THEM?! 380

CHAPTER TWELVE 388
PARENTING'S 21 MAGICAL SECRETS

CHAPTER THIRTEEN 418
PARENTING'S 21 UNIVERSAL PRINCIPLES

    CONCLUSION 455
    WITH GRATEFUL THANKS 458
    BIBLIOGRAPHY... 465
    ALSO BY KATHY FRAY:... 478

Dedicated to my husband who married my spirit.
Dedicated to my kids who nourish my soul.

Author's note

Perfect parents are a pain in the arse. Perfect parents are annoying and make the rest of us feel bad . . . [parenting should be] about how to be a 'good enough' parent, because good enough really is good enough. Any better than that and you start getting irritating.

Nigel Latta, *Before Your Teenagers Drive You Crazy, Read This!*

On library and bookshop shelves, there exists a multitude of honourable parenting books, containing numerous researched theories, and copious amounts of virtuous advice. On internet websites and profuse Google searches, there exists a multiplicity of guides, containing abundant proven philosophies, and many options of worthy parental recommendations.

And this is another one.

Oh shit, no! Let's start again . . .

On groaning library shelves, vibrant bookshop shelves, and too bloody many online parenting websites, there exists a multitude of goody-goody parenting information, containing numerous sanctimonious theories, and copious amounts of holier-than-thou advice ... nearly always stating their theories are proven. And let's face it, we all have to ask just how their theories are proven ... quite how did they get some University ethics committee to approve, and parents to volunteer their children as

Author's note

guinea-pigs: "Would you like to participate in this double-blind trial to see if this parenting theory positively or negatively affects your child?" *Yeah, nah!*

So folks, this book is categorically not another one of those manuscripts. Thank cripes. Just like Parents Inc founder Ian Grant says "I'm just one beggar telling other beggars where the bread is".

As brand new parents most of us had the highest of expectations at first — we dreamed we'd be fantastic parents — the best parents we could possibly be! Then, not long into the journey, we started to discover our own limitations and imperfections. And between impossible expectations and financial stresses, we became exhausted. A few weeks or months or years down the track, we may have found ourselves internally thinking within those dark musty caverns of guilt, that we are oftentimes behaving like pretty average parents, even though we were trying our darndest to get it right. Then again, sometimes we're not trying our darndest at all, 'cause we're just plain over it. We've bought rubbish takeaways for dinner for the second night in a row; there's a mountain of washing with our name on it; there's a message on the voicemail we don't want to know about; we've got to leave early the next morning for an irritating meeting; the cat's spewed another gross fur ball on the carpet; and we've just yelled at our kids when they were hardly doing much wrong.

If there's one thing my husband Mark and I have discovered for sure, we definitely ain't the perfect parents, and are highly unlikely to ever be. We're simply nice, kind, caring and emotionally insecure people, who are working frickin' hard at trying to raise nice, kind, caring and emotionally secure kids. We regularly stuff it up, and occasionally really fuck it up. But we've learnt that's actually okay, 'cause most of the time we're either bloody great parents or good-enough parents, and that's all any of us should ever really expect of ourselves!

At about this point, you're likely starting to wonder who the heck is Kathy Fray anyway?? Why should I read her book? Why would she know what she's talking about? Good bloody question. (Well firstly, yes I do swear, but you will be relieved – or disappointed – to find there isn't really much swearing in the rest of this book – it's pretty tame in that way.) I describe myself as a wife, mother, midwife, author, founder of BabyOK Products, director of SOMCANZ conference on integrative maternity healthcare, lover of hatha yoga, and general work-in-progress.

Anyho', for those who don't know me, my first claim to fame was a book titled *"OH BABY…Birth, Babies & Motherhood Uncensored"*. I am a kiwi (New Zealander) and OH BABY has been our country's No.1 best-selling guide to childbirth and infants since 2005. For those who don't know, NZ has what is globally regarded as the best maternity care health system on the planet, with some of the very best rates of natural labor (and subsequent normal births) in the world (and consequentially low rates of fetal and maternal morbidity and mortality). So although OH BABY is a universal read, for sure, it also could be a challenging read for mums-to-be in some countries, such as USA, Brazil, France, South Africa etc, where the rates of childbirth medical intervention are so insanely high, and so normalised. It's hard to keep a normal thing normal, when the cultural environment is to treat normal as abnormal. We have a saying in NZ "Pizzas are delivered, strong women give birth". So for those moms-to-be who yearn to give birth spontaneously, devoid of the cascade of interventions, then do, do, do buy my book. It's honestly the best guide I know (bias opinion, obviously).

After the release of my first book OH BABY I received many ego-boosting emails from wonderful readers referring to me as their parenting 'guru' asking for a sequel. Now, don't get me wrong, like anyone I love having my pride stroked, but I also ain't comfortable with being held up as parenting perfection personified. I'm just like everyone else, probably in more ways than you can imagine. Let me tell you, when other parents had our young kids over (they're young adults now), and later reported back, "They were great, easy to have around, friendly, happy and polite, no problem at all" — well, that's the time I hear KA-CHING! Because I know all that enormous, obstinate and relentless parenting effort on our part, day in and day out — exhausting, arduous, gruelling — is finally paying the dividends: our kids are demonstrating glimmers of mastering self-sufficient independence, and becoming appreciative, passionate, truthful and loving human beings. *Woo hoo!!*

However, I'm not like everyone else because of my inexplicable passion that has forced me to spend great chunks of the past years gone by researching to exhaustion the plethora of parenting philosophies, to attempt to refine them into plausible print, culminating in this book, which — as my literary agent described it — releasing "basic problems from the shackles of ignorance". And what I can tell you, is we have actually managed to turn out brilliantly capable, independent and achieving teenage young adults – who have tremendous innate empathy, and intuitive instinct, and inbuilt self-motivation, and unquestionably confident self-esteem, and brilliant moral compasses. Of all of that, there is no doubt. And I put it down to one thing: TRIADIC PARENTING.

We have focused *equally* on parenting their physiological bodies with good nutrition, and their intellectual minds with good education, and their spiritual essences with mindful soul. And today, in my observation, it is that third aspect that seems, so often, to have gone by the wayside. On-trend parents are all about organic food and best grades – but failing to talk with their kids about *who they are*, and *what they stand for.* Or the few that actively do, are doing it from an extremist fundamentalist perspective, which can be out of whack with the child's own life-force (and often out of whack with society's chi too).

So we end up with Children of the Void – a generation of Millennials & Beyond, who have experienced parents who have focused too much (in my opinion, and I'm allowed to have an opinion, so are you) on *good diet* and *good education* – and have had almost no direct conversations on how to be a *good person*. Do they hope it will all just happen by osmosis?

When I hear a parent say "I just want my child to be happy" I just want to scream "No you don't!" You want your child to experience happiness and sadness, joy and grief, winning and losing, succeeding and failing, being liked and being disliked. It's the yin and the yang. If you only want them to be happy, they won't know how to cope with being sad ... thus contributing to the senseless levels of teenage suicide. I digress.

So what the heck is *OH GROW UP: Toddlers to Preteens Decoded*. It's a parenting guidebook like no other parenting guidebook in existence. Truly. It's an eclectic collection of rational and radical theories, and conservative and revolutionary advice ... all tied up together to create an innovative and unconventional paradigm, leading you from the simple to the complex, in an exciting and extraordinary parenting journey. In plain English ... it's about going back to the *real* and *authentic* basics!

Pieces of *Oh Grow Up* may be perceived as alternative, marginal or unconventional — but that's only what they seem to be. In reality, this book is fundamentally about rediscovery. Nothing is truly new or novel — nearly all of it is ancient, and much of it is long forgotten.

I've had my writing style described as being punchy, direct, frank, honest and radical — which is great, as that's my intention. What I also know for sure is that anyone taking the time to read this book is obviously trying — like us — to raise a child who eventually possesses an innate character of joy, with a core essence of purpose. You and I, have probably already realised by now that *gratitude, joy* and *purpose* are what bring all humans happiness.

But here's the foundation of this book: such an outcome is just not so easy, when we as parents only focus on our children physically, or only mentally/emotionally, or only spiritually. This book, more than anything, is a guide about parenting the *whole* child — the body, mind and spirit.

Author's note

It is a great hope of mine that this book will appeal specifically to the hordes of middle-of-the-road parents who don't wish to convert to any specific parenting ideology or doctrine. So within this book there will be concepts you utterly agree with, because they are already rudimentary to how you parent. That's brilliant, and just as it should be. As author and reader, we *must* be on the same page on some issues, otherwise you won't like the book at all. Then there will also be concepts you partially agree with, but, right here and right now, they're just a tad too out there or new to your thinking. That's fantastic, and also just as it should be. We *must* all continually redefine who we are and what we believe in, otherwise we become stagnant and don't evolve. Then there will be concepts you may passionately disagree with, because they fly in the face of your own strong beliefs. That's perfect too, and also just as it should be. We *must* maintain some integrity to our own fundamental values, otherwise we're potentially just blind followers of the whimsical notions of a particular author.

But there will also possibly be concepts that blow your mind away. Mind-boggling knowledge that staggers and amazes you; answers to questions about your child you never thought could be answered; incredible insights into your child you never dreamt could be realised; even, perhaps, life-altering philosophical wisdom that revolutionises your long-term, big-picture thinking.

There could also be stuff that motivates you, stuff that soothes you and stuff that plain pisses you off. *Brilliant! All just as it should be.*

So, is this book a masterpiece, my life's magnum opus? No, hardly; I've too much wisdom yet to acquire. All I've really done, as with OH BABY, is spend considerable time investigating the often unintelligible research, then interpreting and regurgitating it to you in some vaguely comprehensible and graspable way. *Ta da!*

So I'm a translator who's deeply honoured to get to do this job — and I couldn't have done it without you, the reader. (Now, just imagine we're on our deck, laughing and giggling as we're having a whinge with our wine – Pinot Gris? Pinot Noir?) So cheers! Let the journey begin . . . I've got so much incredible and fascinating stuff to tell you!!

Kathy Fray xxx

> *Like all parents, my husband and I just do the best we can and hold our breath and hope we've set aside enough money to pay for our kids' therapy.*
>
> Michelle Pfeiffer (1958–), *American actress*

PLEASE NOTE:

This entire book is a guide only, and includes brief introductory summaries of many much larger topics. The author and publisher can accept no legal liability, including but not limited to health-care matters.

All choices are ultimately the readers' decisions.

Foreword

As author of half a dozen best-selling books myself and CEO of Motivational Press, I'd like to pride myself on recognising a next best-seller manuscript, and there is no doubt *"OH GROW UP...Toddlers to PreTeens Decoded"* falls into that category – and that is why I personally approached its New Zealand author Kathy Fray, asking her to join our elite team of authors. Kathy is a best-selling kiwi author herself in NZ, so it was a simple logical step for us to be able to make her wisdom accessible globally to parents all over the world. We are proud to have created this association with her.

Personally I have a passion for books within the genre of personal development, health and wellness – and without any doubt OH GROW UP absolutely fits that brief, in the extreme. Kathy's writing style is also certainly extraordinary, which is why it caught my eye. She's honest, frank and blunt. She's controversial, provocative and refreshing. She's loving, genuine and authentic. She has no hesitation in telling you what she believes is to be the best way to parent, but in the same breath she makes it totally right for you to not agree with her.

OH GROW UP is fundamentally about what Kathy describes as 'wholistic triadic' parenting. She gives parents virtually all the resources they need to be able to parent their child's *body* with what she terms using *Physiological IQ*. Then she gives parents virtually all the tools they need to be able parent their child's *mind* using *Intellectual IQ*.

Then – the section that seems absent from practically every other Parenting book you ever read – Kathy gives parents the wisdom to be able to parent their child's *spirit* (in a unique non-religious connotation) using what she calls Soulful IQ. Here she outlines her **Parenting 21 Magical Secrets** and **Parenting 21 Universal Principles**. It is absolutely inspirational.

I will conclude with a quote from arguably the most famous literary agent in NZ.

> *Kathy Fray writes with force and conviction in an instinctive manner that readers are finding irresistible ... There is a touch of genius in your work, especially the ability to read and research so widely, to extract the knowledge and wisdom that you discover, and integrate it into a powerful and comprehensive narrative.*
>
> *I have not known another person who possesses that remarkable grouping of qualities.*
>
> *Equally to the point you have friendships and relationships with all manner of people who you talk with, and you consult and quote, and who you retain as close personal friends ...*
>
> *The closest comparison I know is in the books of Bill Bryson ... One impressive lady, as determined as an elephant and as soft-hearted as a bird of paradise.*
>
> Ray Richards ONZM [1921-2013]

Justin Sachs, *Motivational Press CEO & best-selling Author*

Introduction

We are bringing up children in a time of unprecedented change ... As society spins at a giddying pace ... Stripped of ritual, tradition and shared meaning, experience seems to be on fast forward. The innocent merry-go-round of raising kids has morphed into a deranged spin dryer.

Michael Carr-Gregg, Your Child Year by Year

I reckon one of the reasons my OH BABY book is a best-seller, is probably pretty simple — 'cause it was written by a mom, for moms. I was inspired to write it because I was so incensed by the traditional, patronising, pious mothercraft books, with their condescending definitions of the perfect parent. I also think people liked it because it had an undercurrent of spiritual awe for motherhood and life! My writing style is frankly blunt, with brutal but compassionate honesty, and intentionally un-PC (politically correct).

I was inspired to write this book because once again I was so incensed by the traditional, patronising, pious parentcraft books, with their condescending definitions of the perfect parent — and the perfect child. They pissed me off. For me, they went only part of the way to understanding what I call the 'Riddles of Parenting Life'. Heck, even God couldn't stop his own children from being naughty and eating the forbidden apple in the Garden of Eden!

So, again, I found myself writing in my non-PC way for the sanity of both of us. This book moves far and away from spewing out the conventional and traditional. It's eclectic, boundless and liberated; it's eccentric, unconventional, alternative and passionate; and, of course, once again, has an undercurrent of spiritual awe for parenthood and life!

What this book is not

This book intentionally does not cover the topics of:

» Specific types of family dynamics, such as two-parent, blended, homosexual, extended, single-parent and foster-care families.

» Correcting maltreatment, such as indulgent or neglectful parenting, physical abuse, physical neglect, psychological unavailability and verbal abuse.

» Extreme special-needs children, be it dyslexia or dyspraxia, the intellectually impaired or the gifted genius. All these topics deserve way more insight that a few paragraphs from a non-expert like me!

» The differences between mother–father parenting roles — though it's perhaps worth mentioning here research by the renowned American psychologist Urie Brofenbrenner, who discovered the average father spends only 37 seconds a day giving undivided attention to his child. At the end of the day, the need for unified parental leadership is also a given.

What this book is

I believe all truth is supposition — that it is conjecture or speculation, just a guess really. I believe no one person can know it all, because there's too much to know. So this book is not about me, the author, teaching you, the reader, the categorically right things to believe — for I *passionately* believe *there is never one right answer.*

If and when I personally possess a strong opinion on a topic, you'll know it, I'm up-front. But I'm not saying that I'm right and everyone else is wrong. I'm simply saying I'm adamant about some things that I'll personally stick by, but you can take it or leave it. This is not some Bible you must follow. This is a guide you might find useful.

Surely, how to get your child to do what you want them to do is perhaps the oldest parenting question and is also sometimes termed *discipline*. Although this is not specifically a book about discipline, it also can't help but be so! Philosopher and psychologist Paul Faulkner said: 'Without discipline, love is incomplete; without love, discipline is irrelevant.' At the end of the day, any parenting methodology should be all about creating likeable kids.

In my biased (obviously) opinion, a lot of parenting guidebooks are — to quote the iconic Kiwi actress Robyn Malcolm — hideous "with those beatific lobotomised morons on the cover posing as the perfect 'mom' — but these self-appointed experts need to shut up with their 'Right and Wrong' self-righteous patter". Those awful books seem to exude full-of-themselves condescending advice that gets under my skin. Oh, and the ardently emphatic and insistent recommendations get up my nose too. Ah, and then there's the layers of guilt-inducing research that show how unsuspecting parents can negatively affect their always-innocent, naturally perfect children — that really gets my goat too.

Yada, yada, yada.

All too often it's pie-in-the-sky sanctimonious idealism, instead of in-the-trenches realism. Hey, I'm not saying all experts are wrong. Far from it! But I am saying the agendas of some experts reek too strongly of smugness. Some of the rhetoric they use when delivering their strategies is just too intense. All that most of us have by now realised is that we can only ever manage to become 'good-enough' parents.

The great majority of child development books are written by academically qualified professionals, and I suppose, in theory, they should be. Educational psychologists, social psychologists, health psychologists, clinical psychologists, neuropsychologists, paediatricians, sociologists, anthropologists, and then there are also the religious or spiritual zealots... Each is often an enthusiastic aficionado of their own philosophy, from conservative traditionalism to extremist twaddle.

Then again, a handful of parenting guides are absolutely brilliant, and some of my favourite authors include Kiwi super-granny Diane Levy; the politically incorrect parenting-shouldn't-be-so-hard Nigel Latta; Australian Father of the Year Steve Biddulph; non-violent aware-parenting gurus, such as Aletha Solter and my friend the divine Genevieve Simperingham; and many books recommended by the Natural Child Project.

When you think about it, this spectrum of literature also mirrors what we have all heard when other parents verbalise their own parenting philosophies, because some of us aspire to maintain a very high level of convention and conformity, and others of us yearn to remain the extreme avant-garde activist.

However, between the two extremes there is also the realm of the mainstream, typical, middle-of-the-road, 'normal and ordinary' parenting style. But gosh, don't you just want to rebel when you realise you might fall into that 'square', predictable and unadventurous category of the 'normal and ordinary'... *Well, the rebellious bohemian in me sure does!*

This first section of *Oh Grow Up* is a general overview of each **Age Stage**, explaining the general development of children, physically, intellectually and emotionally. Each of these unique age stages can then be combined with the other three sections of the book, which talk about how to:

- » Parent our child's body using Physiological IQ
- » Parent our child's mind using Intellectual IQ
- » Parent our child's spirit using Soulful IQ.

This is a very grounded book on sometimes quite ethereal subjects. It is like a sandwich made of theological bread ('rational probing') with theosophical filling ('speculating about mystical insight'). I have done my darndest to extrapolate from some of the best Thinkers to create a cohesive summary of the complex and complicated.

Confused? Good. You should be. This is only an introduction!

> *Before I got married I had six theories about bringing up children; now I have six children, and no theories.*
>
> John Wilmot (1647–1680), *Second Earl of Rochester*

Section One

AGE-STAGE OVERVIEWS

Chapter One

THE 'TODDLING' TOTS — ONE-AND TWO-YEAR-OLDS OVERVIEW

Most adults like to play by the rules,
whereas children prefer to break them.

Tessa Livingstone, *Child of Our Time*

Ah, the toddler . . . a fully mobile being with virtually no common sense. For most parents — especially the stay-at-home mom — toddlerdom contains some of our most physically busy years: we're up, we're down, and up and down again . . . 'Don't touch Nana's ornament', 'No, no, don't pull the cat's fur!', 'Ah, ah — you mustn't poke your baby sister in the eye', 'Eeek — don't build sandcastles on the lounge carpet'.

With the exception of their afternoon siesta, toddlers can be active all day long! So by the end of the toddler years, most parents are pretty shattered, and by then lots of us have another sweet, innocent baby rapidly mutating into a new adventurous, mischievous toddler. In fact, with three children under five, you can easily endure a decade of parenting toddlers.

The best toddler-tamers tend to be extremely attentive parents because, let's face it, toddlers are a hazard to themselves. However, toddlers are meant to be carefree risk-taking thrillseekers. The toddler years are all about pushing boundaries — it's in their job description. This is when your previously faultless, unsullied and blameless baby becomes absolutely and quite intentionally naughty.

Some parents do have an angelic toddler who is as good as gold, but heaven help the parent who believes it is all to do with their extraordinary parenting abilities. Hardly — it's mostly to do with the luck of the draw.

And some parents have a satanic toddler who is a complete nightmare — and heaven help the world if the parents don't do everything in their power to transform the hitting, biting, spitting creature into something vaguely socially acceptable.

But most parents have a middle-of-the-road toddler who's got oodles of great potential, so long as the parents parent, and not befriend (more on that tricky topic later).

PHYSICAL DEVELOPMENT

> *The common practice of dividing infancy and childhood into age-related units of months and years can distort the realities of human development ... The truly important consideration in assessing a child's development is sequence.*
>
> K Eileen Allen and Lynn R Marotz, *By the Ages*

THE BIOLOGY *(Structural anatomy)*

At birth, a baby's head is a quarter of their total body length. By two, the head is only about one-sixth of body length, and infants have also tripled their birth weight and doubled their length.

Generally, at around two-and-a-half years old, children are approximately half their adult height. There are many formulas in circulation that can be used to calculate your child's estimated adult height, and below is the system promoted by Professor Robert Winston from the *Child of Our Time* TV series:

Girls: two-year-old height in centimetres x 1.17 + 63.5 centimetres

Boys: two-year-old height in centimetres x 1.37 + 57.7 centimetres

Physiological development at this age centres around high levels of activity, because it enhances mood, improves metabolism, increases alertness and assists brain development (that is, it increases the neurotrophin chemicals that proliferate brain cell connections).

At this age physical strength relates more to size than gender.

THE MOTOR SKILLS *(Functional physiology)*

Science knows for sure that hand dexterity and brain development are intricately connected, so it makes direct sense to encourage our toddlers to use their hands in as many different and interesting ways as possible, because we know this stimulates brain growth and hemisphere communication. In fact, between two and four years of age, the brain cells' connections that are responsible for hand movement, within the cortex's primary motor zone, develop particularly profusely — with, of course, the left motor cortex controlling the right side of the body, and vice versa.

Regarding the key milestones, infants start out with very poor balance, mostly because of their top-heavy head. But between around 12 and 18 months they typically start to walk, and are usually running before their second birthday. Then rapidly they're also kicking, hopping, jumping, forward-rolling, catching, tumbling, balancing, twirling and dancing . . . plus walking and talking at the same time, and their throwing improves in accuracy too. 'One handedness' dominance starts to become clear from around 18 months of age.

This is a great age, if not earlier, to introduce them to water — the sea, the pool, rivers and lakes — so they can learn to become at ease in it.

COUGHS, COLDS AND GERMS

Much more on this topic later, but well and truly by this age it is normal for a child to have lots of little coughs and colds (say six to 10 a year), the occasional bout of gastroenteritis (vomiting and diarrhoea), and other miscellaneous spells of disease, such as conjunctivitis (pink eye), tonsillitis, bronchitis and ear infections (otitis media). These are all a very normal part of growing up, and a *very* necessary process for all children to develop a robust immune system.

So please don't go o to the doctor for antibiotics with every routine infection! If you do, you're teaching your child's immune system nothing, and the child will routinely su er recurrent infection, because their body hasn't been able to create immunological memory. (More about this in Chapter Eight.) Children also need exposure to germs, so please don't use sanitary wipes and antibacterial sprays all over the place! The main aspects of household hygiene are washing hands after going to the loo, and following the food-safety Four Cs:

» **Clean:** Wash hands before handling food and after handling raw meat.

» **Cook:** Mince, patties, sausages, chicken and pork should be cooked right through (until juices run clear); and reheat all leftovers until steaming hot.

» **Cover:** Cover and refrigerate leftover food.

» **Chill:** Keep meat, chicken and other perishables chilled in the fridge, and separated until you begin cooking.

INTELLECTUAL DEVELOPMENT

When it comes to emotions, parents of two-year-olds are up against a force stronger than they — the nature of development itself.

Tessa Livingstone, *Child of Our Time*

THE BRAIN *(Neurology)*

At this age, pure brain magic is going on! In fact, a one- or two-year-old's brain is growing faster than any other part of the body, making billions of new connections at an incredible rate every day . . . and compared to the body, the head is still huge! By two years of age a toddler's brain is around 75–80 per cent the size of an adult brain.

THE KNOWLEDGE *(Cognition)*

By one year of age an infant's 'memory banks' are beginning to mature, and experts estimate toddlers learn one or two brand-new activities every day. By 18 months of age, toddlers understand that objects do not vanish when they cannot be seen. But, in general, a two-year-old's memory is still very unreliable — with most toddlers usually forgetting more than they remember. Toddlers are driven by a primitive urge to want to imitate. Then, remembering (committing to memory to imitate later) becomes a major part of their learning. For example, at two, they can leave a game, come back to it later and pick up where they left o , as they are beginning to remember things.

During play and exploration, one-year-olds need 'real' objects — such as trucks or dolls — to play with. Then between one and two years they learn to play symbolically; for instance, pretending that a shoe is a boat and the carpet is the sea — it's dressing-up and role-play time. By the end of the second year, they also start to experiment with conflict, showing anger and aggression (usually due to frustration at their own limitations).

By two years of age they can have wild imaginations. Such imagination opens the doors to special interests; soon you often can't get your toddler out of the Disney princess or Superhero costume.

GREAT TOYS AND GAMES

- » Lift-the-flap books
- » Soft toys, dolls and glove puppets
- » Wooden building blocks
- » Push-along and pull-along toys, such as trolleys and Buzzy Bees
- » A toy tricycle, car, bike or tractor to sit on and push with their feet
- » A mini-chair
- » Stacking cups or rings and shape-sorter cubes
- » Toy workbench with wooden hammer
- » Pictorial wooden puzzles
- » Rhyming poems and songs
- » Arty activities, such as making things with Play-Doh® or finger-painting
- » Imitation and imagination play, such as dress-ups and cardboard boxes
- » Listening to music, playing with toy drums and rattles
- » Physical activities, such as jumping, running, swimming and hopping
- » Bath toys, such as waterproof letters and numbers; toys that float, such as a rubber duck; kitchen colander, plastic funnel, small bucket, small watering can and empty plastic bottles

» Favourite games: chasing blown-up balloons around the room; simple memory-card and counting games; games with rules, such as getting tagged 'out'; and ball games: rolling, kicking, throwing and catching

As for TV ... the average two-year-old spends around 10 per cent of their life watching television ... *wrong*! No, it's right, it's the truth; but yes, it's wrong. Please don't plonk your toddler in front of the box for two hours every day. Think of TV as an end-of-day wind-down reward for good behaviour while you're making dinner, or your babysitter while you shower — but not part of their all-the-time daytime activities.

And please, please, please — *one of my own personal pet peeves, I know* — turn *off* the endless bloody daytime television! I'm not saying that you shouldn't watch a bit of your favourite talk show or soapie while you have a bite of lunch, but don't have the box going *all day long!*

THE LANGUAGE *(Vocabulary)*

The first two years of life are the most important for acquiring language, and learning to respond with language truly begins to develop from between 12 and 18 months onwards.

By 18 months infants can understand hundreds of words, and can speak a handful. And they can say the consonant sounds of B, H, M, N and P.

By two years of age they can say around 300 words and speak in sentences. By three years of age, they are learning up to 10–15 new words every day. Between two and four years of age, they can say the consonant sounds of D, G and K. With verbal language girls take the lead up until around age five. *(Some would say up until age 105!)*

Research shows that children immersed in conversation during the first two years later acquire a wider vocabulary for the rest of their lives. So yabber, yabber and yabber away to your little one. It's like brain food. It *is* brain food. So do be chatty!

However, a big reality check for two-year-olds is their inability to express themselves and be clearly understood. Their capacity to comprehend and understand language (in the brain's Wernicke's area) matures much more quickly than their ability to produce spoken language (in the brain's Broca's area) — plus their vocal cords are still maturing too. This may be why your toddler becomes so angry and frustrated, and this is why teaching your child some simple sign language can be an immensely useful parenting tool.

Most of us teach babies to wave 'bye-bye' from around nine months old, but actually they're capable of so many more useful pieces of non-verbal communication, to indicate thirsty, hungry, more please, yes, no and dirty nappy. Just Google 'baby sign language' and you'll discover the umpteen books available.

Plus, of course, immerse them in books. Read, read and read even more to your child, especially at bedtime.

In our family, from when our kids were a really young age, we'd always had a constant stash of library books in the car. Our kids would devour books during nearly all car rides (and a positive side effect of this is that our kids don't suffer much from motion sickness).

SOCIAL–EMOTIONAL DEVELOPMENT

The key to successful parenting is not found in complex theories, elaborate family rules, or convoluted formulas for behaviour. It is based on your deepest feelings of love and affection for your child, and is demonstrated simply through empathy and understanding.

Good parenting begins in your heart.

John Gottman, *The Heart of Parenting*

Chapter One

THE BEHAVIOUR *(Psychological)*

Most one-year-olds become more demanding as the year goes by, commonly soon after 18 months of age, which is why most parents end up commenting that the 'Terrible Twos' have come early. This is when toddlers do one particular thing for the very first time in their life: that is, *be deliberately and intentionally naughty.* Why? Because they're supposed to. It's called testing boundaries, and it's only the tip of the iceberg.

This can be a shocking moment of truth for a first-time parent; their sweet, perfect infant has vanished in that moment and now standing before them is a defiant little rascal who needs, somehow, to be disciplined. *Bugger!*

By 18 months personality is also beginning to really establish itself. Then, at around two, we often see a dichotomy: your child is both sophisticated and gullible. They can cleverly excel with some deductive reasoning in situations they know well, but at the same time may be easily confused with grasping what can seem like basic cause-and-effect lessons . . . *We told you not to put your finger into the door hinge!*

Two-year-olds mostly play on their own. The reasons for this are twofold. First, toddlers can find it hard to understand and to communicate with each other; and second, they are still totally egocentric, self-centred, selfish and notoriously inconsiderate. But they're learning to socialise, and this process is very much a personality-driven thing too. They will often play in parallel, alongside other children, but primarily solo — otherwise a conflict can ensue. As they start to get a bit older, playing with other children will begin to teach them cooperation and negotiation. Communication skills increase, especially the body language of gestures, such as pointing.

From age two to three, it's a journey of power struggles. These little munchkins love attention, and will do *almost anything* to get it, including misbehaving if that's what it takes — any attention's better than being ignored when you're two-and-a-half. This is a big reason why pushing, shoving and snatching are also all part of the average toddler's tactics, which can also progress into hitting, biting and hair-pulling . . . *Oh the socially embarrassed parent!*

Then of course there are the Terrible Twos' ferocious temper-tantrum hissy-fit explosions, which are usually all about anger and frustration at a lack of independence . . . They want to be understood but can't communicate clearly enough; or they want to do things their way, but aren't old enough to run their life. Potentially, loads of aggression stemming from loads of frustration.

Subsequently, discipline tactics are required from 18 months onwards, with the primary golden rule being *consistency*. It's about maintaining the same predictable boundaries to acceptable behaviour. If you want compliance to 'rules', then you need to set the rules in stone by making compulsory 'no-nos'.

This book won't espouse all the right and wrong ways to discipline your child, but I will tell you that the most common error parents make is confusing their child with inconsistent rules. Trust me, just don't go there!

Work out what is acceptable behaviour in your household, and stick to it. Black and white.

Around this age, it's also usually pretty easy to spot the risky thrill-seekers, with their built-in resistance to the word 'no', and, conversely, the shy bashfuls, who will often demonstrate amazingly focused concentration. With toddlers, around a third are shy, a third are average and a third are bold. Personality is very much involved!

SELF-AWARE SELF-RECOGNITION

Up until around a year old, when an adult points at something, a baby will just look at the finger. But some time after their first birthday, an initial step towards conscious awareness is taken as Bubs learns to follow another person's gaze and looks to where they're pointing.

Then, between one-and-a-half and two years of age, your toddler will start to say 'you' and 'me'. As the baby grows into a toddler, this sense of self and self-awareness begins to develop from two years onwards. They will recognise themselves in the mirror or a photograph, and use the word 'mine'.

By around three years they can usually well and truly tell you their likes and dislikes . . . but they'll still think that no one can see them if they 'hide' by covering their eyes — *so cute!*

Our job as parents is simply to guide this self-recognition, assisting them to become self-aware, so they can understand other people and realise that others have different views from them. This is also when your toddler is starting to develop *empathy*.

Two is very much the right age to begin teaching the difference between right and wrong, and a great place to start is with empathy. *Sympathy* is showing pity for someone, and that's not what I'm talking about. *Empathy* is having the ability to understand another person's situation or feelings or motives; it's being able to walk in their shoes, and get behind their eyes. Empathy is a lifelong skill.

TOILET TRAINING

Oh look, do I really need to give this subject its own heading? I'm reluctant to address this topic because it's in my own 'too-hard basket'. That's not because toilet training our own children was a problem, but because it was pretty jolly easy really. I hesitate to write on this subject because it is a little can of worms, devoid of true 'rights' or true 'wrongs', devoid of a one-size-fits-all panacea, devoid of brilliant wisdom — every child is unique.

But I'm oh so aware that at some stage around this time, usually after 20 months of age, you will probably start to get pretty tired of forking out the money on nappies only to see your little monkey toddler squint their eyes to push out a poo — 'looking like little tubes of toothpaste — squeezing from the top' (to quote Nigel Latta) — followed by them saying to you 'poo-poo nappy'. You're thinking to yourself, this child is *so very aware* of what it's doing, but not aware of the money it's costing. So you may begin your own toilet-training crusade.

Or alternatively, you may be expecting another child — and *really* want the first one out of nappies before the next one arrives.

Whatever your motivation, I am no expert — is there really an expert on toilet training? — but to briefly summarise our experiences (which are kind of interesting crap, 'scuze the pun):

» *Child One:* Aged two-and-a-half years. Several weeks leading up to the big event we prepared the ground by repeatedly saying 'When you're two-and-a-half you'll be a Big Girl and ready to use the toilet and wear undies.' She turned two-and-a-half, we put on the undies, she used the toilet . . . voila! Well, pretty much.

» *Child Two:* Aged two-and-a-half years. Several weeks leading up to the big event we prepared the ground by repeatedly saying 'When you're two-and-a-half you'll be a Big Girl and ready to use the toilet and wear undies.' She turned two-and-a-half, we put on the undies, she used the toilet, erratically, and continued having 'accidents'. We bought lollies, o ering one for a pee, two for a poo . . . voila! Well, pretty much.

» *Child Three:* Aged two-and-a-half years. Several weeks leading up to the big event we prepared the ground by repeatedly saying 'When you're two-and-a-half you'll be a Big Boy and ready to use

Chapter One

the toilet and wear undies.' He turned two-and-a-half, we put on the undies, he used the toilet, erratically, and continued having 'accidents'. We bought lollies, o ering one for a pee, two for a poo. He used the toilet, erratically, and continued having 'accidents'. We filled a small jar with small coins, o ering all the coins at the end of the week for a big treat at the dairy, subtracting one coin for each 'accident' ... voila! Well, pretty much.

At the end of the day, it's going to be a very personal journey for such a personal subject! And probably a journey of endless searching through your repertoire and imagination for potentially viable solutions and worthy incentives.

The two best bits of advice I can o er are: one, wait until the time is right for you, for your child, for your household — don't let other family members (such as mothers or mothers-in-law) try to hurry you up. Two, ensure your toddler is eating plenty of fibre roughage and drinking plenty of water to enable them to produce beautifully defecatable poo!

POOR SLEEPERS

Toddlers need 14–15 hours' sleep per 24, including one afternoon sleep that ends at around 3–4pm.

If you haven't yet taught your baby great sleep habits, then, oh heck, before it becomes a fully fledged toddler, *get it sorted*! Otherwise your poorly sleeping toddler will rapidly turn into a sleep-resistant preschooler ... and that directly a ects their ability to be happy and their capacity to learn.

Of course, some children are naturally great sleepers and some are naturally not so great; but it's also a fact that some households successfully teach all their infants how to become good sleeping toddlers, and some households inadvertently teach all their infants how to become sleep-resistant night-wakers, also known as sleep-inducement junkies. These are the two-year-olds routinely energetic after 9pm, because they don't know how to fall asleep when they're tired and on their own; they only know how to fall asleep exhausted, with the number-one teddy, special blankie, right dummy, night light, favourite CD and über cuddles. If this is what it takes for them to fall asleep at 10pm, then you can pretty much guarantee this is what it takes for them to fall asleep at 3am too.

Please, please give your child the *gift* of learning how to become a great sleeper. I'm *passionate* on this topic! Especially as the repercussions of long-term parental sleep deprivation are also so hideous ... It can ruin marriages, lead to depression and absolutely impact on the joy you get from parenting. In *Oh Baby* I have a whole wonderful chapter on the topic, including my 12 Golden Rules, 12 Magical Secrets and 20 Dos and Don'ts to infant sleep. I'm not going to repeat all that wisdom here (continual 'fan mail' confirms that it works), but the main crux of any bedtime routine is that sleep is the only option. And the main crux with a sleep-resistant toddler is that a parent hasn't yet got to the point where they're desperate enough to tough it out for the three or four nights it will take to finally establish good sleep routines. Here are the four basic steps:

» *Step 1:* Get rid of all distractions, such as toys in the cot.
» *Step 2:* Use a routine: dinner, bath, story, bed.
» *Step 3:* Stop the use of all sleep props and inducements, such as special music, night lights, dummies, bottles, boob or cuddling.
» *Step 4:* If under two years of age, use a BabyOK Babe-Sleeper attached sleep-bag to protect them against falling or climbing out of the cot, and to teach them bedtime is sleeptime.

That's it — there is no more. Just get on with it.

To quote my colleague Nigel Latta, 'Sleep, or rather the ability to settle oneself into sleep, is something you have to *teach* your kids ...

Chapter One

There is no way around the fact that the road to good sleep is paved with tears.' Sorting out sleep issues is one of those basic steps to humdinger happiness.

SUMMARY

Having children makes you no more a parent than having a piano makes you a pianist.

Michael Levine (1964–), American composer

In this section of Oh Grow Up I've returned to the middle-of-the-road basics, because kids don't really come 'fully assembled' while their brains are still maturing. No, kids come in 'kitset form', ready for us to mould into good behaviour. With toddlers, as Dr Harvey Karp comments in his bestseller *The Happiest Toddler on the Block,* it's all about appreciating that we need to think of our toddler as a caveman — our own primitive Neanderthal who will zip through the five major achievements it took prehistoric man five million years to accomplish: walking, talking, manipulating things with their hands, figuring things out and forming friendships.

At this age, your toddler has a natural drive to find out, find out and find out some more, to extend the boundaries and discover the rules. Learning by experimentation is the quickest way they learn.

So all we parents really need to do is make sure they're given adequate boundaries and adequate freedom to explore, so they can discover that all their actions have consequences.

Their job is to push the limits, our job is to enforce the limits.

Chapter Two

THE 'PLAYFUL' PRESCHOOLER — THREE- AND FOUR-YEAR-OLDS OVERVIEW

> *The child, compared to us, is not only purer but has mysterious qualities, which we adults as a rule cannot perceive, but in which we must believe with faith.*
>
> Maria Montessori (1870–1952), *The Secret of Childhood*

Oh my word, these little gals and guys are generally so cute! They can be such interactive, energetic and interesting balls of fun. This is of course also dependent on inborn personality and inbred behaviour.

Good parenting requires fortitude; we have to be able to stick to our guns and mean what we say. It's critical. Because toddlers who have been allowed to develop ingrained misbehaviour nearly always as preschoolers have become increasingly di cult to manage, because of their constant defiance and disobedience.

We all know those kids: they're the ones the whole preschool is thrilled about when they leave to start school — *because they'll finally no longer be around to upset everyone.* If those wayward imps are created due to timid, submissive parenting, well, shame on the parent. Research shows the main influence on three- to four-year-olds is learning in the home.

But back to the 'good kids'. Oh, these preschoolers can be just so great. They do have some common sense now; they can follow instructions; they can cooperate and please; and they often have a great sense of humour . . . they can be really funny!

In very general terms, the girls mature faster than the boys; often at four- and-a-half, girls appear extremely ready for school, yet at six years many boys still seem hardly ready to leave Mom's side.

My best advice: have fun with your preschooler — it's your last years of massive influence and leading by example. *Party on!*

PHYSICAL DEVELOPMENT

> *Our exaggerated sense of personal responsibility turns the discovery of the preschooler's potential into a frustrating, discouraging, anxious, exhausting, conformist, competitive frenzy.*
>
> Polly Berrien Berends, *Whole Child/Whole Parent*

THE BIOLOGY *(Structural anatomy)*

Up until age three, a toddler's brain is twice as active as an adult's, and by age three, their brain is almost fully grown (which is why their head still looks large in proportion to their body). From age three onwards, the brain starts to prune back the neuron connections that infrequently function, thus 'killing' some brain cells that aren't being used. But that's okay, because it's exactly how things are meant to be; pruning is how talent (specialisation) can develop.

Diet-wise, up until the age of three the daily energy expended physically has continually increased, but at this age appetite begins to plateau until around age six. So, four- and five-year-olds typically eat a fairly similar amount; whereas a six-month-old and an 18-month-old have completely different food-volume needs.

From age four until puberty, children grow slowly but steadily at a rate of around four centimetres in height a year. Shoe size also changes slowly, but somewhat unpredictably — one pair can be rapidly outgrown, but the next will still fit even though holes have been worn in the soles.

THE MOTOR SKILLS *(Functional physiology)*

By the age of three, around three out of 20 children prefer to use their left hand more than the right. Researchers continue to look into the proverbial chicken-or-egg question in regard to 'handedness': does the use of the right hand create brain development in the left hemisphere and vice versa, or does brain growth create dominant hand use? At the moment the jury is still out.

By age three, balance is much better, so your preschooler is less clumsy. At this age you can also start to teach a child how to hold a pencil, and some can produce recognisable drawings — usually girls, because their hand-eye coordination develops earlier than boys. They also may blink heaps when they're concentrating, which is normal.

Before the fifth birthday, coordination skills have usually improved, and most children have learnt, to varying degrees of skill, the key milestones of how to run, jump, hop, skip, catch balls, kick a ball and throw a ball over-arm (still inaccurately). They can dress themselves with a bit of help, and possibly tie their shoelaces. They can also have a pretty good attempt at using scissors.

Before they start school, make sure they can do all the basics, including using the toilet independently, putting items into their backpack, putting on a jacket and Velcro-fastened shoes, asking and answering questions, telling someone their full name and age, sitting still when required, and coping with lunchbox items. It's very much our job as parents to ensure they know how to do these nuts-and-bolts tasks *before* sending them to school.

INTELLECTUAL DEVELOPMENT

> *This was his reaction when I told him we were going to have ice cream and handed him a Popsicle instead. 'Mom, this is not ice cream. This is a Popsicle, and it is similar to ice cream. Can you taste the difference, Mommy?'*
>
> HubPages.com, *Quotes from a four-year-old*

THE BRAIN *(Neurology)*

At age three, preschoolers need around 14 hours' sleep per 24 hours, probably still including an afternoon nap. At age four, preschoolers need around 13 hours' sleep per 24 hours, usually dropping the afternoon nap.

If you *still* haven't taught your preschooler great sleep habits then, oh man, frickin' sort it out before they start school! No excuses! Otherwise your poorly sleeping preschooler will rapidly turn into an always-stay-up-late grumpy schoolkid, probably with learning difficulties. As I said earlier, research shows beyond any doubt whatsoever that poor sleep directly affects their ability to be happy, their capacity to learn and their resulting IQ. Remember, get rid of all sleep crutches, stick to a routine and be absolutely resolute that at bedtime, *sleep* is the only option!

Subject to getting age-appropriate amounts of sleep, by three the brain starts to lay down long-term memories, and it starts to be able to 'time-travel'. That is, a preschooler can recall the past, and imagine the future.

Imagining the future enables planning the future, and this is a huge life skill to gain, because it leads to the ability to strategise. Research shows the earlier this is learnt, the more successful your child will be later in life, both socially and academically. So encourage your preschooler to think ahead, which of course also involves learning the lessons of *consequence.*

Four-year-old brains are also very capable of interconnected thoughts involving memory, speech and rationale — with an increasingly sophisticated ability to remember, which brings with it the realisation of also being able to forget. So this is the time to develop responsibility: 'Wipe your shoes', 'Hang up your coat', 'Put away your toys', 'Feed the cat', and learning to pass on messages.

THE KNOWLEDGE *(Cognition)*

Three-year-olds show abundant enthusiasm for knowledge, but the average three-year-old watches TV for three hours a day — *arrggghhhh!* Halve it please, *at least,* and make sure what they're watching is somewhat educationally beneficial, such as sing-along DVDs.

For four-year-olds, life is all about learning and thinking. The average four-year-old can particularly enjoy alone-time play, sometimes for hours, talking to themselves in make-believe scenarios. At this age, they begin to learn the final 'tool' in their toolbox for learning, and that is *conscious learning.* This means they choose to concentrate on a topic or interest that takes their fancy, such as dinosaurs, Lego, soccer or ballet. So help them pursue their delight in their developing interest, without the fatal PPS (Pushy Parent Syndrome) . . . *eekk!*

Preschoolers are super imaginative, and so fantasising and creativity are essential normal activities for them. They usually have great interest in pretend-play, exploring, listening and doing. At age four they can also sort objects into pairs or groups, such as cup and saucer, or sock and shoe.

When you read a bedtime story, feel free to add in your own commentary, and ask them abstract questions that force them to really think. They love it. In many ways, the preschooler still needs emotional involvement — rather than plain intellect — to problem-solve.

Without doubt, children of all ages can enjoy totally free, unorganised play, but especially at ages three and four. However, this doesn't mean play activities should always be instigated by the child. Our own children have had broad preschool years, from highly structured Montessori to zero-structure kindergarten, to childcare facilities, to home-based childcare services. At this age a preschooler's thirst for knowledge is also all about avoiding boredom. So please don't go too far into the 'free unorganised play' philosophy and forget to actually lead by example. I've seen the uninterested, bored-to-tears, fed-up looks on children in some kindys that overtly tout the free-unorganised-play mantra, with preschoolers wandering around aimlessly, wishing some adult would finally suggest an activity: 'Today we're all going to make . . .' or some similar level of structured, organised play.

Guided play is my favourite philosophy, and much research backs this approach.

GREAT TOYS AND GAMES

Choose toys that are robust and versatile, so they will last for a few years. Make sure the toys leave some room for the imagination. Some favourites include:

- » Dolls, bricks, balls and books
- » Painting and drawing, especially with felt-tip pens
- » Big wheelie vehicles
- » Simple jigsaw puzzles
- » Construction toys

- Play-Doh, clay and mud pies
- 'Snap' card games, ones that use animals and numbers
- Magnetic letter, wooden alphabet and number-game puzzles
- Singing nursery rhymes
- Glove puppets and finger puppets
- Dominoes or Snakes and Ladders, with an adult
- Making things, gluing and cutting with children's scissors
- Cotton reels and thread toys
- Pop-up tunnel, for crawling through
- Large Lego blocks
- Musical instruments, toy tambourines, drums, triangles, xylophones and sleigh bells
- Plastic animals, especially dinosaurs, insects, reptiles or a farm set
- Make-believe and role play. Girls frequently act out domestic scenes, and boys tend to play characters from books, TV or the movies. They can really enjoy dressing-up clothes, and play kitchens with fake food, saucepans and cleaning utensils, or a play shop, with fake cash register, items to buy and money
- Things that develop their sense of humour, funny things that make them laugh such as silly word-play, slapstick routines, simple jokes, whoopee cushions; preschoolers can laugh 300 times a day!

Many children of this age — mostly first-borns, and especially girls — like to play with imaginery friends; and if they insist they can see their imaginary friend, please don't be flippantly dismissive.

Remember *not* to financially invest too heavily in special-interest hobbies, such as buying expensive equipment or uniforms, as at this age their interest can be fickle and fleeting — gymnastics today, but hip-hop in two months' time. At this stage, they're still 'finding their thing'. For example, our eldest practised playing the drums for the first year using old phone books, after which he'd well earned his first set of second-hand real drums . . . this a much better idea than buying a brand-new drum kit at the start of the first lessons, which, after a few months or weeks, just accumulate dust in the corner.

It's virtually impossible for a four- or five-year-old to appreciate the financial price tag of purchasing hobby equipment — heck, they've never had to go to work to earn money. But they are capable of learning the reward of conscious effort.

THE LANGUAGE *(Vocabulary)*

Language is now blossoming! Typically, in the fourth year there's an explosion of language, with your child learning new words after only hearing them once or twice. They're also getting more familiar with concept words such as 'before', 'after', 'morning', 'afternoon', 'later', 'soon', 'more', 'less', 'bigger', 'smaller', 'heavier', 'lighter', and 'in an hour'. A four-year-old can usually name many colors accurately, and is beginning to know the names of shapes.

At three to four years of age, children start speaking in three- to five- word sentences and sometimes use 'and' to construct even longer sentences. Between two-and-a-half and four years of age they can say the consonant sounds of F and Y, and between ages two and six the sounds of T and Ng. They learn vocabulary and grammar simultaneously.

Preschoolers start making new language errors of grammar and syntax, because their brains are moving from straight mimicking of words to beginning to grasp the complex rules of their mother tongue, for example, saying 'I runned and catched the ball', or 'Look at the fishes and mouses', or 'I go'd to the playground'. But it is this hard-wired process of acquiring grammar that crucially distinguishes we humans from our chimpanzee primate cousins who, when taught sign language, never manage to grasp grammar.

These language skills are all due to the fact that by around four the regularly activated brain circuitry has grown, and the rarely activated circuitries are being pruned. This is partly how a child becomes fluent in their mother tongue.

By age four, they're usually speaking pretty clearly, excluding the sounds Ch, J and L, which are normally mastered by age five. Most of the time they know how to say what they want to say, and they're adding 'when', 'if' and 'but' to short sentences, turning them into longer stories.

THE ART OF COMMUNICATION

Some people are naturally great communicators, and some people ain't. If you're the former, such as the chatterbox conversationalist or narrating raconteur, this can't help but rub o on your children. Evidence shows that being talkative is one of the best things parents can do to help their child's vocabulary. Some research demonstrates that by age three, children from a talkative household will have heard around 40,000 more words spoken — and so will have developed a wider vocabulary than other children.

On the flipside, if we're naturally uncommunicative, such as the reticent and silent or reserved and withdrawn parent, then this too can't help but rub o on our child. Children tend to imitate their parents' communication style. Luckily, in our family we happen to be both — the wildly chatty mother and moderately talkative father, so our children have a broad spectrum of examples to follow.

The issue I have observed as somewhat more challenging for some children to deal with is the introverted and bashful child with two extroverted and sociable parents. They're the quiet-as-a-mouse 'cling-on' at barbecues, rarely venturing from Mom or Dad's side. But typically, between seven and nine years of age, they turn out just fine, and are happily running around playing with all the other kids with normal levels of confidence. And on the other side, there's the extroverted and gregarious child with introverted and timid parents, but I've only seen that rarely (the parents don't get out much). These children also seem to end up just fine.

Nevertheless, whether we believe ourselves to be great, or not so great, communicators, we can still teach our children the *art* of good communication, such as clear speech, honest emotions, attentive listening, friendly body language and gestures, responsive warmth, and showing generosity of time. So I encourage you to use abundant facial expressions, liberal emotional tones and empathetic and sympathetic listening with your child, because body language and sentiments are intrinsically a part of learning the *art* of communication.

We all hope our children will be socially charming, and that requires charisma, which means using responsive expressions, animated body language and eye contact. It's about being an interesting personality, by learning to be an interested person.

TO READ OR NOT TO READ . . . *that is the question!*

A love of books and reading can be built from around just three years of age. Use nursery rhymes, nonsense rhyming games and funny songs, as they all teach your child so much about language. But the debate continues as to when it is best for children to formally learn to read.

I wish I could refuse to enter this debate, but in this book I can't bury my head in the sand that much! So, here goes.

Generally speaking, the pro-early-reading believers have two major philosophies. First, there is the 'Matthews Eect', which states that over time early readers become richer learners, and late readers become poorer learners. Second, long-standing, broad research studies prove that the younger we activate that area of neural circuitry, the easier it is to learn the complexities of language. This is due to physiological changes in the brain that modify its development.

In the opposite camp, Steiner–Waldorf education is renowned for intentionally deferring reading and writing until around age seven, preferring to emphasize creativity and love-of-language techniques, such as first learning to become great listeners. Steiner–Waldorf adherents routinely cite evidence of late readers catching up over a couple of years to the reading levels found in conventional schools, then typically taking o and ultimately faring better than early readers.

Then there's also the long-standing argument that children learning to read under age five end up preferring to read much more than children taught after age five. Well, I would need to question any research on such evidence as I've seen all sorts of results: learn early and love it; learn early and abhor it; learn late and love it; learn late and abhor it. With any methodology, I suggest you encourage a *love* of reading — the rest can come down to the child's personality.

Regardless of what when-best-to-learn philosophy we personally believe in, we can probably all agree that when children know they are a better reader than their peers, this can impact on their sense of accomplishment, and when a child knows they are a poorer reader than their peers, this can a ect their self-esteem and confidence. And, at the end of the day, eventually gaining a good ability to read is perhaps the most critical academic skill a child ever learns! So do what you believe is right for you and your family, for research evidence shows pros and cons for both early- and late-reading learning styles. Where you end up standing on this spectrum will be just one of a great multitude of parenting philosophies that will ultimately define your unique parenting style.

Our children all spent some time attending the same preschool my husband went to as a boy with his brothers — with the same head teacher — a lovely, sweet, old-fashioned preschool. There, *all* children learnt to read confidently and write competently well before starting school. Children can be capable of much, given the opportunity.

WRITING AND COUNTING

A majority of four-year-olds can be taught to hold a pencil fairly well, draw something that vaguely resembles a person, and with encouragement write their name.

Alongside learning to read and write is learning to count. I say count, count, count with your child, anything and everything, anytime and every time. Our kids still remember counting the eggs in the cartons at the supermarket every time we shopped. Learning to count comes solely from practice. It is repetitious rote learning, and most four-year-olds can count up to 20. You can also sing a counting song to the traditional tune of the ABC alphabet song:

1, 2, 3, 4, 5, 6, 7

8, 9, 10 and 11.

12, 13, 14, 15, 16

17, 18, 19, 20.

Now I know my 1-2-3.

Won't you come and sing with me.

SOCIAL–EMOTIONAL DEVELOPMENT

We're willing to work as hard as we have to to get the happy ending. So it is no wonder we feel annoyed at being mercilessly lampooned in books, magazines, movies and television programs; as caricatures like the Power Mom tooling around the suburbs in her sport utility vehicle sipping Starbucks, zealously contemplating weighty matters like which local gymnastics programs will give her agile four year old the best edge in future competition. Who wouldn't resent being sneered at as superficial and out of touch, particularly by those who've never walked a mile in our Nikes?

Alvin Rosenfeld and Nicole Wise,
The Over-Scheduled Child

THE BEHAVIOUR *(Psychological)*

The most important change taking place in three- or four-year-olds is that they are beginning to understand their own and others' emotions. They can begin developing empathy, which is a two-sided coin, as it also brings with it the need to judge oneself.

Three-year-olds will generally play a game in their own way, following their own set of rules, as they're starting to develop a sense of integrity. This is why they are more likely than younger toddlers to do what they're told, and why they're less likely to break rules when parents are not looking. (*And no, it doesn't stay that way, so just enjoy it while it does.*) Four-year-olds are at the beginning of their lifelong journey of learning to understand objectivity, such as societal rules and when it's appropriate to break them, but of course most of this is still way over their heads. So our job at this stage is to give them greater opportunities, by teaching them well and feeding them nutritionally.

Between three and four years of age is a great time to go to playgroups such as the local crèche or playcentre, because this is the period when children begin to comprehend that other people have their own minds.

By age four, most preschoolers have grasped the knowledge that others may have different beliefs from their own, and their social skills improve as they become more aware of what other people are thinking. Sometimes they can be very altruistic, such as unselfishly giving up a toy — then 10 minutes later they're completely egocentric and really struggling to put themselves into someone else's shoes. They have learned that not everything belongs to them, and the skill of sharing their possessions is developing.

From the skill of learning to understand others — while sometimes still enjoying playing on their own — friendships become more and more important, and most children by age four have learnt how to make friends. Boys tend to play in bigger groups, and will argue about the rules. Girls tend to play in smaller groups and argue less, but can get way more upset when they do. And with both sexes, friendships can be pretty fluid.

At this stage, personality-wise, children can be noticeably the limelight-seeking top-dog leader, or popular and confident, or anxious and shy. But unless they're impulsive, aggressive or antisocial, then it's generally best to leave them to play uninterrupted with their friends.

Some children can be neglected, singled out or bullied because complex hierarchies are already developing. However, a good preschool teacher will help these children stick up for themselves and resist the taunting jibes before they affect their self-esteem, though it is also perfectly normal for self-esteem to go up and down at this age.

At the end of the day, learning to negotiate a social life, how to fit in and join in ('inter-personal skills IQ' as the academics say) is one of the most important things we all have to learn. Preschoolers also know, if taught, what manners are and what is taboo, which is why burping or farting make them giggle.

Of course some children are naturally more sociable than others, especially when they have an imaginative, amusing or humorous personality. But regardless of personality or shyness, the warmth, affection and laughter they gain from friendships are important to boost self-confidence. From age three children are ready to make friends and play cooperatively with other children. By age four, they can really look forward to regularly seeing one or two particular friends, and one-third choose close friends of the opposite sex. They can also really enjoy you making time for them to play with their close buddies outside preschool.

One of our big parenting tasks is to teach our children to be cooperative, helpful and considerate, with enough self-sufficient independence to be tough enough, or cheeky enough, to stand up to intimidating bullies. Some personalities get this real quick. Some souls will always be struggling, and that's probably meant to be part of their journey.

A side effect of all this understanding-of-other-people is that the pre-schooler can start to become much more self-conscious with 'let's pretend' fantasy play.

As our children become older and more perceptive, our own role-modelling becomes even more important. For example, I believe they need to see us socialising and enjoying a good laugh, because frequently seeing us having a good time with great friends is priceless. Socialising at least once every weekend is pretty much our golden rule — sometimes more, rarely less.

Well-socialised adults can't help but generally produce well-socialised children who want to join in without being aggressive or disruptive. If you as an adult have debilitating shyness, toilet-bowl self-esteem, or some other socially inhibiting handicap that has transformed you into a loner, then I'm rather ruthless on this one: you need to get your issues sorted, so you are able to help your children conquer their shyness too. Seek counselling if that's what's needed, then join a club or something, and finally ask people over for dinner. Remember the ratio of two ears and one mouth is the way to socialise; when people listen twice as much as they talk, they're routinely described as great conversationalists.

Before age five, children can become more self-conscious, and this is all part of working out where they fit in. Certainly a smart appearance, nice haircut and a joy for life always add to their ability to be liked by others.

Some say that in the time-starved world of today, our job is also to teach them to be organised and time-smart. But at this stage I say it is of more importance to teach them how to stay in the 'Now', rather than always looking forward to what's coming up next.

Do you realise the average Western four-year-old watches four hours of TV a day — that's one-third of their waking life! *Cripes! What's happened to parents?*

SEARCH FOR THE HOLY GRAIL: 'WHO AM I?'

Yes, at three or four years of age we all begin the big journey towards understanding *who we are.* You see, because preschoolers are starting to think about what others feel, they also begin to learn to understand who they are, realising that we all have separate minds and feelings, which can be quite different to each other. *But of course this takes years to perfect — and we all know lots of adults who have never perfected it!*

By three years of age, children start to evaluate themselves, potentially self-criticising, particularly if they're often failing. And when this happens, which it will, our job is to show them how worthwhile and valuable all their efforts are; how invincible, lucky and blessed they truly are; and to make them laugh so they know joy and gratefulness again. That's what returns self-esteem from its time in the dungeons. We adults can struggle to find 50 things a day to laugh about, but preschoolers can potentially find 400!

CONSEQUENCE AND DISCIPLINE

As toddlers, children begin to learn about *consequence,* but as preschoolers it does become increasingly important kids are given the opportunity to experience 'consequence' (the PC term for what used to be called 'punishment'). Kids shouldn't be mollycoddled by overprotective, cosseting parents who continuously pamper, indulge and humour their child 'to protect self-esteem'. No, that teaches them that they can't cope on their own.

We need to begin to teach our preschoolers consequence, so they are better equipped for the big wide world of school. Learning to be able to predict the consequences of their actions is a huge part of the whole growing-up process. You see, part of growing up is learning that bad choices produce bad consequences.

There is, however, a bit of a golden rule that goes along with learning consequence; don't blame the child — only ever blame the child's *behaviour*. For example, don't say, 'This has happened because you were so naughty' or 'disobedient'. Instead say, 'What you *did* was naughty.' And never, ever, ever utter those heinous words: ' *You're stupid*' or *'Don't be so dumb'*. Those phrases really stick like glue, forming deep-fissured scar tissue, and could result in hours on a psychiatrist's couch in adulthood!

Entering the fourth year is about embarking on the learning curve of natural and logical consequences. From the parents' perspective, it's about genuinely respecting a child's wrong decisions so they can find out the hard way. It's not about lessons motivated by anger and revenge, and it's not about a mocking or gleeful 'Told you so, stupid' mentality. It's about us wanting to teach our children by giving them age-appropriate choices, and the alternative consequences, because from around three-and-a-half years most children can well understand the di erence between right and wrong.

Here's another tip: when you're annoyed, don't generalise. Don't say, 'I'm so annoyed at you,' instead try 'I'm very annoyed that you broke my favourite vase.'

And the golden, golden rule: if you say it, mean it. Children soon see through idle threats and hollow pressures to comply, or can be utterly frustrated with rules that constantly change depending on the parent's mood. My recommendation for great behaviour strategies is to have a general expectation for children to do as they are told, obediently and with good manners, first time, every time. If it doesn't happen, then there are immediate consequences, first time, every time. *Simple!*

There is no doubt that statistically children who are allowed to habitually misbehave and be aggressive troublemakers go on to become antisocial adults. So again, it is our job as parents to do everything in our power to address the problem.

Here are some 'multi-disciplinary' or holistic recommendations:

» *Rubbish In = Rubbish Out:* Wholesome food only, and preferably organic, especially fruit. No junk food, except as a treat if behaviour has been exemplary.

» *Food Treats = Treat Foods:* I don't mean sit still for 20 minutes at the supermarket and earn a lollipop at the checkout. No! I mean, show model behaviour all afternoon, then you've earned the lollipop bought earlier that day at the supermarket.

» *Responsibility = Reliability:* Give your preschooler simple daily chores, not as a punishment but to begin to build their sense of responsibility, autonomy, self-confidence and ability to helpfully contribute. It's all about their journey to becoming a self-sufficient, reliable, independent individual.

» *Concrete Warn = Instant Scorn:* Being told off needs to stop them in their tracks, with the toy or suchlike *gone* instantly to a high shelf for 24 hours. It's about getting abruptly serious about the consequences.

» *Meekly-Weakly = Wishy-Washy:* Tell them in black and white the level of acceptable behaviour you expect. Concrete boundaries provide enormous freedom, as they can behave in any way they want, within the limits of clearly known acceptable behaviour.

» *Still Having Problems?* Talk to your child, talk to their innate spirit. Have a good old deep and meaningful conversation. Go to the beach and get your bare feet in the sand or go for a bush walk, but both of you should get grounded. Then ask questions and really listen to their answers.

» *Still Having Problems?* Do all of the following:

» Take your child to a classical homeopath, as they can perform incredible miracles, softening the edges of extreme personalities and balancing equilibrium, levels of personal happiness and overall personal contentment.

» Take your child to a cranial osteopath, naturopath, chiropractor or acupuncturist. It may be simply about getting the physical body in balance.

» Review the personality information in Chapter Nine.

» Read all the bestselling books on disciplining children, and think of the advice as products in a supermarket shelf. Choose the philosophies that sit right with you.

In my opinion, eliminating aggression, lies and stealing is rarely accomplished by discipline, time-out or incentive star-charts. It's about taking a holistic mind-body-spirit approach.

SUMMARY

Having a family is like having a bowling alley installed in your brain.

Martin Mull (1943–), *American actor*

The preschool years are all about the emergence of the coherent personality. These children are on the cusp of change, between cute cuddles, and autonomous independence. We're just along for the ride as the helper, comforter, healer and teacher.

And lest we forget, generally speaking, the temperament of the three-year-old typically becomes the temperament of the adult!

Chapter Three

THE 'EDUCATED' NEW ENTRANT — FIVE- AND SIX-YEAR-OLDS OVERVIEW

The reason grandparents and grandchildren get along so well is that they have a common enemy.

Sam Levenson (1911–80), *American humorist*

This is the age when we all have the most adorable and endearing kids at the school, because our kids are the littlest, weeniest, sweetest young new entrants, whom the big kids and teachers refer to as cute.

Stereotypically, the move to school makes little difference for dads. Stereotypically, the move to school makes a mammoth difference for moms.

It can seem so gut-wrenchingly hard to drop them off at school, to allow some strange teacher to take ultimate responsibility for their 'upbringing', every day, Monday to Friday. Research tells us that for five- and six-year-olds, as formal education becomes such a major part of their life, learning outside the home takes on much more significance. So we agonise, 'The teachers can't possibly care for my child as much as I do.'

Often our daughters enthusiastically bounce into class, yelling 'Bye Mom!' without a longing backward glance. Often our sons attempt to cling to us like Velcro, forcing us to rip them off our legs. We return home, finding ourselves taken aback at how deafeningly quiet the house is. And then it happens, like magic: inside ourselves we hear a guilt-infused acclamation bubbling up . . . *Woo hoo! I'm free!*

Welcome (back) to rediscovering your Self. *Yay!*

For many women, when their last child starts school, *everything* changes. Oh, such emancipation! No more talkative child yabbering in your ear all day. No more preschool lunchtime pick-ups or drop-offs dividing every day in half. Wow! Such incredible freedom: around six hours every day *child-free*. Brisk walks, gym workouts, uninterrupted coffee conversation with a girlfriend, finally starting that cottage-industry business, or, at last, the joy of being able to wear a white blouse and dryclean-only suit. It can all feel so wonderfully liberating.

Then again, for many already working moms, their munchkin starting school can actually bring on a whole set of new problems: you can't drop them off at 7.30am and pick them up at 6pm any more. And what the heck do you do with all those jolly weeks of school holidays? Juggle, juggle, toil and trouble.

PHYSICAL DEVELOPMENT

THE BIOLOGY *(Structural anatomy)*

Welcome to the world of the sociable, communicative, physically active, well-coordinated, lively and enquiring new entrant! Their faces are slimming down, fat is getting replaced by muscle, and growth is happening in spurts. For five- to eight-year-olds, wiggly teeth become an exciting sign of growing up. Milk teeth fall out, and the tooth fairy visits (don't stress if the tooth fairy is a day or two late; our kids adapted just fine to waiting a few forgetful nights during the tooth fairy's 'busy season'). It is also normal for kids' secondary teeth to be more yellow, rather than pearly white, because they have darker enamel.

THE MOTOR SKILLS *(Functional physiology)*

At five years of age, your child's hand-eye coordination may be getting quite good and their fine-motor skills are getting better, which means they can enjoy spending hours doing simple puzzles, coloring-in and drawing — but things like shoelaces can still be tricky. They may also be able to catch and throw a large ball — or even a smaller tennis ball.

By six years of age, their hand-eye coordination may be improving hugely, making them even better at coloring-in 'between the lines', and making them way more accurate in sports play. Typically, around this age children can adeptly run, jump, stand on one leg, use a scooter, jump over a skipping rope and ride a bike with or without training wheels.

The functional physiology of motor skills can be very culturally dependent. For some societies, learning to herd cattle or ride horses is far more important by this age than learning to read and write — and kids are capable of both.

INTELLECTUAL DEVELOPMENT

THE BRAIN *(Neurology)*

By age five, the brain is almost adult-size; and by age six, the brain's development is 95 per cent complete. This is the time during which long-term memories start to get stored, such as a holiday at the beach, or a particularly magical Christmas, or the first day at school. For most of us, our earliest scratchy memories go back to around age three or four, but we usually have clearer childhood memories from around age five or six.

Of course such brain maturation is also dependent on adequate sleep, and at age five to six a child needs around 11–12 hours' sleep overnight — again, because it's essential for the brain's development and general personal contentment levels.

But in most cases the fundamental academic milestones for a new entrant are starting school and learning to read.

THE KNOWLEDGE (Cognition)

The leap from four to five can make the child almost unrecognisable, especially girls, because everything starts to 'click' in their mind. They know their colors, can copy alphabet letters, will point out specific words, and their masterpiece drawings can include houses with a door and chimney, and people with hands and feet. By six, some children can count to 100, and some are starting to learn to tell the time. They can also begin to develop an interest in particular activities.

Their improved focused concentration span, combined with greater dexterity, means they can physically carry out more precise tasks, like using scissors and using a knife to cut their own food.

For those parents who are religiously inclined, this becomes a very important age for religious education as well, such as attendance at Christian Sunday School, or Islamic Koran classes, or Hebrew lessons at the Jewish synagogue, or young Thai boys joining the local Buddhist monastery.

For many in the Western world, this is the age at which computer games become increasingly important to the child. Yes, we've all heard the statistics that demonstrate children who are skilled at computer games can become adept at developing quick reactions, very good peripheral vision and great information-processing skills. *Yada, yada,*

yada. But let's be real about this. Computer gaming is not the real world. So I believe such toys should always remain a treat, not an adrenaline-fuelled addiction. In our household, when homework or chores became arduous, computer games went away until these regular real-life tasks no longer felt laborious. And also, there was generally no electronic or computerised game-playing until their room was tidy and they've had a good play outside.

That's us; these were our policies. You do what's right for you.

GREAT TOYS AND GAMES

Toys, toys and more bloody toys. As Western parents we know the number of toys in our households can be bordering on insane. Between birthdays and Christmas, with a loving family, good friends and some spare change in our pockets, our children can accumulate a wealth of toys that can be beyond their ability to manage.

Then there is the 10-year-old girl just down the road who owns only one doll, or the 12-year-old boy still riding a bike designed for a much younger child. Then there is the four-year-old, just over an ocean away, who is dying of diarrhoea and needs no toys as he no longer has the energy to open his eyes.

The dichotomy of our world's extremes seems so senseless. But in the meantime, we need to deal with raising our children in a democratic, capitalistic and materialistic country, rich with inexpensive and expensive toys. Heck, McDonald's is the biggest toy seller in the world, just through their Happy Meals!

The Austrian educator and philosopher Rudolf Steiner (1861–1925) advocated 'natural' toys made from wood and organic fibres, such as handmade folk-toys, but in the current world it is di cult to avoid forever the requests to Santa for Barbie, action heroes, battery-operated plastic gadgets, and of course Lego. Often parents want to tone down the aggression by having a 'no-toy-gun' policy; but boys will just use sticks as make-believe guns and say 'bang bang'!

Then there's the overindulged way of life that today in the West is so routine. The gluttonous hedonism of excess toys is not often seen for what it actually is. I agree with Laura Schlessinger in *Stupid Things Parents Do to Mess up Their Kids* when she writes, 'Giving your kids whatever they want pushes them to become morally and philosophically aimless.' It's just not healthy.

At the end of the day, we should look at the middle path and ask ourselves: 'What does the child learn from this toy?' (Knowing they always learn something!) And 'Does this toy utilise my child's imagination — or replace it?' The middle path can be turning o the electronic entertainment — the TV, PC, Mac, Nintendo Wii, PlayStation, PSP, Xbox and touch-screen gaming apps. We want our children to be electronically savvy, but achieving balance is simply about moderation. If you want a specific recommendation, I suggest an hour a day maximum, and only when chores and homework have been done willingly and happily.

Below are some of my favourite toys and games for new entrants:

- » Creative activities, such as drawing, coloring, painting and clay modelling
- » Traditional games such as hopscotch, marbles, skittles, dominoes, jacks and pick-up-sticks
- » Simple board games, such as Ludo and Snakes and Ladders, then more strategic board games such as Connect Four
- » Memory games
- » Logic/problem-solving games
- » Role-playing games, complete with hand-me-downs for costumes
- » Physical games, involving equipment such as a ball and bat

- » Trampoline, with a safety net to avoid broken bones
- » Team sports at a local club.

THE LANGUAGE *(Vocabulary)*

The average five-year-old may have a vocabulary of 15,000 words, and they may especially love the word 'because'. They're also usually capable of memorising their personal details, such as address and phone number, and can probably recite all the characters' names from their favourite TV show. By their seventh year, their vocabulary will have doubled, their speech should be clearly understandable, though their grammar can still be confused. They are usually able to say the consonant sounds of R, S and Z between three and eight years of age, Sh between three-and-a-half and seven years, L, Ch, J and V between four and eight years, and Th between four-and-a-half and eight years.

Undoubtedly learning to read and write are two of the most significant tasks we will ever have to undertake but, unlike speech, they must be taught and consciously learned. At age six it's pretty normal if their writing is fairly rudimentary, and if some letters are backwards. This is all par for the course, and not necessarily an indication of dyslexia. They'll also begin to learn to spell, making lots of mistakes — English is a challenging language!

Regarding naming body parts, so long as their age consists of one digit, then I reckon easy words like 'boobs', 'belly button', 'tummy', 'bottom', 'fanny', 'willy' and 'balls' should be quite acceptable. Later, once children hit double digits and need to learn about the birds and the bees, it makes sense to teach more anatomically correct words, such as 'breasts', 'naval', 'stomach', 'buttocks', 'vagina', 'vulva', 'penis', 'scrotum' and 'testicles'. (A personal pet peeve is the double-standard parents who happily use casual colloquialisms for almost all body parts except the genitalia, where they insist their three-year-old says 'vagina' and 'penis'.)

Chapter Three

SOCIAL–EMOTIONAL DEVELOPMENT

Children with a sense of humour are good at amusing their peers and can gain a great deal of prestige for doing so. Childish jokes like pulling funny faces and memorizing rude rhymes and bad words are valuable currency in the playground.

Tessa Livingstone, *Child of Our Time*

THE BEHAVIOUR *(Psychological)*

At this age, children's behaviour, opinions and personalities get increasingly shaped by more and more people (children and adults) outside the family home, because children will adapt to fit in. Their personality of course is also shaped by their temperament, and is a result of inborn tendencies combined with family reactions (as well as many other complexities; see Chapter Nine).

By around age five, a child's personality characteristics and nature are usually fairly similar to what they will be in adulthood, though a tad more extreme around the edges with unexplainable fears, unpredictable fickleness, destructive, aggressive frustration, and powerful, demanding pestering. Plus they can be competitive, ungracious losers, approval-seeking junkies and Energizer bunny rabbits. Oh, and almost nothing can make them dissolve into fits of giggles more than the taboo of 'toilet humour' — burps and farts especially.

In reality, most six-year-olds do know what's expected of them and do know how to behave — wanting to do so, though, is an entirely different matter! You see, at six they can start to assert some pretty firm opinions about likes and dislikes, and may not have much hesitation in obstinately arguing the point.

FORMING FRIENDSHIPS

By age five, children usually have a fully developed sense of *self* and sense of *consciousness*, with a resulting sense of *self-consciousness*. This enables five-year-olds to be able to consider another person's point of view, which is part of a steep curve of learning to understand their own, and other people's, feelings. Of course, this is a really important part of forming friendships, because by age five, school friendships are usually just as influential as home life for children's social, intellectual and emotional development.

Also by age five, game rules tend to become absolute and must be followed the same way by everyone, with no exceptions. For example, Dr Charles E Schaefer and Theresa Foy DiGeronimo in *Ages and Stages* point out that when five-year-olds are asked if children in a different country play their games with the exact same rules, they will typically insist that they must! By age six, friends are becoming even more influential. Kids of this age can usually share quite well, and can really enjoy the company of their own friends. Girls typically have one or two close friends, and boys typically play in large groups. They all tend to love games with rules and like fair play. Predictably, teasing and name calling has also begun.

HANDLING SCHOOL

As a very generalised observation: if the child has had a structured pre-school environment, such as Montessori or a reading-writing focused pre-school, they tend to glide on into a conventional school setting without issue, especially girls who characteristically are *very* ready to be the 'big' schoolgirl. If the child has had a highly unstructured preschool or a play centre environment, often they can integrate into a conventional school setting with not too much issue. But also not uncommonly they, boys especially, can appear not quite so ready to be the 'big' school pupil, and are still just a tad voluntarily attached to the apron string.

If the child has never successfully sat still on the mat listening to their preschool teacher, they can really struggle with the expectation of sitting still to do 'work'. And their frustration at their inability to play-play-play can result in pretty disruptive behaviour in class.

But whatever you decide regarding education (there's more on this in Chapter Nine), we all need to remind ourselves how very, very fortunate we are to be the parents of children who can be educated — in China alone, 80 per cent of rural kids, well over 100 million children, don't ever get to attend primary school.

HOMEWORK AND AFTER-SCHOOL ACTIVITIES

Between extracurricular after-school activities and extracurricular schoolwork (homework, argh! At this age, I absolutely abhor it), there must be plenty of time to muck around and waste time. It's so important kids have time to be childish: going to the creek, skateboarding or rollerblading at the park, riding their bike on their street. People, it's called 'having a childhood'.

This is a great age for regular activities such as gymnastics, dancing or soccer, but I recommend *no* after-school activities for at least the first half of the year after starting school, as initially our little pipsqueak new entrants can be *shattered* at the end of their long, busy school day. When this time is up, maybe add in one activity a week after school, and perhaps a second activity the next year. But, oh please, don't hyper-schedule your children — not unless they very clearly have their own passion and the talent to do a particular activity.

SEARCH FOR THE HOLY GRAIL: AUTONOMY

A child needs independence to gain understanding of living by their wits — that is, learning to have and use common sense. Common sense is only gained by experience.

Five-year-olds are usually chomping at the bit to get some autonomy! So it's time to begin giving them small tasks using practical skills, such as helping clear the dinner table, taking out rubbish, raking leaves, joining Scouts, helping to look after younger siblings or doing the washing up. Certainly, in more traditional societies, many five- and six-year-olds are expected to make bigger contributions to the family workload. We in the West can so tend to baby our babes!

CHORES AND POCKET MONEY

On the can-of-worms topics of chores and pocket money, there are endless simple and complex possibilities for how this can work in your household. I will concede that we tried *numerous* systems, most of which failed due to their over-complexity or sheer inconvenience.

With school-age children, I believe honest work deserves honest income.

As a guideline, the real and meaningful daily chores our children are expected to happily do earn a monthly payment of twice their age in dollars. So the five-year-old gets $10, the 10-year-old gets $20. And it cannot be spent solely on junk food and junk toys.

If one of our children has lost or broken something by being irresponsible — such as their school eraser or swimming goggles — they're expected to pay for the replacement. They are also expected to put aside most of their money for a specific item they wish to save for. For example, at age seven-and-a-half, our youngest decided he wanted a motorbike. By age eight he had enough saved to pay half, and we paid the other half of a 49cc child's motorbike for his birthday. *Well done, Angelo!*

This is the chore system that we've finally settled into:

» *1–2 Daily Chores:* Making own bed, feeding the pets, watering the plants, emptying the dishwasher, setting the table or clearing the dinner dishes.

- » *2–3 Saturday Chores:* Cleaning own bedroom, changing bed linen, cleaning the kids' bathroom, vacuuming, hanging out the washing, bringing in washing, cleaning pet cage or fish tank, or mowing the lawns.

- » From age 10, cooking one dinner a week, including increasing the pocket-money to shop alone for the ingredients. (I appreciate some people can find this idea too much for this age - but it's not - kids are as capable as we expect them to be, and they all adore some autonomy.)

I am not suggesting that this is the *best* system for chores or pocket money — not at all. There are numerous brilliantly conceived reward schemes, and it can be a matter of trial and error. Find your own groove for what works for your family.

TARGET- AND GOAL-SETTING

With regard to formal target- and goal-setting, I believe this concept has become a somewhat irritating bane of our primary school parenting experience. I just don't reckon any child under 10 should be forced to set targeted academic goals they're expected to achieve in order to be taught about 'success'. At that age I want them just *to be*. That's all. Just be, in the *now*, not the future. Enjoying today, not thinking of tomorrow.

Because their little lives have *so many* academic and educational targets and extracurricular goals constantly set by their teachers, I always want home to generally be a goal-free *haven* from their achievement-oriented school lives.

So we didn't set goals at home with young children. We have crystal-clear expectations of acceptable behaviour, and chores that earn pocket money. But if their age consists of *only one digit*, then we didn't focus on targets and goals. But that's just me and one of my little pet peeves. I'm not saying I'm right. I'm just saying I'm adamant.

The exceptions set by parents are general life-skills: things like reading, times tables, riding a bicycle without training wheels and swimming without floaties. Hopefully kids won't need incentives for any of these, but a well-earned reward also isn't out of the question.

The other exceptions, determined by the children, are whatever goals they wish to set themselves . . . Some young children are very self-motivated, natural goal-setters — and if they are, support them to go for it.

Chapter Three

SUMMARY

Today's children are born into a period of excess as offspring of The Simpsons, graduates of crèches, and products of working families, post-modern theory, and a wireless interactive webbed world. Parents may have a broader experience than Shakespeare or Tolstoy, but breadth of experience is not necessarily accompanied by depths of perception. Instead it is common for parents to experience fragility, leaving them vulnerable to crackpot theories and new fads.

Michael Carr-Gregg, *Your Child Year by Year*

There really are just three traits we should want to develop and enhance in all our new entrants: happiness, confidence and success.

Teaching happiness is about teaching joy, through pretty much one powerful tool: demonstrating gratitude.

Teaching confidence is about turning the scary unknown into the comfortably familiar, through pretty much one powerful tool: knowledgeable awareness.

Teaching success is about knowing success and failure, through pretty much one powerful tool: first-hand experience. Success and failure are the yin and yang of the human journey, and the only way to truly know success is to know failure.

Chapter Four

THE 'WANNABE TALENTEDS' — SEVEN- TO NINE-YEAR-OLDS OVERVIEW

You must train the children to their studies in a playful manner, and without any air of constraint, with the further object of discerning more readily the natural bent of their respective characters.

Plato (427–347 BCE), *Greek philosopher*

These are typically some of the most pleasurable parenting years we can experience. Our munchkins are no longer helpless babes, yet also not quite hormonal whiners. This is the era when their competence grows into confidence. *So parents everywhere . . . enjoy, enjoy, enjoy your seven- to nine- year-olds!*

These are generally the last years of true, uncomplex childhood. The final stage in which our kids possess intrinsic trusting childish innocence and perhaps display the last snippets of their genuine, naïve and unsophisticated personalities — before they so often become complicated with the hormones of peripuberty. In an ideal world, all our seven- to nine-year-olds would be vivacious, uninhibited and constantly excited about living their lives! They may be mischievous, adventurous and audacious, and more than a tad impudent, foolhardy and bold. You'll probably find them exploring the local creek, climbing old trees, cycling with great gusto, perfecting their cartwheels, attempting roller-blading, giving soccer a go or learning to play an instrument.

This is not to say that seeing your preteen begin to blossom into a young adult isn't potentially glorious; it simply acknowledges that the concluding years of the single-digit ages are precious and fleeting — for both the child and the parent. *So again, parents everywhere . . . enjoy, enjoy, enjoy your seven- to nine-year-olds!*

PHYSICAL DEVELOPMENT

> *If there's one thing I've learned since becoming a mum, it's to be embarrassed of all the things I said I would never do. My wide-eyed Neverland idealism has transmogrified into cold, hard humble pie and I am eating it, baby.*
>
> Enzed Girl, 'Neverland', www.mumsontop.co.nz

THE BIOLOGY *(Structural anatomy)*

Children all grow and develop at different rates — and girls faster than boys — so don't compare or despair. But certainly our kids sometimes despair: big differences in height — or lack of it — can especially become an issue, a problem that usually sorts itself out during puberty. Increases in 'puppy fat' from about eight years of age can also be normal, especially for girls. And by eight, most children have around 12 permanent teeth.

NOTE: If puberty begins before the eighth birthday in girls (breasts budding, pubic hair sprouting, hips widening) or before the tenth birthday in boys (genitals enlarging, pubic hair sprouting, voice deepening), then this is early, and is termed 'precocious puberty'. It would be wise to have things investigated by a doctor. You can also balance out any treatment with holistic therapies, as precocious puberty can have psychological implications too. (See Chapter Five for more information on puberty.)

THE MOTOR SKILLS *(Functional physiology)*

By seven and eight years of age, most children have a well-developed sense of physical balance and good control of their finer motor movements, such as those needed for riding a bicycle. With improved strength and better hand-eye coordination, they can really begin to master key physical activities such as cycling, swimming, skating and bat and ball skills. All these tasks, though, need a lot of practice.

They may love challenges that test their agility and strength; climbing is almost always a favourite (as, it would seem, is consequently falling from trees and fracturing their arms — all part of childhood). Their stamina and competitive spirit are increasing.

Thirty years ago most children walked to school; today most children don't. Children have never been so sedentary. So we must encourage them to cycle, walk, swim, run, play ball games and practise cartwheels. It blows my mind when I hear intelligent, articulate parents encouraging their children to be sedentary, like reminding them to bring their electronic hand-held games to a park picnic. *I mean, really?!*

Another point we all need to remind ourselves of is that at this age children in traditional rural societies routinely, and out of necessity, contribute to the household economy. In fact it's estimated 100 million children globally are in paid employment, such as carpet weaving, with little time to play. Many more hundreds of millions of other children of this age seriously assist every day with household chores, such as fetching water, laying traps, digging fields and catching fish. Can we not expect our children to empty a rubbish bin or at least take out the recycling?

This age stage is all about starting to hand over the baton, and turning their competence into confidence.

INTELLECTUAL DEVELOPMENT

> *Teacher: 'You must follow the Ten Commandments, so then you will go to Heaven.'*
>
> *Seven-year-old: 'I'm definitely not doing that! I want to go to Heaven 'cause of old age!'*
>
> Our son Angelo

THE BRAIN *(Neurology)*

At seven, children have a hunger to learn, can think more logically, can be more systematic and can concentrate for longer, so altogether are becoming more able to solve complex matters. Yes, hands-on learning is still important (and always will be), but now they can also use *brainpower* to tackle abstract problems.

By eight, the brain has done most of its growing but is continuing to create pathways which will become permanent. This is one of the reasons why this age group may start to show talent or interest in particular academic subjects, or in the arts, or in sports — some of which can turn into lifelong passions. Between the ages of seven and nine, a child's brain needs around 10–11 hours of sleep a night... and you know by now what sleep deprivation does: it reduces learning potential and increases discontentment.

THE KNOWLEDGE *(Cognition)*

At seven years of age they can really begin to enjoy educational computer and electronic games, which are great for fine-motor skills. Just be careful about the content. Research shows that the 'broadband babysitter' exposes one-third of our children to porn, and almost one-tenth to harassment.

This is a great age to enhance their appreciation of Mother Nature. Take them to visit the city zoo or a petting farm, explore forests, investigate rock pools at low tide or grow veggies. This is also a great age to increase their understanding of practical things, like weighing baking ingredients, using a tape measure, helping with simple DIY tasks, like repairing a bike-tyre puncture, and general building and making 'stu '.

Seven-year-olds should have their simple addition and subtraction sums sussed, and perhaps a little multiplication or division, and maybe even more complex mathematical concepts like rudimentary geometry. At eight years old, they can usually start to add up columns, learning to 'borrow' and 'carry over'. Their grasp of counting, and numbers in general, is way more confident. By nine years old, they're usually doing routine multiplication and division, as well as understanding simple fractions, pie charts, bar graphs and more geometry.

GREAT TOYS AND GAMES

» Board games requiring logical decision-making and problem-solving, such as draughts/checkers, Chinese checkers, Cluedo, chess, backgammon, mahjong and mancala
» Card games, including solitaire/patience
» Sudoku
» Activities requiring patience and accurate hand-eye coordination, such as beading, knitting, sewing and cross-stitch

Chapter Four

THE LANGUAGE *(Vocabulary)*

The jump in speech between six and seven years can be huge — as can the increase in their vocabulary. Many seven-year-olds are confident independent readers. Baby-babble mispronunciation of consonants has significantly improved, more conceptual terms are understood better, and their vocabulary is accumulating adjectives... but English is so complex, and with all the new words, correct grammar can still be a bit of a struggle. You might hear your child say things like 'I finished the homework sheet what I needed to do'.

By eight, handwriting may really be improving, and children start to get their 'pen licence', when their teacher allows them to use ink instead of pencil. Plus, they'll probably be learning italic (joined-up) writing (extra tricky for the left-handed), though these days it's generally taught by adding 'flicks' to the end of each letter.

With all the improved vocab and logic, their questions are becoming clearer and more intelligent. In fact, speech and language continue to blossom in great leaps, with improved grammar, imaginative creative writing and dramatic storytelling, complete with a wishful melding of reality and fantasy.

TV — OBSESSIVE COMPULSION

This is also the age when the average Western child spends more than 1000 hours a year watching TV — in fact, more than six hours a day on non- physical media-related activities.

To quote Stephen Covey in *The 7 Habits of Highly Effective Families*: 'Just think about it: The average child spends seven hours a day watching TV and five minutes with Dad. Unbelievable!... Suppose you were on your deathbed. Would you really wish you'd spent more time watching TV?' *Arrrgggghhh! #?@%!*

All this TV watching is occurring when your child is truly beginning to understand, grasp and figure out the concepts of living and paradigms of life. We're mucking with their brains — one hour of TV a day is surely enough!

JOKIN' AROUND — LEARNING HUMOUR

This is an area in which my husband Mark especially excels: *kidding around*. Research shows there's a positive correlation between joke comprehension and cognitive maturity. So go ahead, pull their leg! Learning to understand humour is well documented as highly educational, because it assists children in becoming more sociable and outgoing.

CAUSE AND EFFECT — LEARNING CONSEQUENCES

Cause-and-effect learning is taking the lesson of consequence one step further.

From as young as age seven, given the opportunity, children are capable of persevering with tasks and developing reasoning skills to enable them to work out problems for themselves. There are some marvellous games of logic, which can assist children brilliantly with mastering this, including chess, backgammon, mahjong and mancala. They all help to develop strategy, mathematical skill, concentration and logical thought. This is the age when they really begin to learn the skills of problem-solving and decision-making. *Encourage, encourage.*

MUSIC — A VEHICLE TO LEARNING SPACE AND TIME

Seven years of age is when children can usually learn to sing in tune. Learning keyboard, and music in general, is enormously brain enhancing. In fact, the non-profit research institute MIND (Music Intelligence Neural Development) claims that its cutting-edge research into neuroscience and education demonstrates that learning music, such as piano or keyboard, and using its innovative and distinctive visual approach to learning, stimulates higher brain functions, such as those required for maths, chess, science and engineering.

Research explained in Dr Gordon Shaw's book *Keeping Mozart in Mind* documents how investigations have shown that just six months of piano or keyboard training can dramatically increase children's spatial-temporal reasoning and ability to learn difficult mathematical concepts. There's also compelling evidence that listening to Mozart can improve how children think, reason and create, because music is a 'window' to higher brain function.

This is also a fabulous age to begin many other wonderful left-brain/right-brain activities, such as playing drums, tap dancing and gymnastics. It all enhances brain development, and at this age, kids can love the ritual of weekly habits involving timetabled activities. (But don't go nuts over-scheduling them; just a couple of things a week can be plenty . . . they still need time to get up to childhood mischief!)

If your child can't stand music lessons and practice, then ditch things for now, and reconsider in a few months' time.

What if your child is demonstrating real talent? Perhaps they understand the complex abstract, will concentrate intensely during practices, have a broad spectrum of interests, can think critically, and can articulate very well for their age . . . then maybe you do legitimately have a 'gifted' child. If so, then it's time to start learning more about gifted children — Google and the library are good places to start.

HOMEWORK WORKSTATION — THEIR OWN 'SPACE'

At age seven, children become even more skilled with their hands, such as improving their typing and drawing skills, and their writing is becoming more legible, especially among girls, and has fewer back-to-front letters. So another wonderful thing we can do for our seven- to nine-year-olds is to make them a brilliant little workspace for brilliance to shine — a little place, say in their bedroom, that creates an atmosphere for learning, that is a dedicated work area place they can call their own. It doesn't have to be fancy or expensive: simply a small desk, a chair, a place to put things, paper to write on and pens to write with. I also had two *strongly recommended* golden rules regarding homework:

» Homework is never done in front of the TV, ever.

» No TV until homework is done, always.

SOCIAL–EMOTIONAL DEVELOPMENT

The child who seems miraculous in his precocious intelligence . . . the rich child who prefers disciplined work to frivolities of life, are normal children . . . Thus the deeper nature of the child returns to the surface not seven times but seventy times seven, however it be repressed by the adult.

Maria Montessori, *The Secret of Childhood*

THE BEHAVIOUR *(Psychological)*

At this age, children may start to get embarrassed by their parents' behaviour. They may reject any public a ection such as a kiss or cuddle, but can still be so lovingly a ectionate at home. They can abhor wearing certain clothes, usually because they're desperate to conform. One day they can be brimming full of loud bravado, then that night they refuse to allow you to see them naked . . . and they don't appreciate you poking around among their bedroom possessions anymore.

They can control most of their emotions, so are capable of pretending they don't care, are also ready-loaded for a battle of wills, plus all their pragmatic bargaining and negotiating can really do your head in. But at the end of the day, they still need our attention and affection, because they are still really struggling to contain genuine anger and distress; for instance, self-criticism at not being the best in the class at something.

Well, not all wannabe talented's are like all of this, but most of them are, and at this age, their most important role model — the one they tend to copy the most — is their same-sex parent. In fact, at this age, receiving of genuine praise from their parents is *by far* the most influential aspect in building self-confidence and subsequent self-esteem.

Psychologically, the dominant behavioural learning curve during this period is learning *sharing* and *cooperation,* as gradually children become more mature, and more at ease with themselves.

They can know their own mind: they may love books, they may have very specific hobbies and interests. Seven- to nine-year-olds may also love to collect things! Who knows what, it all depends on personality: stickers, shells, toy cars, cards for swapping . . . all precious treasures!

At this age, life can stop being quite such a carefree existence as worries and anxieties begin to creep in, such as friendship quarrels, school tests, failing in a sport, or home-life dramas. And, although a vast improvement on toddlerdom, they can still be rather impatient.

As their sense of identity grows, they also start to compare themselves to others, becoming aware of what they're good at and not so good at. And that's totally okay. We all can't be good at everything. It's normal, and it's important children learn that lesson: *no one's great at everything.* But don't demean them when they're distressed or worried, as their awareness of their failure isn't minor to them.

FORMING FRIENDSHIPS

From seven years of age, by being better able to see another person's point of view, children can start to develop deeper and longer-lasting relationships. They are also learning how to negotiate. At this age, friendships are still often made and then broken, and they probably have 'best friends' they routinely fall out with. But arguments with their friends may feel like the end of the world to them, so don't trivialise the issues.

At around eight years of age, team games can be especially beneficial — such as cricket, soccer, softball, football, hockey — so long as they're having pleasurable fun, and aren't being driven by an insanely over-competitive parent who is potentially implanting an inferiority complex in their child by incessantly yelling directions from the sidelines. Sporting activities should be about learning how to cooperate and contribute as part of a team, and learning the good sportsmanship of how to lose gracefully.

Usually, by the ninth year friendships really start to grow in terms of loyalty and commitment, and their social life is likely to become of central importance at school. They want to feel popular and included . . . *don't we all?*

Girls continue to tend to stick together in groups of two or three, playing turn-taking sorts of games. Boys continue to tend to hang out in larger groups, often playing in team competitions.

EN ROUTE TO SELF-SUFFICIENT INDEPENDENCE

For most children, getting to and from school may be the only time in their little lives they're free of adult supervision. *(Yay!)* But even then many children don't get the opportunity to act responsibly and do the right thing, because so many moms pick them up and drop them o at the school gate. *Aarrgghh.* I understand circumstances dictate bussing/walking/cycling is not always feasible, but if it is possible, and you're still driving them in the car . . . then shame on you! *Is this too judgemental?*

Yes, I get that they're safer with you. I well remember the phone call when our 12-year-old was hit by a car on a zebra crossing and the phone call when our 10-year-old was accosted by a strange old man. But as a society we also need to overcome our high levels of neurotic and intense overprotection. We have to return to the reality that our job is to teach them independence and self-sufficiency. Our job is to teach them how to eventually not need us.

Personally, at age five all our kids rode the school bus and made their own beds. At eight, they'd get themselves ready for school; getting dressed, making their breakfast and packing their lunch, plus bussing themselves to after-school activities, and on the weekend vacuuming their bedrooms. At 11, they'd cycle half an hour to school, mow the lawns, and weekly cook a family dinner. Ask them if they disliked it. Hell no! They loved having so many moments when they felt in charge of their lives.

It's not unreasonable for an eight-year-old to be given the responsibility of doing unsupervised things outside the home, such as outdoor play with the neighbourhood kids, or an errand to the dairy for milk. As parents, we must let go of the apron strings, and cut the umbilical cord. Not from cruelty, but from respect for their capabilities. Show them you know they're more than capable of exceeding your expectations! If you're feeling like their slave, then perhaps you're *way* overdoing stuff, and inhibiting them from becoming organised and self-sufficient individuals.

FANTASTICAL FICTION OR FUNDAMENTAL FACTS

As an aside, what is my opinion regarding Father Christmas, the Easter Bunny and the Tooth Fairy? Oh, what a little hornet's nest of a topic.

I will let Noell Hyman in Dale McGowan's *Parenting Beyond Belief* answer on my behalf: 'I love Santa and the Easter Bunny. I cannot imagine my childhood without those wonderful nights of exhilarating anticipation. They brought a joy that only Disneyland could match. Discovering they were not real did no damage to my psyche. It was more like discovering the secret to a great magic trick.'

To avoid your children potentially being mocked and ridiculed at school, I recommend the truth is explained to them before their tenth birthday, as a coming-of-age ritual.

MORAL DEVELOPMENT

> *Every so often I'll encounter someone at a seminar or on the radio who will ask, 'How can I get my child to not cross the boundaries?' The answer is always, 'That's her job! Crossing boundaries — testing the limits — is your child's job. Your job is to be on the other side of the crossing and to make it unpleasant for her when she does.'*
>
> Henry Cloud and John Townsend, *Raising Great Kids*

GROUND RULES

By age seven, a child has reached the age of reason, the time for developing their moral compass. Most understand the rules of their home, their school and the general rules of their community, such as that the police are an authority. At this age they typically know the rules of routine, such as 'put your schoolbag away', and the rules of household values, such as not to touch the ornaments on the top shelf.

They know the basics of rights and wrongs, and are likely to do the right thing, but more from motivation to avoid punishment than out of motivation to be especially generous or kind.

By this stage we should expect them to always use 'please' and 'thank you' — good manners help them get on in life. It's also time to start expecting some displays of selflessness — being considerate just to be considerate.

Our seven- to nine-year-olds, hopefully, will have been surrounded by sound values all their lives, such as that stealing is wrong and racism is not tolerated. But now it's time to start to consciously teach morals .

. . which, let's face it, most of us spend the rest of our lives perfecting. Our morals are constantly being refined, as life erodes away previously ill-founded notions, or at other times life cuts great slashes into our groundless notions of 'right' and 'wrong'.

But we've all got to start somewhere, and it should well and truly have begun by the time kids have been at school for a couple of years! And remember, the more we protect them from outcomes during childhood, the less practice they have amassed for dealing with the consequences of their own behaviour in adulthood.

HAIL MOTHER, FULL OF WISDOM! AND OUR FATHER, WHO KNOWS SO MUCH!

This is a play on two traditional prayers and the 'told-you-so' line, and they are a couple of the idiosyncratic adages that have developed to become part of our quirky family's eccentricities. Let me explain . . .

Some parents have too little concern about how their children should best do things — they don't give a damn, which of course is horrid. Other moms and dads feel compelled their entire lives to continually tell their children how to do things. But heck, making decisions and learning by mistakes is what childhood and adolescence is all about.

As parents, Mark and I never say 'Ha! Told you so!' to our kids. Instead we just smile wryly and say, sometimes quietly, sometimes profoundly, 'Hail Mother, full of wisdom!' or 'Our Father, who knows so much!' All this means is that at some earlier moment in time we had pointed out the obvious and inevitable. But who are we to ruin the surprise!

SEX EDUCATION: PART ONE

On or around your single-digit child turning into a double-digit child is the age when I recommend, and plenty of experts back me, that it is time — *eeek* — to have the first birds-and-bees conversation. Make it an introductory basic sex talk about boys' and girls' bodies, the mechanics of making a baby, periods and 'getting to know' your genitals.

Children shouldn't be heading into intermediate or middle school without knowing those life basics. We want to be their main sex educators — not misinformation from their friends. Information does not equal permission; information is what they need to be able to make wise decisions. We must start early, and try our best not to sound like a complete prat or a 1950s sex-ed film. It's about us making sure our kids know we're always open to further conversations with them on the topic — any topic, almost any time — and that we can answer any of their questions — no matter how shocking — without judgement.

Sex ed is not one conversation. This is simply the first conversation of many over the years ahead.

SPECIAL ASIDE: DON'T BE THE ENTITLED PARENT

We live in a western world with a hideously increasing amount of adults feeling ridiculously 'entitled', demonstrated blatantly through their (your?) trigger-happy knee-jerk over-reactionary levels of complaining endlessly about the service they received not meeting their expectations ... the midwife seemed too tired, the doctor was too busy, the teacher didn't teach right, the coach didn't coach right ... the adult levels of whinging and whining and griping and criticizing is insane, and the subsequent parental levels of bad-tempered fault-finding nit-picking is ridiculous. WHY are your kids entitled to fabulous education and wonderful teachers? They're NOT entitled, at all. They're just as entitled as the average Somalian child who only has two years of schooling, or the typical Congo child where their household annual income is US$100, or the Angolan child who has a one in five chance to not even living until age five. Your kids – our kids – none of them are entitled to the incredibly wonderful, joyful, nourishing and magical childhoods they have. So make sure you teach them to realize they are blessed - not entitled - and some of the luckiest children on our planet!

SUMMARY

She will be curious about the world and begin to think and act more independently. The greatest challenge will be finding a balance between her need for family and a desire for freedom.

Carol Cooper, Claire Halsey, Su Laurent
and Karen Sullivan, *Your Child Year by Year*

Dr Christiane Northrup is a renowned holistic physician who has been a pioneer in partnering conventional and complementary medicine. In her encyclopaedic *Mother-Daughter Wisdom*, Dr Northrup divides childhood into three seven-year cycles of maturation, which are also acknowledged by an impressive number of world traditions: 0–7 years, 7–14 years and 14–21 years.

Corresponding research shows beyond any doubt that it is from seven years plus that our children's self-esteem and well-being can be formed from skills such as physical prowess, social competence, self-discipline, self-trust, financial literacy, developing individual talents and positive self-image. Then there is Ron Clark, author of the *New York Times* bestseller *The Essential 55*, who describes in his follow-up book *The Excellent 11*, what he believes are the qualities teachers and parents should use to motivate, inspire and educate children. The first 10 are enthusiasm, adventure, creativity, reflection, balance, compassion, confidence, humour, common sense, appreciation and resilience. But he concludes, 'Of all of the wonderful qualities that are mentioned in this book, no word better personifies a teacher than the word *passion*.'

Our job is to be passionate parents — not fiery, quick-tempered hot-bloods, but fervent, ardent and loving parents. Our job is to help our wannabe talenteds discover their talents.

Chapter Five

THE PUBESCENT PRETEEN —
10- TO 12-YEAR-OLDS OVERVIEW

Don't laugh at youth for his affectations; he is only trying on one face after another to find a face if his own.

Logan Pearsall Smith, *Age and Death, Afterthoughts*

Although this chapter is not designed to be about growing *teenagers*, in reality, our *prepubescent* 10-year-olds are simply still behaving like prepubescent nine-year-olds. For it is the biological process of *adolescence* itself which profoundly changes our child physically, emotionally and socially: it is adolescence's period of puberty that transforms the nine-, 10- or 11-year-old prepubescent child's body and mind into the 10- to 12-year-old pubescent preteen.

As a result, you can write about a typical five-year-old, or a typical eight-year-old, but when it comes to writing about 'be-tweenies' it is impossible not to merge into writing about the topic of *teenagers*. You've got the 11-year-old girl looking and acting like she's 14, complete with eyeliner, handbag, and high heels and you've got the 12-year-old girl still looking and behaving like a shy and petite nine-year-old. You've got the 10-year-old boy stuck behaving like an irresponsible eight-year-old ragamuffin; and you've got the 12-year-old boy rapidly sprouting into a young gentleman — plus everything in between.

In reality, for most children, puberty, defined as the beginning of the functioning of the sex organs, begins before they officially become a teenager. However, we can never know in advance quite when puberty will begin, or how long it will last. It is *hormones* that cause our sons and daughters to morph, inside and out, and their brains to temporarily seem to be no longer the 'whole walnut'. It is the surging oestrogens and testosterone that are the biggest influence over our 10- to 12-year-olds' development, as they begin to dip their toes into the murky waters of becoming an adolescent.

Welcome to the challenging parenting-a-pubescent-preteen roller-coaster world, where your bubbly, energetic and enthusiastic child begins to switch unpredictably between an uncertain child and a mature adult, where a fun-loving youngster may often be replaced by a downcast, forgetful grump, suffering from anxiety and fluctuating moods, and who has difficulty with focused concentration. Or to quote Nigel Latta, this stage is 'the rise of the Neanderthal, and the bitchy physics of the Girl-niverse'.

So in this chapter my goal is not to tell you what your 10- or 11- or 12-year-old 'betwixt tweenager' will be like — *only God knows* — or how you should parent them. For you know your child best. But what I do wish to do is release basic misconceptions from the shackles of ignorance. I just want to help.

PHYSICAL DEVELOPMENT

> *They're also insightful individuals who carry in their heads the answers to many of the questions we have about them and who can show us the way forward if we will only pause long*

enough to ask the question . . . and then wait graciously (and silently) for the answer.

Celia Lashlie, *He'll Be OK*

Surges of sex hormones initiate the start of the adolescent's pronounced growth spurt and period of sexual development called puberty. As growth rate reaches its maximum, fat gain reaches its minimum.

The forehead grows significantly, with the development of the frontal sinuses and the brow ridges, plus the upper and lower jaw project forward to a greater degree, more so for boys.

Because girls' growth spurts start at the beginning of puberty, and boys' growth spurts don't occur until well into puberty, it is common that preteen boys can be shorter than preteen girls.

DENTAL NOTE: By age 12, most children have their adult molars, and by age 14 they usually have their 28 adult teeth. The final four wisdom teeth appear later in their teens or early twenties.

GIRLS INTO WOMEN

Driven by oestrogen released by their gonads (ovaries), puberty for girls usually starts at around 10 or 11 years with breast development. Their breasts bud and nipple areolas enlarge; their arms and legs get longer, with their limbs becoming fatter; they become more shapely as their hips and shoulders widen; their torso grows taller; and their feet reach adult size before the rest of their body. Somewhere between 11 and 14 years is when girls typically grow the fastest, increasing in height by around 25 centimetres in two to three years (or around eight to 12 centimetres per year).

Girls also of course develop the capacity to bear children at this stage: the ovulation cycle and menstruation cycle (or 'periods') usually begin at around 11 or 12 years — though some girls begin their periods as early as eight years, and some as late as 16. This can be weight related; they usually need to be at least 45 kilograms to menstruate. First periods typically last for two to seven days of bleeding, every 24–34 days. Over time, periods gradually establish themselves into the average five days per 28-day cycle. Girls are likely to have period pains, some bad enough to absolutely deserve analgesic pain relief such as paracetamol. Girls can also occasionally experience heavy periods (menorrhagia), but this shouldn't be happening every month. Today, some Western girls are experiencing their first periods on average between ages eight and 11 years; in our grandmother's day, it was between 12 and 14 years.

By 11, some girls may have pubic hair, which on average takes around three years to fully develop to an adult level, but generally appears somewhere between ages 12 and 18. Around 18 months after pubic hair appears, armpit hair develops, taking one to one-and-a-half years to fully develop. The hormone oestrogen usually surges at around 12 years and peaks at 14. Their hips continually widen until their late teens, but once their periods have begun girls will most likely grow no more than another six centimetres in height.

BOYS INTO MEN

Driven by testosterone released by their gonads (testes), puberty for boys usually starts a couple of years later, at around 12 or 13 years, or even as late as 14. This is when, after a slowed period of growth as they reach an advanced stage of puberty, they have a pronounced, rapid growth spurt, usually growing 12 centimetres in a single year, and almost 30 centimetres over a couple of years.

Their growth also happens 'outside-in' — that is, hands and feet first, then arms and legs, and then the torso. Sometimes there's a bit of breast enlargement until testosterone levels rise. Although muscles are thickening, boys typically become gangly because their bones are growing faster (and thinner), but not as fast as their muscles. As a result they can become clumsy, because their brain has to relearn how to balance.

At around 13 or 14 years, boys' testes enlarge, then their penis lengthens and the scrotum skin changes. They also develop the capacity to father children, called spermarche, which is the beginning of sperm production in the testes. However, 'wet dreams' (ejaculating during their sleep) and involuntary daytime erections can begin to occur as early as age 10.

At around 14 or 15 years, their vocal cords enlarge, doubling in length in a single year, often quite suddenly lowering the pitch of their voice by several octaves.

For boys, testosterone typically surges at around age 14, then peaks at 16, causing the development of acne and pubic hair, and then two years later facial, armpit, arm and leg hair. Their face also changes shape, with the jaw becoming squarer, shoulders broaden, and muscles continue to fill out until the late teens.

Once in his twenties, after his growth has begun to plateau, a young man's muscular strength begins to peak.

INTELLECTUAL DEVELOPMENT

Raising teenagers is like trying to nail Jell-O to a tree.

Author unknown

THE BRAIN (Neurology)

Just before puberty, at age 10 or 11, the brain's frontal lobes have a rapid spurt of growth in relation to its inter-neuron connections. But during adolescence some of this activity reverses as connections are pruned back, with the teenager's prefrontal cortex — the area responsible for policing emotions — shrinking. Thus, you get teenage mood swings and frequent temper tantrums while this part of their brain is readying its circuits for survival and reproduction.

It's not until at least 18 years of age, past the turbulent teenage period, that the brain, as an adult brain, finally stops developing and pruning neuron connections. However, the frontal lobes don't fully reach maturity until our early twenties. I remember years ago being told by someone wise: 'Never marry a man before he's 25 — he's too young to know his own mind.' (It seemed like good advice, and I married Mark at 26, but actually it's very sound advice indeed.)

By age 11, a child still needs nine to 10 hours' sleep a night, which reduces to around nine hours by age 15. It's not until our twenties that we need just eight hours nightly, and about seven by our thirties.

THE KNOWLEDGE *(Cognition)*

By 11 or 12 years a child's levels of understanding have usually improved so they can better analyse problems, solve hypothetical challenges, take pride in their abilities and be eager to master new skills. So, from 10 years of age, this more sophisticated logical thinker can develop more focused attention on particular interests.

As explained by the renowned Professor Robert Winston, because of the brain's 'rewiring' during adolescence, the part of their brain that enables teenagers to read facial expressions is one of the areas affected. As a result, younger children are more skilled than the average teen at recognising the emotions on faces, such as happy, sad and angry expressions. They do regain this skill as they mature, but during the peaking periods of adolescence, don't expect them to know your thoughts just by your facial expressions alone!

THE LANGUAGE *(Vocabulary)*

Ten-year-olds can talk and talk and talk, and especially love dramatic adjectives. They can also become rather smooth operators. To quote *Your Child Year by Year*, 'He may have the negotiation skills of a car salesman, managing to get what he wants by striking at the right time, and hitting the right notes'. At this stage, it's about teaching them the skills to transform their tantrums, complete with slammed doors or huffy sulks, into an opportunity for reasoning, debating and negotiating. Although sometimes they can't control their emotional outbursts, they are getting better at trying to stay in control.

This is also very much the right age for children to learn to appreciate the courtesy of not just saying 'Sorry', but of saying 'Sorry for blah blah blah'; and not just saying 'Thanks' but saying 'Thank you for blah blah blah'.

Around this age, oral vocabulary directly reflects the amount they've read; it's no surprise that the more they read, the wider the vocab. This is also when they'll start to make sexual jokes, use swear words and use dating talk among their peer group.

At age 11, our testy, touchy, irritable grouch can snap with quick-tempered sarcasm, for they understand the paradox of irony, the symbolism of metaphor and the comedy of humour — and they'll get back at you by debating logic to turn the tables. They're often confused about peer pressure, 'coolness' and their desire to please, so may need, girls especially, to vent their feelings.

SOCIAL-EMOTIONAL DEVELOPMENT

> *Teenagers are people who act like babies if they're not treated like adults.*
>
> Alfred E Neuman, *MAD magazine mascot*

SELF-AWARE vs SELF-CONSCIOUS

At 10, growing self-awareness means they will be cognisant of their values and talents, and they will begin to compare themselves to others ... which in turn makes them feel more self-conscious than ever before. Their identity among friends and family is being carved out: Leader? Follower? Joker?

At 11, they are developing clearer ideas of what is right and wrong, good and bad, normal and abnormal.

The pubescent, adolescent teen increasingly mixes more with the opposite sex; will want to spend more time with friends and less time with family; will be becoming increasingly influenced by their peer group (values, appearance, interests); and will experience mood changes, for which their surging hormones are mostly responsible, especially in girls.

In general, the preteen and teenage years may be confused, frustrated and moody times, as the frontal lobes sprout new neuron connections. Our adolescents have greater difculty judging others' emotions, and become renowned for their insensitivity and social awkwardness.

INDUSTRIOUS vs INCOMPETENT

When it comes to solving problems, let kids brainstorm to try to solve many of their own problems themselves ... it's the only way they'll learn how. Research by psychologist Wulf-Uwe Meyer found that by 12 years of age, children might actually see praise not as a good sign, but as an indication that praise is required because they lack ability and need encouragement. On the flipside, criticism may also convey to the child that they can perform better.

TIME MANAGEMENT

Are you an adult who is hopeless at time management? If so, then you can't expect your preteen to be better. Some naturally will be, but you have no reason to expect them to be. So my advice is that you need to get good at time management yourself, or at least *appear* to be good at it in front of the kids. It's about walking the walk, not just talking the talk. Adults who habitually run late are actually being disrespectful of other people's time, and that's not okay — so don't lead by poor example.

My motto for scheduling is: *don't waste brain space with diary space.* In my life, if it's not written down, it probably won't happen. I write it down in my diary, then I can stop trying to remember it. But encouraging our children to have good time-management skills is quite a different topic to hyper-scheduling your kids.

In today's busy society, being proficient at time management is a great life skill to teach our preteens. For example, in any reasonably sized intermediate or middle school, they will already have specialist-topic teachers, each handing out homework unaware of what their colleagues are also assigning — and so our preteens need to start to learn to become time efficient. Or perhaps they need to learn to do the week's homework on Mondays and Wednesdays after school, because on Tuesdays and Thursdays they enjoy after-school activities — and who the heck wants to have to do homework on a Friday night or on the weekend, eh?

TARGET- AND GOAL-SETTING

These words are back in our lives again, but now at an age-appropriate time. At a double-digit age, it is time to face the truth and rise to the challenge of living in a target-setting, goal-orientated world — and it's time for our soon-to-be-teens to start to 'get with the programme'.

What can we parents do to help?

Well, a 'not negotiable' is leading by example; getting things done yourself is another way to teach your kids how to become self-reliant. Yes — *yuck, eeek* — but yes. By this 'mature' age, your word as parents now has bugger-all credibility if you only talk the talk. As parents of preteens we must all walk the walk.

It's about creating visible, self-assigned goals — it's the only true way to lead by example. Maybe it's completing a university degree *(like I did, God help you, literally)*, but it doesn't have to be that big. It could be losing 10 kilograms, or competing in a local triathlon, or learning belly-dancing, or religiously walking 45 minutes every morning, or working overtime to save for a new car, or the family going without treats to save for a holiday, or finally finishing the garden, or at last completing the kitchen refurbishment. Whatever. But target- and goal-setting is one of the 'see-and-be-seen' activities of parenting. If you're slack at it, then the kids have all the excuses in the world to be slack at reaching their targets too.

If you've never specifically set goals in your life but want to demonstrate this to your kids, then here are my recommendations. It's really important that our preteens *see* us fulfilling our own dreams:

- » Decide on a goal and break it down into short-term and longer-term parts.
- » Use visualisation, such as making a dream board, or sticking a picture on the fridge. Do something that shows your goal publicly to the kids.
- » Celebrate reaching pre-decided stages with mini-rewards; the 'accomplish that & receive this' incentives.
- » Remember the adage: *Goals in concrete, plans in sand*. Appreciate that goals can sometimes need refining.

RISK-TAKING BEHAVIOUR

Apart from moodiness, the other dominant pubescent trait is risk taking. Oblivious to potential dangers, adolescent risk-taking behaviours can become seriously hazardous activities, especially when combined with hour-to-hour fluctuating moods.

When we ask adolescents 'Why'd you do *that*?!', the answer is typically 'I dunno'— which can be an honest answer. A leading reason for such behaviour is because their brain has not yet fully developed its capacity to assess threats. All in all, pubescent risk taking can lead to a relentless testing of limits and experimentation with inexplicably stupid and dangerous stunts.

Then there are the powerful sexual urges, and an adolescent's ghastly, lonely struggle with their sense of identity, a constant tug-of-war of childish versus adult behaviour. Boys can act aggressively macho; girls can act sexily feminine.

There's also using dress style to identify and express their group 'membership', as well as characteristically refusing to fit into societal norms, and revelling in some sort of 'antisocial' socialising. Oh, the birth of the rebellious youth! Sex, driving, smoking, alcohol, drugs — why do they do it? *(Why did most of us do it?)*

By the way, it seems that for most of us our frontal-lobe activity increases as we get older, making us generally less and less inclined to take risks. What sensible, logical, rational and level-headed (boring) grown-ups we all must resign ourselves to eventually becoming! But as Dr Who famously said, 'There's no point in being grown up if you can't be childish sometimes.' Or as my fab brother-in-law Peter says, 'If you can't be good, be careful. If you can't be careful, be memorable!'

MORAL DEVELOPMENT

My father didn't tell me how to live; he lived, and let me watch him do it.

Clarence Budington Kelland (1881–1964), *American writer*

FREEDOM AND RESPONSIBILITY

The freedom-loving 10-year-old child loves to push boundaries — all kids do — but this begins to amplify in preteens. They strive to be more independent, yearning for the watchful eye of supervision to look the other way.

But whether puberty has commenced or not, our double-digit children need to be ready to be entrusted with more freedom and relied upon to do more chores around the home. They can become especially capable in helping out in their community, such as assisting a neighbour, being in charge of recycling or being involved in local fundraising work.

With freedom comes responsibility — in our household that motto has been hammered into our preteens, including the ground-rule responsibilities of honourable ethics and common sense!

COMMON SENSE

Your preteen is a pupa; they are no longer the larva that's been munching away during childhood on information, information and more information. Now, your preteen is assimilating all this information. Sure, they're gathering more, but they're no longer primarily about accumulating, especially from parents. Now they're primarily about integrating everything they've learnt so far into their person, and developing their own set of consolidated morals.

At this time, more critically than ever before, we as parents need to be black and white on what our own ethics and morals are, relating to our partner, children, parents, family, colleagues, neighbours, community and environment, locally and globally.

Do we clearly accept our responsibility to be good, for our own spirit (and our God/Creator if we believe in one)? Do we overtly accept our responsibility to do the right thing for our own soul (and our fellow earthly creatures)? Do we show gracious respect for cultural di erences and considerate regard for individual di erences? Or maybe not?

We owe our children the right to have parents who have overtly blatant ethics and evidently explicit values. But we also must not expect our kids to create their own set of moral values as simply cloned facsimiles of our own — that would be expecting the impossible, and humankind wouldn't continue to develop and evolve. All we must do, should do, have to do, is provide them with the gift of a robust backbone, so they know 'This is who my parents are, that is what they believe is right and wrong, for these are their morals and values.'

While your preteen is a pupa, your morals can be a protective cocoon. As the renowned talkshow host Dr Phil says over and over again, 'Bad things happen when you put yourself in bad situations . . . You have to take care of yourself, before you can take of others . . . The number-one way we can protect our children is to teach them to self-protect.'

For example, we must teach our preteens to be aware of their surroundings, as most youth crime involves teenager against teenager. It's the obvious things like walking alone at night; like appreciating that being out of it on alcohol or drugs dramatically increases anyone's vulnerability to risk; like realising that headphones and earphones takes away the safety aspect of hearing. So, of course, walking alone at night listening to your iPod is just a really dumb thing to do! Add into the mix an iPod-listening youth stopping in the evening at a poorly lit ATM machine — and well, hey presto, it's a victim waiting to happen.

An absolute 'not negotiable' in our household is that our preteens (and teens) must let us know where they're going, and who they're going to be with. This is not because we don't trust them; it is because we don't trust the crazy people out there. We explain that it's like cyclists wearing reflective jackets: it's not because the person is a bad cyclist — it's because they don't trust the idiot drivers. Teach them that having someone of importance in their life who knows where they are going and who they'll be with is just one of those staying-safe things we all do. Later, when they're grown up, it could be a flatmate, work colleague or partner. But until the law of the land deems them to be an adult, then it's our legal parental responsibility to know where they are. We trust them. We just don't trust every other reckless idiot or creepy nutcase or careless dumb-ass . . . and there are plenty of those around!

Your preteen is metamorphosing into a young adult, and it is awareness of your moral values that can enable him or her to emerge from the cocoon as a beautiful and awe-inspiring young person, fully equipped with all the wisdom we can give.

SEX EDUCATION: PART TWO

A child today faces more sexual signals and temptations on the way to school than his grandfather did on Saturday night when he was looking for them.

Josh McDowell (1939–),
American Christian evangelist and writer

The main point to realise with preteens is that if you think you don't know what's going on in your kid's sex life, then you're probably quite right — and if you think you do know, then you're probably quite wrong. We need to tell our preteens that no question is o -limits. Sex education is not one big talk at 13 or 14 years of age, it's an ongoing conversation from 10 or 11 years onwards.

At around 10, puppy-love crushes can begin, so it's not uncommon for 10-year-olds to be experimenting with some kissing and cuddling of the opposite sex. Then from around 11 years of age, previously platonic boy-girl friendships can become even more serious kissy-cuddly early romances. True love, or just a crush? One thing is for sure: any indication from you that it isn't the 'real thing' can make your preteen think that you don't understand their feelings.

There are differences these days from what went on in 'our day'. For example, sadly, 'sexting' has become a popular activity from intermediate/middle school onwards. Sexting is sending sexy text messages and nude pictures via mobile phone. But at this age, most sexy-pic senders don't realise the receiver will often show the saucy naked photos to all his or her friends too, and most preteens don't appreciate that cybersexting (even sending or receiving pictures of themselves) is actually illegal porn. Plus when those pictures make their way onto the internet (which they invariably do) they're there for time immemorial, never going away. The implications are that years later a university or employer could Google a course or job applicant and find their teenage nude pictures on the worldwide web. We must teach our kids that the minute they send it, they've lost control of it.

This book advocates open and honest communication. And perhaps no topic more than *sex* will define, in the parent-child relationship, just how transparent communication is in a family. Your goal — all our goals — is to make your kids always feel that nothing will be swept under the rug, for no topic is taboo.

NOTE: Cyberbullying is also illegal. If anyone receives four unwanted text messages in seven days — which they don't reply to — they can contact the mobile phone company, who will send a warning or bar the offender from their network — or, in even more serious cases, may assist with law enforcement.

LOOKING TO THE FUTURE — IDENTITY VS ROLE

The most important thing that parents can teach their children is how to get along without them.

Frank A Clark (1915–2003),
police chief and congressional Democrat

Today's Western youths have more freedom and less responsibility than generations of their predecessors — *and it's not natural*.

We've got eight-year-olds who've never set and cleared the dinner table, nine-year-olds whose moms always tidy their rooms, 10-year-olds who've never emptied and stacked a dishwasher, 11-year-olds who've never used a vacuum cleaner, and 12-year-olds who've never cleaned a toilet or mopped a floor. If we don't give our younger children responsibilities, then later we can't entirely blame the 13-year-old who refuses to mow the lawns, or the 14-year-old who doesn't know how to cook a family dinner, or the 15-year- old who's more interested in the TV and computer screens than ever getting o his or her chu to enjoy the income from an after-school job — because we've failed to teach them a basic work ethic.

Many people say our kids are growing up too fast these days. I think many smother-mothered kids are actually growing up way too slowly. Sixteen and 17-year-olds used to be viewed as young adults, and it is only in recent decades they have come to be seen as irresponsible teens. Our modern culture has created that twisted vision. It's our society that has so painstakingly taken away responsibility after responsibility — and subsequent respect — from our budding adults. Let's face it, even the eighteenth birthday sure as heck ain't respected by our community as the entry into adulthood — we see it as legally letting loose yet another bloody pub-drinking, beer-swilling, car-racing hooligan on our community.

I believe as parents of today's Alpha Generation-Z children, we *must* take earnest responsibility to ensure we take every opportunity we can to give our child-like dependents tastes of adult-like independence, responsibilities and freedom. Lest we forget, making our dependents independent is the whole purpose of our role as parents! It's about instilling in our younger children a 'with freedom comes responsibility' ethos, so eventually our teens are able to experience adult-like responsibilities, before they can legally drink, vote or drive a car. It's about them experiencing their roles, so they can discover their identity. And it all needs to begin in childhood.

SUMMARY

Our youth now love luxury. They have bad manners, contempt for authority; they show disrespect for their elders and love chatter in place of exercise; they no longer rise when elders enter the room; they contradict their parents, chatter before company; gobble up their food and tyrannize their teachers.

Socrates (469–399 BCE), *Greek philosopher*

As David Walsh writes in *Why Do They Act That Way?*, 'Adolescence is not a problem to be solved. It is an experience to be lived.' Puberty, the adolescent transition to adulthood, is about autonomy with a safety net, it's about learning to handle adult responsibilities while still having the back-stop of connectedness with family.

Do I know how close I personally came to not making it through those years intact? *Hell yes!* I pashed boyfriends at 11 years, smoked cigarettes at 12, was regularly paralytic at 13 years, and had the police arrive at my fourteenth birthday. By 15 I was routinely toking marijuana and acid- tripping on LSD, and by 16 I had shifted out of home to set up flat, waiting for my boyfriend to get out of jail (not the man I married) . . . And I knew lots of people my age doing the same things — and worse. By the way, my parents were a loving, church-going couple, who scrimped and went without to send me to a respected private school — there was *no* dysfunctional family home to blame, I was simply a rebellious youth on a journey of self-discovery.

I remember so vividly, as a hippy extremist, sauntering around with my equally extremist hippied-out friends, decked out in velvet and lace, brightly tie-dyed muslin, gypsy skirts, beaded headbands and handmade jewellery — and loving that we turned every conservative head to stare at us in shocked disapproval. We were a sight. We knew it. And we didn't care what anyone thought. We hated conservatism and loved intentionally 'freakin' out the oldies'.

So yes, today I truly, deeply realise the enormous impact my own parents' concrete fundamentals of strong ethics had in preventing me from derailing irreversibly. You see, I always knew that much of what I was doing was wrong, even if many of my 'friends' didn't.

It is so vital we all lay down for our children, while they are still children, immensely strong foundations *before* they enter puberty. Because once surging hormones arrive on the scene — oftentimes before they formally become teens — our children begin to 'disappear' for a few years into the mostly inaccessible and unreachable zone of the zitty-faced, hate-myself anguishing youth. By the time they're 10, they need to know with unequivocal certainty who their parents are, and what they stand for.

Alas, it is not for us to tell our children who they should be or what they should believe in, because to do so is almost guaranteed to create a rebellious youth. Instead it's about us demonstrating our own strong morals and principled ethics, while at the same time giving them self-sufficient, independent opportunities to act responsibly, so they can truly begin to fathom who they are, and what they stand for. With the end goal that between 18 and 20, our kids will have become fully self-aware, socially confident young adults, who are pursuing passionate personal interests, developing rewarding careers and experiencing loving relationships.

Am I advocating all teens should experience something similar to my own journey? *Hell no! My poor parents!* But do I honestly regret those years? *Hell no! I had a blast!* And perhaps more than anything else, I'm still that eclectic hippy bohemian at heart. Peace and love, man.

Section Two

CHILDREN'S BODIES

Parenting using Physiological IQ

Section Two Introduction

LIVING IN A TOXIC WORLD

> *We are living in a world today where lemonade is made from artificial flavors and furniture polish is made from real lemons.*
>
> Alfred E Neuman, *MAD magazine mascot*

The top six essentials to human survival are oxygen, water, sleep, salt, potassium and movement — without these, we die pretty quickly. Of course, in reality, we possess an incredibly complicated human body, which has 11 complex systems continuously working in synchronicity to attempt to maintain our homeostasis (equilibrium). Understanding our body's structure is *anatomy;* understanding its function is *physiology*.

Our body systems are:

- » Integumentary (skin)
- » Skeletal (bones, joints, cartilage)
- » Muscular (muscles)
- » Nervous (brain, spinal cord, nerves, sensory receptors)

- » Endocrine (glands)
- » Cardiovascular (heart, blood vessels)
- » Lymphatic (immune system)
- » Respiratory (lungs)
- » Digestive (alimentary canal)
- » Urinary (kidneys, ureters, bladder, urethra)
- » Reproductive (female or male).

The entire physical body is actually composed of tubes — macroscopic and microscopic. As the charismatic 'Indiana Jones' of whole-food healing Don Tolman preaches: 'Tubes minus Obstruction = Vitality'.

From our body's 80 trillion cells, we get entirely new skin every month, a new stomach lining every four days, a whole new liver every six weeks — in fact 98 per cent of the molecules in our bodies weren't there a year ago.

So how is it possible that our bodies continually regenerate disease? Much of the answer is quite simple — because of the rubbish we feed our bodies as metabolic fuel.

OVERFED YET UNDERNOURISHED

Our modern Western diet is commonly so diabolical that most people every day consume double the sugar, almost double the protein, and triple the fat of an ideal diet. Additionally, we routinely eat just eight per cent of the optimum amount of wholegrains, and less than one-sixth of the ideal quantities of fruit and veggies.

Consequently, today Western societies have exponentially escalating levels of much chronic disease in childhood, including recurrent ear infections, tonsillitis, bronchitis, asthma, and the rate of 'old-age' type-2 diabetes appearing in our young people, especially among indigenous and lower-demographic peoples. And what of ADHD (Attention Deficit Hyperactivity Disorder)? In America around ten million children have been diagnosed as having ADHD, with more than half (around six million) on Ritalin or equivalent medication — and similar statistics are found in most Western countries.

We don't really have a health-care system at present; we have a disease-care system.

In our modern world, cardiovascular disease has become our biggest killer: coronary heart diseases, such as high blood pressure and congestive heart disease, have become such common chronic diseases that they have reached epidemic proportions. Cardiovascular disease leads to the number-three cause of death for Westerners, which is strokes (blood clots in the brain) and our number-one cause of death, which is heart attacks (blood clots in the heart) . . . and for 50 per cent of these patients, their first symptom is death. Today, in the industrialised world, our number-two cause of death is cancer . . . and cancer is also the *biggest* killer of all Western five- to 65-year- olds. Around 100 years ago it's estimated just one in 8000 Westerners died of cancer, but now it's one in three, and in the United States alone it has become a US$200 billion dollar a year chemo-radiation, pharmaceutical Goliath. If a proven inexpensive cure for cancer was confirmed, it could potentially bankrupt much of the pharmaceutical industry.

But do you ever wonder why members of isolated pockets of ancient indigenous cultures continue today to routinely live into their hundreds, free from cancer and cardiovascular disease? It's no secret; it's primarily diet. The research has been done, it's just being ignored. Today in our modern hospitals, we are still routinely feeding seriously unwell patients sandwiches made of white bread, soggy overcooked vegetables and gelatinous non-nutritious desserts — personally I believe it's a reprehensible failure on the part of contemporary medicine.

We're all aware our society desperately needs to consume less sugar, animal protein and fat, and consume more fruit, veggies and wholegrains — and it is our healthcare system that should be leading by example.

GLOBESITY

Obesity is the condition of excess subcutaneous adipose tissue . . . in other words, *fat*!

On this planet for the first time in human history, there are now more obese people than hungry people: 10 per cent of Western children are obese by age five, including 18 million preschoolers and 20 per cent of all North American teens. But can't parents see their child's tummy getting tubbier and tubbier? Don't they notice their son developing 'man boobs'? Childhood obesity is an area that parents need to take direct responsibility for, as it is we who stock the pantry, fridge and fruit bowl; it is we who supply breakfast, lunch and dinner; and it is we who provide pocket money. If our children are fat, it is generally our fault; we can hardly blame the child who often simply doesn't know better.

Research has shown children perceive tubby kids to be sadder, less likeable and bigger liars. It takes dedicated hard work to educate yourself on how to feed your family healthily, and it takes conviction to be a 'mean' mom. It takes energy and passion for education to ensure your child understands the basics of eating healthily.

EXERCISE vs ACTIVITY

For me to explain to you, as a parent bothering to read this book, the necessity of exercise for our children is probably a case of preaching to the converted. So alas, I won't deliver that sermon, because I honestly don't believe that exercise is essential for healthy children! Our kids don't need to get a flat, firm, chiselled mid-section with a revolutionary Ab Roller, Ab Slide or Ab King Pro. They also shouldn't need to say goodbye to their bulging love handles, to sculpt shapelier legs or firmer glutes, and they sure as heck hopefully don't need resistance training for a 'total body aerobic workout'! No, all our kids need is simply *activity*... just getting o their butts and *doing* something. Exercise for children should not be exercise at all, it should be *play*, and loads of it.

It's not about the non-sporty child learning to become adept at an activity — that's new-millennium born-again-parenting dogma. The reality is today's parents need to fight a new battle: the war against electronic gadgets. We have to intentionally limit our children's hours of access to their TV, PC, XBox, PlayStation, Nintendo, Smartphones gaming apps. They're so addictive!

On the other hand, physical-activity-based electronics such as Wii Sports and other motion-controlled games are a lot of fun, and are 'exercise' per se.

Exercise for children these days involves primarily limiting access to sedentary non-physical-activity play and instead allowing kids to be childish.' Cause when you take away their gadgets, hey presto (from rapidly looming boredom), most kids find their soccer ball to kick around, or hop on their bike and go for a ride. It's not rocket science.

BODY IMAGE vs SELF-ESTEEM

Is it too early for me to talk about the self-esteem related to body image? Hardly! Not when statistically two out of five primary-school-age girls yearn to be thinner. In the seventies, the average age of a girl starting her first diet was 14 years; today it is eight. Research shows that four out of five young girls are afraid of becoming fat, with most more afraid of being fat than even a nuclear war, cancer or losing their parents — now that's really twisted. And, yes, it is mainly a girl issue, though not exclusively. Unlike teen girls who feel they can't be too skinny, teen boys find themselves caught in the crossfire of trying to walk the gauntlet of the balance between being 'too fat' or 'too skinny'.

It's perhaps little wonder, then, that apparently two out of five women, and one out of five men, would trade three to five years of their life for a better body! Cripes, I remember shopping on one of my 'thin' days when the snooty C-cup stringbean behind the counter condescendingly explained to me that in their boutique, size 12 (US size-8) meant Size Large. *Blimmin' heck.*

It's all so hideous, but hardly a shocking surprise when we realise the average woman is 165 centimetres tall, a size 14 (US size-10 - also known as 'Large') and weighs almost 65 kilograms, yet the average model is 180 centimetres tall and weighs less than 55 kilograms. In fact, models are thinner than 98 per cent of the population — and if we had the same dimensions as Barbie, we'd weigh 45 kilograms!

So it's no surprise that most girls end up feeling like they want to lose the 18–20 kilograms they naturally gain from eight to 14 years. But the end result is that at any on time more than half of all teenage girls are on a diet or are thinking they should be on one; and almost one in 20 girls (and half as many boys) go too far, and end up becoming anorexic or bulimic. (Devastatingly, up to 20 per cent of people with severe eating disorders will die: I well remember the head girl at our school dying after her struggle with anorexia.)

There is little we as parents can truly do to stop the media bombardment of size-0 bodies, but there are strategies we should put in place. The four specific tactics I believe we as parents must use are:

- » *Teach Lifestyle-IQ:* Nurturing nutrition, exercise activities, restful sleep and joyful contentment — more later in this book.
- » *Live Lifestyle-IQ:* We as parents living by example, including nurturing nutrition, exercise activities, restful sleep and joyful contentment.
- » *Teach Gratitude:* Making sure our children are aware of the blessings they have with their beautifully functioning, wonderful bodies.

» *Live Gratitude:* Making sure our children are aware we too know how blessed we are to have our own beautifully functioning, wonderful bodies. Monkey see, monkey do.

ORGANIC FOOD

The type of food human beings have always eaten — until around 50 or 60 years ago — is now fashionably named organic or biodynamic food, meaning it is grown without synthetic fertilisers, insecticides, herbicides, post-harvest fungicides, growth-promoting hormones or antibiotic growth promoters. Processed organic food is also made without artificial colorings, flavour enhancers, preservatives or other synthetic additives, and contains no genetically modified or irradiated ingredients.

The topic of organic food is a can of worms because some of the people who are very 'pro' can, inadvertently, come across as evangelistic, back-to-nature ideologists with a reactionary, alarmist stance. But now it is commonly accepted that the coloring-rich ice-cream, chemically filled biscuits and highly processed chippies routinely fed to children are a ecting their behaviour, health and ability to learn. Heck, even most animals in our zoos are fed organic food.

PESTICIDES

Do you realise that a lot of the beautiful-looking fruit and some vegetables in our supermarkets are sprayed with wax to improve their appearance — just visit an organic produce shop and you will see what apples naturally look like. (Washing does not remove the wax coating.) Our apples can be sprayed with various chemicals 15–20 times before harvest.

Washing and peeling removes some pesticide residues, but many are systemic (they penetrate into the cell structure of the plant). Additionally, after picking, some produce is also drenched in fungicides.

Breads and cereals can also contain high levels of pesticides due to the insecticides used on wheat.

Innumerable studies have linked pesticides to cancer (especially exposure to insecticides). Quite a number of commonly used pesticides are also considered 'probable' human carcinogens and even more are thought to be 'possible' human carcinogens (substances known to cause Cancer).

Pesticides have also been linked to reproductive abnormalities, and may interfere with the endocrine system, the nervous system (memory, alertness, attention, concentration) and the immune system. Pesticides may also affect sperm count, with studies showing that men who eat only organic produce have higher sperm counts.

GROWTH HORMONES

On the whole meat is much less contaminated with pesticides than fruits and vegetables — but it contains, instead, antibiotics and synthetic growth hormones (including testosterone and progesterone), which alter the animal's oestrogen levels.

Did you know that more than half the world's supply of antibiotics is used on farm animals? And a large proportion of these antibiotics are growth promotants (called feed enhancers) that are fed to animals specifically to make them grow faster, rather than to treat disease.' In just the last 20 years, the average age of a Western girl's first period has changed from 12–14 years to 8–11 years. It has been strongly suggested this relates to diet, with improved nutrition, but also to the chemicals and hormones found in modern food. Girls under 10 are way too young to have to deal with the side effects and responsibilities of menstruation!

Scientists are also warning that the practice of continuously feeding antibiotics to animals is producing strains of antibiotic-resistant bacteria that can easily be passed on to humans. Veterinary associations are saying nature's resistance to antibiotics (and other animal treatments such as anthelmintics used to control worms) is developing so rapidly it is outstripping scientists' ability to develop new antibiotics.

GENETICALLY MODIFIED FOODS

Enormous corporations like Monsanto create genetically modified organisms (GMOs) to grow 'bigger and better' crops, while also controlling the natural cycles of food production. Genetic engineering usually relies on bacteria to 'ferry' engineered DNA through the cell walls of a plant, and a 'virus promoter' is used to turn on the new genetic characteristic. Often a 'suicide' gene is also present, which means that farmers have to buy new seed stock annually.

What happens to our bodies when we eat these genetic instructions containing bacteria, viruses and antibiotic-resistant characteristics?

FLUORIDATED DRINKING WATER

Oh, this topic is also a right hornet's nest!

There are now vast amounts of information from scientists, doctors, Nobel Prize winners in medicine and chemistry, dentists, environmentalists, researchers and governments, all opposing the use of fluoride in drinking water. In fact, a landmark European Court ruling has spelled the end to water fluoridation in Europe, stating that flouride must be classified as a medicine, and cannot be used in prepared foods.

Although fluoride received topically (externally through direct contact with the tooth, such as in toothpaste) can potentially help prevent tooth decay, fluoride that is ingested (introduced internally into the bloodstream through drinking) does not hinder tooth decay. In reality fluoride is more toxic than lead, and anything but benign.

MERCURY (AMALGAM) FILLINGS

The use of inexpensive, practical and durable amalgam (liquid mercury and powdered alloy) dental fillings has been controversial since it was first introduced 150–200 years ago. You see, mercury is the most poisonous natural, non-radioactive substance on our planet, and is far more toxic than even arsenic, lead or cadmium — and removed amalgam fillings are considered hazardous waste.

Poisoning from amalgam fillings has been linked to serious disease including chronic fatigue, depression, memory loss and Alzheimer's, and some countries have now banned the use of mercury in all kinds of health-care. Today it appears much wiser to ask for the more expensive white composite cavity fillings — which are a mixture of powdered glass and plastic resin — especially for children!

HOLISTIC HEALTH

The World Health Organization's constitution states: 'Health is a state of complete physical, mental and social well-being, and not merely the absence of disease.' Yet, in practical terms our modern medical doctors have become specialists in illness, not wellness.

Although modern medicine talks of the body naturally seeking balance (homeostasis), conventional medical training focuses on homeostatic health only for a small portion of the first year in medical school. Then, from that point onwards, the focus is on pathophysiology (disease in the body) and inhibiting disease symptoms.

As medical doctors become more highly qualified, unless they enter general practice, they also become more specialised: cardiologists, cytologists, dermatologists, gynaecologists, haematologists, hepatologists, immunologists, nephrologists, neurologists, oncologists, perinatologists … and so modern medicine can tend to view the patient as a 'collection of individual parts' rather than an integrated whole.

We are reasonably aware that if we feed the body rubbish, it affects brain function, and so causes mind stress — and if we stress the mind with too much anxiety, it affects the body, and creates body disease. So why is it that around half our globe's 'enlightened' population continues to be routinely unwell with either physiological disease or psychological disease, or both? I have a hypothesis.

Just over a century ago, exponents of hard-nosed empirical medicine began to realise the shortfalls of concentrating on curing just the *physical* — so the 'pseudo-science' of mental health was established. Now, in the West, mental health is no longer regarded as a pseudo-science, but a fully well-recognized branch of medicine.

Less discussed in the Western world — simply because it is far less understood by Western medicine — is the indigenous knowledge that if we ignore our spiritual well-being it will have an impact on both our mind and our body.

Fortunately, some Western doctors have begun to realise the limitations of curing just the physical and mental, and so now the 'pseudo-sciences' of holistic healthcare (that is, remedies that seek to collectively heal body, mind and spirit) are becoming increasingly mainstream, and there is a growing appreciation for the curative abilities of acupuncture, chiropractic, osteopathy, homeopathy and yoga, for example. Let's finally face it: we are utterly kidding ourselves if we believe that current allopathy (modern orthodox medicine) is the universal magic-potion panacea.

I utterly believe in years to come more and more holistic therapies are destined to become further endorsed by empirical Western medicine. I utterly believe, fundamentally, we are triadic beings — that is, a *body*, a *mind*, a *spirit* — and the practices of naturopathic holistic medicine (dominantly from the Orient) are inextricably intertwined with mind-body-spirit wellness.

True health must be simultaneously achieved physiologically, psychologically and spiritually.

In addition to all this physiological disease is rampant psychological disease. Statistics show that a phenomenal quarter of the Western adult population are annually prescribed antidepressants, including almost one-third of our working mothers, with full-time stay-at-home mothers statistically even more at risk for depression. (And then, of course, there's the horrific ever-escalating teen-suicide rate.)

Cognitive-behavioural therapy, drugs, psychotherapy and counselling all have their place — mental health matters. But we have to seriously question why the heck we have become the saddest generation of humans ever to have roamed this earth, when human life has never had so many labor-saving luxuries; and why the heck we have become the sickest generation ever to exist, when it's never been so possible to be healthy.

Our world is full of entire nations of overfed, undernourished, recurrently diseased and desperately depressed people. To quote the philosopher Jiddu Krishnamurti, 'It is no measure of health to be well adjusted to a profoundly sick society.'

Chapter Six

'WHOLISTIC' NUTRITION FOR PHYSIOLOGICAL WELLNESS

Parents need to fill a child's bucket of self-esteem so high that the rest of the world can't poke enough holes to drain it dry.

Alvin Price, *parenting author*

Let's face it: we all know that 'you are what you eat' . . . and it all begins in childhood!

Of course food matters.

NUTRITION IQ
WHOLE FOODS vs REFINED AND PROCESSED FOODS

The term whole foods simply refers to foods that have not been refined by any processes. For example, corn on the cob is a whole food, but popcorn is not. Strawberries are a whole food, but strawberry jam is not. Or a pork chop is a whole food, but ham and salami are not.

Processed food is food that has undergone some manufacturing refinement, such as enzymes being removed, preservatives added to extend shelf-life, or chemicals included to enhance color, flavour or taste.

Today, so very much of our modern food is 'man-made' (refined by processes), and the result is that for many Westerners their diet contains little, if any, actual 'living' whole food. And the really sad thing is that much of the advertising and marketing of these man-made foods is so aggressive, many people actually believe some of these products are healthy and nutritious . . . even though they lack active enzymes, and contribute to all sorts of complex health issues.

In fact, it's not uncommon anymore for Westerners to go days — or weeks — without managing to actually eat any *real* food, while at the same time be under the utterly misguided belief that they have good nutrition. Let's all face it, food that is processed at a factory, stacked on shop shelves, then stored in our pantries for weeks is far, far removed from being 'whole food'.

The question is, how much of it even still qualifies to be called 'food' at all?

CARBOHYDRATES

Carbohydrates are the body's most preferred fuel for conversion into cellular energy, which we need for physical movement and internal functions, such as brain function, cardiac function and respiration. The body metabolises (chemically converts) starch, fructose, sucrose and lactose into glucose (blood sugar), and then the pancreas produces insulin to enable glucose to enter bodily tissue for use as cellular energy. Our dietary intake of glucose is ideally sourced almost exclusively from three main foods: plant starch, plant fructose and dairy lactose — not from refined sucrose (white sugar).

COMPLEX 'SLOW-RELEASE' CARBS

» *Plant starch:* Unrefined carbs such as dried beans and peas, wholegrains, potatoes, rice, pasta, bread, couscous, polenta, and all cereals such as maize corn, wheat, barley, oats, rye and millet.

SIMPLE 'FAST-RELEASE' CARBS

» *Plant sugars:* Fructose from fruits and vegetables, and refined sucrose such as sugar cane.
» *Dairy sugar:* Lactose from milk and other dairy products.

When we consume more sugar than our body needs, it stores the glucose as glycogen in the liver and muscle cells for later use. Once those 'storage containers' are full, the body then stores excess glucose within adipose tissue as fat. Unfortunately for the overeating Western world, the body *never* treats glucose as an excess waste product that requires excretion — our bodies are programmed to always utilise, or store, all glucose.

When we consume too little glucose (as when dieting) the body will catabolise (break down) the stored fat to supply the body with energy, which is why we lose weight.

PROTEINS

Proteins are amino acids, and amino acids *are* our *body*. They're the building blocks of human life, because amino acids are the body's structural material: blood, skin, muscles, organs and so on. Our body is constantly repairing and replacing cells; for example, our body makes more than two million new red blood cells every single second! Proteins are also the body's regulatory chemicals, such as enzymes, hormones and antibodies. Essential amino acids are proteins that we must source from our diet. Non-essential amino acids can be sourced from our diet or our liver can manufacture them. There are two kinds of proteins:

- » *Complete proteins:* Animal-based proteins, such as meat, seafood, eggs, milk, cheese. These provide humans with the nine essential complete amino acids our bodies require.
- » *Incomplete proteins:* Plant-based proteins, such as dried beans and peas, nuts, cereals, peanuts and lentils. Individually these are missing some of the essential amino acids, but combining them, for example eating rice and beans in the same meal, provides a complete protein. Vegetarians need to plan their diet to prevent protein malnutrition.

LEGUMES

Legumes are divided in two groups: 'forage', such as alfalfa, and 'grains', such as pulses, beans, lentils, peas and peanuts. Legumes are some of the most nutritious foods Mother Earth grows — plus they're inexpensive. Using a food processor, it is easy to 'hide' legumes in cooking, and you're adding fantastically to the nutrition and flavour of meals.

Ideally, legumes need to be soaked, as our ancestors traditionally did, to neutralise anti-nutrients, which interfere with nutrient absorbtion, and phytic acids which chelate minerals blocking mineral absorption in our gut. Some 'healthy'-eating Westerners can still be mineral deficient because of their intake of incorrectly prepared legumes.

NOTE: Peanuts are not 'nuts' at all; they are a member of the pea family. They are commonly fumigated with highly toxic antifungals to stop them going mouldy, and generally speaking it is these sprays that most people allergic to peanuts are actually reacting to. It's best to go organic with peanuts.

FATS AND OILS

Fats, oils, lipids, triglycerides, saturated fats, unsaturated fats, mono-unsaturated, polyunsaturated, long-chain essential fatty acids, good cholesterol, bad cholesterol, trans-fats . . . *where do you start?* When it comes to the topic of *fat,* even some experts are confused, and certainly many experts have conflicting opinions!

The bottom line is that every cell wall in the entire human body is made of phospholipid fats, and its shape is held together by cholesterol fats. Fat is also needed for many other functions, including blood clotting, transporting vitamins, insulation of nerve fibres, cushioning for organs, protection against cold temperatures, hormone production, and general growth and development. Good fat is even crucial for the transport and breakdown of bad fat. *We do need fat in our diet!*

However, fats are never excreted by the body as wastes — because our caveman body sees them as precious, precious, precious. So we store, store, store fats for general functional use and/or for conversion later into blood glucose during the lean times. *(Oh, but we don't seem to have many true 'lean times' these days.)* So, consumption of excess fats (excess to our needs, that is), as we know, is a major issue. But not all fats are bad!

Fatty acids or *lipid fats* are both in general terms fats and oils, and they are essential for the body's anatomy and physiology. In general:

» *Fats* are solid.

» *Oils* are liquid.

Triglycerides are three fatty acids attached to one carbohydrate molecule, and they make up about 95 per cent of the fat molecules found in our food and stored in our body.

Fatty acids can be either saturated or unsaturated.

SATURATED FATS

Saturated fats are stable (solid at room temperature and don't become rancid), and are found in animal-based foods, such as those in meat and some dairy products, and tropical oils such as coconut. Traditionally we have been told that saturated animal fats should be eaten in moderation as they cause blood-cholesterol levels to rise, thus hardening arteries and causing heart disease. The exceptions here are eggs, seafood and raw dairy foods (e.g. butter), which contain 'good' saturated fat.

However, that conventional hypothesis conflicts with much current research. In reality, during the rapid increase of heart disease during the twentieth century, Westerners' consumption of saturated animal fats actually declined. But what did increase was our consumption of industrially processed hydrogenated vegetable fats.

Even the basic theory that it is saturated fat which clogs arteries is under question. When the fat found in clogged arteries is examined, usually three-quarters of it is unsaturated, of which almost half is polyunsaturated, which is supposedly the 'good' fat. Animal fats also contain many nutrients that protect against heart disease and cancer, and improve the conversion of fatty acids. So don't get sucked into the idea that using margarine avoids cardiovascular heart disease, for that claim is seriously under debate!

UNSATURATED FATS

Unsaturated fats come in two varieties, *monounsaturated* and *polyunsaturated* — both are liquid at room temperature, and both are traditionally linked with promoting heart health by increasing 'good' (HDL) cholesterol and lowering 'bad' (LDL) cholesterol.

» *Monounsaturated-Rich Foods:* Include olive oil, peanut oil, sesame oil, nuts and avocados. Olive oil is a delicate oil that is wonderful to drizzle over cooked food, to make dressings with, or add to your smoothies. Cooking with oils at high temperatures destroys their goodness, so I recommend cooking with grapeseed oil, which has a higher heating point. Heating oils during their extraction process also destroys goodness, so always look for oil labels that say virgin or cold-pressed. Store all oils away from light and away from heat, for example in the fridge.

» *Polyunsaturated-Rich Foods*: Include nuts and seeds eaten raw or made into oils, such as flaxseed/linseed oil, sunflower oil, avocado oil or evening primrose oil, and oils from cold-water oily fish such as tuna, salmon, sardines, trout, kippers, mackerel, herrings and anchovies. This polyunsaturated group also contains the two *essential fatty acids* omega-3 and omega-6.

TRANS-FATS

Trans-fats are artificially created fats that are synthesized by the hyd- rogenation (heating to a high temperature to add hydrogen atoms) of inexpensive vegetable oils to convert them into colorless and tasteless solid fat that has an extended shelf-life.

Partial hydrogenation transforms polyunsaturated vegetable oils into monounsaturated 'plastic oils' (such as vegetable oil margarine spreads). More hydrogenation eventually transforms them into a totally mutated variety of saturated-fat shortening lard.

Why is it done? Because it is cheaper to make trans-fats than to buy genuine solid animal-based saturated fats. They are most commonly used in synthetic margarines and shortenings; deep-fried foods such as takeaways and fries; and commercially baked goods such as biscuits, cakes and pretzels.

Trans-fats should be avoided at all costs. Steer clear of them — as if your life depends on it, which it does — for they are an utterly foreign fat that our human biochemistry is not at all equipped to deal with, resulting in toxic, damaging 'free radicals' which can degenerate artery walls and increase the risk of heart disease.

So avoid margarine, canola oil, corn oil, soy oil and trans-fats. Instead, try making your own easy-spread butter by combining 500 grams butter with

½ cup flaxseed oil and ½ cup olive oil.

Always read labels and if it says trans-fat, partially hydrogenated or hydrogenated then *don't eat it — it's poison!*

VITAMINS

Vitamins are various plant- or animal-based nutrient compounds sourced from living organic food sources, which contain carbon and various other elements. Our bodies require vitamins in small amounts for healthy growth, development, vitality and general well-being. Vitamins are the spark plugs that enable our bodies to convert the macronutrients of carbs, proteins and fat into energy.

With few exceptions the body cannot manufacture or synthesise vitamins, and so relies on our diet to provide these essential nutrients. No one food contains all the vitamins the body needs, which is why a varied diet is necessary. A single vitamin deficiency can endanger the entire body, which is also why complementary therapies of vitamin mega-doses can potentially cure multiple medical complaints simultaneously.

PARENTING GOLDEN INSIGHT NO. 1

Fill your child's petrol tank with premium fuel, especially organic fruit, veggies and wholegrains.

MINERALS

Minerals are various soil-based elements that are inorganic (do not contain a carbon molecule) and are required by our bodies for healthy growth and development. All minerals must be obtained from our diet, as our bodies cannot synthesize any minerals. The main sources of soil minerals in our diet are milk, meat, bread, vegetables, peas, beans and cereals.

Minerals are especially important for the composition of body fluids, the formation of blood and bone, the maintenance of healthy nerve function and the regulation of muscle tone, including the heart muscle. Our bodies require around 15 essential minerals to function optimally, the most important being calcium, phosphorus, potassium, sodium, magnesium, iron and zinc. In addition, we require the trace elements such as copper, chromium, iodine, chloride and sulphur.

An issue with current nutrition is that modern farming methods deplete our soil of minerals and thus our food. Combine this with a routine lack of eating organically grown foods and the result is escalating levels of mineral deficiency within our Western population.

FIBRE *(Roughage)*

Fibre (roughage) is the cellulose found in the cell walls of plants, and is primarily indigestible to humans. However, our large intestine (colon) needs dietary fibre as a bulking agent to soften stools, assisting movement along the digestive tract, and to form defecatable faeces (not hard, constipated rocks). Dietary fibre is also an important disease inhibitor, so fibre-rich foods can keep us healthy and slim.

Roughage-rich foods include wholegrain brans, such as rye, oats and barley; wholemeal or wholewheat products, such as bread, pasta and breakfast cereals; brown rice; vegetables and fruits, especially dried figs, dried prunes, prune juice and kiwifruit; legumes and pulses, such as peas, beans, lentils and nuts and seeds.

DAIRY: PASTEURISED, HOMOGENISED, A1 AND A2

Pasteurisation is the process that uses high temperatures to slow the growth of disease-causing micro-organisms in our food — so long as the pasteurised product is refrigerated and consumed before its expiry date. Milk is the most commonly pasteurised food we consume. Long-life UHT milk is processed with an 'ultra-high-temperature' method of pasteurisation to provide extended shelf-life.

Homogenisation is the process of making a mixture the same throughout. With milk, it means breaking the fat globules into smaller sizes to prevent the milk from separating (that is, stopping the cream floating to the top of the milk bottle). By homogenising the milk, it is then possible to sell non-separating milk of varying fat content, such as one or two per cent. There is some controversy associated with homogenised milk as studies have shown that the subsequent health risks to our body can cause disease.

The most common cow's milk proteins are beta casein A1 and beta casein A2, and all cows produce a higher level of one or the other. The A2 protein is the original one that cows have produced for thousands of years, and A1 is a more recent sort of modern, mutated protein (which has been around for the past 1000 years or so). It is known to cause increased health problems, including insulin-dependent childhood diabetes and heart disease, and has possible links to autism and schizophrenia. The majority of our supermarket milk contains a mixture of the A1 and A2 proteins. However, in organic shops and some supermarkets you can get purely A2 milk, produced by herds of A2-dominant cows for general household consumption.

FERMENTED FOODS

Foods can be fermented by various means. The process was originally used to preserve out-of-season foods and for long journeys. Today, as in the past, fermented foods can provide many extra health benefits.

Generally speaking foods rely on micro-organisms in the fermentation process: Eg yeast ferments fructose (fruit sugar) into alcohol, and acidophilus bacteria ferments lactose (milk sugar) into yoghurt.

The other forms of fermenting are pickling (also known as brining or corning), which uses brine (salty water) to produce natural acids that preserve the food, such as salted pork and corned beef. Some vegetables that naturally contain a lot of moisture often only need to be salted to draw out enough excess water to create the pickling brine, such as sauerkraut or Korean kimchi. There is also the souring process, when the food is marinated in vinegar's acetic acid or some Asian oils.

Additionally, herbs and spices are often added in pickling, not just for flavour, but also for their antimicrobial qualities, such as mustard seed, garlic, cinnamon and cloves. Fermentation temperature can also play a big part in determining which micro-organisms dominate, and the end-result flavours. Health-wise, fermentation can improve the nutrient levels of the final product (especially the amount of vitamins it contains). The microbes contained in fermented products can also contain acidifying enzymes that the human body is incapable of synthesising, thus improving digestion in the same way that natural antibiotics and bacteriocins benefit intestinal flora. And of course the fermentation process also potentially destroys many bacteria that cause food poisoning.

Research has also begun to discover medical benefits from eating fermented foods, including lowering cholesterol and providing protective effects against the development of diabetes and cancer. Fermented foods — such as vinegar, pickled vegetables, quark, crème fraîche and sour cream— are also believed to be wonderful immune-system boosters. And loads of health benefits, such as aiding digestion and potentially preventing cancer, have been attributed to kimchi.

GLUTEN

Gluten is a mixture of the plant proteins gliadin and glutenin, which are found joined to starch in the endosperm of some cereal grass grains, especially wheat, rye and barley. It is the glutenin in wheat flour that gives kneaded dough its leavening and elasticity, translating into the pleasant chewiness of baked goods. Globally, gluten is an important source of nutritional protein.

However, it's estimated about one per cent of our population has coeliac (or celiac) disease, causing the immune system to inappropriately respond to gluten. Coeliac disease shouldn't be confused with a wheat allergy. The most effective treatment is simply a gluten-free diet.

CALORIES/KILOJOULES

Calories and metric joules are units of the *energy* contained in food, meaning they measure the amount of energy available from the food via digestion. Energy is primarily provided by carbohydrates. (1 calorie = 0.004 kilojoules, or 1000 calories = 4.2 kilojoules approximately.)

'Empty calories' is a term that refers to foods that offer high instant energy but low nutritional content, such as sweets, soft drinks, white bread, white rice, margarine, fried food and alcohol. The goal of any healthy diet is to eat plenty of nutrient-dense food and avoid empty-calorie foods, because such foods actually 'leach' or 'steal' minerals from your bones and tissues when they are assimilated into the body during digestion.

GLYCAEMIC INDEX

The GI or glycaemic index is a measure of how ingested carbohydrates affect our blood-sugar levels (because carbohydrates convert into blood glucose). Carbs that break down quickly (e.g. refined sugar) are said to have high GI and create a high insulin demand, potentially leading to insulin resistance, i.e. type-2 diabetes.

NITRATES

Processed meats, such as ham, bacon, salami, pastrami, pepperoni, bologna, corned silverside, spam and saveloys, contain the preservative sodium nitrate (or its close relative sodium nitrite) to keep them a red color, and to inhibit the growth of bacteria which cause botulism, a serious form of food poisoning. Science shows that nitrates and nitrites are carcinogens (cancer-causing substances), but the jury is out on quite how harmful these are in foods, and what (if any) are acceptable levels.

My advice is to buy nitrate-free processed meat whenever possible, and eat other processed meat in moderation.

SUGAR AND SUGAR ALTERNATIVES

Big Sugar, like Big Tobacco and Big Pharmaceuticals, has a filthy history. The sugar industry was built on slavery and many of the people working in the industry today still remain on the precipitous edge of survival. Today the United States government pays several times more than the rest of the world for its sugar due to subsidising, to the tune of $1 billion annually, a crop of no nutritional value. Big Sugar can even wangle things so that soft drink costs less to buy than plain water — *how is that feasible?* Because Big Sugar makes Big Money, which means the sugar barons are able to continue to make famously large donations to buy big political influence . . . but that's a whole other book.

Sugar (especially refined white sugar) deserves the name 'kiddie cocaine', because its intense, short-lived, fizzing-at-the-bung 'highs' are addictive. Today, it is common for Westerners to consume more than their entire body weight in refined sugar each year. In the United States over half of all teenagers drink at least one can of soft drink every day. In fact, kids in industrialised countries are drinking twice as much soft drink as milk.

Let's face it, even 'healthy' modern childhood diets can be *so* full of sugar! Several teaspoons at breakfast (sugary cereal with sugar sprinkled on top), several teaspoons at lunch (sugary sandwich spread, sham 'muesli' bar and fake fruit juice) and several teaspoons at dinner (a glass of cordial and tinned fruit soaked in sweetened fruit syrup) all add up!

Sugar increases the risks of obesity, dental cavities and diabetes. In reality, all our body's energy requirements can be obtained from a healthy diet of wholefood carbohydrates — without the roller-coaster highs and lows of refined sugar. Each *teaspoon* of this kiddy cocaine takes a child's body three to four hours to process. And it is this subsequent extreme workload on the pancreas which is creating the runaway numbers of children developing the old-person's disease of type-2 diabetes.

So please eliminate processed sugar as much as possible from your children's diet — it has no nutrients (all the vitamins, minerals and enzymes have been stripped away during processing). But the body has to use umpteen vitamins and minerals to digest these empty calories, thus creating the commonly malnourished Western child (overfed but undernourished). **Always read labels** and if it says anything ending in '-ose', such as sucrose, dextrose, levulose or galactose, or corn and rice syrups, then *avoid it*. Refined-sugar highs are *so* rampant in our society — they directly contribute to our epidemics of obesity, diabetes, heart disease, asthma, eczema and learning disorders.

GOOD SUGAR ALTERNATIVES

» *Honey, Maple Syrup and Molasses:* All very obvious natural sweeteners. Make sure the maple syrup is real, not artificial.

» *Stevia:* Originating from the Paraguay–Brazil region, this perennial shrub is also known by other names such as 'sweetleaf', 'sugarleaf' and 'sweet honey leaf', as it is around 300 times sweeter than sugar. Yet stevia has no calories and is safe for diabetics. It has a '0' glycaemic index, plus it is heat-stable, so suitable for cooking. Also, as the body does not digest or metabolise stevia, it is not converted into glucose blood sugar.

BAD SUGAR ALTERNATIVES

» *Aspartame Acesulfame:* This artificial sweetener, used in products such as NutraSweet and Equal, deserves a whole book in itself. *Avoid, avoid, avoid!*

» *High-Fructose Corn Syrup (HFC):* This is natural corn-starch fructose that has been converted into a crystal-clear syrup of artificial 'high fructose'. It's commonly used in soft drinks and tricks the liver into triggering your body to store fat. It can also contain traces of mercury. *Avoid, avoid, avoid!*

» *Saccharin:* Another artificial sweetener that has been connected to itching, rashes, eczema and bladder cancer. *Best avoided.*

» *Sucralose:* An artificial sweetener; its long-term use may potentially cause chronic immunological and neurological disorders. *Avoid.*

» *Tagatose:* A low-calorie sugar ('cousin' to fructose) that is derived from dairy whey and provides 90 per cent of the sweetness and 30 per cent of the calories of ordinary white table sugar. Gastrointestinal problems can occur with consuming large amounts of tagatose. *Use in moderation.*

» *Xylitol:* Popular with many dental associations, this artificial sweetener is derived from rice or corn, and contains 40 per cent fewer calories than sugar. Xylitol has few of the major health concerns associated with some artificial sweeteners but, like other sugar alcohols, consumption can result in bloating, diarrhoea and flatulence (farting). *Use in moderation, but with reasonable confidence.*

PARENTING GOLDEN INSIGHT NO. 2

Feed moderate-low levels of 'kiddy cocaine': swap sugar for stevia

---

DUMP THE JUNK — DAILY DIET STRATEGY FOR YOUR FAMILY

> *If I recommend to you ... to drink water or eat a ripe tomato and you take it upon yourself to do so without supervision of a licensed medical doctor you do so at your own risk. The publishers, the author, the bookstores, the distributors, the marketers present this material for educational purposes only. Duh.*
>
> Don Tolman, wholefood guru, *Farmacist Desk Reference*

Epigenetics is the study of how our environment can change our phenotype appearance; that is, how our genetic DNA sequences are modified by outside influences. In other words, this new science is beginning to attempt to understand how our cells are affected by a lifetime of consuming foods rampant with heavy metals, antibiotic growth-promotants, pesticides, herbicides, insecticides, nitrogen-based fertilisers, synthetic additives of colors and flavours, and of course artificial sugar. It's a *massive* onslaught to our health.

We also have to continually ask ourselves: how old is our food? At the best of times 'fresh' food can be five to seven days old before we buy it, then it can sit in our fridge or fruit bowl for another few days. How much nutrition do we get from food like that? About 40 per cent if we're lucky. And if we boil it for 10 minutes, we've lost most of the remaining goodness.

Add to that the nutrient-depleted soil our food was grown in, and the multiple toxins it was sprayed with, then even the seemingly best of diets can leave the body nutritionally deficient ... let alone the routine breakfasts of white toast laden with trans-fat-rich marg and smothered in sugary jam, washed down by a sweetened cup of tea. Then there's the mochaccino, and cake with our lunch, and fast-food, instant-heat takeaways for dinner. We're killing our cells, we're killing our selves.

At the end of the day, what you feed your child is all about you, and not about me. These are simply my opinions, based on my experiences, my philosophies and extensive research. You could utterly disagree with many of my sentiments — and crikey, that's your call. Who's to say I know it all — not me. However, I know bits and pieces and, with assistance from some great specialists and experts, I'm confident that in general terms, I've hit the nail on the head.

The reality is that *nobody* knows it all when it comes to nutritional information; there are so many varying opinions that nutritionists themselves can no longer 100 percent agree. So you need to adapt the ideas to suit you as a parent, your children, your family dynamics, your values, your beliefs and your preferences. It's all about you and your family.

But here are my best basic recommendations — and I believe it's all about helping our children form healthy relationships with food, instead of rampant childhood addictions to nuggets and noodles.

WATER
The main drink all day and offered at every meal

When babies are born they are around 97–98 per cent water, and by adulthood we're about two-thirds or 60–70 per cent water — either way, we're mostly water! So it makes a load of sense that consuming water is important to staying healthy. In reality, water is the source of all life on earth, and without clean water, we cannot maintain optimal health.

Water is the universal conduit for all nutrients, hormones and enzymes, and is the universal detoxifier to clear away wastes; it dilutes, transports and neutralises toxins. The brain is around 93 per cent water washed by cerebrospinal fluid. Blood is 83 per cent water.

Water balances hormone functions and can cure headaches and constipation — H_2O rejuvenates and regenerates! But as a modern society we seem to have lost our ability to di erentiate thirst from dehydration. If our lips are dry we put on lip balm, if our tongue sticks to the roof of our mouth we suck on a mint or chew some gum. And then, when we do finally feel irresistible thirst, we drink diuretics like cola, co ee or beer — which actually increase urine excretion, making us even more dehydrated.

However, there are also some huge question marks surrounding the 'urban myth' preaching eight large glasses of water daily (or two litres per adult) as 'best practice'. It is also important not to dismiss the considerable water contained in fruit and veggies. So perhaps a better indicator of ideal hydration is to think in terms of consuming enough liquid each day to consistently produce clear or very pale odour-free urine; water should be as clear coming out as it was going in — that's the sign of good hydration.

At the end of the day, there are a few people drinking potentially too much water, and many, many people unquestionably drinking too little, especially children — be it plain water or juice from fruit. And how do you get children to drink water over other drinks? Simple — don't routinely serve other drinks!

BREAKFAST — Complex carbs, protein and fibre

At breakfast time, our kids (and we parents) ideally need slow-release carbs, such as oatmeal porridge, wholegrain breakfast cereals, muesli or wholegrain toast; with some protein, such as organic eggs, no-sugar-added peanut butter, lean bacon, quality butcher sausages, probiotic yoghurt or A2 milk; plus the vitamins and minerals and fibre found in fruit and nuts.

What we all really don't need are sweetened cereals with sugar piled on top. Processed foods, especially refined sugars, lack nutritional value, are highly addictive and produce the imbalance of a blood-sugar rush of hyperactivity followed by a blood-sugar plunge of weariness. It's crazy to send our children to school with such non-nutritious fillers in their tank at the beginning of their day of learning.

SNACKS — Morning tea and afternoon tea

Fruit; vegetables; nuts; fat-free popcorn; a hard-boiled egg; 'super foods', such as blueberries, cranberries, organic apples, persimmons, probiotic yoghurt, spirulina smoothies and pomegranate juice; and healthy carbs, such as homemade healthy muesli bars (loads of great recipes are available on the internet) or healthy store-bought muesli bars (look at the ingredients and if sugar is listed in the first five, or ingredient names contain numbers, then they're hardly natural and healthy).

LUNCH — Complex carbs, protein and fibre

Just like at breakfast, at lunchtime we all need the same food-type goodies: primarily slow-release complex carbs, such as wholegrain bread for sandwiches or a genuine muesli bar; some protein, such as meat, eggs, cheese or seeds; plus some minerals, vitamins and fibre, which can be found in fruit, nuts and veggies.

Just one item of refined rubbish is a big enough treat, please, in school lunchboxes.

DINNER — One-third carbs, one-third protein and one-third veg

As adults, our ideal dinner consists of one-quarter carbs, one-quarter protein and half vegetables. But when serving kids you should divide their plate into thirds.

For example, one-third complex carbs, such as skin-on potatoes, brown rice, wholemeal pasta, wholemeal wraps, organic couscous; one-third protein, such as meat, poultry, fish or organic eggs (or at least free-range); one-third veggies that includes varieties in lots of colors for a range of minerals and vitamins; followed by fruit (preferably organically grown) for dessert.

Remember, we all need a minimum of five servings per day of fruits and veggies (a 'serving' is equivalent to each person's own fist size). With fruit at breakfast, lunch and dinner, and veggies at lunch and dinner, this is easily accomplished.

EXTRA TIPS FOR EATING WELL

» Buy veggies from farmers' markets — or better still, grow your own organic vegetables.

» Add in 'super foods' as much as possible, especially the likes of tomato paste, garlic, ginger, ground linseed, green barley and kelp.

» Be generous with herbs and spices (especially fresh herbs, which contain wonderful phytonutrients).

» Cook with grapeseed oil — and dress with olive oil.

» Use refined table salt in moderation; instead use pink Himalayan or Celtic sea salt, rich in minerals.

TREATS

All fatty processed and refined-carb sugary foods are non-nutritious . . . they're *all* junk-food treats . . . including lollies, biscuits, cakes, chocolate, ice-cream, softdrinks, white bread, potato chips and many mass-produced sausages. Yes, they're all indulgent excesses and were never designed to fill tummies. So all these delightful pleasures should be eaten in moderate amounts, and for children should be earned by great behaviour, or a job well done.

Chapter Six

PICKY FUSSPOTS

We all have a varying number of tastebuds, and our genes have an impact on reactions to strong-tasting foods. Some people are 'super-tasters', experiencing taste overload with certain strong flavours, and have a subsequent tendency to be thinner. 'Non-tasters' are dustbin gannets who will eat almost anything, with a tendency to be chubbier. But picky, fussy eating can also be bred! Research shows that the majority of fussy-eating school-age children are actually only picky at home, as children will adapt to fit in socially.

When it comes to fussy, picky eaters, I admit to being stubbornly opinionated, to the point of being potentially offensive and impolitely judgemental on this subject. Our children are fantastically diverse eaters. First, because I served *enormous* varieties of foods and cuisines, and second, because of two dinner-table household rules:

1. You don't have to like it, you just have to eat it.
2. It's fine to leave a mouthful.

Different cuisines are a big part of our household eating. A week of dinners can routinely include an Asian stir-fry, Italian pasta, Indian curry, Mexican chilli, spicy Middle Eastern, and a traditional Sunday roast. I can easily conjure up a month's menu that never repeats — and so can any middle-class parent (though research shows that 90 per cent of English mothers have a repertoire of only eight dinner menus). Making a variety of quick, tasty and nutritious dinners is not that hard, really.

Our first rule, *You don't have to like it, you just have to eat it*, is directly responsible for producing non-fussy eaters who can consequently enjoy an enormous variety of food, who can accept anybody's cooking, who can devour any restaurant plate, and who are happy to try any unknown new dish. During the kids' childhoods we'd all eat together, and we'd all eat the same dinner — routinely.

When you use this as the foundation ground rule, it also allows you to discover tastes a child very genuinely doesn't enjoy. For example, Rickie likes shrimps, but they upset his stomach. Candyce prefers her broccoli without cheese sauce. And Angelo really doesn't like kiwifruit. Fair enough, I don't especially like celery, and Mark doesn't like feta.

The second rule, *It's fine to leave a mouthful*, allows a bit of independent freedom. If it's a mouthful of mushrooms, or a mouthful of Brussels sprouts, we don't care! It's their choice. They just need to eat the rest of the plate.

Is a parent really doing a child any favours when they let them just eat canned spaghetti, or squeal at a mild curry, or have their own special sausages for the barbecue, or don't like drinking plain water? Intelligent parents doing really unintelligent parenting! And we all see such examples a lot of the time. Ask any cook at a school-camp kitchen and they'll tell you there's an enormous number of young school-age kids who 'only eat' chicken nuggets.

And we're responsible for that. We as parents. We're the ones who buy it and serve it. It's not the child's fault. It's not their stubborn personality's fault. It's not their acutely sensitive tastebuds' fault. Yes, these can contribute. But the biggest fault lies with a lack of adequate parental stubbornness to win the battle.

SUPPLEMENTS

Even if you eat a wide variety of organically grown food, it's worth including daily supplement capsules or syrups, which include non-synthetic vitamins, minerals, antioxidants and omega-3 oils. And for sad, grumpy preteens, maybe a ginseng–ginkgo combo (see Trendy Old Natural Depression Remedies in Chapter Seven).

PARDONING EXTRAS

Exercise (especially walking), fresh air, sunlight, non-toxic loving relationships, self-education, meditation, sleep and passion for life can all assist to overcome plenty of transitory dietary sins, to fuel us and keep us going.

READING LABELS

We must know what's in the refined commercially processed foods on sale at the supermarket, because this is fundamental Nutrition IQ.

Ingredients are listed in descending order of volume (from greatest to least), including preservatives, additives and flavourings — all of which are best avoided. So when a 'natural fruit juice' has a first ingredient of water, and second ingredient of sugar, you know without any doubt it is *loaded* with sugar — in fact, it has even more sugar than fruit! Or if a sandwich spread advertises itself as a 'nut spread with a touch of chocolate', yet its label reads 'sugar, cocoa, nuts' then the product is perhaps more accurately described as a 'sugar and chocolate spread with a touch of nuts'!

Remember too that refined sugar can have several names, including corn syrup, fructose, maltose, dextrose and sucrose — and you really don't want the product if one of these sugars is listed in the first five ingredients.

Food-label nutrient charts initially list the amount of calories or kilojoules, followed by a breakdown of the nutritional content into carbohydrates (including sugar), saturated fats (including trans-fats, unsaturated fats, cholesterol), protein, sodium (salt), dietary fibre, minerals and vitamins.

The 'bad' ingredients to limit (things Westerners generally eat way too much of) are primarily the sugars, trans-fats and salt. The overabundance of these ingredients in our diet causes numerous health problems and disease. The 'good' ingredients our diets are commonly lacking include dietary fibre, vitamin C, vitamin A, calcium and iron.

Be very wary, too, of words like 'natural', 'reduced fat', 'light' or 'non-fat' — much of this is simply advertising spin. 'An excellent source of energy' doesn't mean it's actually good for you, it just means it's full of sugars. Remember, '95 per cent fat-free' also means '5 per cent fat', and 'fat-free' doesn't mean sugar-free (such as fat-free marshmallows, which are high in sugar which the body will convert into fat). Also, a 'Healthy Heart Tick' means the product is simply a lower-fat option, but is not necessarily healthy if eaten in excess. Plenty of genuinely healthy food does not have a Healthy Heart Tick due to the cost involved in obtaining one!

A great shopping companion is *The Chemical Maze* by Bill Statham, a guidebook to food additives and cosmetic ingredients. You can also refer to the 'Feed Me Right' Food Additives to Avoid list at the end of the chapter.

A–Z OF EXTRAORDINARY FOODS

ALMONDS *(Raw)*

Store all nuts in the fridge as it keeps the oil in the nuts fresh. Roasting damages the healthy oils. Almonds contain practically no carbohydrates, so can be ground and used instead of flour for low-carb, gluten-free baking. Almonds are rich sources of vitamin E and 'good' fat, which lowers 'bad' fats (cholesterol). Almonds are also traditionally used as a favourable brain and nervous system food, and additionally have health benefits for the complexion, the colon and cancer prevention.

ANTIOXIDANTS

Chemical reactions are essential to life. Oxidation is a chemical reaction of electron transference; a process where an atom or molecule robs another of one or more electrons. Easily recognised examples of oxidation are an apple browning or an iron nail rusting. In your body, the reactive unstable molecules produced by oxidation, called 'free radicals', can damage cells, causing irreversible ageing and disease, and particularly brain degeneration.

Antioxidants are molecules that combat oxidation by slowing or preventing the process, thus minimising free-radical damage. Antioxidants can take the form of vitamins, minerals, enzymes or phytochemicals, such as carotenoids, which are responsible for the red-orange-yellow color of foods (e.g. tomatoes, carrots, pumpkin, red peppers, salmon and some seaweeds). Various herbs and spices are also particularly rich in antioxidants, especially garlic, ginger, oregano, sage, thyme, rosemary, peppermint, lemon balm, allspice, cloves, cinnamon and turmeric. And then, of course, there are the very well-known antioxidants termed the 'ACES' — vitamins A, C and E and the trace element selenium.

APPLES

The apple has a colorful mythical history. Nicknamed the 'Queen of all Foods', or 'Gaia's Milk', the old adage 'an apple a day keeps the doctor away' is very true indeed — as eating an apple daily provides enormous health benefits. In fact, one apple provides enough fibre to meet the suggested daily requirements!

Apples can also protect your heart by preventing cholesterol build-up, and so reducing strokes and heart disease. They contain fibre to aid digestion and prevent constipation and diarrhoea; antioxidants to slow ageing and reduce cancer risk; and phytonutrients to protect against degenerative brain disorders.

BEANS

The term 'bean' refers to the edible legume seeds, or the edible pods with seeds. 'Green' beans doesn't refer to a bean's color, but simply means the young pod of a bean plant picked before it completely ripens and dries — thus being tender when raw or cooked. In general, beans are high in protein, complex carbs and iron.

Examples of popular beans include broad (fava) beans, runner (string) beans, azuki beans, pinto beans, navy beans, lima beans, soybeans, lentils, kidney beans, black (turtle) beans, cannellini (white) beans, great northern (baked) beans, garbanzo beans (chickpeas), sugar-snap peas, snow peas, green peas and lentils.

Beans are a low-fat, protein-laden 'super food' and are great for heart health, blood-sugar levels and combating obesity, and have been associated with reducing cancer. But unfortunately as income levels rise, inexpensive bean consumption tends to decrease — so don't forget the economical bean!

The bean family also includes co ee beans, cocoa beans and vanilla beans — *which combined can make a fabulous mochaccino!*

BEEHIVE PRODUCTS

Beehive products are renowned for their antimicrobial, cholesterol-lowering, anti-cancer, anti-inflammatory, wound-healing and immune-system-stimulating qualities. Apart from raw honey, other health-giving hive products include bee pollen, royal jelly and propolis.

BLUEBERRIES

Blueberries are a 'super food' renowned for providing a long list of health benefits including: preventing and inhibiting urinary tract infections; reducing cholesterol with a natural aspirin (salicylate); lowering the risk of cancer; and reversing age-related physical and mental decline through their antioxidants. Blueberries are an ideal food for diabetics, because of their low glycaemic index properties.

BRAIN FOODS

These are foods high in omega-3 essential fatty acids and traditionally assist in managing anxiety and stress, improving cognitive function (i.e. thinking), and reducing depressive disorders, neurological disorders and sleep dysfunction. Famous brain foods include:

- » Almonds, walnuts and bananas
- » Oily fish such as salmon and tuna
- » Supplements such as Panax ginseng, ginkgo biloba, zinc and complex vitamin B, including B_3 (niacin), B_1 (thiamine), and B_9 (folic acid).

BROCCOLI

Closely related to the cauliflower, broccoli is a vegetable with edible flower heads from the mustard family that has become known as a 'super food'. Along with its high levels of vitamins, fibre and iron, broccoli assists heart health and has potent anti-cancer properties, plus immune-system-response regulators and antimicrobial compounds that kill bacteria responsible for stomach ulcers and cancers.

CALCIUM

By mass, calcium is the fifth most abundant element in the human body, and it is a very important component of a healthy diet. Calcium is a crucial blood-clotting factor, and it's an essential mineral for communication between muscle cells, such as those in the heart. But in our body, 99 per cent of calcium is found in our bones and teeth. Research shows the better our calcium intake in childhood, the stronger and denser our bones in adulthood, and the lower our risk of osteoporosis later in life.

Foods rich in calcium include dairy products, seaweed, nuts and seeds, blackstrap molasses, beans, quinoa, broccoli, oranges and figs ... and interestingly green leafy veggies contain way more usable calcium than dairy.

CEREALS AND GRAINS (OATS, WHEAT AND CORN)

Cereals are grasses, such as wheat, oats and corn. Grains are the seeds of cereal grasses. Kernels are the grain seeds of cereal grasses enclosed in a husk (and also the inner edible seeds of a nut or fruit stone).

Oats are a super food. We can eat them as ground oats, rolled oats (hulled grains rolled into flat flakes) and oatmeal (porridge made from ground/rolled oats). Oats contain more soluble fibre than any other grain — so take longer to digest and leave you 'feeling full' for longer. Oats are also great for blood-sugar regulation and they contain many powerful health-giving phytochemicals.

Wheat grains are ground to produce flour for bread, cakes, biscuits and pasta. *Bran* is the hard outer casing of cereal grains, and is renowned for lowering 'bad' cholesterol. 'Germ', as in wheatgerm, is the vitamin-, mineral- and lipid-rich reproductive embryo within cereal kernels. Endosperm is the starch tissue inside the grain, surrounding the germ.

Wholegrain foods contain the bran, germ and endosperm. *Wholemeal* products are made from wholegrain flour. (White bread is made from flour that has had the wheatbran and wheatgerm removed, leaving only the endosperm.) *Corn (maize)* is actually a grain too, and can be used to make cornmeal, flour and polenta. Yellow corn has significant amounts of health-giving carotenoids.

When reading the labels on baked goods, including bread, crackers, cereals, pretzels and so on, look for ingredients beginning with the word 'whole'. If the fibre content in bread and cereals is less than three grams per serving, then I suggest putting it back on the shelf.

CRANBERRIES

Cranberries are packed full of nutritional goodness, antioxidants, and anti-cancer phytochemicals that benefit the cardiovascular and immune systems. They also protect against the formation of kidney stones and reduce urinary-tract infections.

EFAs: THE REMARKABLE OILS

Essential fatty acids (EFAs) are long-chain fatty acids also known as omega-3 and omega-6 oils, which build healthy cell walls and allow our brain cells to grow and form connections with other brain cells — in fact, our brain is almost 70 per cent fat, and EFAs are *vital* for healthy brain function!

For optimal well-being, we should ingest these two essential oils every day. Good sources include:

- » Oily fish, such as salmon, tuna, sardines, trout, anchovies, mackerel and herring, as well as fish-oil supplements
- » Flaxseed (linseed), either ground (provides extra fibre) or oil (keep refrigerated, not recommended for cooking)
- » Venison
- » Wheatgerm
- » Walnuts.

Research has shown that daily EFA supplements improve children's overall cognitive function and subsequent academic achievement, particularly at maths. Research has also found daily EFA supplements assist in controlling ADHD and other behavioural problems, as well as dyslexia and other learning difculties, help with coordination, reading, handwriting and spelling, and reduce anxiety and aggression.

FLOWERS — Edible

Many, many flowers are edible, and aren't just for decoration. They can be used in teas, juices, salads, stir-fries and desserts. Some edible flowers are: chive, dill, chamomile, daisy, broccoli, cauliflower, mustard, marigold, safron, lemon, orange, coriander, squash/pumpkin, chrysanthemum, rocket, fennel, gladiolus, lavender, mint, basil, oregano, marjoram, garden pea, plum, radish, rose, rosemary, sage, lilac, dandelion, thyme, tulip and violet.

FRUIT AND VEGETABLE JUICES

As promoted by the wholefood selfcare-revolution guru Don Tolman, KABALA juice is great for kids. Just put the following combination of foods through a juicer — it's delicious!

- » K(C) — 1 kg carrots
- » A — 1 red apple
- » B — ½ beet
- » A — 1 yellow apple
- » L — ½ lemon
- » A — 1 green apple

It's always best to add in some of the pulp to any fruit juice, as the fibre slows the uptake of sugar in the bloodstream. Otherwise, a glass of fruit juice without pulp may have a similar efect on blood sugar as a can of Coke!

Another great idea is to add a teaspoon of flaxseed/linseed or coconut oil, to also assist in slowing the sugar absorption, and to make the fruit juice more of a complete food.

GARLIC

Fresh raw garlic (known as the stinking rose or Russian penicillin) has health benefits that have been known for thousands of years.

When fresh garlic is crushed it releases the enzyme allinase, which rapidly changes the garlic clove's alliin to allicin. This famous antifungal and antibiotic therapy is especially useful for treating streptococcus, colds, flus and oral thrush and is great for children whose systems have become antibiotic-resistant. This beneficial chemical compound only exists in this state for a few hours and alters with cooking; however, the sulphur-rich components in cooked garlic also provide many general health benefits to the immune and cardiovascular systems, plus it aids intestinal bacteria and is known to have cancer-fighting properties.

HERBS

Herbs are leafy green plants such as basil, oregano and rosemary, small amounts of which are used for medicinal healing, spiritual ritual and culinary flavouring. Fresh herbs especially can contain wonderful health-promoting phytonutrients.

IRON

Iron-deficiency is common in children with poor diets, such as picky eaters. Low iron levels lead to anaemia (low levels of red blood cells), which leads to low oxygen uptake. Chronic anaemia will lead to slow growth, tiredness, poor concentration, recurrent infections and potentially poor behaviour.

Eating red meat, along with a good variety of dark green leafy vegetables and dried fruits, can ensure adequate iron intake — especially if these iron-rich foods are accompanied by a glass of *real* orange juice, because vitamin C assists iron absorption. If your household doesn't eat red meat, then to ensure adequate iron consumption, you may want to consider a daily supplement of blackstrap molasses or an iron syrup such as Floradix taken as directed.

NUTS AND SEEDS

Not all seeds are nuts, but all nuts are seeds — they're just seeds encased in a hard shell.

Raw, toasted, puréed or ground into flour, seeds add exciting flavours to foods and can be incredibly nutritious — especially raw nuts and oily seeds. A small handful daily can provide great amounts of protein, vitamins, minerals, fibre and oil.

Especially yummy nuts and seeds are walnuts, hickory nuts, pecans, chestnuts, hazelnuts, almonds, pistachios, Brazil nuts, cashews, pine nuts, macadamia nuts, pumpkin seeds, sesame seeds and sunflower seeds. All nuts are best stored in the fridge to avoid becoming rancid.

NOTE: Peanuts are *not* a nut, they are a pea (a Legume).

ORANGES

Most of us know this 'super food' citrus fruit as a potent source of vitamin C, but vitamin C is rapidly excreted from the body, so we need adequate daily intake for optimum health. When buying real orange juice, ensure it includes the pulp, which is much higher in vitamin C than the juice.

Oranges are rich in flavonoids, which are made up of antioxidants and antimutagenics (inhibitors of cancer and other diseases). The flavonoid rutin, found in oranges, is an antiviral, and it protects capillaries from age-related breakdown. Pectin, the fibre in oranges, helps to reduce cholesterol and stabilises blood sugar.

NOTE: When buying vitamin-C supplements, choose ones with added bioflavonoids.

PERSIMMONS

Persimmons are a fruit that looks somewhat like a tomato, with wonderful health benefits because of their high levels of potassium, fibre, minerals and the phenolic antioxidant compounds also found in the other fruit of the gods, apples. Persimmons can be eaten when ripened to orange and slightly softened, then cut in slices like an apple, or when fully ripened to red, and the soft, almost translucent fruit scooped out with a spoon. When in season, they are a lovely alternative to an apple a day, and make the ultimate natural dessert.

POMEGRANATES

Known as the 'jewel of winter', pomegranates are an apple- or orange- sized fruit, with tough dark red or brownish skin. The edible part is the transparent-red, sweet, tangy pulp surrounding the seeds. Pomegranate juice (also known as pomegranate molasses and essence) tastes fab (reminiscent of children's cordial) and is receiving critical acclaim for its antioxidant health benefits, keeping arteries young and reducing cancer rates.

PROBIOTICS *(Good bacteria)*

Friendly 'good' bacteria maintain a healthy balance within our guts, boosting our immune system by providing a vital immunity against bacterial infections.

These 'good bugs' are found in yoghurt *(free from colorings, flavourings and added sugar, please)* containing lactobacillus acidophilus and/or lactobacillus bifidus bacteria — so homemade or organic yoghurt is best.

PUMPKIN

This member of the gourd family has been heralded as a super food because it is inexpensive yet nutritionally valuable. Pumpkin is high in fibre, low in calories, and contains an abundance of disease-fighting nutrients including carotenoids, the powerful antioxidant that wards o various cancers and heart disease.

SALMON

Salmon is a large herring-like game fish with delicate red-pink flesh — they're famous for swimming from salt water to fresh water to spawn. Salmon is classified as a healthy super food because it is an oily fish high in protein, vitamin D and the omega-3 fatty acid.

NOTE: There are some environmental issues regarding farm-raised salmon. To make responsible fish choices, you may want to do a little research, such as visiting the Environmental Defense Fund website at www.edf.org.

SALT

Just like sugar, our craving for salty foods is a built-in survival reflex (from Palaeolithic times), because sodium is an essential ingredient for our body's electrical nerve-signal transmission (the most fundamentally basic function of the human body, after the conversion of glucose sugar to cellular energy). Our blood, tears and urine all contain similar levels of salt. So we do need salt! We just don't need the high amounts found in typical Western food, which become toxic to the body and increase blood pressure.

Modern 'table salt' isn't that great either. First, in an e ort to make it the attractive, uniform white substance that pours out of your salt shaker, it is refined to the point that nearly every beneficial trace element has been extracted — except for the salt itself (sodium and chloride). Then to make the table salt even more free-flowing, aluminium is added as a bleach and anti-caking agent . . . And let's not forget the iodine and iodine stabilisers that are added . . . but it's worth noting iodine is already present naturally in salt before it's refined! *Arrgghh!* Unfortunately, the chemical additives combined in refined table salt make it di cult for our bodies to absorb the salt naturally.

So what to do? Buy good quality salt, which is unrefined and unprocessed, organic and hand harvested, unbleached and unwashed, and contains no additives. My personal favourites are pink Himalayan salt and Celtic sea salt, and they look attractive in the salt grinder and taste way better!

SOY

The use of soybeans, or soya beans, as a food dates back as far as 2000–3000 years, when the Chinese learned to ferment them. Soy is used in many forms, including soy flour, vegetable oil and soy meal (primarily for livestock feed). Soy is also processed into dairy substitutes including milk, margarine, ice-cream, yoghurt, cheese and, controversially, infant formula. Then there is of course tofu (soybean curd), soy-protein powder (used in smoothie shakes), soy nuts, edamame (green soybeans that taste like lima beans), tempeh, fermented soybeans and miso, used to make a tasty soup. Finally there is the salty condiment soy sauce (or soya sauce), made by fermenting the beans.

Some believe soybeans to be a super food, saying they contain all the essential amino acids, and so are a great meat replacement and source of complete protein for vegetarians and vegans. Others vigorously dispute this, saying soy *does not* provide complete proteins. And that is just one of the debates about the advantages or disadvantages of eating soy products. In general, research has found that most modern soy foods do not confer the same health benefits as traditional soy foods, because they are not fermented (to neutralise toxins) and are refined (which denatures proteins and increases carcinogens). Factory-processed soy foods can be nothing like the traditional village-made foods.

SPICES

Spices can be dried, ground or grated, and can come from plant seeds, berries, bark, roots or fruit. Small amounts are used for medicinal healing, spiritual ritual and culinary color and flavouring. Like herbs, spices are also renowned for their disease-fighting potency, from easing arthritis pain to keeping your heart healthy with their abundant antioxidants. The most famous wellness-giving spices include ginger, cinnamon, turmeric, cardamom, cloves, cumin, red chilli powder, yellow curry powder and wasabi.

SPINACH

Spinach has a somewhat mythological reputation as a super food for its iron content. Spinach is also a powerhouse of calcium, folate (folic acid), antioxidants (vitamins A, C and E), vitamin K (essential for blood clotting), fibre and magnesium. Fresh or frozen spinach is a super food that is great for the eyes, strengthens bones, improves memory and helps protect against arterial disease and cancer.

SPIRULINA

Called spirulina because of its spiral shape when seen under a microscope, this plant is one of the group of remarkable single-celled 'blue-green' algaes that have loads of health benefits. This micro-algae certainly can be called a 'super concentrated wonder food' because its nutrient profile is so strong. But is it a food or a supplement? It's a food generally taken as a supplement.

It is very high in protein; rich in iron, which is great for red blood cells and oxygen transfer, both essential for building a strong body system; has great amounts of vitamin B$_{12}$, which is essential for a healthy nervous system; beta carotene, an antioxidant essential for growth, vision and mucous membranes; and an array of amino acids and fatty acids, including rare essential fatty acids that can't be synthesized and are essential for body growth.

SUNSHINE

Although not a food, sunshine is essential for our body's production of vitamin D, and lack of sunshine creates vitamin D deficiencies. Modern society is starting to see increasing symptoms of vitamin D deficiency, such as rickets and osteomalacia, because of our high use of sunscreens, sunglasses, covering up while in the sun and tinted windows.

Dark-skinned people need even higher levels of sun exposure because the melanin in their skin naturally blocks a significant portion of the sun's radiation.

SUPER-SUPER FOODS

Throughout this section I refer to 'super foods' — but there certainly are some even more extraordinary super foods, other than well-known ones such as spirulina, echinacea, ginger, raw honey, bee pollen, royal jelly, propolis, blue-green algae, and the herb goldenseal. Other foods, currently less well known for possessing remarkable levels of vitamins, minerals, enzymes and co-factors (non-protein chemical compounds that are bound to proteins — needed for proteins to perform their biochemical activity) include: wheatgrass, barleygrass, coconut, turmeric, noni fruit, durian fruit, goji berries, açaí berries, raw cocoa, maca powder, dulse (red algae), chlorella (green algae), kelp and seaweed such as kombu, nori and wakame.

These are foods that promote exceptional well-being. But, sadly, because super foods have such extraordinarily good wellness properties and potential disease-eliminating attributes, some have had — and may continue to receive — ridiculous 'bad press'.

TOMATOES

Although botanically a fruit, tomatoes are nutritionally categorised as a vegetable. Tomatoes, especially cooked, are an antioxidant super food that aids in cardiac protection. They contain lycopene, one of the most powerful antioxidants. Lycopene is more easily absorbed by the intestine if it's been cooked, so use plenty of tomato paste, tomato puree and tomato-based sauces in your daily diet.

WALNUTS

The walnut tree grows a round, sticky outer fruit that encloses the nut's woody shell containing its delicious seed. Raw walnuts are rich in omega-3 oil, which is helpful in lowering cholesterol. Store walnuts in the fridge to avoid becoming rancid.

YOGHURT

Yoghurt is produced by bacterial fermentation of any milk, including soy, but most popularly by cow's milk. Live yoghurt is a super food that contains beneficial bacterial cultures, whereas pasteurised yoghurt does not — so do ensure the yoghurt you buy contains live cultures. Natural yoghurts can be sweetened such as with fruit, honey, maple syrup, stevia, vanilla or chocolate.

Yoghurt aids digestion and helps balance good and bad gut bacteria, its calcium content strengthens bones, and it supports the immune system by inhibiting viruses.

'FEED ME RIGHT' FOOD ADDITIVES TO AVOID

Below is a comprehensive list of food additives to avoid, used with permission from *Feed Me Right* by Dee and Tamarin Pignéguy:

- 102: Tartrazine
- 104: Quinoline yellow
- 107: Yellow 2G
- 110: Sunset yellow FCF
- 120: Cochineal
- 122: Carmoisine
- 123: Red food coloring Amaranth
- 124: Ponceau 4R
- 127: Erythrosine
- 128: Red 2G
- 132: Indigo carmine
- 133: Brilliant blue FCF
- 150: Caramel
- 151: Black PN
- 154: Brown FK
- 155: Brown HT
- 160: Annatto
- 210: Benzoic acid
- 211: Sodium benzoate
- 212: Potassium benzoate
- 213: Calcium benzoate

- 214: Ethyl 4-hydroxybenzoate
- 215: Ethyl 4-hydroxybenzoate sodium salt
- 216: Propyl 4-hydroxybenzoate
- 217: Propyl 4-hydroxybenzoate sodium salt
- 218: Methyl 4-hydroxybenzoate
- 219: Methyl 4-hydroxybenzoate sodium salt
- 220: Sulphur dioxide
- 221: Sodium sulphite
- 222: Sodium bisulphite
- 223: Sodium metabisulphite
- 224: Potassium metabisulphite
- 250: Sodium nitrite
- 251: Sodium nitrate
- 310: Propyl gallate
- 311: Octyl gallate
- 312: Dodecyl gallate
- 319: *Tert*-Butylhydroquinone
- 320: Butylated hydroxyanisole
- 321: Butylated hydroxytoluene
- 621: Monsodium L-glutamate (MSG)
- 622: Monopotassium L-glutamate
- 623: Calcium di-L-glutamate
- 627: Disodium guanylate
- 631: Disodium inosinate

- 635: Sodium 5-ribonucleotide
- 950: Acesulphame K/Sunnet®
- 951: Aspartame/NutraSweet®/Equal®
- 955: Sucralose
- Diet/Low-Calorie/Lite/Sugar-Free products containing Aspartame, NutraSweet®, Equall®, Saccharin, Cyclamate, Acesulphame K, Sunnet®, Thaumatin, Alitame and Sucralose.

SUMMARY

Let food be your medicine and medicine be your food.

Hippocrates (450–357 BCE), *Greek physician*

The everyday choices we make at the supermarket determine the future of our food, and the future health of our children. Today, fortunately, the tide is turning, and people are becoming more concerned with the honour, ethics and integrity of our food suppliers. For at the end of the day, the buck stops with us, the consumers. A great place to start informing yourself on this topic is Peter Singer and Jim Mason's shocking and illuminating *The Ethics of What We Eat*.

As my friends, the mother-and-daughter team Dee and Tamarin Pignéguy, write in their fabulous book for children *Feed Me Right*, 'If you fail to plan to eat well, then you plan to fail.'

So how about we really cut the crap, by cutting out the crap. Today, most of us are eating too much of the wrong things and we're not eating enough of the right things. We're primarily eating too much meat, fat, sugar, processed food and fast food. We're doing stuff fundamentally wrong — and everybody knows it.

In all our households, we need to increase high-fibre, high-nutrient, organic plant-based nutrition. Ideally we need 50 per cent of our diet (particularly our children's diets) to be raw, organic, plant-based foods such as fruits, vegetables, nuts, seeds, seaweeds, grasses, sprouts, herbs and super foods. To be honest, we don't eat like this all the time. *Hell no.* But we are striving to!

Chapter Six

To be unavoidably judgemental: if you have a car worth more than $5000; or you have fewer than three children and more than one bathroom; or you pay for holiday accommodation annually; or you eat out fairly regularly; or you have more than one TV or computer in your home — then you can afford to buy great food for your children. Own that fact, take responsibility for it, and go from there. It's only about priorities.

GENERAL RULE OF THUMB: You choose what goes on your children's plates. You are Queen of the Content, and King of the Menu!

I encourage you — *beg you* — to feed your child right. Of course food matters.

Chapter Seven

NATURAL HEALTH — REMEDIES AND THERAPIES FOR WELLNESS AND HEALTH

There can be no denying on my part that the entire topic of wellness versus disease is a colossal pet peeve of mine!

On one hand, I'm a midwife who is routinely required to prescribe and administer drugs such as antibiotics — for there are circumstances where pharmaceuticals are totally warranted. On the other hand, I'm a mother who's passionate about ensuring her children develop robust immune systems. As a like-minded girlfriend once said to me, 'If our kids' immune systems can't handle a bit of tonsillitis or an ear infection, how the bloody heck do we think they'd handle the really serious stu ?'

Mark and I are immensely proud ('scuze the less-than-humble ego) that our children's bodies have ingested *so* few pharmaceutical drugs, apart from the occasional bit of paracetamol pain relief. Yes, not one course of antibiotic drugs for a secondary infection ever — and that's no mean feat these days! This is not because we've refused to administer them, but simply because the right natural remedies can work so well!

Certainly we're lucky none of our children were born prematurely, when antibiotics can save immature immune systems, and they haven't been involved in any serious accidents . . . touch wood. But otherwise, it hasn't been luck — it's been a specific determined strategy of Mother Nature being first cab o the rank.

Consequently, I recommend that every family — just like us — not only has a trusted GP, but also has their own local professionally trained naturopath, competent in both herbalism and homeopathy, who is able to guide them through the labyrinth of amazing complementary therapies available.

In stark contrast, the only medication our GPs can ever prescribe is what is listed on governments' pharmaceutical schedules. For example, as a midwife I routinely have clients who are iron depleted or su ering from iron-deficiency anaemia, to whom I prescribe iron tablets. There are many superior natural products available in health shops to improve their iron levels — but I can prescribe none of them. My hands are tied. And so too are your local doctor's.

Disappointingly, the paradigm of seeking wellness through curing the root causes of disease is still yet to be wholly embraced by Western medicine — whereas that is practically all Eastern medicine has ever tried to do. Today we call the holistic options complementary and alternative medicines (CAMs), because they are di erent to mainstream conventional medicine. However, considering modern medicine is really only about 150 years old, and most herbs have been used for thousands of years with proven track records, then to my mind the names are back-to-front: we should be saying *complementary and traditional medicines*, and *modern medical alternatives*. You see, today's medicine is hardly undisputedly mainstream, because historically mankind's most genuine mainstream medicine has always been herbalism.

So this chapter is dedicated to parents consciously looking for alternatives to medical, pharmaceutical drugs, not just for their young children but for the whole family's health. This is why some health problems listed are typically more associated with adult ill-health.

Many of the healing modalities listed in this chapter are 'holistic' — that is, they heal the body-mind-spirit, because holistic health is about healing the *core imbalances* to enable long-term well-being. They have the ability to improve all disease and can completely relieve some specific diseases. This is often a process of folding back the layers, much like peeling an onion, to get to the root cause of disease.

Our bodies are amazing machines, specifically engineered and beautifully designed to heal themselves, especially when encouraged to have a robust (experienced) immune system. The beauty for holistic practitioners who work with children is that their innocent state means everything sits closer to the surface and they often respond very quickly to such therapies. Adults tend to have a few more layers!

OUR VIBRATIONAL BODY

Our bodies are, roughly speaking, one-half oxygen, one-quarter carbon, 10 per cent hydrogen, and the remainder more than a dozen other kinds of molecules. Molecules themselves are simply cocktails of various elements, and elements are simply combinations of various atoms, and atoms are simply a central nucleus of protons and neutrons, with electrons whirling around them at an inconceivably high velocity. But, *between* the atom's whirling electrons and the nucleus is simply vibrational space . . . not even air (for air is full of molecules). You see, at our core, humans, and everything on earth, and in fact everything in the entire universe, consists mostly of space, of this vibrational energy. So how does the discovery of this pure energy relate to health? There is massive evidence human beings can experience improvements to well-being and reduction in disease, not just through molecular input (such as ideal nutrition and pharmaceutical drugs), but also through manipulation of energy. Many ancient therapies, such as acupuncture, and new non-conventional treatments are based on the principle that our bodies are not simply chemical — we are actually, *primarily*, energy.

Chapter Seven

PARENTING GOLDEN INSIGHT NO. 3

Explain to your child we are all interconnected with the universe ... many say from our molecular structure to our collective consciousness.

'WHOLISTIC' WELLNESS PLAN FOR CHILDREN

In our quest for 'wholistic' parenting, this is my recommended general strategy for all children's care:

- » Routine infancy wellness checks with a classical homeopath and a naturopathic herbalist.
- » Substantial, directed effort to teach infants how to develop excellent sleep habits, to create well-rested children.
- » Breakfasts of complex carbs, avoiding sugar-high rubbish cereals; nutritious lunches, including carbs, protein and fruit; and dinners of *immense* variety, including healthy carbs, moderate amounts of animal protein, loads of veggies and fruit for dessert.
- » Water as the main drink all day, every day — except for occasional treats.
- » A few small sugary-chocolatey treats once or twice a week, which are only ever well earned and well deserved.
- » A takeaways/junk-food dinner maximum of once every couple of weeks.
- » Quality daily supplements, including omega-3 oil.
- » A well-stocked pantry, free of non-nutritious rubbish 'food'.
- » A maximum of about an hour a day of sedentary TV/computer/gaming blobbing.
- » Regular physical after-school activities, such as dancing/sports lessons, biking to the park, skateboarding to the creek, swimming at the beach, karate, soccer or similar.
- » Dirt is okay. No antimicrobial spray-and-wipe-type cleaners (apart from bleach for the toilet bowl). Unless kids are visibly dirty or noticeably smelly, they do not have to bath/shower every single day.
- » Kids feeling unwell? First ports of call: rest and hydration, then appropriate homeopathy and naturopathic GROOVEyS (see page 149).

TRENDY OLD NATURAL HEALING REMEDIES

I give this section the name of 'trendy' not out of disrespect to these wonderful remedies, but because most of these ancient medicines are presently particularly popular, and are often highly recommended for any household's first-aid kit.

PARENTING GOLDEN INSIGHT NO. 4

Consider naturopathic remedies first instead of only pharmaceutical drugs.

ALOE VERA GEL

Although aloe plants look similar to cacti, they are actually members of the lily family. The healing properties of the gel inside the leaves of the plant were discovered centuries ago. Aloe veras are easy to grow and it's a great idea to have a plant growing in a pot inside or outside in the garden — when you need some, you only need to break o a leaf.

Aloe vera gel has wonderfully restorative e ects on skin as it has a pH level almost identical to human skin. It is particularly good as a remedy to help soothe and heal minor burns, itchy insect bites, nappy rash, cuts, scratches and sunburn, and can also be taken internally for colds, ear infections, sore throats, toothaches and asthma attacks. (If you don't have a plant, you can buy the gel.)

ANTISEPTICS *(Natural options)*

Many natural topical (skin) antiseptics are available in place of pharmaceutical lotions or alcohol wipes. My personal favourites are:

» Hypericum

» Aloe vera

- Tea-tree
- Bee propolis ('beehive glue')
- Manuka-oil
- Honey
- Calendula
- Papaw
- Colloidial silver

ARNICA

Probably the best known of all homeopathic-based remedies, arnica is derived from the herb *Arnica montana* (mountain daisy), and comes in various forms including sprays, drops and tablets for taking internally, and creams and gels for external use.

Arnica is globally renowned for its anti-inflammatory properties, and is used for bruises, sprains, strains, sore muscles, fractures, pain, swelling, traumatic injuries, concussion, insect bites and stings, nose bleeds, and pre- and post-surgery. (It should not be applied to broken skin.)

CALENDULA

Known as the homeopath's antiseptic, calendula is derived from the herb *Calendula officinalis* (marigold), which is available in various remedies, including drops for taking internally and creams and gels for external use. Calendula is an antiseptic and analgesic (pain reliever) and is used to heal skin wounds and rough, dry, chapped skin, and for cuts, abrasions, rashes, blistering and minor burns. It also helps stop bleeding and promotes healthy skin texture and tissue repair to reduce scars.

COLLOIDAL SILVER

Silver has been used for thousands of years as a natural antimicrobial healing remedy, as it has antibacterial, antiviral and antifungal qualities. It is a powerful preventative against infections because it works as a catalyst to disable the oxygen-metabolising enzyme in single-celled bacteria, fungi and viruses.

Colloidal silver is made up of ultra-fine molecules of silver suspended in water. When taken internally, colloidal silver confers tremendously positive effects on the body's immune system, and used typically assists in generating less scar tissue due to its rapid healing qualities. Short-term use of colloidal silver is non-toxic — except to single-cell micro-organisms such as viruses, fungi and bacteria.

Colloidal silver is reputed to have very positive effects on many body functions including cell regeneration, and on many conditions including acute toxicity, sinusitis, hayfever, sore throats, staphylococcus, streptococcus, stomach flu, tonsillitis, all viruses, yeast infections, cuts, abrasions, open wounds, eczema, itches, acne, insect bites, septic infections, colds, flus, burns, allergies, boils, dermatitis, cold sores, parasitic infections, conjunctivitis, glue ear, nappy rash, thrush, bladder infections — plus about 600 other conditions.

It is tasteless, doesn't sting and does not interfere with other medications.

ECHINACEA

Native to America and commonly known as the purple coneflower, echinacea is harvested for its roots, seeds, flower heads and juice, and was a main medicinal remedy used by the American Indians. Colonial settlers introduced the herb to the rest of the world and by the early 1900s echinacea had become the most popular prescribed medicinal herb, and within three decades was being exported in great quantities to Europe.

Echinacea is one of Mother Nature's natural antibiotics, and is an excellent remedy to help rid the body of microbial infections. It has also traditionally been used for treating insect bites, teeth or gum pains, colds, measles, mumps, bacterial and viral attacks, boils, laryngitis, tonsillitis, nose and sinus problems, septic sores and cuts, streptococcus and staphylococcus. Echinacea has excellent immune-system-stimulating properties too, as well as 'cleaning' the lymph and blood systems.

Echinacea can be used when the body is sickly, run-down or has a sluggish immune system that is struggling to fight such conditions as a lingering cold or recurring thrush, and as an alternative to antibiotics. Even the (conservative) World Health Organization (WHO) supports the use of echinacea for colds, flus, infections of the respiratory and urinary tracts, poorly healing wounds and chronic ulcerations.

The root is considered to be the more potent part of the plant, with herbalists using upwards of 3g daily, compared to much smaller doses found in over-the-counter products.

GARLIC

The health benefits of garlic have been known for thousands of years, but now science is paying garlic more attention, and research is providing some astonishing results. Garlic's only negative side effects seem to be its taste and odour! When fresh garlic is crushed it releases the enzyme allinase, which rapidly changes the clove's alliin to allicin — the compound that contains garlic's antibacterial and antifungal properties.

Mixing a little fresh, well-crushed raw garlic into children's milk, juice or food releases this plant's fantastic antifungal and antibiotic powers, and can be used to treat streptococcus, colds, flus, oral thrush and infections in children whose systems have become antibiotic-resistant. And of course the sulphur-rich components of cooked garlic provide many general health benefits, including boosting the cardiovascular and immune systems.

The scientific research into garlic continues.

GOTU KOLA *(Indian pennywort)*

Gotu kola is one of Indian Ayurvedic medicine's primary rejuvenating herbs (nicknamed 'food for the brain'), and in China it was recorded 2000 years ago as a herbal medicine. In India, gotu kola can also be called brahmi because it 'brings knowledge of the Brahman' (a Hindu high-noble priest). Besides improving brain function (such as memory), gotu kola also has positive effects on the circulatory system, improving blood flow and strengthening arteries, veins and capillaries, and is traditionally described as a blood purifier. In addition, it improves digestion disorders, strengthens the immune system and fortifies the nervous system. Gotu kola is also renowned for its superb skin-healing qualities.

These are some of Mother Nature's best non-drug antimicrobials:

Grapefruit Seed Extract (GSE)

Olive-leaf Extract (OLE)

Oil of Oregano

Vitamin C

Echinacea

Silver (Colloidal).

GRAPEFRUIT SEED EXTRACT *(GSE)*

Like so many complementary and alternative medicines, there is well-publicised controversy about the use of grapefruit seed extract, alongside enormous support for the product. Its main claim to fame is its antimicrobial qualities as an antibacterial, antiviral, antifungal and antiseptic. So GSE has been traditionally recommended for the treatment of colds, flu, coughs, throat infections, earache, bronchitis, thrush, urinary tract infections, diarrhoea and suchlike.

One note of caution: grapefruit does interact with a number of pharmaceutical drugs — so if this might be an issue you're best to check its use with a naturopath.

HYPERCAL/HYPERICAL

Hypercal is a homeopathic remedy of calendula and hypericum. It comes in various forms, including oral drops, and creams and gel for external use.

Hypercal is globally renowned for calming and healing skin infections, injured skin, cuts and sores. It helps the skin recover quickly, promoting healthy, rapid healing. Hypericum is a natural antiseptic and analgesic healing agent, which stops bleeding, relieves sharp pain, infection, nerve damage and pain from tail-bone falls.

KOREAN or CHINESE GINSENG *(Panax ginseng)*

Derived from the Greek words 'akos' (cure) and 'pan' (all), panax ginseng comes close to being the perfect herbal cure-all. It helps to restore the physiological balance of the body's mental and physical capacities — aiding the body to heal itself.

An Asian herb exalted in mythology, it has been used as a medicine for thousands of years. Its influence is gentle, slow, cumulative and broad. The constituents of panax ginseng are remarkably complex and its workings are still an unsolved mystery to modern science. (Natural white ginseng is steam-processed to produce the higher-potency red ginseng.)

Panax ginseng is commonly used to boost energy (treating weakness, exhaustion and fatigue); to sharpen the mind (treating loss of concentration); to reduce stress; to boost the immune system (enhancing immune responses); to modulate blood pressure; to regulate blood-sugar levels (such as in diabetes); to strengthen the cardiovascular system; to raise athletic stamina; as an anti-inflammatory; as an antioxidant; and as a supplemental cancer therapy. The WHO formally recognises its unique qualities.

OIL OF OREGANO

Studies have found oil of oregano (a different *Origanum* species to the oregano herb used in cooking) to be an antioxidant, anti-inflammatory and potent antimicrobial (antibacterial, antiviral, antifungal and antiparasitic). The oil's thymol and carvacrol are believed to be the main sources of its benefits.

Oil of oregano is most widely known for its ability to reduce digestive problems, such as infections, gastrointestinal upsets and indigestion, and for generally aiding digestion. But the oil is also used to treat sore throats and skin infections, such as athlete's foot and dandruff; increase joint/muscle flexibility; relieve migraine headaches; improve breathing problems and respiratory health, such as coughs or sinus and lung congestion; and generally strengthen the immune system.

OLIVE-LEAF EXTRACT *(OLE)*

The olive tree, referred to in the Bible as the 'tree of life', produces fruit and leaves that have been used since Egyptian times for their healing power. And today's scientists are now discovering that OLE is one of nature's *best* broad-spectrum antimicrobial medicines. Among other things, modern research has found that it is particularly effective against viruses, bacteria, fungi and worm parasites, and aids coronary blood flow. It is particularly wonderful for colds and flu. Available as syrup and capsules.

PAPAW OINTMENT

Papaw (pawpaw) ointment, especially the Lucas brand, has a growing reputation as a wonderful mildly antiseptic healing cream. It is made from papaya and can be used for haemorrhoids, eczema, dermatitis and many other skin conditions.

TEA-TREE OIL

Tea-tree oil is recognised as a very e ective antiseptic, fungicide, antibacterial and germicide, and it also promotes tissue regeneration. It must only be applied externally.

Tea-tree oil has many uses including treating burns, thrush, cuts, nappy rash, earaches, insect bites and stings, pimples, scaly scalp, sinus and bronchial congestion, eczema, splinters and sunburn.

URTICA URENS CREAM

Urtica urens treats urticaria — meaning this homeopathic aqueous ointment, made from the dwarf stinging nettle plant, treats nettle rash or hives, and is very soothing for any hot, red, burning or itchy skin eruptions. *Urtica urens* is also soothing for minor burns such as scalds, sunburn or blistering, and allergic reactions to insect bites, stings, shellfish and plants.

TRENDY OLD NATURAL DEPRESSION REMEDIES

Statistics confirm depression is now the number-one health issue in the Western world, with its insidious low mood, low self-esteem, insomnia and loss of ability to experience pleasure from normally enjoyable activities. The WHO predicts that by 2020 this rampant disease will be the second highest cause of death and disability in the world! So sad, literally.

Research shows childhood stress leads to childhood depression, and conversely childhood depression is the leading cause of childhood stress

— both resulting in children who are more irritable than 'down', and often described as clingy, demanding, dependent, insecure or ADHD. They are typically uninterested in school and decline academically, with the potential to develop self-destructive behaviour.

We now know rates of depression in the adult populus are doubling every year, but a study at Harvard Medical Center found *childhood* depression rates are increasing by more than 20 per cent annually! *It's a really, really twistedly insane situation.* Other hideous statistics state one in four English children suffer from depression, with its subsequent displays of irritation and anger. Even in God's Own, (what locals call New Zealand) it is estimated one in four kiwi children are likely to experience some kind of significant mental health problem before they reached adolescence. *One in four! Do we have a problem? Hell yes!*

Unfathomably, preschoolers are now the fastest growing global market for the popular antidepressant pharmaceutical drugs called Selective Serotonin Reuptake Inhibitors (SSRIs) — even though a review in the *British Medical Journal* concluded SSRIs were ineffectual for preschoolers, and the United States Food and Drug Administration (USFDA) have warned SSRIs are leading to increased suicide in children. *How sick is that?*

Stressed-out parents are more inclined to medicate their children. In fact, the use of pharmaceutical medication on children is estimated to have increased 500 per cent in the past 20 years. As a midwife asking newly pregnant clients their health history, I estimate two out of five have been treated with SSRIs — and these are only women in their twenties and thirties, many of whom are yet to even truly experience some of the most horrid shit life can dump on us as a 'grown-up'.

Today, in the doctor's arsenal, SSRIs have become the cure-all for the frazzled businessman, languishing housewife, brooding teen and moping child. These drugs, such as paroxetine (Aropax, Loxamine), fluoxetine (Prozac, Fluox), sertraline (Zoloft) and citalopram (Celapram,

Cipramil), all block the brain cells' reabsorption of the neurotransmitter serotonin, thus increasing the availability of serotonin inside the brain and prolonging its action. Response to treatment typically takes two to six weeks and during the early stages there is increased risk of suicide ideation. A common adverse reaction is insomnia — which in itself is crazy, because it is during sleep that our body should primarily produce its own supplies of serotonin. Because SSRIs structurally alter brain cells, discontinuing their use requires a gradual reduction of dose to minimise withdrawal symptoms, because going 'cold turkey' on them can lead to an even worse level of Depression.

It's essential today's parents have an arsenal of options to holistically treat their children to e ectively prevent childhood stresses mutating into childhood depression. It's also essential today's parents have an arsenal of alternatives to pharmaceutical SSRI drugs, to stop their own adult stresses warping into the cesspool of full-blown depression.

The crazy aspect of it all is that in the 'good old' Dark Ages, when almost everybody's life sucked big time — with smallpox, not enough food and countless persecutions — living was still understood to be nowhere near as bad as dying and God sentencing you for eternity to the damnation of Hell. Life was horrid, but you had to harden up, and just get on with it.

Whereas today the societal expectations hammered into us relentlessly (like nails into our co n) are that we should thoroughly enjoy our lives; that we are each entitled to our own rightful share of happiness — complete with loving partner, adorable children, beautiful home, caring family, loyal friends, rewarding career, good health, fulfilling sex life and adequate retirement savings. If you're missing any of this, then life may suck, because you've failed to reach your 'potential'. The depressed have an inability to construct their future — then again, people can be in love with their particular life drama.

Today, we don't think we're asking too much to 'have it all', for that's what we're told we're entitled to — happiness and joy — and everyone's telling us it's possible. Everyone's striving for it. It's our democratic right, our industrialised entitlement — and our Western obsession. So when we don't get it we're bummed out, sometimes clinically. For with the modern, harsh 'winners make their own luck' philosophy, if the successful merit their success, then the unsuccessful must merit their failure.

I think if we were able to time travel to experience the hardships of the Dark Ages, or even to our great-grandparents' era, it would allow us to return to our current lives — complete with all their setbacks, defeats, frustrations, disappointments, disasters and disillusionments — and be able to appreciate all of the beauty of our lives and to finally feel contentment and gratitude for what we do have. Alas, today it seems that many, many people never stop thinking of all the good things they *don't* have. There is no denying every generation have their own societal problems. For our Gen-Z's it's especially economical and environmental but they're mostly not such life-threatening as their ancient relatives concerns! Argh, 'first-world problems' aye.

I'd like to hypothesize, as many have before me, that maybe this entire 'loving our perfect life' lark makes the biggest contribution of all to our society's escalating rates of depression.

Perhaps actress-singer Vanessa Williams is right: 'The greatest gift parents can give their children is to love what we do, and love who we are.' Perhaps journalist-writer Maria Shriver (Arnold Schwarzenegger's wife) is right: 'It's very important for your children to see you living your life, loving your life, because that gives them permission to do the same.' Probably Buddha was right: it's overcoming craving that brings Nirvana. Probably Jesus was right: the kingdom of Heaven lies within us.

God knows!

But what I do know is that ungratefulness makes me sick and tired.

I believe it's actually all about acceptance . . . because feeling like a piece of shit, and feeling that we are unique and wonderful are intimately interrelated. We can only truly appreciate feeling happy when we intimately know what it's like to feel sad.

So, keeping this in mind, this section is all about me helping you to learn about some of the wonderful natural therapies available for any family member who may be feeling low or stressed out — though, as always, it can be wise to see your naturopathic herbalist for recommended doses.

5-HTP *(5-Hydroxytryptophan)*

In biology, a 'precursor' is a substance from which another, more biologically active substance is formed. L-tryptophan is the essential amino acid that the body converts into 5-HTP, and 5-HTP is the precursor of serotonin (5-HT) and melatonin. Serotonin is the main neurotransmitter that controls both mood regulation by combating anxiety and depression, and impulse control by combating aggression and promoting sleep. 5-HTP supplements are derived from the seeds of the West African medicinal plant *Griffonia simplicifolia*.

Taking 5-HTP supplements can work well to fight mild to moderate depression by increasing the production of serotonin. 5-HTP has also been shown to increase the activity of dopamine and adrenal noradrenaline, which help regulate alertness and mood. 5-HTP can relieve depression, improve mood, treat anxiety, enhance sleep quality, improve cognitive abilities and suppress the carbohydrate cravings typical of depression. Many are heralding 5-HTP as Prozac's 'true alternative'. It should not be used in conjunction with a pharmaceutical antidepressant.

ESSENTIAL AMINO ACIDS

Your liver manufactures about 80 per cent of the amino acids your body needs — the other 20 per cent can only be supplied by diet, and are therefore called 'essential' amino acids. Amino acids are the building blocks of protein chains, and having low levels of certain amino acids can depress a person's mood. For example, low tyrosine or phenylalanine can create abnormal levels of mood-regulating chemicals in the brain such as dopamine. Low levels of S-adenosyl methionine (SAM-e) can imbalance catecholamines, which can depress the mood. Depleted levels of 5-HTP affect production of the powerful neurotransmitter serotonin, which affects mood, such as a reduced sense of satisfaction and well-being. This causes depressed moods including anxiety, insomnia, reduced appetite and lowered libido.

Taking an essential amino acid supplement can be positively mood-enhancing, and is especially advantageous if combined with vitamin C and vitamin B6.

GINKGO BILOBA EXTRACT *(GBE)*

Ginkgo biloba is thought to be the oldest species of tree — and one tree can live a thousand years. Ginkgo biloba extract (GBE) is a refined mood-enhancement supplement that is a very effective treatment for depression. This natural antidepressant is said to stabilise cell membranes, inhibit lipid breakdown and aid the cells' use of oxygen and glucose. It is also a mental and vascular stimulant, which normalises blood circulation (especially in the brain's hippocampus and striatum), and so protects the brain, liver, eyes and blood vessels.

GBE is used medicinally for a wealth of mental-function problems, including depression (increasing neurotransmitter production), mental concentration (giving a clearer mind) and Alzheimer's. It also helps to reverse mental deterioration (such as that caused by strokes). In some Western countries, it is often prescribed by doctors and has almost immediate effects.

KAVA

Found throughout the South Pacific islands, the 'dirty water', peppery drink made from the kava root has been used for centuries as part of the local cultures' expressions of village camaraderie, jovial friendship and welcoming hospitality.

In recent times, kava supplements have gained a strong reputation as a tried-and-true natural calming treatment for anxiety, nervous unrest, and minor depression. Therapeutic doses do not dampen alertness or interact negatively with mild alcohol consumption, plus, unlike synthetic tranquillisers such as pharmaceutical benzodiazepine drugs, kava is not addictive.

As kava is a mild skeletal-muscle relaxant, it can also be a useful treatment for muscle-spasm conditions such as neck-tension headaches.

PSYCHOSOCIAL TREATMENTS

Psychotherapy's cognitive-behavioural therapy (CBT), which focuses on our belief systems and the role of our thoughts, can be especially successful in assisting children to learn life and stress-coping skills and aids them to think about things from a better perspective. Interpersonal therapy (IPT) may also be helpful, with its emphasis on coping with relationship conflicts. Family therapy focuses on the psychological health of the entire family relationship. Psychotherapy's 'play therapy' can help children get past inner anxieties created by emotional di culties.

Psychotherapeutic counselling can include some psychological therapies, but is mainly about supportive listening and providing practical problem-solving information and coping strategies for the child to gain better abilities to relax, be assertive and socialise.

ST JOHN'S WORT *(Hypericum perforatum)*

St John's Wort derives its name from its annual blooming time in Europe, which is around the feast day of St John the Baptist. St John's Wort has been known as a medicinal herb for centuries, and has a long, magical and fabled history.

Also known as the Devil's Scourge, St John's Wort has been used by 'wise women' and midwives for many hundreds of years, to 'chase away the devil of psychotic madness' and other illnesses of the imagination and understanding, such as melancholia and anxiety. Even soldiers in the Crusades would drink it with wine to steady their nerves. This mood-enhancing natural antidepressant increases the availability of serotonin in the neuron synapses; of norepinephrine, which improves alertness and increases energy; and of dopamine, which increases the feeling of well-being.

St John's Wort is a legitimate alternative to pharmaceutical antidepressants and in some Westernised countries it is more popularly prescribed than the drugs Zoloft and Prozac. It is also very popular for treating insomnia, mood swings, fatigue, PMS and menopause.

As with pharmaceutical antidepressants, the e ects of St John's Wort take six weeks to become fully apparent. It should not be used in conjunction with a pharmaceutical antidepressant drug or the oral contraceptive pill.

SIBERIAN GINSENG

Although Siberian ginseng (*Eleutherococcus senticosus*) is not a 'true' panax ginseng, it is a distant relative and shares similar properties. As a mood-enhancement supplement, Siberian ginseng provides marvellous protection against stress.

This natural antidepressant can help to combat depression, insomnia, moodiness, fatigue, poor memory, lack of focus and mental tension, is an immune-system booster, improves the balance of the brain's important neurotransmitters, and increases physical performance and endurance.

A–Z OF NATURAL HEALING THERAPIES

A confusing aspect of holistic therapies is that so many practices talk of their capacity to produce very wide-ranging cures, which can make it extremely perplexing for today's parent to actually decide which therapy is best suited to their individual child's needs. So this section is about *options* and choosing the most appropriate healing therapies — it's an attempt to narrow things down for greater clarity. I've also included therapies such as pilates, yoga and tai chi because all are holistic and none are simply about flatter abs or improved cardiac output. They are mind-body-spirit forms of exercise, with local studios these days often o ering classes for children and adolescents.

PARENTING GOLDEN INSIGHT NO. 5

Consider natural healing therapies for maintaining health and wellness.

ACUPUNCTURE

Acupuncture is an ancient traditional form of Chinese medical treatment that aims at treating the whole person as well as the disease. Acupuncture is based on the belief that illness occurs when some factor disrupts the normal flow of life force (qi) through the energy pathways of the body. The acupuncturist inserts very fine needles into carefully selected specific points on the body to stimulate a natural healing response. Treatment is used as a preventative as well as a healing process, including alleviating disease and relieving pain.

IDEAL USES

Acupuncture is part of a complete system of medicine and as such can assist with most health issues. To name a few: contagious diseases such as colds and influenza, nose and ear infections, phlegm, eczema, sleep difficulties, teething pain, digestive problems, chronic pain caused by headaches, arthritis, back pain, ulcers, menstrual cramps, muscle strain, hypertension, nausea, vomiting, asthma and addiction cravings. Acupuncture is a safe and effective method of treatment for children and babies, and as the needles are very fine and generally painless, children are usually happy to be treated.

ALEXANDER TECHNIQUE

The Alexander technique uses guided experimentation to recognise (and reactivate) habitual limitations of thinking and movement. It is taught in one-to-one lessons, combining verbal instruction and hand contact. The aim is to free oneself from unintentionally self-imposed limitations, and so teach the body-mind unit the ability to make new choices.

Children of all ages can benefit from learning the Alexander technique, as it can give them a sound awareness of how they control their postural development and prevent them developing bad postural habits as they grow. To paraphrase Glynn MacDonald in *The Complete Illustrated Guide to the Alexander Technique*, the Alexander technique can help children by preventing them from developing harmful ways of using their bodies as they grow. It is concerned with the quality of learning and respects the fact that every individual learns differently. When children go to school they are under pressure to master a skill and produce work that gains approval, which may cause them to develop habits of tension. The Alexander technique can prevent harmful reactions.

IDEAL USES

For back and neck pain, RSI, stuttering/restricted breathing, balance, posture, mobility problems, phobias and depression, and to improve self-awareness, creativity, clarified objective thinking, sports or artistic prowess.

AROMATHERAPY *(Essential oils)*

Odours have an enormous impact on our body-mind-emotion balance. Aromatherapy uses essential oils, which are extracted from plant material such as flowers, berries, leaves, wood, bark, roots, seeds or peel. Some are inexpensive, some are very expensive; with essential oils there is the 'get what you pay for' aspect, in that if one brand is cheaper than another, it will usually be of a less pure quality. It is best to seek the most pure, and ideally organic, oil possible, rather than a blend — though the more expensive oils such as rose and neroli can be diluted with a vegetable or nut cold-pressed carrier-oil such as grapeseed or almond. (Due to their concentration, never apply oils 'neat' to skin — except tea tree and lavender.)

You can use aromatherapy at home by burning oils in a di user, or placing a few drops of oil in water and heating it with a candle. Aromatherapists also use essential oils in a base carrier-oil for the likes of a full-body massage, as well as prescribing oils for baths, compresses and di users. Some will even use the oils internally. The key point is to ensure your aromatherapist is fully trained.

IDEAL USES

There are too many ailments aromatherapy can be used for to list them all, but it can be especially great for arthritis, bronchitis, catarrh (thick phlegm), colds, constipation, urinary tract infections, dermatitis, diarrhoea, eczema, headaches, hives, flu, laryngitis, nausea, skin conditions, sinus and throat infections, tonsillitis, muscular tension and sprains/strains. It can also be used to stimulate digestion, give your immune system a boost, balance hormones and reduce stress, anxiety and fear.

Aromatherapists can create special blends customised for children to combat many issues, such as for clearing snu es, aiding concentration, relieving anxiety, alleviating irritability, inducing sweet dreams and reducing tears to bring joy. Many wonderful aromatherapy self-help guidebooks are available.

AYURVEDA *(Indian medicine)*

Ayurvedic medicine is a 4000- to 6000-year-old intricate holistic system of medicinal healthcare that's still in daily use by hundreds of millions in India, Nepal and Sri Lanka. The word 'ayurveda' translates as 'life-principle knowledge'. This globally respected 'science of life' focuses on the body, sense organs, mind and soul to obtain physical, mental, social and spiritual harmony. Ayurveda centres on the unique foods and lifestyle best suited to each person's individual constitution in order to maintain health, based on ancient knowledge of the energetic forces that influence us, particularly those that a ect the mind-body connection.

IDEAL USES

Innumerable, including treating fever, diarrhoea, boils, childhood diseases and diseases of the eyes, ears, nose and throat; detoxifications; and boosting the immune system.

BACH FLOWER REMEDIES

These remedies are 38 flower essences discovered and categorised by London physician Dr Edward Bach (1886–1936). Using a similar vibrational principle to homeopathy, the remedies extract the flower essences into spring water, then brandy is added as a preservative, and the mixture diluted for medicinal use. This type of remedy is very safe, because it does not contain any chemicals except a very small amount of alcohol. Bach flower remedies treat the body on an emotional level to alleviate unhappy feelings and unblock the body's natural restorative abilities.

IDEAL USES

Flower remedies are incredibly effective and wonderful to use with children. Some examples are: larch for lack of confidence in children who underrate their own capabilities; holly for children who are jealous or hostile, perhaps towards a younger sibling; mimulus for shy children, and those with fears or phobias related to a known cause such as animals or the dark; and clematis for children whose concentration is poor because they daydream a lot.

RESCUE REMEDY

Perhaps the most famous of Bach's combination preparations, Rescue Remedy is an essential for the first-aid box. It is immediately calming and emotionally stabilising, and is good for recovery from frights, shocks, tantrums, arguments, anxiety, irritability, nightmares or overtired sleeplessness.

BIOFEEDBACK and NEUROFEEDBACK

Traditional biofeedback is a technique using sophisticated instruments to monitor the body's autonomic nervous system, allowing the person to gain control over involuntary body responses such as breathing, heart rate, skin temperature and muscle tension, and the sympathetic nervous system's dualistic fright response (fight or flight). The more recent neurofeedback (specifically brainwave biofeedback) is becoming increasingly popular with parents and children. Neurofeedback typically uses an EEG (a machine that detects the brain's electrical activity), and is gaining favour as a non-drug treatment for ADHD.

IDEAL USES

Biofeedback can assist with hypertension, migraine headaches and anxiety. Neurofeedback for ADHD involves down-training slow brain waves (such as theta) associated with spacing-out or inattention; and up-training beta waves associated with cognitive tasking and executive function.

BOWEN THERAPY

Bowen therapy was pioneered by Thomas Ambrose Bowen in Australia. After working in di erent laboring jobs as a young man, he developed a great interest in massage and body work. Eventually Bowen's subtle, relaxing and painless technique became immensely popular.

Bowen therapy should not be confused with massage, as there is no use of oils or rubbing. Instead, the practitioner uses their fingers and thumbs in a type of rolling movement over the muscles, tendons and ligaments, which releases this soft tissue, allowing the body to realign itself. It is a straightforward, no-nonsense remedial therapy that is non-intrusive, gentle and e ective. With Bowen therapy, the *whole* body is treated — regardless of the ailment — and it promotes general healing, pain relief and recovery of energy.

IDEAL USES

Back pain; whiplash, shoulder and elbow problems; RSI and carpal tunnel syndrome; tennis or golfer's elbow; coccyx, sacroiliac, sciatic and pelvic problems; pain in hamstrings, knees and ankles; restless legs; respiratory and digestive problems, including asthma and colic; headaches and sinus problems — plus almost any soft-tissue injury or discomfort.

CELL SALTS

A 'cousin' to homeopathy, the cell salts are 12 biochemical, inorganic tissue salts, developed by physician Samuel Hahnemann (1755–1843) and Dr Wilhelm Heinrich Schuessler (1821–98), that are used to support the utilisation, absorption, activation and function of important mineral salts present in human cells. This treatment acknowledges the basic premise that imbalances of any form cause disease.

IDEAL USES

There are a multitude of uses for cell salts, including the treatment of colic, headaches, diarrhoea, itching, fluid retention, colds, sinus problems, muscle twitching, mild fever, sore throats and so much more. Get yourself a cell salt first-aid kit! Definitely a great purchase for the household.

CHIROPRACTIC

Chiropractors use their extensive knowledge of anatomy and physiology (alongside X-rays) to address disease and dysfunction in the human system. Chiropractic works on the principle that abnormally disrupted nerve functions result in diminished health and increased disease, because the central nervous system controls virtually everything in our entire body. The chiropractor uses manual adjustments to relieve nervous-system dysfunctions and rehabilitate the spine and associated joints, thus enabling the body to heal and repair itself.

There are typically two types of chiropractors. The first group are those who primarily deal with painful joint movement (termed biomechanical joint dysfunction). Second, there are those who offer an integrated wellness approach, encompassing regular tune-ups to the spine and the spinal column, nutritional support, lifestyle advice, education and health enhancement. Chiropractors working in the wellness area typically involve children, adolescents, adults and the elderly in regular care.

IDEAL USES

Integrated health and wellness; treatment of migraines, headaches, back pain, sluggish immune system, lethargy, insomnia, poor posture, reduced mobility, ADHD, asthma, recurrent childhood ear infections, respiratory infections, bed-wetting; enhancing sporting performance and more.

CRANIOSACRAL THERAPY *(CST)*

In the 1970s, while assisting during spinal surgery, the American osteopath Dr John Upledger first observed the movement of the craniosacral system (the meningeal membranes and cerebrospinal fluid). His curiosity led to decades of clinical trials and research resulting in craniosacral therapy — a gentle hands-on therapy that works closely with the body's natural healing abilities to facilitate change through bone and soft-tissue release.

IDEAL USES

In addition to increasing energy and resistance to disease, CST can help with a wide range of problems, including neck and back pain, digestive problems, fatigue and lethargy, insomnia and sleep difficulties, stress and tension, headaches and migraine, TMJ (temporomandibular joint) dysfunction, and pre- and post-surgery care. Encompassing mind, body and soul, CST can improve both emotional and physical ailments.

FELDENKRAIS METHOD

The Feldenkrais method of 'somatic education' involves gentle movement lessons that awaken the person's system to new options for posture and movement. Its applications are wide.

IDEAL USES

In general, Feldenkrais is commonly used for musculo-skeletal problems such as back or neck pain or stiffness and to improve posture in adults and children. It is also used for rehabilitation after injury or joint surgery, and for performance improvement in sports, dancing, voice and acting. In children, it is used where there are developmental difficulties — in fact, its creator, Russian-born physicist Moshé Feldenkrais became famous for working with children with cerebral palsy.

FENG SHUI

Feng shui (pronounced fung-shway) is the very ancient Chinese practice that uses the laws of heaven and earth regarding the placement of buildings and objects in space to achieve environmental harmony. The fundamental theories of feng shui include the qi (chi) flow of energy, the polarity of yin (female, negative, yielding) and yang (masculine, positive, thrusting) balancing all the points of the compass, and an octagonal bagua ('key' diagram of the eight areas of a space).

IDEAL USES

Used to achieve optimum health, wealth and well-being in all areas of life, including interpersonal relationships. The same applies to children, with feng shui creating spaces that are vibrant, joyful and restful, to help ensure you have aspiring, intelligent, healthy children and enhanced family relationships.

HERBALISM

Many of us believe that Mother Nature has provided the cure for almost every natural disease in existence — it is just a matter of knowing all her medicines, and herbalism can be the key that unlocks her secrets! Herbalism (or herbology) is the traditional botanical medicine system derived from plants and plant extracts. It uses botanical remedies rich with vitamins, minerals, lipid fatty acids and protein amino acids, but also most importantly phytonutrients, which are the medicinally active ingredients in herbal medicines (and food). All components in these medicines work together, amplifying the effect of the whole herb on human tissue, which is termed synergy.

IDEAL USES

Daily supplements for overall health and well-being; specific therapeutic remedies for specific diseases; plus herbal teas, particularly for children, for example chamomile and lemon balm for calming and assisting digestion and peppermint for cooling and stimulating digestion.

HOMEOPATHY *(Classical and first aid)*

Initially developed by German physician Samuel Hahnemann (1755–1843), homeopathy uses 'potentised remedies' that treat like with like. Homeopathy remains popular because, quite simply, it works — whether or not science can ascertain *how* it works. In the past, homeopathy was an aristocratic medicine endorsed by royalty, and today many countries around the world (especially in Europe) still include homeopathy under their national health schemes.

Homeopathic first aid can be self-prescribed for relieving acute symptoms; however, for chronic conditions it is essential to receive a full diagnosis and ongoing prescriptions from a classical homeopath.

Store homeopathic medicines in a cool dark place. Avoid having homeopathics around strong odours that neutralise remedies, such as mint, eucalyptus, caffeine, cigarettes or camphor. Only take homeopathic remedies for a day or two, and stop when symptoms improve.

IDEAL USES

Innumerable. A huge number of conditions respond well to homeopathy, including ear infections, tonsillitis, bronchiolitis, bronchitis, chickenpox, colds, coughs, croup (barking cough), diarrhoea, glue ear, hand-foot-and-mouth disease, flu, measles, mumps, sore throats, thrush, vomiting, eczema, allergies, asthma, cradle cap, colic, diabetes, fevers, gastroenteritis, jaundice, vaccination reactions, hormone rash, nappy rash, teething, hyperactivity, antisocial behaviour, bedwetting, anxiety, irrational fears, timidity, low self-esteem, super tantrums, ADD, ADHD and more.

HOMEOPATHIC ESSENTIALS IN THE FIRST-AID BOX

- *Arnica (sprays, drops, tablets, creams, gels):* Taken internally or externally for bruises, knocks, sprains and strains (don't use on broken skin).
- *Calendula (drops, creams and gels):* Taken internally or externally for cuts, scrapes and painful injured skin; ideal for nappy rash.
- *Hypercal (drops, creams and gels):* A combination remedy (hypericum and calendula) taken internally or externally for painful or infected skin.
- *Kali Bich (drops and tablets):* Taken internally for green snotty noses.
- *Aconite (drops and tablets):* Taken internally for the sudden onset of sore throat, cough and earache symptoms.
- *Belladonna (drops and tablets):* Taken internally for fevers, earaches and teething, especially when cheeks are red.

HYPNOTHERAPY

Hypnotherapy is a natural yet altered state of consciousness, in which the critical part of the mind is quietened and access is given to the most powerful part of the subconscious mind. During this altered state our brain is extremely active, which has been documented and measured through PET, MRI and detailed EEG scans. Generally the hypnotherapist uses deep relaxation and focused concentration to assist people into the hypnotic state. Hypnotherapy is a safe and powerful tool for enhancing focus and overcoming psychosomatic issues, unwanted habits, phobias, feelings of uneasiness and self-esteem issues.

IDEAL USES

Enhancing study/learning, concentration and sports performance; anaesthesia/pain-relief management (chronic, surgical or dental pain relief); breaking unwanted dysfunctional habits such as smoking, overeating and nail-biting; and modifying emotional behaviour, such as anxiety.

IRIDOLOGY AND SCLEROLOGY

Iridology and sclerology are not forms of treatment — they are diagnostic assessment tools. Iridology reads the colors and characteristics of the iris, and sclerology examines the red lines in the whites of the eyes.

The sclera is divided into four quadrants, each of which relates to specific areas of the anatomy. It is used as a second witness to diagnostic findings in the irises, or on young children (below five) whose irises still aren't properly formed.

Iridology can provide a lot of information about genetic predispositions, as well as current health challenges, and sclerology gives very specific information about current health issues and the causes at an anatomical level. As iridology is not a treatment, most iridologists have also studied a complementary medicine, such as naturopathy, in order to treat disease.

IDEAL USES

Iridology and sclerology can be used to diagnose toxins, inflammation, inherent weaknesses, biochemical deficiencies and general health status, and can often be especially helpful with chronic and 'undiagnosable' disease or general unwellness. Many health-food stores have a resident or visiting iridologist who can assist with health maintenance.

LIVE BLOOD ANALYSIS

On the basis that blood is the essence of health, the technique of 'live blood analysis', such as Hemaview®, involves taking a tiny 'pin-prick' of blood from the finger and examining one or two drops under a special diagnostic microscope. Live blood analysis is not a healing therapy, but a screening tool based on the medical science of haematology, investigating the size, shape and ratio of the red cells, white cells and platelets in blood. It is used to assist in the detection of inflammation, toxicity, oxidative stress, free-radical damage, nutrient deficiency, microbial infections and more. It translates that information into an analysis of immune competence, nutritional status, liver health, functional imbalances and degenerative changes.

IDEAL USES

Live blood analysis does not 'treat' unwellness. It is simply a screening tool that gives the practitioner more information about what is happening in the blood at that point in time, to provide a better understanding of the person's overall health, so suitable therapies can be administered.

MEDITATION

Meditation was developed more than 7000 years ago by people who sought a deeper understanding of themselves and life. It has since been incorporated into many Eastern and Western spiritual paths.

Meditation is the practice of directing the mind inward to a single focal point. Depending on the technique practised, the focus may be on the breath, body sensations, visualisation or a mantra. The experience during meditation depends on both the technique used and the individual meditator. Scientists are just starting to explore the many physical and mental benefits of meditation, but so far, amongst other things, they have found that it lowers stress-hormone levels and improves the immune system. These days it is also easy to download guided meditations to listen to.

IDEAL USES

As a busy parent, it is important to take precious time out to recharge yourself — and to maintain your sanity! Meditation is often used as a means of reducing stress, bringing mental peace or obtaining spiritual enlightenment. It has also been proved to reduce heart rate and blood pressure. The benefits of meditation translate into your day-to-day life, bringing clarity, intuition and inner strength to face all of the challenges that come with raising children.

Like adults, children too can benefit from knowing how to meditate; perhaps it is part of the reason depression is almost unheard of in Eastern children who are skilled in meditation. And these days it's so easy to play YouTube guided meditations on your phone ... I try to meditate at least 10-20mins every day. It just becomes part of how you function.

NATUROPATHY

Naturopathy, also known as 'natural medicine', is an 'umbrella' term that refers to a practitioner formally trained in a variety of treatments, with an overall focus on a holistic approach. Naturopathy was the forerunner of modern medicine, and today still aims to treat the causes of disease rather than inhibit symptoms. The naturopathic therapy of herbal medicine has been used for centuries and is still used by the great majority of the world's population — because in general terms it is safe, e ective and children especially can respond beautifully to it. Naturopaths may be qualified to prescribe herbal remedies and a range of micronutrients, including herbs, vitamins, minerals, Bach flower remedies and homeobotanicals. They can o er nutritional advice, and may have a minimal involvement with homeopathics. Naturopaths are also often trained in healing therapies such as massage, Bowen technique, reflexology and aromatherapy and assessment tools like iridology.

IDEAL USES

Although somewhat the natural equivalent of a GP, naturopaths do not diagnose as such. Instead they look at the overall wellness of a person, rather than treating symptoms. My recommendation is that along with a family GP for diagnosing illness, you also have a naturopath for complementary and ancient medicines to promote wellness. Seeing a great naturopath for everyday health concerns and health maintenance can be an excellent family health investment. (Like medical doctors, some naturopaths go on to specialise in particular fields, such as allergies, infertility, pregnancy and childbirth.)

NATUROPATHIC ESSENTIALS IN THE FIRST-AID BOX

» *Aloe vera gel:* Soothes minor burns and insect bites.

» *Colloidal silver (liquid or cream):* Taken externally or internally as powerful antimicrobials and preventatives against infection, with hundreds of uses.

» *Echinacea (tablets or drops):* Natural immune system stimulant, especially ideal for assisting recovery from measles, mumps, boils, laryngitis, tonsillitis, thrush, streptococcus, staphylococcus,

- » respiratory and urinary tract infections — and to boost a run-down, sluggish immune system.
- » *Olive-leaf extract (capsules or syrup):* Broad-spectrum natural antimicrobial, wonderful for fighting viruses, bacteria, fungus-yeast infections, worm parasites, colds and flus.
- » *Cat's claw:* An incredibly powerful herb particularly good for chest, especially upper respiratory, infections.
- » *Thuja occidentalis (Thuja):* Fantastic for skin warts and plantar (sole of foot) warts but never take it orally unless specifically instructed by a qualified herbalist. Mix with a vitamin E cream and apply topically to the warts and watch them literally fade away.
- » *Bach's flower Rescue Remedy:* For upsets, accidents and falls.
- » *Manuka or tea-tree oil:* Topical antiseptic.

NEURO-LINGUISTIC PROGRAMMING *(NLP)*

NLP originally developed in the 1970s; 'neuro' means brain or mind, 'linguistic' means language or speech, and 'programming' means instruction. In other words, NLP is a behavioural science of how people think, feel and behave in their everyday life — our beliefs, values, attitudes and spirituality. Since the 1980s, NLP has had an enormous impact on the corporate world but can also be used in a family dynamic as well.

IDEAL USES

Applications of NLP are wide and varied, but in general the improvement in the way one thinks, feels, acts and learns can be used in a wide range of self-improvement avenues, including business, healthcare, sports and personal development. When taught in a fun, child-friendly way, NLP can be just as effective for children and teens, and can aid in increasing confidence, gaining motivation and improving communication skills, as well as helping with common childhood problems such as exam stress, low self-esteem and reversing negative attitudes.

OSTEOPATHY

Osteopathy is a hands-on practice, using extensive anatomical and physiological knowledge and observation to treat the musculo-skeletal system and thus improve health and well-being. The gentle art of cranial osteopathy is particularly popular for use on newborns, though it is suitable for all ages.

IDEAL USES

Treatment of back pain, neck pain, headaches, asthma, middle-ear infections, menstrual pain and respiratory infections; and disease prevention.

PHYSIOTHERAPY

With extensive biomechanical and medical knowledge, physiotherapists or physical therapists use various treatments to rehabilitate people with injuries to muscles or joints, neurological problems and cardio-pulmonary disease. Physiotherapy includes therapeutic exercise, nerve stimulation and joint mobilisation.

IDEAL USES

Treatment of orthopaedic and neurological movement dysfunction, sports injuries and cystic fibrosis; and the prevention and treatment of 'lifestyle diseases' of the twenty-first century.

PILATES

Pilates is a body-conditioning system of physical fitness developed in the early twentieth century by Joseph Pilates (1880–1967), which teaches mind-breath awareness and strengthens the body's core postural muscles for improved spinal alignment, to maintain body balance and reduce back pain. Joseph Pilates believed physical and mental health are entwined, so the exercise includes yoga-like principles of concentration, control, precision, breathing and flowing movement. It has grown immensely in popularity over recent years.

IDEAL USES

Therapeutic uses for Pilates include alleviating and preventing back pain, improving mental and physical well-being, increasing flexibility, and strengthening postural muscles, as well as sculpting the body.

QIGONG

Qigong (ch'i kung), which means 'vital-energy work', originated several thousand years ago. Qigong practitioners develop the ability to feel the movement of qi (chi or vital energy) along the channels of the body to assess the state of the body, including the e ects of qi flow to the organs. It is thought that this was how traditional Chinese medicine developed.

Di erent qigong styles have evolved, influenced by the di erent schools of Daoism, Buddhism and Confucianism. Although the martial arts may have subsequently influenced some styles of qigong, they themselves are often a derivative of qigong, which pre-dates them. (Qigong does get confused with martial arts — especially tai chi — but its movements are much slower.) Today there are thousands of styles of qigong, and all are slow, graceful exercises designed to work on qi to improve overall health. Breathing techniques are often involved.

IDEAL USES

Qigong has much to o er, including gaining strength, improving health, reversing disease and increasing spiritual connectedness. Some qigong practices encourage healing of minor injury and illness, and can even be used for more serious situations as one's practice and understanding develops. Because children are so open, they very easily benefit from qigong.

REFLEXOLOGY

Reflexologists apply finger pressure to the feet (and hands and ears), on the basis that di erent areas or reflexes (especially of the foot) correspond with di erent areas of the body. Reflexology relieves nervous tension and stress, inducing relaxation. It also improves circulation, revitalises qi (life-force energy) and improves the general equilibrium, health and well-being of people of any age.

IDEAL USES

Multiple uses, including treating migraines, back pain, arthritis, sleep disorders, hormone disorders and digestive disorders. Reflexology can be very e ective when used on babies for minor upsets such as reflux, colic and sleeplessness.

REIKI

Developed by Mikao Usui (1865–1926), reiki translates as 'universal life-force energy' and is a spiritual practice that treats physical, emotional and mental disharmony and/or disease using qi or healing energy. Reiki has gained great credibility because of its amazing, often inexplicable, results. Reiki is a totally non-invasive healing technique, using a gentle-touch or non-touch methodology of relaxation and healing, working towards a balanced harmony of mind, body and soul.

IDEAL USES

Reiki is primarily used for prompt stress reduction, pain relief and accelerated tissue healing. Reiki can also improve problem-solving abilities and enhance creativity. As reiki is simple to learn and easy to use on yourself, family, friends, animals and plants, it is a cost-effective and immediate way of gaining enhanced health, peace of mind and well-being. A deep state of relaxation occurs easily and with it physical, mental and emotional feelings of calmness, peace, optimism and energy renewal. Reiki is always done with the client fully clothed and is an excellent complementary therapy for cancer patients, pregnant moms, the elderly and babies, as it is non-invasive and physically non-stimulating.

ROLFING

Created by Ida Pauline Rolf in the 1950s, 'Rolfing' is described as 'structural integration soft-tissue manipulation' — but it is a lot more than simply massage. Rolfers palpate (touch) the tissue to feel for imbalances, then use deep-tissue massage to holistically balance the body. It is said that afterwards clients can stand straighter and move better. As Dr Rolf said, 'Anyone can take a body apart, very few know how to put it back together.' It's about realigning the body for long-term structural health.

IDEAL USES

Rolfing® can be used to treat back pain, RSI and muscular trauma, and to enhance vitality and decrease postural asymmetries. For children, Rolfing can assist posture, growing pains, emotional stress, scoliosis, club feet, cerebral palsy, self-esteem/confidence issues and attention focus, and is ideal for broken limbs or after accidents, assisting the healing of supporting connective tissue, for improved range of motion.

SHIATSU

Shiatsu is Japanese for 'finger pressure', and is based on principles of Chinese medicine. Practitioners use palm and finger pressure to massage key energy channels in the body, releasing tension and stimulating flow within the system — it feels great. Your limbs are gently rotated and stretched, and palm and finger pressure release muscular tension.

IDEAL USES

Considered a preventative treatment, regular shiatsu sessions may alleviate stress, stimulating the body's immune system in both adults and children. Shiatsu massage may be particularly helpful for children and teenagers who suffer from headaches, asthma, eczema and repeated ear infections, or have difficulty in concentrating. Best of all, Japanese modesty requires that you keep your clothes on!

TAI CHI

Tai chi chuan is the traditional 'internal' Chinese martial art of hard and soft techniques. Tai chi chih is a Western, standardised version of tai chi chuan, which features a series of 19 movements and one pose, creating a meditative version focusing on developing and balancing chi spiritual energy.

IDEAL USES

Maintaining health and longevity, reducing stress and relieving minor ailments. For children, tai chi can be particularly helpful in improving concentration, balance, flexibility, focus, attention, learning, behaviour and fitness.

TRADITIONAL CHINESE MEDICINE *(TCM)*

TCM is based on many interconnected philosophies, including

yin and yang (unity of opposites), qi (life force), the five elements (water, metal, earth, wood and fire), and the body's energy pathways (meridians). TCM observes that human bodily processes interact with, and are interrelated to, the universal environment. Practitioners recognise the signs of imbalance or disharmony in order to diagnose, prevent and treat illness and disease, believing that optimum health results from living harmoniously.

TCM is mainstream medicine in China and Taiwan, and includes therapies such as herbalism, acupuncture, moxibustion (the burning of 'moxa' or mugwort herb), tui na (bodywork massage), qigong, tai chi, feng shui and Chinese astrology.

IDEAL USES

TCM is particularly useful for long-term treatment of chronic conditions, cravings, and for general health and well-being. In China, TCM uses at least 500 herbs and more than 400 patented herbal remedies — not all are available internationally. For children, TCM's soft and gentle tui na massage and herbs in low dosage can be especially helpful.

YOGA

Yoga is an enormous topic in itself, so this is very much a simplified introduction. Yoga had its origins in India more than 5000 years ago and its aim is to lead one to self realisation, and ultimately to 'God' realisation. Today in the West, however, we associate the word yoga with flexible hamstrings and a tight butt, but the word actually refers to many disciplines. Just one, hatha yoga, is the yoga of controlled physical postures that the West is most familiar with. Hatha yoga has many varieties, including iyengar, ashtanga and bikram.

IDEAL USES

Yoga works on mind-body rejuvenation, preparation for meditation, improved flexibility, greater strength, better posture, increased circulation, stress reduction, general well-being and health promotion. It can also help to remedy some emotional disorders, and to heal certain chronic problems, especially relief of back pain, chronic headaches, joint pain, general stiffness and weakness. Popular styles include:

- *Iyengar:* Strong classical yoga involving the long holding of poses and focusing on correct bodily alignment. It encourages the use of props such as belts, bolsters and blocks to compensate for lack of flexibility and to gain maximum benefits from each pose. Ideal for beginners, and people with back or joint problems.

- *Hatha:* A general term traditionally meaning many types of physical yoga, but classes termed 'hatha style' generally provide a gentle, mellow, comfortably paced introduction to basic yoga postures, focusing on breathing and meditation. Ideal for winding down at the end of a tough day.

- *Ashtanga:* Physically demanding 'power yoga' style, which is fast-paced, moving quickly from one pose to the next in a continual flowing sequence and focusing on breath. Light on meditation and heavy on developing strength, stamina and flexibility.

- *Bikram:* 'Hot' yoga done in a room 38 degrees Celsius or higher, allowing muscles to loosen and the body to sweat, and thereby cleanse. Bikram focuses on 26 very physical poses of high intensity.

- *Kundalini:* Combines precise poses, sounds and breath control, incorporating meditation, mantras (chanting), visualisations and guided relaxation to heal and 'purify' the mind, body and emotions, and naturally release endorphins

SUMMARY — THE FUTURE OF MEDICINE

When health is absent, wisdom cannot reveal itself, art cannot manifest, strength cannot fight, wealth becomes useless, and intelligence cannot be applied.

Herophilus (335–280 BCE), *Greek physician*

At this time, modern science gropingly struggles to understand how ancient, natural and traditional medicines do what they do, because, of course, modern science doesn't yet understand how many of its own patented drugs do what they do. So right now modern pharmaceutical medicine and *vis medicatrix naturae* (the healing power of nature) are at great odds with each other.

Fortunately increasing numbers of individuals have become interested in finding out what optimum holistic health means and how to obtain it. Simultaneously, many forward-thinking, broad-minded and revolutionary medical experts are pioneering a new scientific matrix based on equal parts of ancient wisdom and modern medicine that I faithfully believe will eventually transform mankind's collective understanding of individual health and wellness.

It's about remembering the role of the human spirit in health and healing, for as Austrian philosopher Rudolph Steiner so aptly said, 'Any science that considers only the physical understands only the corpse.'

Chapter Eight

DISEASES, DRUGS AND NATURAL ALTERNATIVES — THE GOOD, THE BAD AND THE UGLY

Obviously there is a place for physicians in treating many acute illnesses and conditions such as seizures, fractured bones, serious infections and abscesses, congestive heart failure, strokes, etc. For less serious problems, and for a majority of chronic difficulties, home remedies and common sense may often offer the best approach.

Dr C Norman Shealy,
The Complete Family Guide to Natural Home Remedies

Without any doubt, modern medicine is outstandingly brilliant in several specific areas: improving infant mortality rates, attending to accidental structural damage to the body (such as broken bones), spectacularly intricate surgery with often miraculous outcomes, and the occasional transformation of acute disease.

But, also without any doubt, conventional medicine does not do so well when it comes to genuinely curing most chronic disease. Instead, modern drug-based medicine specialises in suppressing symptoms, encouraged and supported by the multi-billion-dollar industry of Big Pharmaceuticals. Often, simply blocking the symptoms does little to facilitate real permanent healing cures.

A PILL FOR EVERY ILL, AND A BILL FOR EVERY PILL

BIG PHARM *(Big pharmaceuticals)*

'Action unknown' is an extremely common phrase used in pharmaceutical drug handbooks and drug data sheets, because it is very basic laboratory knowledge that medical science does not yet have the skills to identify many of its own patented and prescribed drugs' microbiological biotransformations (termed a drug's pharmacodynamics and pharmacokinetics). This means the medical profession doesn't truly know what the drugs it's prescribing are doing to the body and what the body does to the drugs.

Pharmaceutical drugs always have side effects (technically termed adverse reactions), because every drug is a synthetic molecule, and every synthetic molecule is foreign to our body — so our body will always react to unknown molecules. Enormous amounts of pharmaceutical drugs are intentionally prescribed specifically for their discovered side effect reactions, and many other pharmaceutical drugs are most commonly prescribed purely to counteract the side effects of other prescribed drugs such as an antiemetic (anti-vomiting drug) to counteract the adverse reaction (in this case vomiting) of a first drug.

Big Pharm are in the business of making money — they are a half-trillion-dollar-a-year huge conglomerate of international corporations, with duties to their shareholders to make a profit. Consequently, there is gigantic incentive for the pharmaceutical industry to 'pooh-pooh' the curative abilities of all their natural competitors. Big Pharm denigrate, ridicule and belittle almost all nature-made medicines and holistic healing therapies — even though most of the natural remedies have had thousands of years of use, and much current research proves beyond doubt their substantial ability to arrest and treat disease.

I am not criticising all pharmaceuticals. Without any doubt whatsoever (*hear me roar*) modern drugs definitely do have their place. We absolutely do need analgesics and anaesthetics for pain management (interestingly, the most effective are still nature-copied opioids). We absolutely do need antibiotics, especially for prematurely born babies' immature immune systems (interestingly, the most effective is still nature-copied penicillin). And yes, we definitely do need a wide variety of drugs for short-term, acute, life-saving events, such as the cardiac medication Digoxin (interestingly, a compound originally discovered in the foxglove plant).

However, it is the long-term, years-upon-decades of prescriptions for chronic lifestyle-related disease which is abhorrent to me, and for which conventional medicine should be professionally embarrassed. Our medical doctors — most untrained in curative nutrition — are missing the boat and failing to tackle the underlying problems.

Fortunately, growing numbers of GPs are realising, with escalating frustration, that their medical training is simply pharmaceutically based disease management — *reducing symptoms* rather than *curing disease.* So today more and more doctors are 'turning to the dark side' by also becoming trained in naturopathic herbal medicine, to provide them with more effective knowledge on how to activate the body's inherent healing mechanisms to *cure* its own disease.

So, to the growing numbers of medical doctors who are training in holistic medicine, beyond any doubt, you are the heroes of future modern medicine!

Thank you! Thank you!

VITAMIN AND MINERAL MYTHOLOGY

There is a widespread assumption that if vitamin and mineral supplements were miraculously wonderful for us, we'd be hearing about it all over the news. *Wrong!* There is also pervasive misinformation that if vitamins can cure disease, then the wrong dose must be like the wrong drug dosage, which can cause harm. *Wrong!*

Evidence does not back such suspicion, because (unlike man-made drugs) vitamins and minerals are substances our body naturally metabolises. As Don Tolman writes in the *Farmacist Desk Reference*, 'The idea of minimum or maximum amounts of any nutrient is utterly ridiculous! We've gotten so chemically smart we're stupid.'

In fact, orthomolecular (vitamin-mineral) medicine has well and truly proven that mega-doses of vitamin therapy can often prevent and treat much illness, with few if no side e ects. 'The reason one vitamin can cure so many illnesses is because a deficiency of one vitamin can cause many illnesses,' says Andrew Saul, the renowned therapeutic nutritionist. But ... Big Pharm won't invest serious research funds into organic healing remedies, because they can't earn royalties on molecules naturally found in nature.

BACTERIA

Bacteria are micro-organisms, usually one-celled and of various shapes, that live in the earth's soil, water and air. Our ecosystem relies heavily on bacteria, especially for the recycling of nutrients such as carbon, nitrogen and sulphur. Most bacteria on our planet are highly beneficial.

We absorb millions of bacteria daily through inhalation, ingestion, direct contact and insect bites. But occasionally, a bacterium can be parasitic to humans, animals or plants, causing us disease that potentially leads to infection (invasion of the body by harmful organisms).

VIRUSES

Too small to be seen with a regular microscope, viruses are minute particles that can replicate, but only within cells. Viruses infect animals, plants and micro-organisms, causing many diseases, including influenza, mumps, hepatitis and polio. Viruses can remain in a dormant state for long periods without causing disease, until they are stimulated months or years later; for example, cold sores or a dormant chickenpox virus reactivating as shingles. A 'retrovirus' contains RNA that converts into DNA, integrating itself into the host cell chromosome, for example the HIV virus.

Although pharmacologists have produced numerous antibacterial drugs that kill bacteria, science has been somewhat less successful in creating antiviral drugs that kill viruses. What does exist is a limited range of antiviral drugs that *inhibit* viral activity, such as Acyclovir for herpes.

THE IMMUNE SYSTEM

The immune system is the name given to the bodily system that protects us from microbials, such as bacteria and viruses. The immune system is responsible for pretty much every runny nose, sneeze, cough, upset stomach causing vomiting or diarrhoea, and fever, which are all responses to unwanted germs. In fact, with every scratch, cut, bruise, rash or zit, it is our immune system that is involved in healing.

The key point to remember is that no drug ever truly cures a person: it is the person's immune system that cures the person. Certainly, copious pharmaceutical drugs mask or inhibit symptoms, and many naturopathic remedies assist and boost the body to heal. But at the end of the day, only our own body truly cures our own body ever!

Our body's constant protective response is two-fold:

- » *Non-specific first-line of defence:* Prevents entry and spread of microbes by our intact skin, intact mucous membranes (lungs, urinary tract, mouth and anus) and the inflammatory healing response (redness, swelling, heat and pain).

» *Specific second-line of defence:* Attacks particular foreign particles with the immune system's white blood cells, which are involved in producing antibodies and macrophages (scavenger cells that destroy foreign particles).

Antibodies are our immune system's major defence mechanism and we have millions of di erently shaped ones constantly circulating in our blood. *Antigens* are di erently shaped foreign molecules (germs) that find their way into our body. Our body matches the antibody to the corresponding antigen in a key-and-lock type system, rendering it harmless. The body doesn't normally attack its own cells, because every one of our own cells has a kind of molecular name-tag, which is biologically unique to each of us, and is recognised by our immune system.

IMMUNE-SYSTEM BOOSTERS

Many health-shop items are described as immune-system boosters, such as vitamins A, C, B_6, E, niacin, riboflavin, zinc, honey, fermented foods, probiotics, amino acids L-Arginine and glutamine, echinacea, royal jelly, maitake mushroom extract, aloe vera, grapefruit seed extract, and kombucha (Manchurian tea). But at the end of the day, simply a healthful organic based diet, including fresh greens, garlic, nuts, seeds and fruits can probably replace a long list of over-the-counter immune-system boosters.

ANTIMICROBIALS

Infection is the invasion of the body by pathogenic microbes (harmful micro-organisms) such as bacteria, viruses, fungi and protozoa (for example, amoebae). Both pharmaceutical drugs and naturopathic remedies use the following terms regarding antimicrobial qualities:

- » *Antibacterials:* Destroy or inhibit growth of bacteria.
- » *Antibiotics:* Substances derived from one micro-organism that destroy or inhibit growth of another micro-organism.
- » *Antivirals:* Inhibit the replication of cellular DNA to inhibit viruses.
- » *Antifungals:* Destroy or inhibit fungi, e.g. the Candida yeast infection thrush.
- » *Antiseptics:* Destroy or inhibit bacteria on the surface of the skin (e.g. alcohol wipes or ointments) by sterilising the environment, such as around the site of a wound.

VACCINES

The topic of immunisation is an absolute hornet's nest. And although included under the umbrella of modern medicine, it is not a medicine at all. *Immunisation* is the normal process the body continuously uses to activate its immune system to create immunological memory, while *vaccination* is the artificial stimulation of immunological memory through *inoculation*. How immunisation occurs through exposure to antigens is quite miraculous and part of the body's innate intelligence, which is very difcult to copy. Vaccinations attempt to achieve immunisation; however, as every person's immune system is unique, full immunity does not always necessarily occur.

Today there are the 'pro' lobbyists, who use third-world statistics to promote vaccines to the developed-world market, while ignoring and denying almost all connections between vaccinations and adverse reactions.

Then there are the 'born-again' anti-inoculation activists, who quote dramatic horror stories, often with great bias and outdated information.

Vaccinations are not a topic on which this book can or will give a definitive answer. But it is prudent to provide you with some basic information regarding the body's defence processes.

Vaccines actively and artificially expose the immune system to disease-causing pathogens, with the specific purpose of generating protection against that specific disease. Some vaccine inoculations provide lifetime immunisation, and some a limited period of protection — with no guarantees at all, because every body's immune system responds differently.

Each time a new antigen is introduced into the body (this happens to us constantly, day in and day out), then a new antibody (immunoglobulin) is 'switched on', and the body creates immunological memory — that is, it duplicates many identical antibodies for a stronger and faster response when the body encounters the same antigen in the future. This is how our body develops a robust immune system.

Logically, the body cannot particularly distinguish between an antigen introduced naturally from the environment and one introduced artificially via a vaccine injection; it is simply one of the thousands of antigens it is dealing with at any one time.

The earliest vaccines were whole-cell — that is, they contained the complete dead organism of the disease, requiring the body to produce say 50–60 different kinds of antibodies. However, with advances in science over the last 20–30 years providing a better understanding of the process, many current childhood vaccines provide only the crucial piece of the disease cell, thus requiring the body to produce only a couple of types of antibodies to create immunological memory against the entire disease organism. Another point is that vaccines do not guarantee immunisation — because every person's immune system varies in its efficiency. Some children can be immune after the first vaccine; others may not still be fully immune, even after two to three vaccines.

To assume all vaccines are perilously dangerous is reactionary. Yet to assume all vaccines are unequivocally safe is naive.

Like *so* many parenting philosophies, this is another black-and-white decision you will need to make, based on information that only comes in shades of grey. It is important to get all the facts from both sides of the fence to make a truly informed decision.

Anti-vaccines, books by Beyond Conformity's Peter and Hilary Butler, *Just a Little Prick* and *From One Prick to Another,* include some interesting virological research, and as the Butlers themselves say, 'The bottom line is, make up your mind what *you* are going to do, when you are satisfied with the level of information you have thought through, and have strong enough convictions about what you are going to do, either way. And then take possession of your own decisions.'

WHAT TO DO IF YOU DO WISH TO IMMUNISE

Below are suggestions and recommendations from vaccine providers, doctors, naturopaths and homeopaths — this book is neither formally endorsing nor dismissing them. Parents need to do their own investigative homework.

- » Give children vitamin A after receiving the pertussis (whooping cough) inoculation.
- » Give children a good dose of vitamin C before receiving any vaccine.
- » Administer no vaccines when the child is ill or sickly — only when they are very healthy.
- » Ask that inoculations be split up as much as possible, leaving a gap of at least one month between vaccines.
- » Visit a professional homeopath to obtain tinctures (such as hypericum and ledum) to give to a baby before and after

- inoculations, to counteract the severity of adverse reactions.
- » If your family has a history of immunological problems, such as allergies or previous vaccine reactions, or neurological problems, such as epilepsy or convulsions, then do particularly thorough investigative research to ensure you make a well-informed decision.
- » Breastfeeding is advantageous in reducing reactions to immunisation.

O cially report any vaccine adverse reaction event to the correct authorities so it can be added to statistics.

PARENTING GOLDEN INSIGHT NO. 6

Strongly consider natural healing therapies as your first go-to for treating disease and unwellness.

A–Z OF DISEASES, CONDITIONS, DRUGS AND NATURAL ALTERNATIVES

POINTS TO NOTE

- » To clarify and remove confusion, 'anti-' or 'ant-' means preventing or counteracting. However, 'ante-' means before, such as 'antenatal', meaning before birth.
- » Always do refer to medicine packaging and/or manufacturer instructions and/or consult a qualified doctor, pharmacist, herbalist or naturopathic health professional.
- » Many well-documented common adverse reactions (side e ects)

to pharmacological drugs are listed below; however, numerous other well-documented but generally less common adverse reactions also exist.

» Only main drug brand names are provided; often many brand names exist for the same drug.

» For information on specific doses of supplements and herbs, an excellent start is Lani Lopez's *Natural Health: A New Zealand A–Z Guide*, or Karen Sullivan and C Norman Shealy's *The Complete Family Guide to Natural Home Remedies*. Alternatively, visit the herbalist at your local health shop or have a formal naturopathic consultation, as some natural remedies are best used under a health professional's supervised recommendations for achieving the most effective doses.

ADD/ADHD

ADD/ADHD (Attention Deficit Disorder with or without Hyperactivity) is characterised by distractibility, short attention span, impulsive behaviour, moody irritability, potential low self-esteem and learning disabilities — what some people used to term a 'naughty, unmanageable child'.

ADD/ADHD is defined as a neuro-developmental psychiatric disorder, and is one of the fastest-growing 'childhood diseases' in the Western world, reportedly affecting an astounding 10+ percent of all school-aged children in the United States!

ADHD has become synonymous with the cerebral cortex psycho-stimulant methylphenidate (Ritalin) — a cousin to 'speed'. You see, paradoxically, children with genuine ADHD respond to this 'upper' by becoming less hyper. But methylphenidate has many common side effects. Yes, it can help a child to stay focused in class and write on a straight line, but at the same time, he or she can become serious, sullen, rarely laugh, and may have a low appetite. The happy energy and giggles can vanish.

Astoundingly, use of Ritalin in the United States is said to have increased by 1000 percent since 1990s, with more than ten million prescriptions being written annually. If Ritalin doesn't work then it's usually on to stronger drugs such as the tricyclic antidepressant Clonidine (also used for opioid withdrawal). Many around the developed world are instead defining ADHD as the 'artificial diet hyperactivity disorder' — for the body is a rubbish-in-rubbish-out metabolic factory.

Hyperactivity is commonly one of the body's negative responses to food hypersensitivity. Naturopaths can often assist greatly to pinpoint the culprit, thereby avoiding an ongoing cycle of doctor's visits and medications with unpleasant side effects. Just daily doses of Fish Oil have been very well documented to oftentimes 'cure' ADHD.

COMMONLY PRESCRIBED PHARMACEUTICAL DRUGS

BRAND NAMES: *Concerta, Ritalin, Rubifen*

DRUG NAME: *Methylphenidate*

DRUG TYPE: *Central nervous system stimulant*

MAIN USES: *Treatment of ADHD and narcolepsy (extreme sleepiness).*

COMMON ADVERSE REACTIONS: *Headaches, insomnia, drowsiness, dizziness, emotional changeability, anxiety, nervousness, irritability, aggression, cough, fever, increased heart rate (tachycardia), heart palpitation arrhythmias, altered blood pressure, dry mouth, gastrointestinal upsets, decreased appetite, hives, joint pain (arthralgia), hair loss and tics.*

ADD/ADHD TOXIC SUBSTANCES

» Food additives, such as preservatives, food dyes, artificial flavourings and artificial coloring.

Chapter Eight

- » Refined sugars and aspartame (artificial sweetener).
- » MSG, gelatin, caffeine, soft drinks, lollies and junk foods.
- » Household chemicals, tobacco smoke and perfumes.
- » Heavy metals (iron, lead, copper), mercury (from dental fillings) and fluoride.
- » Industrial pollutants in the air or water (insecticides, pesticides).

ADD/ADHD DETOX FOODS

- » Apples, apricots, celery, cherries, grapes, limes, lychees, nectarines, peaches, pears, plums, prunes, rhubarb, spinach, strawberries and tomatoes.
- » Cayenne pepper, garlic, fennel, flaxseed, sage, sunflower seeds and tahini (sesame seed paste).
- » Nutritional yeast, evening primrose oil, flaxseed oil, ginkgo biloba, ginseng, grapeseed extract, hemp seed oil, lecithin, raspberry leaf and wheatgerm.

ADD/ADHD NATURAL THERAPEUTIC REMEDIES

- » *Drink:* Filtered water, rice milk, nut milks, spirulina, fresh homemade fruit and vegetable juices.
- » *Eat:* Whole foods (especially raw fruits and vegetables), wholegrain bread and brown rice, and home-made nut butters such as almond and cashew.
- » *Avoid:* Cooked dairy and animal products, which may contain hormones, pesticides, antibiotics and animal disease.
- » *Supplements:* Omega-3 fish oil; phosphatidylserine (from lecithin); 5-HTP (5-Hydroxytryptophan); Cell Salts kali phos, mag phos and silica; calcium, boron, chromium, magnesium, lithium (trace

amounts), vanadium and zinc.

» *Herbs:* The many options and the condition warrant a consultation with a medical herbalist.

» *Homeopathy:* The many options and the condition warrant comprehensive assessment with a classical homeopath.

» *Acupuncturist:* Visit routinely.

» *Neurofeedback therapy:* As a non-drug treatment.

» *Lifestyle:* Sensible bedtimes; daily outdoor exercise; not storing food in plastic containers (because of plastic's potential chemical by-products).

ADD/ADHD LIFESTYLE FURTHER READING

» *No More Ritalin* by Mary Ann Block, *Ritalin-Free Kids* by Judyth Reichenberg-Ulman and Robert Ulman, *Fed Up* by Sue Dengate and *Indigo Children* by Lee Caroll and Jim Tober.

» *Online:* Investigate and get knowledgeable about alternatives to Ritalin, such as by contacting your local holistically-minded ADHB organisations.

» *Education:* Consider mainstream alternatives, especially Montessori and Steiner-Waldorf.

ALLERGIES *(Hypersensitivities)*

Allergies are an abnormal immune-system overreaction to things that are typically harmless. When the body is hypersensitive to a particular foreign molecule (allergen), it then provokes the same reaction each time the allergen is encountered. Allergies are when the body's immune system causes itself tissue damage by its attempts to fight o a 'perceived threat'. Allergic reactions can be localised, such as conjunctivitis or insect bites; general, such as asthma, eczema, dermatitis, hayfever runny-nose, itching, hives, diarrhoea or vomiting; and severe, such as an asthma attack or anaphylactic shock.

Susceptibility to allergies can be hereditary. However, exposure to germs (bacteria, viruses), either through a large family or daycare, actually reduces the likelihood of allergies (as does six to 24 months of breastfeeding).

Food allergy hypersensitivities can get confused with food non-allergy hypersensitivities, which are more accurately termed food intolerances because some of the body's negative responses to food hypersensitivity express themselves as asthma, eczema and hyperactivity.

COMMON ALLERGENS

- » Foods such as dairy, eggs, wheat, soy, peanuts, shellfish, honey and bananas.
- » Insect bites and stings.
- » Airborne particles such as dust mites, mould spores, animal hair and pollens.
- » Chemicals such as cosmetics, perfumes, laundry detergents, dyes, household cleaners and pesticides.

COMMONLY PRESCRIBED ANTIHISTAMINE PHARMACEUTICAL DRUGS:

BRAND NAMES: *Allerid-C, Cetrizine-AFT, Zyrtec*

DRUG NAME: *Cetrizine*

DRUG TYPE: *H1-receptor antagonist*

MAIN USES: *Relief of allergic reactions including hayfever, itching and hives.*

COMMON ADVERSE REACTIONS: *Dry mouth, fatigue, somnolence (drowsy sleepiness).*

BRAND NAMES: *Claratyne, Loraclear, LoraPaed*

DRUG NAME: *Loratadine*

DRUG TYPE: *H1-receptor antagonist (non-sedating)*

ALSO FOUND IN: *Clarinase, Maxiclear*

MAIN USES: *Relief of allergic symptoms including hayfever with sneezing and runny nose, burning itchy eyes, itching and hives.*

COMMON ADVERSE REACTIONS: *Rare.*

BRAND NAME: *Histafen*

DRUG NAME: *Chlorpheniramine*

DRUG TYPE: *H1-receptor antagonist*

ALSO FOUND IN: *Codral, Codrex, Demazin, Robitussin, Sinutab and Sudafed*

MAIN USES: *Relief of allergic reactions including hayfever with sneezing and runny nose, itching, hives and insect bites.*

COMMON ADVERSE REACTIONS: *Sedation (drowsiness, sleepiness, weariness) and dry mouth.*

BRAND NAME: *Phenergan*

DRUG NAME: *Promethazine*

DRUG TYPE: *H1-antagonist (Phenothiazine)*

ALSO FOUND IN: *Tixylix*

MAIN USES: *Relief of allergic reactions, including respiratory and skin conditions; allergic reactions to medicines; surgical pre-medication sedative.*

COMMON ADVERSE REACTIONS: *Drowsy tiredness, dizziness, restless hyper-excitability, nightmares and gastrointestinal upsets.*

NOTE: If you choose pharmacological antihistamines for the treatment of allergies, this book recommends opting for a single-ingredient, low-dose chlorpheniramine formulation such as Histafen to minimise adverse effects.

NATURAL THERAPIES FOR ALLERGIES

- » *Eat:* Lots of vegetables, especially leafy greens and onions; lots of fruit, especially apples, citrus, rockmelon, strawberries and tomatoes; and legumes and wholegrains.
- » *Avoid:* Refined sugars, white flour and white rice.
- » *Supplements:* Flaxseed oil, barley grass, wheatgrass and apple cider vinegar, quercetin, lactobacillus rhamnosus, vitamin C and zinc.
- » *Herbs:* Echinacea, baikal skullcap, astragalus, boswellia and nettle.
- » *Homeopathy:* Apis, Rhus Tox or NaturoPharm's Allermed or Sinumed Relief.
- » *Nasal decongestants:* See Colds.
- » *Topical: Urtica urens* ointment.
- » *Breastfeeding:* Lactating mothers should remove dairy and other allergenic foods from their diet, and delay weaning to formula. (If using a cow's milk formula for feeding swap to an alternative such as goat's milk formula. Refer to my book, *Oh Baby,* for more information.)

ANALGESICS — see Pain and pain-relieving drugs

ANAPHYLACTIC SHOCK

Anaphylaxis is a potentially fatal condition resulting from an immediate allergic response to a stimulus to which the body has become intensely sensitised, most commonly peanuts, beehive products and bee stings. The body's inflammatory reaction sends blood to the extremities, causing a sudden drop in blood pressure. Emergency treatment is an adrenaline (epinephrine) injection ('epi-pen') to send the blood back from the peripherals to the trunk's vital organs. Seek medical treatment immediately.

ANTIBIOTICS *(Antibacterials)*

With bacterial disease, it can be normal medical best practice to initially issue a broad-spectrum antibiotic at the same time as taking a sample of the o ending bacteria for a culture and sensitivity test at the local medical laboratory. First, the lab cultures the germ to identify its species. Then the germ's resistance and sensitivity to various antibacterial drugs are tested. In this way, the medical doctor can later modify the patient's initial prescription to a narrow-spectrum antimicrobial treatment, which is already proven to e ectively target the particular germ.

The developed world now unquestionably prescribes copious amounts of drugs such as antibiotics. Cumulatively, this massive global overprescription has resulted in many microbes evolving to become antibiotic-resistant, or 'superbugs', which is a gargantuan health concern. Because of the widespread overprescription of antibiotics, performing a culture and sensitivity test becomes even more important.

Antibiotics were initially derived from nature's penicillin mould and chances are we will need to return to nature for better remedies. We need to remind ourselves: if possible, it is best to avoid antibiotics. A healthy child has a huge ability to combat bugs without intervention, resulting in a stronger immune system.

ANTIBIOTICS COMMONLY PRESCRIBED FOR CHILDREN

BRAND NAMES: *Amoxil, Augmentin**

DRUG NAME: *Amoxicillin (* with clavulanic acid)*

DRUG TYPE: *Broad-spectrum aminopenicillin*

(*Augmentin contains beta-lactamase inhibitor that increases effectiveness by deactivating part of a disease defence mechanism)

MAIN USES: *Respiratory infections such as pharyngitis, tonsillitis, pneumonia and ear infections; skin and soft tissue infections; urinary tract infections.*

COMMON ADVERSE REACTIONS: *Gastrointestinal upsets, rash. (Should be taken with food.)*

BRAND NAME: *Ranbaxy*

DRUG NAME: *Cefaclor*

DRUG TYPE: *Cephalosporin*

MAIN USES: *Respiratory infections such as pharyngitis, tonsillitis, pneumonia and ear infections; skin and soft tissue infections; urinary tract infections.*

COMMON ADVERSE REACTIONS: *Diarrhoea; increased white blood cells (eosinophilia).*

BRAND NAME: *Trisul*

DRUG NAME: *Sulfamethoxazole with Trimethoprim*

DRUG TYPE: *Sulfonamide (also contains dihydrofolate reductase inhibitor that increases effectiveness by deactivating part of a disease defence mechanism)*

MAIN USES: *Bronchitis and gastrointestinal, genital, urinary tract and ear infections.*

COMMON ADVERSE REACTIONS: *High levels of potassium in the blood (hyperkalaemia); headaches; gastrointestinal upset; superinfection.*

Discontinue at first sign of skin rash. (Should be taken with food.)

NOTE: AAD (antibiotic-associated diarrhoea) is common and usually mild. Consuming probiotics such as acidophilus yoghurt in conjunction with antibiotics is recommended. Antibiotics kill all colon flora, good and bad, and countering this with probiotics can reduce the severity of AAD. Any diarrhoea fluid loss should also be compensated by increased fluid intake to reduce dehydration and its subsequent potentially serious side effect of electrolyte imbalances.

ANXIETY

Levels of anxiety in modern life can be ridiculously high, with rampant anxiety attacks, fears and phobias; we worry about 'everything'! Fuelling these peaking anxiety levels is society's obsession with perfection.

At a physiological level, anxiety produces stress-coping hormones, but the human body is not designed to cope continuously with stress, and soon this manifests as sickness, either in an isolated place or systemically.

Sadly, many of our children are rapidly being sucked into the stress culture forced upon them: five-year-olds being required to goal-set at school; seven-year-olds requiring mandatory multi-week after-school lessons; and nine-year-olds' schoolbags overladen with homework. How did we get to this point?!

NATURAL ANTI-ANXIETY THERAPIES

» *Drink:* Lots of water (1–2 litres a day for an adult and the equivalent for a child depending on their size). Remember, when water comes out as clear as it went in, that demonstrates great hydration.

» *Eat:* Six smaller meals (rather than three large meals) throughout the day, including a banana a day (bananas are high in potassium, which is great for beating stress).

» *Avoid:* Caffeine, cola drinks, chocolate, alcohol, tobacco and black tea.

» *Supplements:* Omega-3 oils, such as fish, flaxseed/linseed, evening primrose or borage; 5-HTP; royal jelly; melatonin (must be prescribed by a medical doctor); comprehensive daily multi-vitamins and minerals, including all the B vitamins.

» *Herbs:* Skullcap, valerian, kava, passionflower, licorice, panax ginseng, St John's wort, lemon balm or California poppy.

» *Homeopathy:* Aconite, Arsenicum, Gelsemium, Arg Nit and Lycopodium (depending on symptoms); and NaturoPharm's StressMed Relief, Panicmed Relief or Restore-med.

ASTHMA

Asthma, with its signature dry, unproductive cough, is rife in the developed world. There are complex theories as to why this is the case, including the excessive use of paracetamol during infancy and childhood. Asthma is another hypersensitivity disease and is extrinsic (caused by external allergens such as dust), intrinsic (caused by internal non-allergenic triggers, such as exercise) or both.

During an asthma attack, the body's cells are stimulated to release inflammation mediators (such as histamines and prostaglandins). This causes the bronchial muscles in the lungs to narrow, plus excessive mucous secretions and bronchial oedema (swelling), which further narrows airways.

On inhalation the bronchi over-expand so air can reach the lungs, causing wheezing and nostril-flaring. On exhalation the gas pressure in the lungs closes o the bronchi, causing a lengthened expiration and wheezing. This can subsequently lead to a 'tight chest', severe anxiety, labored, di cult breathing (dyspnoea), increased breaths (hyperpnoea) and potentially fatal hypoxia (lack of oxygen).

Asthma treatment generally includes education, fitness, relaxation, allergen avoidance and pharmaceutical therapies. These drugs are described as 'relievers', to rapidly relax acute attacks of bronchial muscle spasms; 'preventers', long-acting anti-inflammatory corticosteroids; and symptom-controlling bronchodilators as 'maintenance treatments' for reversible obstructive airways diseases (ROAD), of which asthma is one.

The drugs work by stimulating the sympathetic nervous system and opening the airways (beta-agonists), and inhibiting the opposing parasympathetic nervous system by relaxing the muscles (anticholinergics). Corticosteroids are inhaled to replicate the powerful chemicals naturally produced by the adrenal gland's cortex, such as glucocorticoids which have powerful anti-inflammatory effects.

Unfortunately one of the side effects of asthma medication is immune-system suppression, specifically increased susceptibility to respiratory infections. So maintaining a healthy lifestyle and nutritious diet become even more important.

COMMONLY PRESCRIBED RELIEVER (BRONCHODILATOR) INHALERS

BRAND NAME: *Apo-Prednisone*

DRUG NAME: *Prednisone*

DRUG TYPE: *Glucocorticoid*

MAIN USES: *Steroid-responsive conditions.*

COMMON ADVERSE REACTIONS: *Numerous.*

BRAND NAME: *Atrovent*

DRUG NAME: *Ipratropium*

DRUG TYPE: *Anticholinergic*

MAIN USES: *Management and prevention of bronchospasms associated with chronic bronchitis and asthma.*

COMMON ADVERSE REACTIONS: *Headache, dry mouth, gastrointestinal upset.*

BRAND NAME: *Bricanyl*

DRUG NAME: *Terbutaline*

DRUG TYPE: *Beta2-agonist*

MAIN USES: *Relief of asthmatic bronchospasms and preventor for known inducements of asthmatic bronchospasms.*

COMMON ADVERSE REACTIONS: *Headache, nausea, nervousness, increased heart rate (tachycardia), heart palpitations, tremor and continious muscle spasms.*

BRAND NAME: *Combivent*

DRUG NAMES: *Salbutamol and Ipratropium*

DRUG TYPE: *Beta2-agonist with anticholinergic*

MAIN USES: *Relief of moderate-severe asthmatic bronchospasms.*

COMMON ADVERSE REACTIONS: *Headache; dizziness; nervousness; throat irritations such as dry mouth, cough or hoarseness; increased heart rate (tachycardia); heart palpitations and tremor.*

BRAND NAMES: *Respigen, Salamol, Ventolin*

DRUG NAME: *Salbutamol*

DRUG TYPE: *Beta2-agonist*

MAIN USES: *Management and prevention of mild asthmatic attack; treatment of acute moderate-severe asthmatic exacerbations; prevention of allergen/exercise-induced asthmatic bronchospasms.*

COMMON ADVERSE REACTIONS: *Headache, increased heart rate (tachycardia) and tremor.*

COMMONLY PRESCRIBED PREVENTOR (MAINTENANCE) INHALERS

BRAND NAME: *Flixotide*

DRUG NAME: *Fluticasone*

DRUG TYPE: *Corticosteroid*

MAIN USES: *Management and prevention of asthma.*

COMMON ADVERSE REACTIONS: *Throat irritations, such as oral thrush, hoarseness or contusion trauma.*

BRAND NAME: *Oxis Turbuhaler*

DRUG NAME: *Eformoterol*

DRUG TYPE: *LABA (long-acting Beta2-agonist)*

MAIN USES: *In conjunction with corticosteroids in treatment and prevention of ROAD.*

COMMON ADVERSE REACTIONS: *Headaches, palpitations and tremor.*

BRAND NAME: *Pulmicort*

DRUG NAME: *Budesonide*

DRUG TYPE: *Glucocorticoid*

MAIN USES: *Maintenance of asthma by controlling airway inflammation.*

COMMON ADVERSE REACTIONS: *Headache; light-headedness; throat irritations such as oral thrush, dry mouth, cough, hoarseness and bad taste; gastrointestinal upset; weight gain; tiredness and psychiatric behavioural disturbances.*

BRAND NAME: *Seretide*

DRUG NAME: *Fluticasone and Salmeterol*

DRUG TYPE: *Corticosteroid and LABA (long-acting Beta2-agonist)*

MAIN USES: *Treatment of ROAD, such as asthma.*

COMMON ADVERSE REACTIONS: *Headache; throat irritations such as oral thrush and hoarseness; heart palpitations; muscle cramps; rash and pneumonia.*

BRAND NAME: *Serevent*

DRUG NAME: *Salmeterol*

DRUG TYPE: *LABA (long-acting Beta2-agonist)*

MAIN USES: *In conjunction with corticosteroids for asthma management, chronic bronchitis and prevention of exercise- or allergen-induced bronchospasms.*

COMMON ADVERSE REACTIONS: *Headache, heart palpitations, tremor, muscle cramps. Use with caution.*

BRAND NAME: *Symbicort, Vannair*

DRUG NAME: *Budesonide and Eformoterol*

DRUG TYPE: *Glucocorticoid and LABA (long-acting Beta2-agonist)*

MAIN USES: *Part of regular combination treatment for asthma.*

COMMON ADVERSE REACTIONS: *Headache; throat irritations such as oral thrush, hoarseness and coughs; heart palpitations and tremor.*

NATURAL ASTHMA COMPLEMENTARY THERAPIES

- *Drink:* Lots of water, plus green tea, spearmint tea and papaya juice.

- *Eat:* Lots of garlic and onion; high vitamin-C foods and juices such as rockmelon, strawberries, tomatoes, fresh red-skinned potatoes and green leafy vegetables; spicy foods, such as Tabasco sauce, cayenne pepper, jalapeno peppers and horseradish; high-chlorophyll foods such as parsley, celery, alfalfa sprouts and cabbage; high-selenium foods such as Brazil nuts; and in general a high vegetarian diet with lots of celery.

- *Avoid:* Hyperallergenic foods, such as those containing food colorings, especially yellow; preservatives, especially sulphite; dairy products, eggs, soy, wheat and yeast.

- *Supplements:* Omega-3 oils, such as fish, flaxseed/linseed, evening primrose or borage; olive-leaf extract and echinacea combo to boost the immune system; vitamin C, helps to suppress asthma (and too little of it seems to aggravate asthma); and comprehensive daily multi-vitamins and minerals, especially those containing magnesium, manganese, zinc and potassium.
- *Herbs:* Marshmallow root, licorice, boswellia, perilla, eyebright and/or fenugreek. I advise against self-prescribing herbs for asthma; it is best to see a qualified medical herbalist.
- *Homeopathy:* Various remedies depending on specific symptoms. Asthma definitely warrants full assessment by a classical homeopath.
- *Aromatherapy:* Essential oil of citrus.
- *Breathing methods*: Dynamic breathing techniques, such as Bradcli , Buteyko and Sudarshan Kriya.

BONE FRACTURES

Breaking a bone — hairline or complete fracture — is generally treated by realigning the bone and immobilising it with external splints or internal fixation while it heals.

BENEFICIAL THERAPIES FOR BONE REPAIRS

- *Eat:* Grains, nuts, seeds and fresh pineapple.
- *Avoid:* Preserved foods, co ee and soft drinks.
- *Supplements:* Silica, calcium, magnesium and potassium.
- *Homeopathy:* Arnica, Hypericum or Bryonia (depending on symptoms), then after setting Symphytum and Calc Phos.

BRONCHITIS *(and bronchiolitis)*

Bronchitis is the inflammation of the lung's bronchi (large airways) due to a viral or bacterial infection, causing excess mucous secretions, swelling, bronchiole constriction and its characteristic cough. The symptoms of bronchitis include cold and flu symptoms before onset, such as a runny nose, fever, chills, tiredness and feeling unwell; breathlessness, wheezing, rapid shallow breathing and a tight chest; coughing, sore throat and excessive mucus; a cough that brings up yellow-grey-green mucus; and the retraction of the lower ribs and sternum when inhaling.

Bronchiolitis is the inflammation of the lungs' bronchioles due to a viral or bacterial infection, and occurs most commonly in infants. Because an infant's bronchioles are so tiny, even minor swelling can produce problems and may require the administration of oxygen.

NATURAL BRONCHITIS THERAPIES

- » *Drink:* Plenty of fluids, such as vegetable juices, soups and herbal teas.
- » *Eat:* Lots of onion, spinach, sesame seeds and almonds.
- » *Avoid:* Sugar, including restricting intake of honey and fruit, refined carbohydrates, dairy and egg whites.
- » *Supplements:* Vitamin C, zinc, vitamin A and bromelain (pineapple enzyme).
- » *GROOVEyS:* Natural antimicrobials (see page 149).
- » *Herbs:* Licorice, fenugreek, white horehound, thyme, hyssop, wild cherry bark, marshmallow root, coltsfoot, mullein, elecampane, kumerahou, euphorbia, wild indigo, sundew, wood betony and yarrow.
- » *Aromatherapy:* Menthol, pine, eucalyptus, basil, wintergreen, chamomile, thyme, lavender, rosemary.

- » *Homeopathy:* Various remedies depending on specific symptoms; bronchitis definitely warrants a full assessment by a classical homeopath.
- » *Lifestyle:* Rest and sleep.

BRUISING/HAEMATOMAS

When the body receives a whacking thump, its blood vessels rupture, causing the escaping blood to leak into the surrounding tissue thus creating a red contusion (bruise). If the accumulation of blood clots to form a solid swelling, this is called a haematoma.

Over the following days, as the body 'reabsorbs' the leaked blood, the bruise discoloration gradually changes to purple, blue, black and finally greeny-yellow.

The standard treatment for contusions is RICE: Rest, Ice, Compression bandages and Elevation, plus the use of non-steroidal anti-inflammatory drugs (NSAIDs) such as ibuprofen (Brufen or Nurofen). NSAIDs are also analgesics, so provide relief from pain or discomfort. After the first day, hot compresses can also assist the reabsorption of the blood by increasing circulation to the area.

NATURAL THERAPIES FOR BRUISES

- » *Eat:* Fruits high in vitamin C and bioflavonoids, such as berries, cherries, capsicum, citrus fruits and kiwifruit.
- » *Supplements:* Multi-vitamin and mineral formulas, especially vitamin C; ProenOthera; bioflavonoids such as hesperidin, rutin and quercetin; glucosamine and chondroitin combo; bromelain (pineapple enzyme); or Calc Fluor cell salt.
- » *Herbs:* Gotu kola, horse chestnut, butcher's broom, arnica, Bach Rescue Remedy, witchhazel cream or lotion, peppermint oil, comfrey or sweet clover.

- *Homeopathy:* Various remedies depending on symptoms, especially Arnica and Bellis Perennis, and the combination called Traumeel.
- *Poultice:* Putty-like compress of lemon juice and grated raw red potato.

BURNS

First-degree burns, such as sunburn, affect the skin's epidermis. They are generally red, tender and dry, and heal in around 48–72 hours.

Second-degree or partial-thickness burns affect the dermis and are painful and moist, with blisters. They heal in around 10–14 days. Both first- and second-degree burns can be termed *superficial* burns.

Third-degree or full-thickness burns destroy the entire epidermis and dermis, and fourth-degree burns extend into the muscle or bone. Both can be termed *deep* burns, and cause considerable scarring. Burn surface tissue can become weepy, which is why extensive fluid loss occurs with severe burns, depleting the blood volume and causing potentially fatal cardiovascular shock. The loss of skin integrity also exposes the body to massive potential infection.

FIRST-AID TREATMENT OF BURNS

- Immediately cool the burn for 10–15 minutes to remove irritants, decrease inflammation, constrict blood vessels and reduce swelling—cold tap water is perfect.
- Don't pop blisters; they're protecting sensitive healing skin from damage and infection.
- Always seek medical attention for second-degree burns, particularly of the face, hands, feet or genitals.
- Always seek hospitalisation for third-degree burns, especially for pain relief and potential skin-grafting.

NATURAL THERAPIES FOR MILD BURNS

» Aloe vera gel provides almost instant pain relief and reduces inflammation.

» *Other Topical remedies:* Lavender oil diluted in aloe gel, cooled chamomile tea, witchhazel ointment or cooled tea all reduce pain and inflammation; calendula is antiseptic and anti-inflammatory; comfrey ointment improves healing and reduces scarring; colloidal silver spray is an antibiotic and disinfectant; sliced raw potato and honey fight infection and promote healing; the inside layer of ripe banana skin soothes burn sting; radishes crushed in the food processor soothe sting and reduce infection; tannic acid (acorn extract); *Urtica urens* ointment.

» *Eat:* Blackberries and watermelon.

» *Supplements:* Antioxidant vitamins A, C and E.

» *Homeopathy:* Arnica, Cantharis, Arsenicum and Kali Bich (depending on symptoms), or NaturoPharm's Burnmed Relief Gel.

COLDS, FLUS AND COUGHS

When people have a cold, they often comment that they've 'got the flu', but when people have full-blown influenza, they actually usually feel like they're dying! Colds are minors. Flus are majors! But the symptoms of both are similar.

Cold viruses typically produce a runny nose, sneezing, mild fever, fatigue, headache and possibly a sore throat and dry, unproductive cough. Flu viruses typically produce a moderately high fever, chills, red face, generalised aches and pains, and probably a runny nose, headache, persistent dry cough and sore throat. (Influenza is of particular concern to people who already have a weak immune system, such as infants, the elderly, diabetics and asthmatics.) Modern pharmacological medicine o ers virtually nothing to assist in the cure of viral colds and flus — and 95 per cent of upper respiratory tract infections are viral, and therefore don't need antibiotics. So instead, pharmacology o ers a plethora of options to attack the symptoms of coughs and colds, primarily:

- *Antitussives* to suppress coughing.
- *Mucolytics* to break down and dissolve thick mucous lung secretions.
- *Expectorants* to thin and increase lung secretions to improve productivity of coughing.
- *Decongestants* to reduce and relieve stu y-nose nasal congestion.
- *Antihistamines* to reduce the body's allergy-based histamine reactions, such as a runny nose.

COMMONLY PURCHASED OVER-THE-COUNTER COLD OR COUGH SYRUPS

Listed are the common adverse reactions for each product:

- *Benadryl Chesty Forte* (expectorant and mucolytic): gastrointestinal upset.
- *Benadryl Dry Forte* (antitussive): diarrhoea.
- *Benadryl Nightime* (antitussive and antihistamine): drowsiness.
- *Benadryl Original* (expectorant and antihistamine): cough, sneezing, runny nose and watery eyes.
- *Demazin* (decongestant and antihistamine): central nervous system disorders such as drowsiness, sedation, dizziness, weakness, headache, insomnia, unsteady walk and pupil dilation; gastrointestinal upsets, such as nausea; cardiovascular disorders, such as increased heart rate and heart palpitations; insomnia and excitation.

- *Dimetapp Elixir and Infant Drops* (decongestant and antihistamine): drowsiness, weariness, dizziness, nausea, dry mouth, decreased mental alertness, pupil dilation, irritability, excitation and high blood pressure.
- *Dimetapp Cold and Cough* (antitussive, decongestant and antihistamine): drowsiness, dizziness, reduced mental alertness, emotional changeability, dry mouth, pupil dilation, gastrointestinal upset, high blood pressure, increased heart rate, irritation, agitation and excitation.
- *Duro-Tuss Chesty* (mucolytic): diarrhoea.
- *Duro-Tuss Chesty + Nasal* (mucolytic and decongestant): diarrhoea and sleeplessness.
- *Duro-Tuss Cough Expectorant* (antitussive and mucolytic): headache, vertigo, perspiration, rash, respiratory depression and altered liver function.
- *Duro-Tuss Dry Cough* (antitussive): gastrointestinal upset.
- *Gees Linctus* (opiate squill antitussive): not for children.
- *Phensedyl Dry Cough* (antitussive, decongestant and antihistamine): drowsiness, insomnia and constipation.
- *Philcodine* (antitussive): drowsiness, gastrointestinal upset such as nausea and constipation; restlessness and respiratory depression.
- *Robitussin Children's Night* (antitussive, decongestant and antihistamine): drowsiness, dizziness, vertigo, headache, nervousness, tremor, increased heart rate, dry mouth, gastrointestinal upset, rash, excitability and insomnia.
- *Robitussin DX Extra Strength* (antitussive and decongestant): headache, drowsiness, dizziness, sedation, vertigo, anxiety, insomnia, high blood pressure, increased heart rate, dry mouth, gastrointestinal upset, rash and blurred vision.

- » *Robitussin Paediatric Drops* (expectorant): headache, dizziness, gastrointestinal upset and rash.
- » *Tixylix* (antitussive and antihistamine): dizziness, sedation, restlessness, gastrointestinal upset, blurred vision and habitual dependence.
- » *Vicks Formula 44* (antitussive): adverse reactions are rare.

PHARMACEUTICAL COLD AND FLU TREATMENTS NOT RECOMMENDED, ESPECIALLY FOR CHILDREN

- » Any prescription-only pharmaceutical drugs for treating the common cold symptoms of a stuffy nose, fever or non-productive cough.
- » Any oral treatments (pills or syrup) for nasal decongestion, because they treat systemically rather than locally, and are often amphetamine-like (with adverse reactions such as jitteriness, sleeplessness and potential heart problems).
- » Any antihistamines for colds and flus, because histamine blocking does not cure a cold, and has sedative effects and umpteen other adverse reactions.
- » Any antibiotics for sore throats — unless the sore throat is strongly suspected or has been demonstrated by a culture and sensitivity test to be strep throat.
- » Any cough suppressants for a productive cough: never suppress a cough that is bringing up phlegm.
- » Any cough-cold medications containing the cough suppressants dextromethorphan or diphenhydramine, or the expectorant guaifenesin — there is little strong evidence that these ingredients are effective.
- » Any cough-cold medications that are combinations of antihistamines, decongestants and/or cough suppressants, because they are 'shot-gun' recipes with higher risks.

RECOMMENDED RELIEF FOR COLDS AND FLU

Single-ingredient options, such as a nasal spray for a stu y nose, Histafen (chlorpheniramine) for allergies, and natural non-medical cough remedies.

- » *General cough suppressants:* Warm water with honey and lemon juice (increasing fluid consumption is nature's best expectorant, loosening up mucus); natural cough syrups, such as Weleda's Organic Cough Syrup or NaturoPharm's Coughmed Relief; herbal syrups containing mullein, elecampane or hyssop; or fresh ginger-root tea.
- » *Dry cough:* Homeopathic Bryonia or Pulsatilla (depending on symptoms).
- » *Loud, rattling cough:* Homeopathic Ant Tar, Drosera, Ipercac, Hepar Sulph or Kali Bich (depending on symptoms).
- » *Croup cough:* Homeopathic Aconite, Hepar Sulph, Lachesis or Spongia (depending on symptoms).
- » *Thick lung mucus:* Room humidifier or steam vaporiser to moisten air; homeopathic Aconite, Arsenicum, Gelsemium, Pulsatilla, Silica, Kali Bich or Natrum Mur (depending on symptoms).
- » *Stuffy blocked nose:* Inhalants such as eucalyptus, lavender, Friar's Balsam or Karvol capsules; chest rubs such as Weleda, Ethics, Tixylix or Vicks VapoRub; nasal sprays containing oxymetazoline or xylometazoline, such as Dimetapp, Drixine, Vicks Sinex or Otrivin (but don't use for more than three days as they then promote congestion); eat spicy food; NaturoPharm's Sinumed Relief; or Homeopathic Merc Viv, Pulsatilla, Silica, Kali Bich or Lycopodium (depending on symptoms).
- » *Runny nose:* Saline nasal spray to dry mucous secretions.
- » *General fever, headaches and body aches:* NaturoPharm's Coldmed Relief.

- » *Moderate fever:* Homeopathic Belladonna 30c drops.
- » *High fever (more than 38.5°C):* Paracetamol as directed.

NOTE: Fever is part of the body's natural defences that kill bacteria, so it is important not to take paracetamol for mild fevers, as this will prolong the cold/flu illness.

NATURAL COLD AND FLU THERAPIES

- » *Drink:* Lots of fluids, including water; herbal teas such as thyme, rosemary, sage, lavender or chamomile, perhaps with a little catnip; and vegetable and fruit juices such as orange, tomato, grapefruit, pineapple, apples, watercress, carrot, beetroot and silverbeet. Drink enough water a day for the average adult to produce around one and a half litres of urine and the equivalent for a child, depending on their size — remember when water comes out as clear as it went in, it demonstrates great hydration.
- » *Eat:* Lots of vegetable soups containing green capsicum, broccoli, Brussels sprouts and tomatoes; loads of healing herbs and spices such as parsley, basil, cinnamon, fenugreek, ginger, horseradish and wasabi, and lots of garlic and onions; soft stewed fruits.
- » *Avoid:* Sugar, bananas, dairy, refined carbs, egg whites, honey for toddlers and babies, and excessive wheat products.
- » *GROOVEyS:* Natural antimicrobials (see page 149).
- » *Supplements:* Vitamin C (daily 500 mg per year of age, to a maximum of 5g a day); consider vitamin A or its precursor beta carotene; and multi-mineral formulas high in zinc, copper and magnesium.
- » *Herbs:* Astragalus, pau d'arco and St John's wort.

» *Homeopathy:* Apis, Belladonna, Silica, Bryonia, Gelsemium, Merc Viv, Silica, Arg Nit, Hepar Sulph, Lachesis, Lycopodium or Phytolacca (depending on symptoms), Kali Bich for green snotty noses; NaturoPharm's A.G.E. and Flu Guard; and Aconite, especially for the sudden onset of symptoms such as sore throat, cough and earache.

» *Lifestyle:* Reduce exercise and rest in bed or on the couch for around one to three days; dress warmly but still get fresh air by opening windows or using ceiling fans to move the stale air; place a cooled cloth or chilled wheatie-bag on the forehead; use hot saline footbaths.

NOTE: Flu viruses are highly infectious — so stay at home!

SEE THE DOCTOR FOR

» High fever above 38.0°C–38.3°C after taking paracetamol or if fever goes above 39.0°C–39.4°C.

» Common cold symptoms that don't improve after three to five days, or symptoms worsening.

» Coughs that bring up greenish, yellowish or foul-smelling phlegm; a cough accompanied by high fever that lasts a few days; coughing or breathing causing sharp chest pain; shortness of breath and coughing up blood. (Such symptoms may indicate a secondary bacterial infection such as bronchitis or pneumonia, which may require antibiotics.)

» Sore throats with yellow-white spots filled with pus on throat or tonsils; accompanied by high fever; with swollen or tender glands (bumps in the front of neck); with a rash during or after sore throat; if the patient has a history of rheumatic fever or exposure to someone with strep throat. (Such symptoms may indicate the secondary bacterial infection strep throat, which requires antibiotics to avoid rheumatic heart disease.)

CONSTIPATION

The colon (large intestine) is the organ that reabsorbs water before we defecate (poo out our waste). When food remains too long in the colon, too much water can be reabsorbed, resulting in stools (poos) that are hard and difficult to pass. This is constipation.

Constipation can be caused by disease, a sedentary lifestyle, and by many medications—antacids, antihistamines, analgesics, antispasmodics, anti-depressants, anticonvulsants, diuretics, tranquillisers and iron supplements, to name a few. But constipation is most commonly caused by a diet too high in animal fats and refined sugars, and too low in water, dietary roughage and essential fatty acids.

Symptoms of constipation include difficulty passing stools and a low frequency of bowel movements (less than three times per week). Associated symptoms can include bad breath, nausea, fatigue, colicky pain, bloating, mucus around stools, and headaches.

COMMONLY PRESCRIBED PHARMACOLOGICAL TREATMENTS

BRAND NAME: *Duphalac Syrup*

DRUG NAME: *Lactulose*

DRUG TYPE: *Hyperosmotic laxative*

MAIN USES: *Constipation.*

COMMON ADVERSE REACTIONS: *Flatulence (farting) and intestinal cramps.*

NATURAL THERAPIES FOR CONSTIPATION

» *Drink:* Increased water (warm) and raw juices such as prune, celery, spinach and/or grapefruit juice.

» *Eat six times daily:* Increase fibre, such as wholegrain bread, muesli, oats, beans, brown rice, green leafy veggies, peas, bifidus-acidophilis yoghurt, dried figs, prunes, kiwifruit, grapes, bran muffins and bananas.

» *Avoid:* Faecal-softening or laxative-stimulant drugs such as docusate or bisacodyl. (If you have a diet high in fibre and liquids you should not need these drugs.)

» *Fibre supplements:* 1–2 tbsp per day of apple pectin, marshmallow root, chitosan, LSA (ground linseed, sunflower seeds and almonds), or LSAP (LSA with ground pumpkin kernels).

» *Supplements:* Inositol, iodine, iron, potassium, vitamins C, B_1 and B_{12}, folic acid, magnesium, papaya (papain), chamomile, dandelion root, black walnut, barberry and boldo. For chronic 'bound-up' constipation, consider castor oil, alder buckthorn and rhubarb root; senna and/or cascara sagrada for short-term use only, as we can become dependent on these supplements.

» *Herbs:* Bitter digestive stimulants such as gentian, dandelion and globe artichoke will increase bile flow and digestive enzymes, in turn stimulating digestive function.

» *Homeopathy:* Bryonia, Nux Vom, Silica, Lycopodium, Natrum Mur, Sepia or Sulphur (depending on symptoms).

» *Laxatives:* Ginger, ginger tea, apple cider vinegar, aloe vera juice, dandelion, slippery elm and carob.

» *Over-the-counter bulk-forming soluble fibre:* Psyllium, such as Metamucil, Mucilax, Normacol or methylcellulose in moderation — these take around 12 to 72 hours to take effect.

PREVENTATIVES FOR CONSTIPATION

- » *Drink:* Generous daily fluid intake especially water; juices such as apple, prune, carrot, beetroot, spinach and aloe vera; herbal teas such as chamomile, peppermint, ginger, wild yam and Swedish bitters; or dandelion root co ee.
- » *Eliminate:* White flour, white rice and white sugar.
- » *Reduce:* Eggs, dairy (especially cheese), heavy protein such as red meat and fried food.
- » *Try:* Gluten-free foods and soy/rice milk substitutes.
- » *Eat fibre-rich foods:* Especially wholegrain flour, brown rice, bran cereal, nutritional yeast, legumes and wheatgerm.
- » *Eat fruit:* Especially prunes, raisins, apricots, figs, kiwifruit, bananas, strawberries, persimmons — and an apple a day.
- » *Eat vegetables:* Especially broccoli, cabbage, cauliflower, zucchini, spinach, carrots, beets, rhubarb, sweet potatoes, garlic, peas and beans.
- » *Supplements:* 1–2 tsp of monounsaturated oil such as olive or canola, and LSA, which can be easily added to cereals, salads, smoothies, soups and stews.
- » *Exercise:* At least 30 minutes three times a week.

COUGHS — *see Colds, flus and coughs*

CYSTITIS — *see UTIs*

DEPRESSION — *see depression remedies in Chapter Seven*

DIABETES MELLITUS

Insulin is a hormone produced in the pancreas, which regulates our blood sugar (glucose levels) by enabling cell-tissue absorption of glucose for energy. Diabetes mellitus is a disease of insulin deficiency, or increase of insulin resistance, and has two main kinds, plus a third only seen in pregnancy:

» *Type-1 insulin-dependent diabetes mellitus (IDDM):* Insufficient insulin production from pancreatic beta-cells. It is typically discovered in childhood or adolescence.

» *Type-2 non-insulin-dependent diabetes mellitus (NIDDM):* Insufficient insulin from insulin resistance or abnormal insulin secretion levels.

It is typically related to ageing or obesity and if poorly managed can progress into IDDM.

» *Type-3 gestational diabetes mellitus (GDM):* NIDDM or IDDM that develops during pregnancy, when the woman's body is unable to produce the required increased amounts of insulin (typically self-resolves shortly after childbirth).

Because its cell tissue is 'starving' for energy, a diabetic's body increases blood-sugar levels; however, without insulin, the cell tissue remains 'starving' while the blood-sugar levels increase. The cell tissue is still glucose-hungry, so the body releases even more glucose into the blood, eventually causing hyperglycaemia (excess blood glucose). If left unmanaged, diabetes will lead to a potentially fatal coma.

Diabetics must regularly monitor blood-sugar level, eat a personalised meal plan, routinely exercise, and possibly be prescribed insulin medication.

Subsequently, it is important to appreciate that diabetic children must monitor what they eat and may need to eat outside of set school break times; they will need to learn to prick their fingers to check their blood-sugar level with a glucometer, and perhaps may need to inject themselves with insulin.

Symptoms of unmanaged diabetes mellitus include excess urination, excess thirst, excess hunger, weight loss, fatigue, weakness, nausea, dry itchy skin, frequent skin infections, discomfort in the genitalia and vision changes.

MANAGING DIABETIC BLOOD SUGAR LEVELS

- *Vigilant adherence to:* Diet, exercise, blood-sugar-level monitoring and lifestyle regimes as recommended by medical health professionals.

- *Drink:* Lots of water and green tea.

- *Increase:* Vegetables such as salad greens, celery, onions, garlic, asparagus, alfalfa sprouts, broccoli, fennel, parsnips, spinach, sweet peppers and parsley; legumes such as black beans and navy beans; fish, fresh or canned; non-sweetened yoghurt; raw nuts and seeds; soy products; ginger and cinnamon; and most fruit, especially avocados, citrus fruits, strawberries, cherries, berries, stone fruit and olives.

- *Eat:* A daily fist-size (depending on blood-sugar numbers) of dense breads, wholegrains, textured wholemeal, wheatbran, wheatgerm, oat bran, long-grain rice such as basmati, brown rice, rye, kumara, taro, yam, noodles, barley wheat, bulgur wheat, porridge or muesli.

- *Add in:* Spirulina, nutritional yeast, linseed/flaxseed, dandelion, guarseed, fenugreek seeds, ginseng, goldenseal or licorice root.

- *Replace:* Refined oils with unrefined oils such as sunflower oil.

- *Avoid high GI (glycaemic index) foods:* Sugars, maltose, corn syrup, sucrose, honey, maple syrup, golden syrup, white bread, pumpkin, most potatoes, most cereals and crackers, tropical fruit, soft drinks and some dried fruit including raisins.

- » *Avoid refined carbs:* White flour, short-grain white rice such as jasmine, pasta, cakes, biscuits, pastries, pies and breadcrumbs. (Shirataki noodles have virtually no carbs.)
- » *Avoid saturated fats:* Animal fats, processed meat such as sausages and salami, fried foods, butter, margarine and coconut products.
- » *Avoid artificial sweeteners:* Use stevia instead.
- » *Supplements:* Multi-vitamin and mineral formulas that contain chromium, vanadium and zinc; antioxidant formulas; omega-3 and -6 oils such as evening primrose, fish and flaxseed; and fibre supplements such as linseed, guar gum, psyllium, pectin and slippery elm.
- » *Herbs:* Many, many options — make an appointment with a naturopathic herbalist.
- » *Homeopathy & Acupuncture:* Many, many options — make an appointment with a classical homeopath.

DIARRHOEA

The colon is the organ that reabsorbs water before defecation, so any condition causing food to rush through it will result in watery stools. This could be a bacterial, viral or parasitic food-poisoning gastroenteritis, food sensitivity intolerance, chronic disease or adverse reaction to medication. Diarrhoea is a common problem that can cure itself. However, diarrhoea can also be very serious in children (especially infants) as it can quickly result in dehydration, causing subsequent potentially life-threatening electrolyte imbalances. Symptoms of diarrhoea include loose watery stools three or more times a day or stools increasing in volume, frequency, urgency and fluidity.

BENEFICIAL THERAPIES FOR DIARRHOEA

- » *Rehydrate:* Replace fluids with salted vegetable soup broths, herbal teas, flat lemonade, ice-blocks, diluted fruit juices such as blackberry and commercially prepared electrolyte rehydration solutions available at pharmacies (as they include sodium, potassium and chloride).

- » *Reduce symptoms:* Mix 3 tsp carob powder with heated soy milk and sweeten with stevia.

- » *Eat:* Starch and simple proteins; the BRAT diet of Bananas, plain Rice, Apple sauce and Toast; as well as ginger, blueberries, bananas, pineapple, bifidus-acidophilus yoghurt; cooked fruits such as blueberries, bananas, pineapple and apple; and foods rich in L-glutamine amino acids such as fish, red meat and beans.

- » *Increase fibre:* Flaxseeds, pectin, psyllium or LSA.

- » *Replace:* Dairy products with soy or rice milk.

- » *Avoid:* High-sugar foods and drinks; excessively salty foods; white flour; fatty or greasy foods; spicy foods; hard, solid foods; caffeine; tomato-based foods; processed foods; artificial additives; and MSG— they all can aggravate diarrhoea.

- » *Avoid:* The opiate derivative and anticholinergic drug Diastop (diphenoxylate and atropine) because of potential adverse effects — in fact, the WHO has warned against this drug's use in children.

- » *Supplements:* Multi-vitamin and mineral formulas, digestive enzymes, garlic, bee pollen, bitter melon, and/or L-glutamine and probiotics are essential.

- » *GROOVEyS:* Natural antimicrobials (see page 149).

- » *Herbs:* Slippery elm, meadowsweet, cloves, wormwood, black walnut, goldenseal, marshmallow root, chamomile, fennel seeds and/or aniseed.

- » *Homeopathic remedies:* Arsenicum, Chamomilla, Gelsemium, Arg Nit, China or Sulphur, depending on symptoms; NaturoPharm's Diarmed Relief, Digest-med and Nausmed Relief.
- » *As diarrhoea subsides:* Add potatoes, crackers and carrots to the diet.

SEEK MEDICAL ATTENTION FOR THE FOLLOWING SYMPTOMS

- » Severe explosive diarrhoea.
- » Diarrhoea with fever above 38.5°C.
- » Diarrhoea lasting more than two to three days.
- » Diarrhoea with strong abdominal pain.
- » Diarrhoea with dehydration, resulting in confusion, unresponsiveness, dizziness while standing, dry mouth, strong body odour or sunken eyes.
- » Blood, pus or mucus in stools, or black tar-like stools.

EAR INFECTIONS *(Otitis media)*

The *outer ear* consists of the auricle (the part of the ear we put jewellery in) and the external auditory canal (the ear canal you can stick your little finger into). The *inner ear* is the internal part which includes the vestibule, semicircular canals and cochlea, which are responsible for equilibrium and balance, and for the conversion of vibrations into sounds. In between is the *middle ear*, which is the pea-sized tympanic cavity containing the body's three smallest bones, the ossicles (nicknamed the hammer, anvil and stirrup) that transmit the vibratory motion of sound from the outer ear to the inner.

Middle-ear infections and inflammations, such as glue ear, are a common childhood problem, particularly with under-six-year-olds with allergies, or after an upper-respiratory infection. The resulting earache, fever and hearing loss can particularly affect six- to 20-month-olds, as their ears' eustachian tubes (pressure-equalising passageways to the back of the throat) are shorter and more horizontal, so fluid may not drain and pus can accumulate, filling the middle ear and making the eardrum bulge.

This has historically been treated with recurrent antibiotics, often followed by the too prevalent myringotomy surgery — that is, the insertion of grommets (tiny tubes) into the eardrum so pus can drain from the middle ear to the outer ear. Again, this is modern medicine not actually curing the root source of the problem, but instead treating the symptom.

Symptoms of middle-ear infections include earache (dull pain that can become stabbing), mild fever and general unwellness, diminished hearing and discharge from the ear.

RELIEVING SYMPTOMS OF EAR INFECTIONS

» *Homeopathy:* Weleda's Levisticum, NaturoPharm's Earmed Relief, and Aconite 30c for sudden onset of earache.

» *Pain-relieving drugs:* Paracetamol (also reduces fever) or ibuprofen (also reduces fever and inflammation); use both in moderation.

» *Avoid allergens:* Artificial colors, preservatives, dairy products, wheat, eggs, peanuts, soy, corn, tomatoes, chicken and apples.

» *Reduce:* Refined sugar, including confectionery and soft drinks.

NATURAL THERAPIES FOR EAR INFECTIONS

» *Drink:* Lots of water and carrot juice.

» *Eat:* Lots of vegetables and fruit.

» *GROOVEyS:* Natural antimicrobials (see page 149), especially colloidal silver drops.

- » *Supplements:* Cod liver oil, and multi-vitamin and mineral formulas including zinc.
- » *Herbs:* Wild indigo, goldenrod, goldenseal, eyebright and mullein.
- » *Homeopathy:* Aconite, Apis, Belladonna, Chamomilla, Merc Viv, Nux Vom, Pulsatilla, Calc Carb, Hepar Sulph, Kali Bich, Lachesis, Mag Phos, Silica or Sulphur (depending on symptoms).
- » *Cleanse the ear canal:* Place a drop of garlic oil in the ear canal once a day; or use candling (or coning), the centuries-old gentle remedy of drawing out residue from the ear canal. The patient lies on their side, and a hollow candle (like a straw) is placed inside the exposed ear. Lighting the candle creates a vacuum which slowly pulls out the (sometimes years old) wax, fungus and other debris, with the additional benefit of improving chronic middle-ear infections.
- » *Lifestyle:* Rest and sleep.

ECZEMA

Eczema affects all ages and can be severe, causing extreme pain and debilitation, or mild, with dry, itchy patches. Eczema is a hypersensitivity response (and a 'cousin' to asthma and hayfever), and can commonly be 'atopic' — that is, a reaction to something in the environment such as an allergen. A baby who has eczema may later develop other immune-related conditions such as asthma and food sensitivities.

Symptoms of eczema include skin redness and inflammation, intense itching, tiny moist weepy blisters, or blisters that crust over. There is also the potential for secondary skin infection (e.g. bacterial).

POSSIBLE CONTRIBUTING FACTORS

- » *Environmental allergens:* Animal fur, laundry detergents, soaps, pollen, dust mites and pollutants.

- » *Immune imbalance:* Caused by stress or anxiety.
- » *Food allergens:* Sensitivities to additives. A naturopath can check for any sensitivities with a hair test.

COMMONLY PRESCRIBED PHARMACOLOGICAL TREATMENTS

BRAND NAMES: *DP-Lotion, Lemnis Fatty Cream*

DRUG NAME: *Hydrocortisone*

DRUG TYPE: *Topical corticosteroid*

ALSO FOUND IN: *Micreme-H and Pimafucort, with antibacterials and antifungals.*

MAIN USES: *Skin allergy treatment including eczema and dermatitis (potentially complicated with secondary bacterial or candidal infection).*

COMMON ADVERSE REACTIONS: *Skin atrophy (cell degeneration).*

DRUG TYPE: *Zinc oxide and castor oil*

MAIN USES: *Treatment of chafed skin; protective healing barrier for eczema or nappy rash.*

COMMON ADVERSE REACTIONS: *Rare.*

RELIEVING SYMPTOMS OF ECZEMA

- » *Reduce itching:* Use a mild topical cream or ointment containing coconut oil, coal tar or ichthammol preparations; keep skin well moisturised with extra-virgin olive, coconut or soy cold-pressed oils or ointments; and wear only natural fibres such as cotton next to skin.
- » *Avoid:* Rapid changes in air temperature and clothing made from synthetic fibres.

- *Daily bath:* Fill a bath with 1 cup of baking soda to reduce itching and/or an emollient such as 2 cups oatmeal or colloidal oatmeal.
- *Drugs:* For very acute cases only, use antihistamine medications, immuno-suppressants or topical corticosteroids such as hydrocortisone in the short term and in moderation.

NATURAL THERAPIES TO MANAGE ECZEMA

- *Drink:* Sarsaparilla, carrot juice, spinach juice and/or marshmallow root tea.
- *Eat:* Lots of fish (fresh or canned), fresh vegetables, nuts and seeds.
- *Avoid:* Allergens such as citrus, peanuts, wheat, eggs, corn, tomatoes, food colorings, artificial preservatives, soap, iodides such as iodised salt, bromides such as pesticides, and foods with gluten. (A child that has developed eczema after being introduced to solids may be gluten sensitive. As the blood test can give a false negative, it can be a far better test to go on a three-month gluten-free diet.)
- *Reduce:* Saturated fats from poultry and red meat, refined foods and sugar.
- *Dairy:* Depending on personal allergens, eat only goat's milk and yoghurt, nut milks, white cheeses such as feta, quark, cottage cheese and ricotta, and small amounts of ghee.
- *Supplements:* Calcium and zinc; vitamins C, E and B5; calendula and chamomile oils; boron, inositol, niacin, beta carotene, bioflavonoids, quercetin; and Omega-3 and -6 oils such as flaxseed, borage, evening primrose and cod liver oils.
- *Herbs:* Use those that balance and modulate the immune system, such as milk thistle, dandelion root, yellow dock, cleavers, sarsaparilla, licorice, burdock, perilla, boswellia or chickweed.

- » *Eczema-easing products:* Natural products such as the non-steroidal (non-cortisone) topical anti-inflammatory balm of chickweed, botanical extracts and avocado oil, and herbal formulas available through naturopaths. (Also available as the branded cream Xma Ease.)
- » *Probiotics:* Ethical Nutrient's Eczema Shield.
- » *Lifestyle:* Reduce stress with meditation, tai chi or yoga.
- » *Chronic cases:* Rotate diet, don't eat the same food more than once every four days.

EYE INFECTIONS *(CONJUNCTIVITIS)*

NOTE: The eyes are very delicate organs, and may require antibiotic eye drops if the problem is a bacterial infection.

COMMONLY PRESCRIBED PHARMACOLOGICAL EYE DROPS/EYE OINTMENT

BRAND NAME: *Fucithalmic*

DRUG NAME: *Fusidic acid*

DRUG TYPE: *Antibacterial*

MAIN USES: *Bacterial conjunctivitis (pink eye), eyelid inflammation, stye or keratitis inflamed cornea.*

COMMON ADVERSE REACTIONS: *Burning, stinging eyes.*

BRAND NAME: *Chlorsig*

DRUG NAME: *Chloramphenicol*

DRUG TYPE: *Broad-spectrum antibiotic*

MAIN USES: *Eye infections including bacterial conjunctivitis (pink eye).*

COMMON ADVERSE REACTIONS: *Burning, itching eyes.*

BRAND NAME: *Sofradex*

DRUG NAMES: *Dexamethasone, Gramicidin and Framycetin*

DRUG TYPE: *Anti-inflammatory corticosteroid*

MAIN USES: *Viral or fungal eye disease and eyelid inflammation. (Also used as treatment for otitis external ear-canal inflammation.)*

COMMON ADVERSE REACTIONS: *Burning, stinging, itching eyes.*

ALERT: *Dexamethasone is not recommended for treating infections because it can hide the signs of infection. It may be better to use Soframycin instead, which only contains the antibiotic Framycetin.*

NATURAL THERAPIES FOR EYE INFECTION

» *Herbs:* A herbalist can make a topical eyewash or compress of marigold, goldenseal and eyebright.

» *Supplements:* Goldenseal, eyebright, goldenrod, cleavers, poke root, and/or cell salts such as Kali Mur, Ferr Phos, Nat Phos or silica.

» *GROOVEyS:* Natural antimicrobials (see page 149), especially colloidal silver drops.

» *Homeopathy:* Belladonna 30c drops.

HOMEOPATHIC EYE REMEDIES

» *Inflammation:* Apis, Pulsatilla, Silica or Arg Nit, depending on symptoms. Bathe eyes in tincture of Euphrasia or Hypercal.

» *Injury:* Aconite, Arnica, Ledum, Symphytum or Staphisagria, depending on symptoms.

» *Styes:* Apis or Pulsatilla.

FEVER *(Pyrexia)*

Fever is an immensely important function of the body's defence against, and destruction of, germs. The body uses shivering and chills to increase its core temperature to produce a fever, then later it uses flushing and sweating to reduce its core temperature. During infection, it is important to avoid a life-threatening high fever, but it is also important to allow a mild or moderate fever to run its full course. Unnecessarily reducing fevers can prolong illness. (See Colds, flus and coughs)

GENERAL DEFINITION OF TEMPERATURES

» *Below 36.4°C:* Hypothermia (too cold).

» *36.5°C–37.5°C:* Normal.

» *37.5°C–38.0°C:* Mild fever.

» *38.0°C–38.5°C:* Moderate fever (administer homeopathic Belladonna).

» *38.5°C–39.0°C:* High fever (administer drug paracetamol).

» *39.0°C –39.5°C:* Has little extra germ-destroying benefit, and requires prompt medical attention.

» *39.5°C–40.0°C:* Irreversible cellular damage begins, and requires *urgent* medical attention.

» *Over 40.0°C:* This is 'cooking the brain'!

NATURAL THERAPIES FOR MILD TO MODERATE FEVER

» *Lifestyle:* Rest and sleep.

» *Increase fluids:* Drink water or water with lemon; suck on ice; rehydration drinks from the chemist; or herbal teas such as thyme, chamomile, linden, willow bark and spearmint.

» *Cooling down:* Sponging with tepid wet compresses and dressing lightly (while also avoiding hypothermic cold-stress shock).

- » *GROOVEyS:* Natural antimicrobials (see page 149).
- » *Homeopathy:* Belladonna 30c drops.
- » *Thermometer:* Vigilantly monitor temperature to avoid febrile seizures (fever fits).

SEE DOCTOR IF MODERATE OR HIGH FEVER IS ACCOMPANIED BY ANY OF THE FOLLOWING

- » Vomiting or diarrhoea, from a gastrointestinal infection.
- » Coughing or wheezy breathing from a respiratory infection.
- » Refusing food because of a throat infection.
- » Painful ears from an ear infection.
- » Limpness, malaise or blue-tinged skin.
- » A rash or sore neck — seek urgent medical attention, as this may be meningitis.

FLU (Influenza) — *see Colds, flus and coughs*

FRACTURES — *see Bone/fractures*

FUNGAL INFECTIONS

Superficial (surface only) fungal diseases can often be tinea (ringworm) infections of skin, scalp or nails, such as athlete's foot. These are generally not life threatening, but can be unsightly and sometimes contagious, so do need treatment. Other fungal infections are candida such as thrush, or pityrosporum such as dandru , which can be superficial, but if left untreated can also become chronic.

Drugs such as antibiotics and corticosteroids can cause fungal infections. Environmental factors also play a big part, with infections appearing in warm, moist areas of the body — groin, genitalia, skin folds and mouth — and when wearing sweaty clothes and shoes.

COMMONLY PRESCRIBED PHARMACEUTICAL MEDICATION

BRAND NAME: *Nilstat Oral Drops*

DRUG NAME: *Nystatin*

DRUG TYPE: *Antifungal and antibiotic*

MAIN USES: *Oral candidiasis (thrush).*

COMMON ADVERSE REACTIONS: *Gastrointestinal upsets such as diarrhoea, nausea and vomiting.*

BRAND NAME: *Diflucan Suspension*

DRUG NAME: *Fluconazole*

DRUG TYPE: *Antifungal agent*

MAIN USES: *Oral and systemic candidiasis (thrush).*

COMMON ADVERSE REACTIONS: *Elevated liver functions, gastrointestinal upsets, headaches, acne and rash.*

GENERAL NATURAL ANTIFUNGAL REMEDY FOR SKIN

» Wash the area with apple cider vinegar.

» Then wash with Lugol's iodine mixture (six drops in ¼ cup boiled water).

» Apply colloidal silver cream.

» Mix three drops of Lugol's iodine in ½ cup of warm water. Add 1 tsp of manuka honey and a small capful of apple cider vinegar. Drink three to four times a day for a week.

NATURAL ANTIFUNGAL THERAPIES

» *GROOVEyS:* Natural antimicrobials (see page 149).
» *Alternative wash:* Bathe in Condy's Crystals (potassium permanganate).
» *Eat:* Garlic, ginger, licorice, chamomile, sarsaparilla and goldenseal.
» *Herbs:* Apply thuja, tea-tree oil, myrrh, lavender oil and oregano oil.
» *Homeopathy:* Borax, Ant Tart, Potas Permang, Caps, Kali Chloric, Merc Cor, Ars or Silic, depending on symptoms.

GASTROENTERITIS — *see Diarrhoea and Vomiting*

GASTRO-OESOPHAGEAL REFLUX *(Acid indigestion)*

Gastro-oesophageal reflux (GOR) also goes by the names of heartburn, acid reflux and acid indigestion. This painful condition is when the cardiac sphincter (lower oesophageal valve) at the top of the stomach, which is supposed to stop its contents moving back up the oesophagus, is 'unreliable' (not as tight as normal), and food containing acid from the stomach regurgitates back up into the oesophagus.

However, when symptoms are more severe and interfere with growth and development, or cause serious acidic esophageal ulcerative damage, the condition is classified as a disease.

COMMONLY PRESCRIBED PHARMACOLOGICAL TREATMENTS

BRAND NAME: *Zantac*
DRUG NAME: *Ranitidine*
DRUG TYPE: *H2-Antagonist*
MAIN USES: *Treatment of gastro-oesophageal reflux disease (GORD).*

COMMON ADVERSE REACTIONS: *Headache, dizziness, blurred vision, rash and altered liver metabolism (jaundice).*

BRAND NAMES: *Losec*

DRUG NAME: *Omeprazole*

DRUG TYPE: *Antiulcer PPI (proton pump inhibitor)*

MAIN USES: *Gastrointestinal disorders such as severe indigestion heartburn, GORD, duodenal and gastric ulcers.*

COMMON ADVERSE REACTIONS: *Controversially rare.*

SOME BENEFICIAL THERAPIES FOR GASTRIC REFLUX IN CHILDREN AND INFANTS

» Breastfeeding is strongly preferable over formula because breastmilk is a natural antacid, is more rapidly digested, is more intestine-friendly and produces softer poos.

» Elevate the head-end of the bed to an angle of about 30 degrees, and sleep the child (not infant) on its left side so that the gastric inlet is higher than the outlet.

» Avoid decongestants (which dry mucus production).

» Don't encourage the child to become too 'bonny', as obesity can aggravate reflux.

» Use homeopathic remedies such as Belladonna, Nux Vom, Bryonia, Mag Phos or Staphisagria (depending on symptoms).

» Visit a cranial osteopath and a classical homeopath.

» Try over-the-counter infant antacid liquids, such as Gaviscon or Mylanta.

» In severe cases, try a prescription acid-blocker medicine, such as Losec at night time to reduce stomach-acid production.

- » In extremely severe cases, request a prokinetic motility prescription medicine, such as Prepulsid, which will increase the muscle tone of the lower oesophageal sphincter muscle.
- » Consider a food allergy, such as cow's milk protein allergy. (See Allergies.)
- » Consider a food intolerance, such as lactose intolerance. (See Intolerances.)
- » Get a hair test done by a naturopath for diagnostic purposes.
- » Speak to a health professional about probiotics specific for a child's less mature digestive system.

HAYFEVER — *see Allergies*

HEADACHES AND MIGRAINES

There are many kinds of headaches, from mild tension headaches caused by physical fatigue, heat dehydration, bright lights or sinusitis; to stress-related cluster headaches (severe pain behind one eye); to toxicity/viral/bacterial headaches; to nutrient-deficient or hormone-related migraines that last one to three days (caused by over-dilation of brain arteries); and throbbing one-sided migraines which can be actually symptoms of more serious intracranial disease.

Migraines are different from headaches as they may be accompanied by debilitating nausea, vomiting, an odd sense of smell, aversion to bright lights and even visual disturbances including temporary blindness.

It can be tricky to diagnose headaches and migraines in children, especially when they are too young to have the vocabulary to describe what they are experiencing. The symptoms can be mistaken for something else, or can actually *be* something else. So, in general, head pain with lethargy should always be treated as potentially serious, especially if a fever is also present. Such symptoms require a consultation with your medical doctor for a confirmed diagnosis.

NATURAL THERAPIES TO RELIEVE HEADACHE SYMPTOMS

- *Herb:* White willow and feverfew.

- *Homeopathy:* Aconite, Belladonna, Bryonia, Gelsemium, Ignatia, Kali Bich, Merc Viv, Nux Vom, Pulsatilla, Rhus Tox, Silica, Phosphorus, Natrum Mur, Lycopodium, Sepia or Cocculus, depending on specific symptoms; NaturoPharm's Headmed Relief.

- *Aromatherapy:* Lavender, rosemary and peppermint.

- *Relaxation therapies:* Massage, acupuncture, deep breathing, visualisation and biofeedback.

- *Drugs:* Analgesic pain relief, such as paracetamol (not for long-term use).

NATURAL REMEDIES TO INHIBIT HEADACHES

- *Drink:* Lots of water.

- *Reduce:* Hyperallergenic foods such as sodium-nitrate-rich cured meats like salami, ham, bacon; phenylalanine-rich and tyramine-rich foods wine, beer, pickled foods, wheat, wheatgerm, soy, corn, cheese, ricotta, beef, turkey and eggs; fat-rich foods such as ice-cream, chocolate, nuts and milk; sugar, coee, soft drinks, processed junk food; and artificial, synthetic foods containing preservatives, additives, flavourings, pesticides, MSG and artificial sweeteners.

- *Supplements:* Magnesium, calcium, vitamin B complex, 5-HTP, MSM (methyl-sulphonyl-methane), DIM (di-indolylmethane) or co-enzyme Q10.

- *Herbs:* Feverfew, chaste tree, false unicorn root, dong quai, wild yam, black cohosh (only in the case of hormonal headaches), gymnema, bitter melon, chromium, goldenrod or goldenseal, depending on the type of recurring headache.

» *Lifestyle:* Exercise that includes posture improvement such as Pilates, yoga, tai chi, Feldenkrais, chiropratic and Alexander technique.

HIVES — *see Allergies*

INFLUENZA — *see Colds, flus and coughs*

INSOMNIA

Insomnia is the inability to fall asleep, restlessness while sleeping, or remaining asleep for an inadequate time. In adults it is generally caused by stress, and in children it is generally caused by a lack of being *taught* how to become a good sleeper when young and/or overstimulation and over-tiredness.

Perhaps one of parenting's biggest misconceptions is the idea that infants are born knowing how to go to sleep unaided and devoid of sleep props — that is, believing babies have the innate ability to gently, happily fall asleep without any enticement (such as being rocked to sleep or breastfed to sleep). About one in 5-10 can, but the rest will need varying levels of parental guidance to *teach* them how to fall asleep, without the aid of extreme exhaustion.

Otherwise, parents can soon rapidly — because time flies — discover their poorly sleeping infant has grown into a sleep-resistant toddler, who grows into an always-fighting-bedtime preschooler, who is now completely addicted to the sleep-junkie inducements like their special blankie, special soft toy, night light, dummy, bottle or whatever other bedtime crutches they 'can't do without'.

The long-term accumulation of sleep deprivation can have dire consequences, affecting brain function, especially reducing intelligence and increasing depression. So what are 'normal' childhood levels of sleep?

1- to 2-year-olds: 14–15 hours a day

3- to 4-year-olds: 13–14 hours a day

5- to 6-year-olds: 11–12 hours a day

7- to 9-year-olds: 10–11 hours a day

11- to 14-year-olds: 9–10 hours a day

15- to 19-year-olds: 9 hours a day

NATURAL THERAPIES FOR INSOMNIA

- *Drink:* Milk, dill tea, and fresh lettuce and celery juices.
- *Eat:* Tryptophan-rich foods such as turkey, but also chicken, beef, fish, eggs, milk, cheese (especially Gruyère), brown rice, hazelnuts, sesame seeds, sunflower seeds and soy, including miso and tofu.
- *Supplements:* 5-HTP; melatonin pineal-gland derivative of serotonin (not generally recommended for children and needs to be prescribed by a medical doctor); fish oil; vitamin B6, calcium and magnesium.
- *Herbs:* Californian poppy, valerian, skullcap, Jamaican dogwood, passionflower and chamomile flowers, Bach Flower Remedies.
- *Aromatherapy:* Lavender oil.
- *Lifestyle:* Plenty of exercise, neurolinguistic programming, craniosacral therapy and acupuncture.

INTOLERANCES

Food intolerance is a non-allergic hypersensitivity to certain foods, including the chemicals naturally found in food. In general, intolerances relate to an individual's low levels or absence of a specific enzyme required to digest the food substance. The reasonably common diagnosis of lactose (milk-sugar) intolerance means the person is deficient in lactase, the enzyme that digests lactose. Because the lactose is not being broken down, it ferments in the gut, causing various symptoms. The body is not allergic to lactose — it just can't deal with it. When breastfeeding lactose-intolerant infants, mothers should ensure such a baby gets all the fat-rich hind-milk to aid digestion and delay weaning. (See my *Oh Baby* book for more information on this topic.)

There is also the reasonably common (one per cent of the population) gluten intolerance known as coeliac disease, also called GSE (gluten sensitive enteropathy), which is caused by an abnormal immune reaction to partially digested gluten — not to be confused with a wheat allergy.

A rarer congenital metabolic disorder is phenylketonuria (PKU), which most newborns are checked for via the Guthrie heel prick blood test. PKU is a liver enzyme deficiency that inhibits the metabolism of phenylalanine. It accumulates in the body, leading to brain damage.

Food intolerances are primarily treated by altering diet.

MENINGITIS

Meningitis is the inflammation of the meninges (connective tissue that lines the exterior of the brain and spinal cord) caused by a bacterial, viral or fungal infection. Viral meningitis is rarely life threatening, and usually clears up within about a week. Bacterial meningitis, however, is potentially life threatening because of its dramatic ability to develop, within hours, into septicaemia (blood poisoning), convulsions, delirium and death. It is most commonly caused by the meningococcal bacteria strains A and B, and pneumococcus. The best treatment for bacterial meningitis is urgent hospitalisation for massive doses of intravenous antibiotics.

INITIAL SYMPTOMS OF MENINGITIS

- » Intense severe headache.
- » Fever, nausea and vomiting.
- » Loss of appetite and drowsiness.
- » Intolerance, aversion to or dislike of bright lights and sounds.
- » Rigidity of muscles, especially a sti neck.
- » Flu-like aches and pains.
- » Convulsions.
- » Septicaemia, red-purple rash from broken blood vessels (see Septicaemia).

NOTE: *Bacterial meningitis is a medical emergency.* If you suspect your child has it, you need to seek urgent medical attention by calling your doctor, taking your child to the emergency department of your nearest hospital or calling an ambulance.

MENINGOCOCCAL INFECTION — *see Meningitis*

PAIN AND PAIN-RELIEVING DRUGS

Our bodies have two main types of pain-receptor — some that transmit fast, sharp, intense pain and some that transmit slow dull aches — all ascending from our spinal cord to our brain.

Pain has an important and vital purpose: it keeps us safe. Pain prevents us from continuing to damage that part of our body.

BRIEF SUMMARY OF PAIN-RELIEF DRUGS

Over-the-counter paracetamol (Pamol, Panadol) and ibuprofen (Brufen, Nurofen) work on separate metabolic pathways, which is why they can be combined to enhance overall relief from discomfort. It is important these drugs are taken at regular periods over 24 hours. Instructions of 'three times daily' does not mean with breakfast, lunch and dinner, it means at eight-hour intervals; and four times daily means at six-hour intervals. Pain relievers are categorised as:

- » *Analgesics:* Non-narcotic drugs that block the generation of pain impulses, such as paracetamol and ibuprofen; and opioid narcotics, such as codeine, pethedine and morphine, that also trigger feel-good receptors.

- » *Antipyretics:* Drugs that reduce fever, such as paracetamol and ibuprofen.

- » *Anti-inflammatories:* Drugs that lower inflammation to reduce discomfort, such as ibuprofen (Brufen, Nurofen) and diclofenac (Voltaren, Cataflam); and steroids such as cortisone and prednisone.

- » *Anaesthetics:* Drugs that remove sensation from a part, or the whole, of the body, such as lignocaine injections used for dental cavity repairs, suturing a cut or epidurals during labor; or general anaesthetics used to put us asleep for surgery.

COMMONLY PRESCRIBED PHARMACEUTICAL PAIN-RELIEVERS

BRAND NAMES: *Panadol, Pamol, Paracare*

DRUG NAME: *Paracetamol*

DRUG TYPE: *Non-narcotic analgesic and antipyretic*

ALSO FOUND IN: *Codral, Coldrex, Dimetapp, Lemsip, Maxiclear, Panadeine, Sinutab, Sudafed.*

MAIN USES: *Relief of mild to moderate pain, discomfort and fever caused by teething, immunisation, headaches, colds and flu.*

COMMON ADVERSE REACTIONS: *Controversially rare.*

ALERTS: *Only take a maximum of four doses of Paracetamol in 24 hours. Paracetamol is generally regarded as a safe anti-fever pain-relieving drug, but if used in high doses, long term or combined with alcohol it can become highly toxic, causing permanent liver damage.*

Research is also demonstrating strong correlations between excessive paracetamol overuse for non-life-threatening conditions and increased rates of childhood asthma. Take a look at the Beyond Conformity website, www.beyondconformity.co.nz.

BRAND NAMES: *Brufen, Fenpaed, Nurofen*

DRUG NAME: *Ibuprofen*

DRUG TYPE: *NSAID (non-steroidal anti-inflammatory drug)*

MAIN USES: *Relief of fever, and mild to moderate pain associated with inflammation such as teething, toothache, earache, sore throat, headache, sprains, strains, arthritis, colds and flu.*

COMMON ADVERSE REACTIONS: *Gastrointestinal upsets and bleeding (both very common); ear imbalance such as tinnitus (ringing ears) or vertigo; oedema (fluid retention); headaches; nervousness; skin reactions such as rashes or itching; or decreased appetite.*

BRAND NAMES: *Maxigesic*

DRUG TYPE: *Combo of 500mg Paracetamol and 150mg Ibuprofen*

DRUG TYPE: *Combo of analgesics, antipyretics and anti-inflammatory (refer Paracetamol and Ibuprofen individual descriptions.*

MAIN USES: *General headache. backache, toothache, period pain, arthritis, sinus pain, rhematic pain, sore throat, tension or migraine headaches, muscular pain, dental procedures, cold-flu achy pains and tennis elbow.*

COMMON ADVERSE REACTIONS: *(Refer Paracetamol and Ibuprofen individual descriptions.)*

BRAND NAMES: *Aspro, Disprin*

DRUG NAME: *Aspirin*

ALERT: *Do not give to children under 12 years.*

RASH — *see Allergies and Septicaemia*

SCALDS — *see Burns*

SEPTICAEMIA *(Blood poisoning)*

Septicaemia is the life-threatening, widespread destruction of blood vessels from bacterial infections such as meningococcus, streptococcus and staphylococcus. The main symptom is the tell-tale septicaemic rash (from broken blood vessels). Septicaemia must *always* be taken very seriously, especially in the under-fives! The best hope of treating bacterial septicaemia is urgent hospitalisation for massive doses of intravenous antibiotics.

IDENTIFYING A SEPTICAEMIA RASH — THE GLASS TUMBLER TEST

Press a glass tumbler firmly against the rash. If the pressure doesn't 'bleach' the rash and you can still see it through the clear glass, then seek urgent medical assistance. (On dark skin it can be best to do the tumbler test against lighter areas of skin.)

SINUSITIS — *see Colds, flus and coughs*

SKIN WOUNDS

Skin tissue can regenerate small areas of injured cells, replacing them with the same types of original cells, potentially leaving no trace of the injury. With larger areas of injured cells, tissue regeneration will replace damaged cells with scar tissue. Although scar tissue is strong, it lacks the flexibility and elasticity of most skin cells, and doesn't perform the original tissue's functions.

Chapter Eight

COMMONLY PRESCRIBED ANTIBIOTIC OINTMENT

BRAND NAME: *Bactroban*

DRUG NAME: *Mupirocin*

DRUG TYPE: *Antibiotic ointment*

MAIN USES: *Skin infections.*

COMMON ADVERSE REACTIONS: *Itching, burning, flushing (erythema), stinging and dryness.*

NATURAL THERAPIES FOR SKIN WOUNDS

» *Drink:* Fruit juices high in vitamin C, such as citrus, rockmelon, strawberry and tomato juices.

» *Eat:* Nuts, seeds and grains for the amino acid arginine; foods high in vitamin C such as citrus, rockmelon, strawberries, tomatoes, fresh red-skinned potatoes, green leafy vegetables, onion and garlic; foods high in zinc such as seafood, meat, cereals, legumes, nuts, wheatgerm and yeast; foods high in copper such as liver, shellfish, wholegrains, legumes and meat; foods high in vitamin A such as deep-yellow and deep-green leafy veggies, fish-liver oils, egg yolk and liver; and foods high in vitamin E such as wheatgerm, vegetable oils, nuts, wholegrains and dark-green leafy vegetables.

» *Supplements,* Zinc, bromelain (pineapple enzyme), vitamin B complex, vitamin C, ornithine alpha-ketoglutarate (amino acids ornithine and glutamine), gotu kola, horse chestnut, arnica and bee pollen.

» *Topical creams:* Zinc, aloe vera, chamomile, gotu kola, calendula, hypercal and honey.

» *Homeopathy:* Arnica, Calendula, Hypericum, HyperCal cream and Staphisagria; NaturoPharm's Healmed Relief cream.

- *Lifestyle:* Rest and sleep.

SPRAINS and STRAINS

Nearly all the muscles we voluntarily move are linked to bones, because we move our bones by contracting our muscles. Bones act as the levers that provide muscles with strength, which is why muscle-building exercises also strengthen bones, because bones increased their strength enough to support the demands of muscular activity.

Tendons are the tough, fibrous connective cords that link skeletal muscles to bones. Tendonitis is the inflammation of the tendon from, for instance, excessive overuse.

Strains occur when a muscle has been excessively worked or overstretched, resulting in pain and swelling.

Ligaments are the tough, fibrous connective tissues that link two bones together at a joint. Although ligaments are flexible, they are not elastic; *sprains* can occur from sudden overstretching.

Cartilage is dense connective tissue able to withstand considerable pressure, and it ensures smooth gliding movements. Several diseases, such as osteoarthritis, can damage cartilage.

Because tendons, ligaments and cartilage contain no blood vessels, they all repair slowly.

RICE: TRADITIONAL THERAPY FOR SPRAINS AND STRAINS

- **R**est: Reduce activity to the injured area, for example use crutches.
- **I**ce: Apply an ice pack immediately then intermittently.
- **C**ompression: Use elastic bandages on the injured area.
- **E**levation: If possible keep the injured area above the level of the heart to decrease swelling.

Chapter Eight

NATURAL THERAPIES FOR SPRAINS AND STRAINS

» *Drink:* Pineapple juice for its healing enzyme bromelain.

» *Supplements:* Bromelain.

» *Homeopathy:* Arnica and Traumeel; possibly Bryonia, Rhus Tox or Ruta depending on symptoms.

STINGS and INSECT BITES

Most bites and stings are not serious and simply cause mild irritation, but some children can have life-threatening allergies (see Anaphylactic shock).

In general, children don't need a medical consultation after a bite or sting unless the skin reaction spreads, if it is an open wound or if it becomes infected or is generally becoming worse and failing to heal.

BENEFICIAL THERAPIES FOR STINGS AND INSECT BITES

» Dab household ammonia or a slice of lemon on the sting, followed by *Urtica urens* ointment.

» Put ice cubes or packets of frozen vegetables on the sting to deaden pain, reduce swelling and reduce venom spread.

» Make a poultice paste from water and baking soda to place on the sting or bite, and allow to dry. This draws out and neutralises the poison, as well as reducing itching.

» Later, heat can feel good. Try running the affected area under warm water or aim a hairdryer at it.

THROAT INFECTIONS —
TONSILLITIS, STREP THROAT and RHEUMATIC FEVER

Some bacterial or viral throat infections (pharyngitis) are associated with tonsillitis (infection of the tonsils). The tonsils are a pair of specialised lymph nodes either side of the throat just behind and above the tongue. Like the adenoids (at the rear of the nose) they are part of our immune system and help to protect us against germs that enter the nose and mouth. Sometimes tonsils can get overwhelmed with infection, becoming swollen and inflamed. But removing tonsils or adenoids is removing part of our immune system!

Symptoms of tonsillitis include a severe sore throat, difficult or painful swallowing, fever above 38 degrees Celsius and/or chills and enlarged, sore glands in the jaw and neck.

BENEFICIAL THERAPIES FOR TONSILLITIS

- *Drink:* Lots of water with lemon; chamomile tea with 1 tsp lemon juice and 1 tsp honey; fresh watercress and apple juice with ¼ tsp cream of tartar; or pomegranate juice.
- *Gargle:* Several times daily with warm salty water: ¼ tsp salt to ½ glass of water.
- *Eat:* Soothing foods such as broths, soups, mashed veggies, soft/puréed fruit, porridge and soft-cooked eggs; cold foods such as sorbet, frozen yoghurt and fruit-juice ice-blocks; healing foods such as garlic, onions, chives, spring onions, figs, beets, horseradish, cinnamon, cloves and pomegranate.
- *Supplements:* Vitamin C and zinc.
- *Herbs:* Echinacea and sage.
- *Homeopathy:* Aconite, Arsenicum, Gelsemium, Pulsatilla, Silica, Kali Bich, Natrum Mur, Bryonia, Nux Vom, Rhus Tox, Ipecac or Eupatorium Per (depending on symptoms) and NaturoPharm's Throatmed Relief.
- *Lozenges:* Especially manuka honey, and Noni lozenges with honey and propolis.

» *Lifestyle:* Rest and sleep.

STREP THROAT

If a sore throat is suspected to be strep throat, then it is best practice for a GP to send a swab to the laboratory for a culture and sensitivity test. I personally do not endorse generalised antibiotic treatment for all sore throats, however, it is important to treat and stop the spread of strep throat as it can lead to rheumatic fever.

Preventing the spread of strep throat

It is very wise for *any* person with a sore throat to always:

» Wash eating and drinking utensils separately.

» Wash their hands frequently.

» Avoid coughing or sneezing near other people, especially children.

» Replace their toothbrush once recovered — and never share toothbrushes.

RHEUMATIC HEART DISEASE

Strep throat is highly contagious, and around 0.5 per cent of strep throat cases result in rheumatic fever, potentially causing rheumatic heart disease within six weeks. Rheumatic fever affects mainly five- to 15-year-olds, and symptoms include fever, arthritic joint pain or swelling, and/or a rash. The heart muscle (myocardium) valves and/or the membranes surrounding the heart (pericardium) become inflamed.

There isn't a definitive laboratory test to confirm rheumatic fever, but instead diagnosis is done by specific tests such as blood counts, throat cultures, ultrasound or an ECG. Treatment usually includes antibiotics, analgesics and a month's bed rest, followed by ongoing antibiotics until 25 years of age!

For 50 per cent of patients, the scarring caused by rheumatic fever can lead to chronic valvular disease (heart murmurs and destroyed heart valves), and not uncommonly heart failure can occur within a decade, which requires heart-valve corrective surgery.

URINARY TRACT INFECTIONS *(UTI)*

Cystitis (bladder inflammation) is a lower urinary tract infection and is commonly caused by bacteria ascending the urethra into the bladder, usually *E. coli* bacteria from the rectum. UTIs are more common for females due to our shorter urethra. *Remind daughters to always wipe front-to-back after using the toilet.*

The main symptom of cystitis is frequent, painful, urgent urinating. A simple urine stick test at the GP can confirm the presence of a suspected UTI, which is then usually followed up by a midstream urine specimen. (This is cultured in a laboratory to identify the bacterial species, then screened for sensitivity and resistance to various antibiotics.)

If symptoms begin to consist of cloudy foul-smelling urine, reddish urine due to blood, fever and chills, or flank pain (rib/back tenderness), then these are signs that the infection has ascended from the bladder up the ureter(s) to the kidney(s) and has become an upper UTI (pyelonephritis), which can cause serious, irreversible renal (kidney) damage.

THERAPIES TO RELIEVE SYMPTOMS OF CYSTITIS (LOWER UTI)

» *Alkalinisers:* Ural powder sachets.

» *Drugs:* Analgesics and anti-inflammatories such as ibuprofen.

NATURAL THERAPIES TO TREAT CYSTITIS (LOWER UTI)

» *Drink:* Alkalinisers such as barley grass and green juices; increased fluids to flush the bladder, including lots of unchlorinated water,

- » *Eat:* Cranberries, craisins (dried cranberries) and blueberries which all inhibit bacteria from attaching to the walls of ureters, bladder and the urethra; adzuki and kidney beans.
- » *Avoid:* Asparagus, spinach, beetroot, raw carrots, potatoes, tomatoes, citrus fruits, strawberries, red meat, milk, ice-cream, junk food and tea and co ee.
- » *Supplements:* Vitamin A (or its precursor beta carotene), MSM (Methylsulphonylmethane), zinc and glucosamine.
- » *Herbs:* Cranberry, bearberry, buchu, goldenseal or gotu kola.
- » *GROOVEyS:* Natural antimicrobials (see page 149).
- » *Homeopathy:* Apis, Cantharis or Pulsatilla, depending on symptoms; or NaturoPharm's Urinary-Med.

barley water and juices such as cranberry, celery, aloe vera or pomegranate.

PHARMACEUTICAL TREATMENTS FOR PYELONEPHRITIS (UPPER UTI)

By using the natural therapies above, it is hopeful that cystitis will not progress on to pyelonephritis. However, if it does, a medical consultation should be sought and prescribed pharmaceutical antibacterial options may include a few days on antibiotics, such as Trisul (sulfamethoxazole and trimethoprim), Augmentin (amoxicillin and clavulanic acid), or probably E-Mycin (erythromycin) for those with a penicillin allergy.

NOTE: If the medication you have been prescribed ends in '-floxacin', it will probably be a fluoroquinolone antibiotic. These are commonly misprescribed for colds, sore throats and bladder infections. With a few exceptions, fluoroquinolones are not the drug of choice, because they are expensive, bacterium resistance to them is increasing and they have potentially serious adverse reactions. Ask for one of the many other e ective antibacterial alternatives.

VOMITING (Emesis)

When the stomach receives something it doesn't like, such as bacterial toxins, it triggers the brain stem's 'launch lunch' function: the diaphragm and abdominal-wall muscles contract, increasing intra-abdominal pressure, the cardiac sphincter (stomach door) relaxes, the mouth's soft palate rises to close o the sinus passages, all in preparation for vomiting. Oh, we are all familiar with the pale face and nauseated feeling before spewing!

Excessive vomiting can be serious in children, as it can quickly cause dehydration, with subsequent electrolyte and acid-base imbalances. In these cases anti-emetics prescribed by your GP may be necessary.

COMMONLY PRESCRIBED PHARMACEUTICAL ANTI-EMETIC

BRAND NAME: *Maxolon*

DRUG NAME: *Metoclopramide*

DRUG TYPE: *Gastrokinetic dopamine-antagonist*

MAIN USES: *Severe vomiting.*

COMMON ADVERSE REACTIONS: *Drowsiness, restlessness, fatigue, lassitude (weariness), and muscle spasms (dystonia).*

NATURAL THERAPIES FOR VOMITING

» *Drink:* Replace fluids and electrolytes, using commercially prepared dehydration solutions available at pharmacies, which include sodium, potassium and chloride. Avoid rehydrating with fruit juice or soft drinks, as they won't provide the necessary electrolytes.

» *Eat:* Starch and simple proteins such as the BRAT diet of Bananas, Rice, Apple sauce and Toast.

- » *Herbs*: Ginger, bee pollen, slippery elm, bitter melon, goldenseal or carob powder.
- » *Homeopathy*: Arsenicum, Nux Vom, Silica, Ant Tart, China, Drosera, Ipecac or Phosphorus, depending on symptoms.

WARTS

Warts are a benign skin growth caused by the human papillomavirus (HPV). They can be firm, horny papules on the fingers, hands, elbows and knees; cluster mosaics of flat, skin-colored warts on the face; or tender warts on the sole of the foot (verrucas or plantar warts). Warts won't harm you but they are unsightly and may be painful.

COMMON WART THERAPIES

- » *Over-the-counter:* Lactic acid or salicylic acid treatments such as Duofilm or Posalfilin.
- » *Cryotherapy:* Freezing them o with liquid nitrogen by a GP.
- » *Topical:* Herbal *Thuja occidentalis* (Thuja) mixed with vitamin E cream.
- » *Homeopathic:* Thuja.

SUMMARY

Natural forces within us are the time healers of disease

Hippocrates (460–377 BCE), *'Father of Medicine'*

Today, a power-to-the-people revolution is going on. People are questioning the previously unquestioned medical establishment. The people — us — are realising that giving the body drugs (synthetic molecules) doesn't automatically promote health, and at best only disguises ill health. The only way things are really going to transform is if we escalate our demands for change and if we take direct responsibility for the health of ourselves and our children.

With the struggle to conceive our first child I discovered I was even more naturopathically minded than I had comprehended. At that time I had no medical training whatsoever. But I soon decided, I would not wish to have unnecessary interventions for my birth. I also soon realized, I would not wish to powerlessly present an unwell child into our Goliath medical machine. So – in an age before Google – I began to read and research and investigate. I began to get knowledgeable about non-mainstream healthcare alternatives. I began to get empowered about complementary options. Little did I realise at that time, that a decade later my first parenting guidebook would be published, or that another decade later on, I would have become the Founding Director of SOMCANZ, a global-first conference on Integrative Maternity Healthcare.

Today our Ritalin and Ventolin-fed hyper-allergenic children are being cared for by their Losec and Prozac-fed parents, and babysat by their Warfarin & Insulin-fed grandparents. We now are entire nations of overfed,

Chapter Eight

undernourished, recurrently diseased, and desperately depressed people. We have to seriously question why we have become the sickliest generation ever to exist, when it's never been so possible to be healthy. And why we have become one of the saddest generations of humans ever to have roamed this earth, when human life has never had so many labor-saving luxuries.

Alarmingly, our children's generation today, are now the first generation ever predicted to have shorter life-spans than their parents!

Section Three

CHILDREN'S MINDS

Parenting using Intellectual IQ

Section Three Introduction

THE MIND'S HARDWARE AND SOFTWARE

Man's main task in life is to give birth to himself,
to become what he potentially is.

Erich Fromm, *Man for Himself*

The mind is mankind's greatest mystery! It's our intellect, imagination, perceptions and cognitive processes. For eons, scientists have been hypothesising and theologians have been philosophising about it.

Some believe love, joy, fear and hate are all part of our mind, while others argue they are simply primitive emotions, and that only memory and reason constitute the mind. However, we can probably all agree that the mind manifests itself as our consciousness; but is our mind a God-given divine connection to our soul, or is it simply an 'epiphenomenon' (a secondary phenomenon resulting from our brain activity)? Regardless, our *thoughts* are definitely our mind, which means no one else can ever truly 'know our mind'!

Our mind's *hardware* is the brain, and the human brain is our galaxy's most complex structure. Because as parents we are in charge of young developing brains, it makes sense to have a basic understanding of the brain's anatomy and physiology.

Our mind's *software* is our personality and intelligence — much stemming from nature, much coming from nurture, much coming from many sources of influence. And because we are the parents of young developing minds, I believe it is also important we have a broad appreciation of each child's unique personality, and a good overview of the many extra kinds of IQ today's children need to possess in order for them to mature into thriving, flourishing young teens.

THE MIND'S HARDWARE: THE BRAIN

THE HUMAN BRAIN: THE GALAXY'S MOST COMPLEX STRUCTURE

Without going quite so far back as the theoretical Big Bang, we need to begin at the beginning. On one level, we're simply a quadrillion-quadrillion atoms of mainly oxygen, carbon, hydrogen and splatterings of other basic elements combined into about 80 trillion body cells.

On the other hand, we are the species *Homo sapiens*: the walking, talking, tool-making, deep-thinking ape, di ering from chimps by just 1.2 per cent of our genes. We also just happen to be the most hazardous, dominant and life-threatening creatures on the planet — well, apart from bacteria!

A tiny human fetus has a brain that grows a staggering 250,000 to 500,000 neurons (brain nerve cells) every minute, primarily in the first 18 weeks. So, by birth, we have an extraordinarily sophisticated wiring system consisting of around 100 billion neurons — most of which will last our lifetime. Unlike most of the cells in the rest of our body that are constantly replaced, it is generally understood that the brain cells we have at birth are all we'll ever have.

During our first decade, the neurons grow steadily in length and weight, and form trillions of connections with other neurons, enabling them to communicate with each other. It is estimated each neuron can link with up to 15,000 other neurons. All up, it's an amazing course of events.

The cauliflower-like structure underneath and at the back of the brain's large cerebrum is the cerebellum, and it is primarily responsible for our body's coordinated movements, posture and balance.

The brain stem connects our brain to its extension called the spinal column; and this 'reptilian old brain' controls our body's most basic functions such as keeping the heart beating and our lungs breathing.

Deep within the brain structure is our limbic system, or 'mammalian mid-brain', which is involved in instinct, impulse, mood and emotion, such as fear and anger, and urges, such as thirst and hunger.

The brain's largest area, the walnut-shaped outer layer called the cerebrum (neo cortex or 'new brain'), is the site of our conscious faculties, where we deal with processing the information received from our senses, such as vision and hearing, and our thinking functions, such as reasoning. The highest functions occur in the prefrontal cortex (behind our forehead), which is the area of our conscious, rational thought processes. Arguably we are the only creatures on earth who can so cleverly plan, empathise and deceive! But our brain is far from fully mature at birth. The reason why children seem so unrestrained in their emotional responses is because their prefrontal cortex hasn't matured enough to control their instinctual urges. This won't happen until they're over the age of 20. This is also why children can have difficulty maintaining focused attention, because their brain's 'reticular formation' is still maturing.

But the obvious question lingers: If we are born with all our brain cells (neurons), how can the newborn's head be so much smaller, at just 25 per cent, than an adult's? The answer is simple: myelination.

Our brain is often nicknamed 'grey matter', and when we are born it is all grey matter. Then, for the next 10–12 years, our brain gradually matures, especially rapidly in the first two years.

Brain cells' finger-like dendrites receive information that is then processed by the nucleus (centre). Brain cells share information through electrical impulses that travel along their axon (long tail) to the axon terminals where they are then relayed across a synapse (tiny gap) to the next brain cell's finger-like dendrites.

As our neurons mature, these axon tails become covered in a fatty waxy sheath of schwann cells called myelin, which insulates the brain cells and dramatically increases the speed of transmission of the electrical impulses. This process, called myelination, gradually expands the physical size of our brain, tripling its weight in just the first year, reaching almost 80 per cent of the adult brain weight by two years old, and becoming almost fully grown by three years. Our brains use about the same amount of electricity that would power a small lightbulb, and consume 20 per cent of our body's oxygen.

There are also brain connections present at birth between the auditory and visual cortices which are later pruned. So it is probable that infants are synaesthetes — that is, they can also hear colors and see sounds. This could be another reason why newborns can become so easily over-stimulated, and thus overtired.

HOW WE LEARN

As we experience life, our brain 'learns' by forming infinite linked circuits between its neurons. Some scientists estimate that a single human brain has more connections than all the atoms of the entire universe. Science is also well aware that a single human brain can store more data and process information at faster speeds than the most powerful computers in existence.

Most of our learning is done by *making associations*. Our brain groups together experiences, sensations, objects or events, pigeon-holing them into categories — and then we relate these new experiences to what we already know.

We also learn through *conditioning*. Our brain links directly associated events with recurring outcomes. This is how we learn to avoid events with unfavourable outcomes, and how we learn to seek out events that have favourable consequences.

We also learn by *imitation*. Our brain compares our actions to the skills of others — in fact, our brain in childhood is hard-wired to learn by mimicking, miming and mirroring others.

We also learn *how to learn*. We learn the art of practice and repetition to develop skills and memorise facts, such as memorising times tables or playing an instrument, embedding these activities into our long-term memory. And ideally, our learning strategies improve as our knowledge of what to ignore increases.

Although it is not precisely physiologically accurate, but also far from a complete lie, challenging our children's brains with difficult work helps them get smarter. Although our brain is not made of muscle cells, learning does exercise the brain like a muscle, directly helping it to work stronger and sharper, through faster inter-neuron connections.

HOW WE REMEMBER

When we're alive, our brain is the consistency of jelly, but it is also 'plastic'. That is, brain-cell connections are constantly rewiring themselves, creating endless new circuits, making the brain impressionable, malleable, alterable, pliable, flexible and putty-like. When the pathways that link neurons are repeatedly used, they become permanent (or hard-wired). By exercising certain parts of the brain we increase the development of that area. Every time we commit something to memory, we're forcing the brain to rewire itself. And each time we refer to that memory, we're making the circuitry connections stronger.

Depending on which theorist you're listening to, we have several memory stores in our brain.

First, our *sensory memory* stores a memory for a few fleeting seconds. Then anything that catches our attention enters our *short-term memory* for up to a few minutes (essential for reading a book or watching a film). But this area has limited space and constantly requires the contents to be discarded, and most of this information is 'lost'. Short-term memory is what we use to actively think about something and to problem-solve. A small child's short-term memory is very limited, and this kind of memory peaks in our teens. Short-term memories that we consolidate are linked with existing memories and encoded by the brain's hippocampus into the unlimited repository of our *long-term memory*. Then every time that 'web cluster' of memory is refired it becomes a stronger and more accessible memory, with memories that can last a lifetime.

Events experienced with intense levels of strong *emotions* (such as joy or shock) are typically stored as amplified permanent memories, with heightened levels of detail. *Episodic* (intermittent) *memories* can include a time and date. *Factual memories* are what we learn academically, and these stores need to be refreshed constantly or the memories fade.

Our long-term memory does not begin to mature until about age three and peaks by age 30, which is why it is difficult to remember life as an infant, and why we can be increasingly forgetful as we age.

Our brain is also designed to retain interesting and unusual memories. So when we, or our kids, forget something, it's generally because the brain has filtered out what it perceives as irrelevant enough to discard. It's all about attention: when you're tired, bored and unfocused, learning and remembering are hindered. *This may go some of the way to explain why kids constantly lose their socks, erasers, pencils, jerseys, raincoats, ATM cards and wallets ... and homework, eh!*

The old adage of practice makes perfect describes how physical skills are learnt. In fact, it's your conscious cerebral cortex teaching your unconscious cerebellum to do things on autopilot, such as learning to ride a bike. But science has also discovered that sleep dramatically assists the learning of physical skills that require practice. Additionally sleep helps with mental problem-solving challenges, such as mathematical puzzles. (Interestingly, it is said to take around 10,000 hours of practice to become expert at something.)

INNATE LANGUAGE

The critical period of learning from sight is the first year of life, but the critical period for learning to speak is the first 11 years of life.

From birth, babies have millions of brain cells that are specifically sensitive to identifying all the different sounds of speech patterns — yet only those nerve cells that are repeatedly activated by the most-used languages will eventually develop into the complex network connections that allow us to master a language. Learning from listening to language begins from day one — even from within the womb.

Language acquisition is a use-it-or-lose-it process. This is why in a bi-lingual household immersing a child in two languages during the baby and toddler years can be so beneficial — these are the easiest ages for our children to become fluently multilingual.

In *The Human Mind*, Professor Robert Winston points out amazing research demonstrating that babies' babbling sounds differ, depending on the native language they hear in their household. He goes on to explain remarkably that 'even deaf babies, born to parents who communicate with them via sign language, will make hand movements identical to the babble of normal babies — suggesting that the seemingly nonsensical speech of infants is in fact a crucial rehearsal for the full-blown use of language'.

SLEEP DEPRIVATION

Science still doesn't fully understand the point of sleep — especially the fact that it consumes about a third of our lives — but suppositions conclude it is for balancing brain chemicals, building connections to become proficient in new skills, and solidifying memories. However, what we know for sure is that lack of sleep makes you bad-tempered, miserable, fatigued, clumsy and inhibits memory, impairs learning, stunts growth, slows healing and increases the risk of diabetes, obesity and depression.

There is no doubt sleep deprivation adversely affects brain function, which is why I've always been passionate about how essential it is to teach infants to become great sleepers, before they grow into sleep-resistant toddlers, because sleep-deprived children develop less intelligent brains — that's the bottom line. (See my first book, *Oh Baby*.)

In fact, a healthy sleep pattern from infancy is one of the greatest ways to enhance a child's intelligence. Children who are found to have excellent intelligence almost always have this one thing in common: healthy sleep habits.

METACOGNITION:
ONLY HUMANS CAN THINK ABOUT THINKING

What sets humans apart from all other animals is our ability to mull over problems, deliberate on solutions, contemplate abstract concepts, reminisce about past events, visualise future events, and hypothesize about the unseen. We are the ponderers, ruminators, meditators and philosophers of the animal kingdom. And science really has little idea how this all functions, except that it always uses the brain's prefrontal cortex. We are capable of thinking about how we think!

Thinking itself is also divided into the *conscious* and *unconscious*. Our limited conscious is the logical and rational decision-making we're aware of at any one moment in time. However, the multi-tasking unconscious is our main thought-processor, with its creative, imaginative and intuitive actions operating below the surface, influencing our ideas and behaviours.

THE CONSCIOUSNESS — AN ONGOING MYSTERY

Consciousness is the sensation of awareness we have while we're awake. It's our personal, and completely private, inner world that includes all our thoughts, feelings, ideas, the imagination of daydreams and the inner voice of decision. It is the 'real you'.

But how does it function? Where is it located? These questions continue to ba e scientists, but they know there is no one separate central headquarters within the brain where our consciousness is processed — and consciousness always evolves into self-consciousness.

For most animals, when they look in a mirror they see a stranger; however, we see ourselves because we have self-consciousness. But such self-consciousness brings with it the interminably perpetual questions of 'Who am I?' and 'What am I here for?' Throughout mankind's history, all societies have asked these meaning-of-life questions, with the majority of the world now believing we each possess a spirit or soul that unites the body and mind. But we don't begin life with a sense of the inner self... or maybe we do.

Most theorists believe that babies' brains don't comprehend that we all have di erent opinions, beliefs or desires — they just know they're cold or hungry or tired. Scientifically, it is generally thought babies acquire self-awareness as they grow into toddlers. Spiritually, many faiths believe quite the opposite: you are born with self-awareness.

THE SUBCONSCIOUS — A CONTINUING ENIGMA

In the past, philosophers have called the non-mindful part of our brain the 'unconscious mind' or the 'preconscious', but today it is commonly called the 'subconscious' and it refers to the part of the mind that operates above the level of conscious perception. The subconscious is the hidden area of the mind we are not entirely aware of when it is working, but we know for sure it exerts enormous influence, affecting all our thoughts, behaviours and actions. It is our subconscious that enables us to competently ride a bike, so we can consciously enjoy the scenery.

Along with academic knowledge of the subconscious comes theorised therapeutic 'expertise', espousing ways to influence the unconscious mind — for it is often said that repetition is the key to overriding the subconscious. These repetitive techniques include hypnosis, subliminal messages or auto-suggestive statements of desired intentions, such as 'I am great at basketball and never miss a three-pointer'. There are many other psychotherapeutic tools, such as tapping energy fields with emotional freedom techniques (EFT), trauma resolving with eye-movement desensitisation and reprocessing (EMDR), or influencing brainwaves with binaural beats.

From a spiritual perspective, many believe the subconscious mind to be our soul, our essence, our divine thought, our Godly part of the universe, our individual piece of universal consciousness. Or, as M Scott Peck says in *The Road Less Travelled*, 'To put it plainly, our unconscious is God. God within us. We were part of God all the time.'

It's important an author admits their own bias, and without any personal doubt, I do strongly believe that our subconscious is a manifestation of our spirit — the universal power that exists inside each one of us — the seat of our perfect soul without our cumbersome body or limited mind. If you are able to hop onboard this premise, I absolutely encourage you. If you are not, then I totally understand. I could be utterly wrong. *God knows, literally!*

THE MIND'S SOFTWARE: PERSONALITY AND INTELLIGENCE

Five hundred years ago, the Italian artist and scientist Leonardo da Vinci (1425–1519) summarised his seven principles of brain development, which are still so relevant today:

- » *Curiosità:* An insatiably curious approach to life and an unrelenting quest for continuous learning.
- » *Dimostrazione:* A commitment to test knowledge through experience, persistence and a willingness to learn from mistakes.
- » *Sensazione:* The continual refinement of the senses, especially sight, as the means to enliven experience.
- » *Sfumato:* The going-up-in-smoke willingness to embrace ambiguity, paradox and uncertainty.
- » *Arte/Scienza:* The development of the balance between science and art, logic and imagination ('whole-brain' thinking).
- » *Corporalita:* The cultivation of grace, ambidexterity, fitness and poise.
- » *Connessione:* A recognition of and appreciation for the interconnectedness of all things and phenomena ('holistic systems thinking').

I believe it is our duty as parents to encourage and to develop all these aspects of our children's minds, regardless of individual personality, culture or religion.

INTELLIGENCE: BORN OR BRED?

For more than a century, scientists have been trying to answer the question: are there 'clever' genes? And why are men's brains bigger (about 20 grams heavier than women's), when this isn't reflected in higher scores on IQ tests? *(There's a potential joke in that fact somewhere ... sorry guys!)*

Some research says that a higher ratio inside the brain of grey matter (unmyelinated neurons) to white matter (myelinated neurons) corresponds to higher intelligence. But that doesn't seem logical, when you consider that myelination protects and speeds up brainwave transmission. *Hmmm.*

Science also shows that identical twins raised separately usually maintain a similar IQ. But we also know that children from unhappy households have lower IQs, and children fed diets rich in Omega-3 can improve their IQ. Obesity and lower IQ can also correlate, but then maybe that's little to do with weight and more to do with poor diet; or maybe it's to do with sedentary lifestyle, as science has proven that regular physical exercise is good for brain function — the old 'healthy body and healthy mind' adage. As the esteemed neuroscientist Emerson M Pugh once said, 'If the human brain were so simple that we could understand it, we would be so simple that we couldn't.'

By the way, we decline cognitively with age but our IQ actually continues to improve — and there's strong evidence that shows the more intelligent we are, the longer we live!

CREATIVITY: BORN OR BRED?

Then there's the question about how we unlock access to the most elusive of all human faculties ... our creativity.

Some define creativity as painting, composing or writing.

Some define creativity as an ability to switch modes between primary conscious and secondary unconscious thought, and between left-brain and right-brain dominance.

Some define creativity as increased cortical brain activity.

Some define creativity as a right-brain activity, freely making associations between seemingly unrelated events.

Some define creativity as sensitivity, personified by the introvert who seeks solace and solitude in an 'inner world'.

I define creativity as simply the Art of passionate Inspiration!

MUSIC AND MOZART

Then there's the famous Mozart E ect, which hypothesizes that listening to this eighteenth-century 'brain music' can transform health and well-being, improve memory, awareness, learning, imagination, creativity and reduce depression. Don Campbell's books *The Mozart Effect* and *The Mozart Effect for Children* provide some fascinating reading about awakening your child's mind, health and creativity with music.

In recent times, Dr Gordon Shaw, emeritus professor of the Center for the Neurobiology of Learning and Memory at the University of California at Irvine, released his landmark book *Keeping Mozart in Mind*, which details 25 years of remarkable research into how music a ects reasoning and learning, and how music is a 'window' into higher brain function, enhancing brain development and influencing how children think, reason and create. Baroque music too is understood to 'work harmoniously' with the brain's natural wave rhythms, encouraging left–right brain connectivity. (Baroque music has strict, chromatic melodies and elaborate, harmonious chords. Famous Baroque composers include Bach and Handel.) I know for sure in our household that as young children, our kids would make more intelligible dinner-table conversation when the classics were playing on the stereo.

But in general terms, music (listening to it, singing to it, dancing to it, and making it) is *great* for the brain, especially our spatial and temporal reasoning — and it helps us emotionally. Personally, our home environment is 'drowned' in a vast array of music ... just feels great for the soul.

BRILLIANCE vs HYPER-PARENTING

There are a few varieties of hyper-parents: the 'helicopters' who are always hovering overhead; the ever-vigilant 'curlers' who frantically sweep away all the obstacles in front of their kids; the 'educationers' who devote untold time to their child's academic education; the 'a uenzas' who are a icted by their desire to keep up with the Joneses; and of course the classic well-recognised 'hypers' who altogether over-parent everything, virtually eliminating unsupervised play.

I've known many three- and four-year-olds who have educational activities scheduled every day ... swimming, baby gym, library storytime, music and movement, and so on. They're exhausted! I've known five- and six-year-olds who have after-school activities booked every single afternoon, sometimes more than one a night, plus Saturday sport of course.

OTT (over the top) doesn't begin to sum it up sometimes, and it's not an exaggeration to say that some of these children almost need to schedule in time in their over-organised, performance-laden lives just to fit in riding a bicycle around their street!

So, dear fellow parent, don't get too sucked into the hyper-parenting way of life, which can develop in our children a type of 'competitive neurosis', as author Steve Biddulph terms it, where life is seen as a desperate race with an aura of anxiety. Or, as authors John and Linda Friel sum up in *The Seven Worst Things Parents Do:* 'Excellent grades, not-so-excellent life.'

Realistically, most parents hope their child will be brilliant at something — not necessarily a gifted maestro, but to have some shining talents come forth. A fairly common sense book on the topic is *Make*

Your Child Brilliant by Bernadette Tynan. And of course there's the old basic rule, that low boredom thresholds can give rise to mischievousness in the classroom, but may also be a strong sign of brilliance!

But, but, but, but, *but!* *Please* don't become obsessed with ensuring your child is all-round gifted — it's genuinely pretty rare. *Please* don't be one of those parents who want to meet with the teacher all the time to discuss little Tristan or Porsche's 'unique wonderfulness' — because, frankly, you really ain't helping the teacher to enjoy their presence in the classroom. Let me tell you, teachers loathe those parents who are obsessed with how darn special they perceive their attention-spoilt, educationally over-stimulated and materially overindulged children to be — most of them are normal and average, good at some things, not so good at others.

We all know parents like that . . . the ones that demand homework, and respond meaningfully all the time to every boring thing their child utters. *How unrealistic!* The trick with parenting is *not* to mismanage our children, either by hypo-parenting them to the point of them losing their will to succeed and their vitality, or to the other extreme by hyper-parenting them so the drive to succeed overtakes the urge to be in the now.

And please, please can we all find the balance between deserved pride in our children and the unpleasantness of the snobby or pompous parents who pretentiously gloat over the grandiose achievements of their probably swollen-headed child. As Polly Berrien Berends observes in *Whole Child/Whole Parent*, 'Through the success of the bright child we expect to demonstrate how knowing and smart and successful and powerful *we* are as both the source of, and the force behind, the child.' *It can make you want to heave!*

None of us want our kids to be stupid or thick, but the fact is that as a general gauge, about half of them must be below average . . . oh, but not yours or mine, of course, eh?

MULTIPLE INTELLIGENCES

It is traditionally said that about four out of five people have an IQ (intelligence quotient) of between 80 and 120, with the average being 100. But the eerie reality is that research over the past 50 years has discovered a remarkable rise in the average IQ score, by around three points per decade. Thus, it could be hypothesized that the average intelligence 100 years ago would today be categorised as deficient — but obviously that can't be completely true. However, certainly improved nutrition and education standards have improved intelligence, which is only common sense.

We know also without any doubt that intelligence is affected by both nature and nurture; that is, the most stable, loving, healthy childhood environments may impact a little on a low IQ; and even in the poorest and most underprivileged environments, naturally bright children can still fulfil amazing potential.

In 1983 Howard Gardner, a distinguished Harvard psychologist, first laid out in his book *Frames of Mind* the seven 'dimensions of intelligence', and followed it up in 2007 with the bestseller *Five minds for the Future*. Over time many other experts have expanded the list of multiple intelligences (and mindsets) needed by 'successful' human beings. Ideally our kids will be adept in all of them! *Fingers crossed.*

But it's not about obsessively demanding that our children are highly intelligent in all areas; it is about having an appreciation and awareness that to be truly 'intelligent' no longer just refers to having a high academic IQ. Multiple intelligences, or IQs, include:

» *Linguistic (Verbal) Intelligence:* Language-smart people are good with words, spoken or written. Generally they read quickly, take in information easily and can express themselves in writing. Linguistic IQ is learned by listening, taking notes, discussing philosophy and debating politics, and incorporates reading, writing, spelling, telling stories, explaining, teaching and orating (speaking). Girls tend to score higher than boys.

» *Spatial (Visual) Intelligence:* Spatial-smart people are good with visualisation (constructing things in their mind) and spatial judgement, have a good sense of direction, can see and turn around shapes in their mind's eye, and can read maps. These people can be talented artists, engineers and architects. Boys tend to score higher than girls.

» *Logical (Mathematical or Numerical) Intelligence:* Maths-smart people have analytical minds that are good with logic, abstractions, inductive and deductive reasoning. Logical-mathematical-numerical IQ is learned through logical-numerical activities such as mathematical calculations, pattern recognition, science, economics, chess and computer programming.

» *Lateral Intelligence:* Creative people with imaginative minds who can 'think outside the square' and 'think laterally' to solve problems.

» *Emotional Intelligence (EQ):* EQ incorporates 'intrapersonal' and 'interpersonal' intelligence, along with stress management, adaptability and general mood. A person with high EQ is good at understanding how other people feel and think.

» *Social Intelligence:* The ability to empathise and work with others — decreed by some to be the most important form of intelligence.

» *Kinaesthetic (Bodily Control) Intelligence:* Body-smart people who are adept at performing physical activities, including those requiring fine motor dexterity. Kinaesthetic IQ is learned through bodily activities, such as building and making things, rather than learning visually (reading) or verbally (being told). These people can be our athletes, dancers, actors, surgeons, builders and artisans.

- *Musical Intelligence:* Rhythm-smart people who have tone and pitch. Musical IQ is learned through formal lessons, music composition, playing musical instruments and singing. These people are our musicians and singer-songwriters.

- *Naturalist Intelligence:* Nature-smart people who are sensitive to nature, with the ability to grow plants and nurture animals, including caring for and taming animals. These people are our farmers, zoologists, veterinarians, herbalists, gardeners and conservationists.

- *Intrapersonal (Self-Understanding) Intelligence:* Self-aware people who understand their own motivations and can control their emotions. A high level of this IQ typically shows an assertive, introvert perfectionist who is self-reliant and so learns best when left alone. These are our psychologists, philosophers and theologians.

- *Interpersonal (Understanding Others) Intelligence:* Socially smart people who can communicate well with others. A high level of this IQ typically shows itself as a sensitive extrovert, who has empathy for others' feelings and motivations, and learns best working in a team. These are people who can be responsible for others, such as our social workers, managers and politicians.

- *Existentialist Intelligence:* Universe-smart people who have the ability to ask profound questions and reflect about life, death and ultimate realities.

- *Spiritual Intelligence (SQ):* This is becoming a formidably popular term. SQ incorporates self-esteem, creativity and gratitude.

- *Fluid Intelligence:* The ability to see, interpret and manipulate relations between things — regardless of experience or practice.

- *Crystallised Intelligence:* The knowledge we acquire through experience and putting thoughts into practice.

- » *Disciplinary Mind:* The ability to master the major schools of thought, such as science, mathematics and history.

- » *Synthesising Mind:* The ability to integrate ideas from different fields and to be able to communicate it to others.

- » *Creating Mind:* The ability to discover new phenomena and to clarify problems and questions.

- » *Respectful Mind:* The ability to appreciate the differences among human beings.

- » *Ethical Mind:* The ability to fulfil one's personal responsibilities as a human being.

- » *G-type Intelligence:* An overall general intelligence of perceptual organisation, working memory, processing speed, verbal comprehension and the ability to overcome distraction.

I would like to build on this base with four additional intelligences our children of today must possess:

- » *Environmental IQ:* Today, 'environmentalism' is no longer just the work of activists, as it has become an everyday concern for regular people who are 'going green'. Our children need a core appreciation of the major environmental issues, especially global warming.

- » *Cosmopolitan IQ:* Today, we live in a multicultural and multi-ethnic world, where globally five out of six people our kids meet will be religious, and two out of three won't be Christian. Our children today need a sophisticated broad-based understanding of the major traditional religions of the world.

- » *Old Age-New Age IQ:* Today, we live in a Western world where there is an en masse humanistic movement, renowned for its rejection of dogmatic doctrine and its human-potential philosophies of seeking 'universal truths'. Our children today need a fundamental grounding in the diverse topics of old age-new age trends.

» *Streetwise IQ:* Statistically, half our teens will experiment with an illegal recreational drug, but some drugs can be heinously addictive. Our preteens today must have the street-smarts to know the di erence *before* they become teens — such knowledge saves lives!

TECHNO IQ

These emoji-expressing Alpha Gen-Z's, with their inherited Millennial Gen-Y's YOLO (you only live once) philosophies, are today living in an era where every twelve to eighteen months computers are doubling their capabilities. This exponentially advancing revolution translates to technology estimated to be a thousand times more cutting-edge in just the next decade. Twenty years out from now, technology is projected to be a minimum of hundreds of thousands of times more advanced. Then in thirty years' from now, 'The Singularity' is predicted to have occurred, when biotech, nanotech, robotics and computers will have all combined into such profoundly advanced technologies, that we don't even possess the language or comprehension right now to understand the actuality.

But will our kids cope? Yes they will, and no they won't – for they will react like all the generations before them. Douglas Adams (1952-2001) best known as author of The Hitchhiker's Guide to the Galaxy summed it up so articulately: "Anything that is in the world when you're born is normal and ordinary and is just a natural part of the way the world works. Anything that's invented between when you're fifteen and thirty-five is new and exciting and revolutionary and you can probably get a career in it. Anything invented after you're thirty-five is against the natural order of things."

SUMMARY

> *The Child Genius Syndrome, where the message that every child is the next genius is drilled into us . . . The old codes of perfection, genius and conformity all merge together like a pressure cooker in every parent's gut. Even when logic should prevail, we still feel the pressure of what our children should be.*
>
> Marilynn McLachlan, *The New Parent Code*

Children can no longer be perceived as empty vessels to be filled with academic education — there's just too much to learn! No, these days it's all about learning *how* to learn. To paraphrase Laura Berk in *Infants, Children and Adolescents,* there is unprecedented expansion and change in theory and research, which is ushering in a wealth of new content and teaching tools. And, as summarised by Rosalind Charlesworth in *Understanding Child Development,* today's schooling needs to celebrate diversity, provide multicultural education and unbiased curricula, that respect and incorporate different cultures, customs and languages.

Without question, long gone are the days of grooming young children into being suitably prepared for conventional foreseeable careers. Occasionally, this will happen because of a child's great passion. But generally, it won't. In 2009, the top 10 most in-demand jobs were ones that did not even exist in 2004.

Today, we are preparing our children for jobs that do not yet exist, where they'll use technologies not yet invented.

Chapter Nine

PERSONALITIES! PERSONALITIES! EACH SO MAGICAL AND MYSTICAL!

> *Creative and intelligent individuals are rich in personality traits that can leave parents exasperated or brimming with a mixture of admiration and fascination.*
>
> Marilynn McLachlan, *The New Parent Code*

We all know what *personality* means; well, we think we do — it's, well, who the heck we are! It's the complete set of traits, qualities, mannerisms, temperament and characteristics of our emotion and intellect; it's our individual motives, choices, abilities and interests; it's what makes each of us distinctly unique people — it's our innate wiring. But if you ask a psychologist what personality means, it would seem most of us know squat, as the majority of us are not conversant in the lingo-gibber of psychobabble.

You see, today the modern science of psychology has engorged itself (like all sciences have) into a vast array of sub-disciplines within an enormous assortment of specialised spheres, including psychiatry, psychotherapy, psychoanalysis, psychopharmacology, psychobiology, psychodynamics, psychometrics . . . *yada, yada, yada* . . . and let's not forget sociology and anthropology!

Then there's the multitude of theories about the developmental and psychopathological processes of behaviour and emotions: Arnold Gesell's 'maturational theory', Sigmund Freud's 'psychoanalytic theory', Jean Piaget's 'cognitive-development theory', BF Skinner's 'learning theory' — the list goes on and on.

So when we want to *read* about the topic of children's personalities, we discover there is a correspondingly vast array of books available, which infinitesimally analyse human psychology using diverse, specific theories — but I have *no* intention of this book becoming yet another!

If you have more than a couple of children — or even if you only have one child — there's a good chance they will have quite a different temperament to yourself and, like stripes and polka dots, a mismatch of personalities can cause quite a clash. So it is incredibly beneficial for parents to have a basic grounding in the understanding of different personality types. As Stephen R Covey writes in *The 7 Habits of Highly Effective Families*, 'The key to your family culture is how you treat the child that tests you the most'!

I also love Polly Berrien Berends' gorgeous saying in *Whole Child/Whole Parent*, 'the best thing to read when trying to raise a child is the child'. Properly comprehending our children's personalities empowers us as parents to understand how our kids tick. We can recognise their thinking processes, grasp what hits their hot-buttons, realise what turns them off, become au fait with their innate emotional hungers and, of paramount importance, figure out why your family interacts the way it does.

But to me, summarising personality only with psychology is like summarising physiology only with anatomy — both are intricately related, but hardly the whole story.

PERSONALITY OVERVIEW

One of the most basic groupings of personalities is simply *Type-A* and *Type-B*. Type-B people are unhurried, patient, relaxed and easy going, whereas Type-A people are competitive, achievement-oriented and highly driven workaholic stress-junkies, who find it difficult to relax and are at increased risk of heart attacks. But let's face it, this classification is way too crude for parenting and doesn't particularly relate to children.

Although definitions are constantly being reassessed, these days there is a general consensus between most experts that there are five main *sliding scales* of personality traits. We're all somewhere along each of these sliding scales, and we all need a bit of each personality trait, but few individuals are truly at the furthest extremes, as follows:

» *Openness:* From the imaginative, curious, independent, adventurous, emotional, spontaneous, art lover who prefers variety and new experiences . . . to the conventional, down-to-earth, conformer who prefers routine and resists change.

» *Extroversion:* From the sociable, fun-loving, energetic, enthusiastic, affectionate, talkative, confident and action-orientated thrillseeker . . . to the quiet, low-key, retiring, sober and reserved introvert.

» *Agreeableness:* From the helpful, soft-hearted, trusting, compassionate, cooperative, considerate, good-natured, honest optimist . . . to the unhelpful, argumentative, uncooperative, unfriendly, ruthless, suspicious and sceptical antagonist.

» *Conscientiousness:* From the organised, careful, dutiful, sensible, reliable and self-disciplined hard worker . . . to the disorganised, careless, weak-willed and compulsive dilettante.

» *Neuroticism (Emotional Instability):* From the calm, relaxed, stable, secure and self-satisfied rational being . . . to the worried, insecure, self-pitying, angry, anxious, sensitive, depressed, reactive and easily upset neurotic.

Chapter Nine

FEELINGS AND EMOTIONS

Another significant part of us all that allows us to express our unique personalities is our individual emotional nature — because emotions are the crossroads of our body, mind and spirit. As Irish writer Oscar Wilde said, 'The advantage of the emotions is that they lead us astray.'

In psychological discourse all emotional responses have generally been grouped into eight categories: love, joy-happiness, surprise, disgust, sadness, fear, anger and shame. Within the brain, strong responses, such as anger, are triggered by a structure within the limbic system called the *amygdala*. The frontal lobes, which are the advanced parts of our cognitive brain that enable us to control, resist or hide emotions, take around 20 years to mature. This is why children and teenagers can have such emotional meltdowns and exhibit uncontrolled anger. In other words, their amygdala is generating strong feelings, but their frontal lobes are not mature enough to control the outcome!

Powerful emotions can also, in a millisecond, trigger our rapid sympathetic nervous system's fright-fight-flight physiological response, bypassing our consciousness as a primal survival shortcut to protect us from danger. Our heart rate and respiration increase, blood rushes to our muscles, our pupils dilate, we sweat and our sensitivity to pain drops. At the same time, digestion goes on hold and our mouth stops producing saliva. And it can all happen in an instant!

But I'd like to put a slightly different spin on it all . . .

I believe *emotions* are simply our *unconscious* reactions: they're our buttons being pushed — especially the emotions of anger, upset, disappointment, anxiety, resentment, conflict, struggle or resistance.

I also believe *feelings* are our *conscious* interpretations: they create positive or negative energy and, when living positively, our *feelings* are what enable us to be in the now.

Let's face it, if life was only about the physical, then physical things would make us happy and complete — but they don't. It's emotions — our *reactions* — that create our 'suffering' and our 'joy'. As the adage goes: illusion is a misinterpretation of reality and reality is what's left when illusion is gone. So we need to teach our children (and ourselves) how to control their reactions to their *feelings*, so they can take charge of their inner states of *being*.

PARENTING GOLDEN INSIGHT NO. 7

Teach your child that the universe's only true emotional feeling is *Love*! The rest are man-made.

BOYS vs GIRLS

Without me going into great depths on the subject of gender differences, this book would be incomplete if I failed to acknowledge the obvious gender differences — much of which is determined by genetics.

Male fetuses experience a surge of testosterone that assists their brain's ability with systemising and spatial tasks, and is evident in the common desire of little boys to play with objects that have a definite purpose, such as toy vehicles and weapons, building things with construction sets or collecting items that require classifications, such as dinosaurs, Pokémon cards or Lego. It is this how-things-work part of their brain that can often lead them into an adult enjoyment of maths, science, construction, engineering and chess.

In girls, their surge of oestrogen assists speech, evident in the common desire of little girls to talk and talk, and it can naturally provide them with a much greater capacity to empathise.

Hormone surges during fetal development are also expressed in finger lengths. A simple experiment to determine if your child had a fetal testosterone surge is to compare the length of their ring finger to their index finger. Most girls and more gentle boys tend to have a longer index finger. Whereas, because of the testosterone surge, most boys and more tomboy-type girls tend to have a longer ring finger, which is also commonly found in great mathematicians, musicians and sporting heroes.

Then of course there's the topic of gender training, such as giving girls dolls and boys cars to play with. We all know such 'conditioning' routinely occurs, and debate continues on the subsequent negative, or positive, influences. Research has proven beyond doubt, with multiples it is very possible to have utterly opposite results from, in principle, identical upbringings.

Once puberty sets in there are two main structural differences between the male and female brains. First, in males the highly testosterone-responsive 'medial pre-optic' area of the hypothalamus is more than two times bigger. This is the area where interest in sex and the opposite sex is stimulated. *Surprise, surprise . . . lock away your girls!*

Second, in females the corpus callosum 'superhighway bridge' (a thick band of nerve fibres that connects the brain's left and right hemispheres) is thicker, subsequently improving the ability for communicative empathy and to express emotions. Literally, in females the right brain's assertive, analytical, vocal extrovert can communicate more efficiently with the left brain's perceptive and sensitive introvert, providing an enhanced ability to understand people and put them at ease.

So when it comes to socialising and detecting the subtle nuances of facial expressions and emotions in people's eyes, it's pretty apparent that in general female brains are innately wired more efficiently for communication. *Well, tell us something we didn't already know.* (This also goes a long way to understanding why our guys can have such a difficult time 'explaining how they feel' — they're just not hard-wired to do it so easily.) Research shows that even as early as just three years old, girls are already generally more empathetic than boys, and boys are generally more aggressive. Men use language to transmit facts and data, and patiently take turns to speak. Women use language to bond and build relationships, and mostly love to talk.

As an aside, when it comes to the social skill of reading complex emotions, autistic boys, such as those with Asperger's syndrome, score worst of all — but they may have enhanced systemising skills, and often develop obsessive interests in the unusual.

We know men have a compartmentalised brain and women have a web-like, structured brain, but did you know the male brain's resting tone is 30 per cent active, and the female brain's resting tone is 70 per cent active — *'What you thinking 'bout, Hubby?' 'Nothing.'* It's true!

LEFT BRAIN vs RIGHT BRAIN

In most people the right hemisphere of the brain thinks spatially, taking in sounds and words. It responds to sound, music, rhythm and tone, and is best at recognising shapes, appreciating musical melody, and understanding the sarcasm and metaphors of jokes. The right brain also controls the left half of the body.

In most people, the left hemisphere of the brain makes the actual rational, logical sense of the sounds it hears, it processes language (grammar, writing, spelling), and is best at hearing the rhythm and pitch of music. The left brain also controls the right half of the body.

Scientists generally acknowledge that individuals commonly have one side which is more dominant.

» *Right-brainers:* The holistic, introverted, passive energy of intuition, receiving, creativity and prosody (the poetical intonation and accentuation of language). These are people who have better language skills and enjoy reading and writing, and dealing with 'approximates'. They tend to have better empathetic understanding of people's feelings, better perceptive reading of body language (for example, they can tell when someone is lying), have better social skills and are able to see the 'big picture'.

» *Left-brainers:* The analytical, extroverted, assertive energy of logic, giving and bringing ideas into action, and verbalising the grammar and vocabulary of language. These are people who enjoy systemising, memorising lists of facts, noticing small details and dealing with 'exacts'. They tend to understand shapes, maps, diagrams of how machines work and technical matters. These are also the best brains to have on your Trivial Pursuit team for miscellaneous fact retrieval!

As an interesting aside, in general, everyone either has a dominant right or left hand, but can have an opposite dominant foot — you can write with your left hand but kick a soccer ball with the right.

Whole-brain 'synergetic' brain development activities are really worth encouraging your child to do. These are activities that stimulate the left brain and right brain to communicate together, such as:

» Physical activities like crawling, walking, running, swimming, cycling and trampolining

» Musical activities, including singing, drumming and tap-dancing

» Poetry, reciting nursery rhymes and children's songs

» Learning languages, brain-teasing riddles and maths

» Drawing and origami.

Montessori expert and Kids Talk columnist Maren Stark Schmidt even advises, when a child is emotionally upset or crying, that you can calm the emotional right brain just by 'softly counting' into the child's right ear, because this stimulates the rational and logical left brain functions.

PERSONALITY TYPING — THE BIG FOUR

Interpreting personalities is a very old science. In fact, it was in the fourth and third centuries BCE that the 'father of medicine', Greek physician Hippocrates (460–377 BCE), and the Greek philosophers Plato (427–327 BCE) and Aristotle (384–322 BCE) all theorised that there are four human temperaments, based on the Western astrological elements of air, earth, fire and water.

Five to six hundred years later, in 190 CE, the Greek physician Galen (130–200 CE) defined human personality traits according to ancient medical theory as the Four Temperaments, famously naming them:

- » *Sanguine:* Courageous, socialising, intuitive, emotional, sensuous, innovative, artistic and artisan.

- » *Melancholic:* Intellectual, seeks facts, ambitious, traditional, economic, guardian, judging, antisocial, sleepless and despondent.

- » *Choleric:* Socially confident, opinionated, idealistic, moral, virtuous, receptive, intuitive, doctrinaire and easily angered.

- » *Phlegmatic:* Calm, easy-going, perceptive, unemotional, logical, theoretical, sceptical and rational.

Then, between the fourteenth and sixteenth centuries, the Renaissance period marked the transition of Western thought into the modern era, with its brilliant revival of worldly learning. German philosopher Rudolph Göckel (1547–1628), first coined the word *psychology* during this time.

Only 150 years ago, in the mid to late 1800s, another German philosopher, Karl Marx (1818–83), was one of the founders of this modern social science.

But pretty much from the birth of the Renaissance until the birth of Marxism, empirical science famously emphasized the body and mind over spirit. The irony was that while most of the empirical scientists did not believe (then or now) in any quantifiable usefulness of spirituality, most of the populace they theorised about attended church each week.

Then by the late nineteenth century psychiatrists and psychologists were unsatisfied with the many scientific, 'mechanical' models of understanding human bodies and minds, and found themselves forced to conclude that man is also spirit. Consequently, we now have *transpersonal psychology,* which incorporates spirituality. Transpersonal psychology's most legendary forerunners were Sigmund Freud (1856–1939) and Carl Jung (1875–1961). Soon an explosion of respected scholars all began to classify personalities and interpersonal skills, nearly always defining types into the original four temperaments.

But regardless of which school of thought you refer to, the concept of every person being a unique combination of four basic personality types is a hypothesis now well entrenched in our psychological understanding of ourselves. And these days personal development gurus have more definitions such as:

- » *THE FOUR Ps:* Powerful — Popular — Peaceful — Precise.
- » *THE FOUR Ss:* Self-propelled — Spirited — Solid — Systematic.
- » *THE FOUR As:* Administrative — Active — Amiable — Analytic.

PERSONALITY PLUS

One particularly powerful guru on personality is the public speaker Florence Littauer, who is also the author of myriad self-help books. She has truly become a legend in her own time.

Without doubt, her most famous books are the bestseller from the early 1990s, *Personality Plus,* and her follow-on book, *Personality Plus for Parents.* In these insightful guides to understanding yourself and others, Littauer goes back to the basics, reviving Galen's ancient classifications of temperament. (Of course, people rarely fit exactly into one categorised mould, but are usually some kind of temperament blend.) One of the most valuable tools her books provide is an easy-to-understand introduction to appreciating the personality types of children (and people in general).

With the assistance of the award-winning motivational speaker, author of *Pressing the Right Buttons* and Littauer protégé, the divine 'people interpreter' Allison Mooney, I can provide the following concise personality descriptions:

PLAYFUL (OLD TERM: SANGUINE)

The social personality — likes the fun way.

» *Overview:* The Playful loves interacting and socialising and gets on great with people. They are flexible and love variety. Playfuls can promise the world and get others excited about goals — for that's the friendly thing to do. They see it as almost part of their role to keep people entertained. Playfuls are flexible and love variety.

» *Weaknesses:* Playfuls think in feelings and talk incessantly, so they tend to go with what feels right, being too permissive and bouncing from one idea to the next idea without completing the first. This means you can't always rely on them to get things done, for Playfuls can overpromise and underdeliver.

» *Strengths:* Playfuls are loving, passionate, positive, a ectionate, artistic, perceptive, confident, courageous, innovative, fun-loving, extrovert, popular, open, chatty, the storyteller, cheerful, friendly, personable, even-tempered, generally optimistic, and can become skilled craftspeople who enjoy life. They are the most optimistic and fun-loving child, who does not sulk and does not hold grudges.

» *Interactions:* Playfuls love people, because they have a high need to be close and included, and love being popular, influencing and motivating others — but they can swing between wanting control and needing dependency. This strong need for acceptance drives them potentially into the youth group, sports club, or gang.

» *Parenting:* The Playful child needs attention from all, approval for everything they do and loads of affectionate touch. This child loves goofing off, and really just wants to be accepted for who they are, and will do anything to get this! So the more you encourage, the more they will do. Avoid criticism and anger, because for them that spells rejection. Warning: they have messy rooms! The Playful child must learn commitment and the discipline of finishing their work.

POWERFUL (OLD TERM: CHOLERIC)

The commander–leader personality — likes their own way.

» *Overview:* Powerfuls are dominant and strong — they are the extrovert equivalent of the Precise. They relate to others on their own terms, and base decisions on their own opinions. This is a strong-willed child!

» *Weaknesses:* Powerfuls can be stubborn, dogmatic, dominant, judgemental, arrogant, bad-tempered and easily angered. Powerfuls want to be close to others, but also desire control, so can step on and 'use' people. They don't understand that being too direct, without grace, can hurt.

» *Strengths:* Powerfuls are great at getting things done, for they are decisive, receptive, intuitive, idealistic, morally virtuous, serious and are confident interacting socially. Powerfuls are high achievers who love to lead and receive loyalty from their 'troops'. These children have the greatest potential for future leadership!

» *Interactions:* They have a low tolerance for control by others. Powerfuls get frustrated by Peacefuls who don't seem to want to get things done right now — but this relationship can work as Powerfuls tell people what to do, and Peacefuls do what they're told.

» *Parenting:* The Powerful child needs a sense of control, and wants appreciation and credit for work well done. They like a fast-paced, stimulating and challenging environment. The Powerful child must learn not to be too bossy or argumentative.

PRECISE (OLD TERM: MELANCHOLIC)

The intellectual personality — likes the right way.

» *Overview:* Precise types come into the world with intensity written all over their faces. They think there is a right way to do everything, and want everything done that exact way. Precises are traditional deep-thinkers who internalise everything. They enjoy assessing and analysing facts, such as economics, and evaluating positives and negatives to reach a conclusion.

» *Weaknesses:* Precises are somewhat antisocial or less social, so their judging-guardian nature can turn them into self-contained loners who are despondent or depressed. Precises can also have unrealistic expectations of themselves and others (the perfectionist), and can end up paralysed by their own over-analysis.

» *Strengths:* Precises have high standards, are orderly and creative, and desire to solve everything. They are fantastic planners and great at making sure things happen, characteristically by making lists and working through them point by point.

» *Interactions:* Precises may have a low need to be close to others, a low tolerance of control by others, and a high frustration level with 'flitty' Playfuls — but they are respectful of other people.

» *Parenting:* The Precise child needs to be shown sensitivity to their feelings as they can easily wound and scar; they need reassurance. They are great students, but can only work well when things are neat and tidy. They love having space to be alone and moments of silence away from other people. The Precise child also needs structure and clear directions, and does not like sudden changes. The Precise child must learn flexibility and optimism.

PEACEFUL (OLD TERM: PHLEGMATIC)

The diplomatic–neutral personality — likes any way.

- *Overview:* Peacefuls are sensitive, caring and relaxed, but seem unexcitable and indifferent. They try not to make decisions, and generally go for the status quo. This is the low-energy and easy-to-please person.

- *Weaknesses:* Peacefuls can be resistant to change, sceptical or lazy, with their shy personality inhibiting their enthusiasm. In fact, their unexcitable personality, indecisiveness, flat indifference and almost 'absence' of temperament can really frustrate people.

- *Strengths:* Peacefuls are good administrators who are accommodating, unemotional, consistent, reliable, dependable, kind, compassionate, observant, affirming, theoretical, logical and rational. Peacefuls are generally self-confident, and don't mind socialising, or not.

- *Interactions:* Peacefuls are calm, agreeable, great listeners and people warm to them. They are good at making friends, are loyal and tend not to actively upset people.

- *Parenting:* The Peaceful child loves problem-solving and thrives in a slow, consistent, unstressful, peaceful and quiet environment, with a steady work pattern. They want to be loved by everyone, and look for appreciation. When the Peaceful feels valued for their self-worth, this gives them self-respect. They also need time to consider and respond to questions. The Peaceful child must learn to be assertive.

We also see the four personalities in lots of children's stories. In *Winnie the Pooh* there is phlegmatic Pooh, sanguine Tigger, melancholic Eeyore and choleric Rabbit. In the Charlie Brown cartoon strip there is phlegmatic Charlie, sanguine Snoopy, melancholic Linus and choleric Lucy.

A wonderful tool to help children understand their own unique personality traits is Gary Smalley and John Trent's book *The Treasure Tree*, featuring Giggles the playful otter, Honey the peaceful golden retriever, Chewy the precise beaver and Lance the powerful lion.

PARENTING GOLDEN INSIGHT NO. 8

Understand your child's personality type:
Playful? Powerful? Precise? Peaceful?

PERSONALITY TYPING — THE SIXTEEN

Fascinated with Carl Jung's work on the four personalities, the mother- daughter team of Katharine Cook Briggs (1875–1968) and Isabel Briggs Myers (1897–1980) developed one of the most well-respected personality typing systems, which is known as the Myers-Briggs Type Indicator (MBTI). Today it is used to test more than two million people each year. The MBTI system is based on four pairs of opposing 'preferences', creating 16 possible personality combinations, summarised as four-letter codes. Of course there is no right or wrong combination, as the world needs the skills and abilities of all 16 personality types. This style of personality typing is currently popularised in the bestselling book *Nurture by Nature,* by Paul D Tieger and Barbara Barron-Tieger.

With the assistance of my wonderful colleague Sue Blair from Personality Dynamics (inventor of The Personality Puzzles), we have put together a summary of the four preference pairs and related them to children:

HOW WE ARE ENERGISED

» *Extroverts:* **E** children have outward energy; enjoy social situations, variety, and action; are expressive and enthusiastic; and speak before they think. These children are energised by social interaction.

» *Introverts:* **I** children have inward energy; enjoy waiting, watching and concentrating on one thing at a time; are private and reserved; and think before they speak. These children are energised by their internal world of ideas, thoughts and feelings.

HOW WE GATHER INFORMATION

» *Sensor:* **S** children are realistic, practical and literal. They notice facts and details, play at a steady pace and ask 'what' questions. These children like real toys that imitate life, enjoy games with rules and accept step-by-step directions.

» *Intuitive:* **N** children are creative, imaginative and complex dreamers. They notice meanings and see possibilities and play in bursts of energy. These children may play with toys in original and unusual ways, enjoy make-believe fantasy games and are interested in how things could be.

HOW WE MAKE DECISIONS

» *Thinker:* **T** children are tough-minded and analytical, making decisions using their logic and objectivity. These children value competency, speak with honest clarity, want praise for independent achievements and are upset by unfair injustice.

- » *Feeler:* **F** children are warm, sensitive, tender-hearted and empathetic, and make decisions using their feelings and values. These children care about relationships, speak with tactful diplomacy, want praise for cooperative contribution and are upset by disharmonious conflict.

OUR FAVOURED LIFESTYLE

- » *Judger:* **J** children are organised, responsible and productive. These children prefer a structured, ordered, predictable world, where they can make plans and decisions, and finish projects.
- » *Perceiver:* **P** children are flexible, curious and playful. These children prefer a world with unlimited possibilities, where they can impulsively experience play without rules, and adaptively go with the flow, starting a multiple number of projects from which they are happy to be distracted.

A common question is: 'How early can I detect my child's personality?' The most accurate answer is unhelpfully vague: 'It depends'. As with walking and talking, there is wide range of 'normal'.

Extroversion and introversion are usually easy to spot from a very young age, even in infants and toddlers, as well as the judging and perceiving temperaments. However, the other two preferences describe mental processes that may take a little longer to accurately detect.

Very generally speaking, and if you know what to look for, by the age of six you could have a good grasp of your child's personality, and by 12 it should be quite clear. But even the experts can get it wrong and even some adults can take a long time to assess and discover their own true personality type. When looking at your children, be open to the fact that you will see all personality preferences at various times, but a closer look will allow you to see behaviour patterns emerging.

Other great books on the topic include *Motherstyles* by Janet P Penley and Diane Eble, which looks at personality type to discover your parenting strengths; *The Developing Child* by Helen Bee and Denise Boyd (from the My Development Lab series); *People Types and Tiger Stripes* by Gordon Lawrence, a practical guide to learning styles; and *Effective Teaching, Effective Learning* by Alice Fairhurst, which makes the personality connection in the classroom. What will probably dictate how deeply you investigate personality type will be either how 'easy' or 'challenging' your individual children's dispositions are, and your own personal curiosity about the children in your care. It can be easier to parent children who are similar to you and harder to parent those who are different. Having a reliable framework to describe personality is a powerful tool when communicating with anyone, but especially helpful within your own family dynamics. Remember, your parenting style also reflects your own personality!

PARENTING GOLDEN INSIGHT NO. 9

Consciously embrace and demonstrate tolerance to all children's personalities different from your own . . . there is no 'normal' as we are all uniquely different!

NEURO-LINGUISTIC PROGRAMMING

Neuro-linguistic programming (NLP) teaches that every person works in one of three internal mental processing modalities (patterns). That is, we are all either *Visual, Auditory* or *Kinaesthetic* learners.

These thinking-learning styles are associated with our main sensory language and they can be fairly easily identified by observing where our eyeballs flick to when we are *thinking*. For Western society's right-handed people the three types of thought processing generally are as per below (the opposite applies to left-handers):

» *Visual:* These people learn best by seeing things, and when they're thinking their eyes flick upwards to the left or right. They relate best to visual words, such as saying 'I *imagine* your point of *view* and *see* the *picture*.'

» *Auditory (or Aural):* These people learn best when listening to someone explain things, and when they're thinking their eyes flick sideways left or right. They relate best to aural (sound) words, such as saying 'I *hear* what you're *saying* and get your *message*.'

» *Kinaesthetic (or Practical):* These people learn best with the hands-on experience of doing things, and when they're thinking their eyes flick down left or right. They relate best to kinaesthetic (touchy) words, such as saying 'I *grasp* how you're *feeling* and I'm very *touched*.'

To work out what internal-processing modality your child operates in, you can simply ask them what happened at school today, or ask them what they might like for dinner on Friday — simply observe where their eyes flick to when they're 'thinking'.

Once you know what main modality your child identifies with, then you are better able to make yourself more clearly understood, simply by speaking in *their* lingo, and assisting them with their best learning style — be it by sight, by explanation or by experience.

Knowing even more about NLP can become an immensely practical parenting tool, too. When you're wondering, for example, if your right-handed Visual child is telling the truth, watch to see if they flick their eyes to up-left (remembering) or up-right (imagining)! But don't distort this theory by teaching children that they are one particular category, and therefore unable to learn under non-preferred modalities — that's drivel. We have a full range of senses, and we learn from all of them!

Chapter Nine

LOVE LANGUAGES

Dr Gary Chapman, associate pastor, radio-show host, marriage and family-life consultant, and author of the bestseller *Five Languages of Love*, originally taught couples how to discover and speak their spouse's 'love language'. He then teamed with Ross Campbell, associate professor of paediatrics at the University of Tennessee College of Medicine and author of the bestseller *How to Really Love Your Child*, to create a 'bible' for understanding your child's 'love language' called *The Five Love Languages of Children*.

The revelations in this wonderful book work on the premise that every person expresses (and best receives) their love through one of five primary 'love languages'. When parents use the right 'love language' for each child, then this is shouting to their souls in their clearest loudest voice '*I LOVE YOU!*' To quote Chapman and Campbell, 'It puts fuel in their tanks', and so provides your children with balance, stability and happiness as they develop into responsible adults.

On the flipside, the authors say receiving the incorrect 'love language' can sincerely hinder a child's development, for they will feel a constant gnawing uneasiness that they're unloved, or not loved enough. As Irish playwright George Bernard Shaw said, 'Do *not* do unto others as you would have done unto you — they may have different tastes.'

It is not very difficult to analyse a child's love language. Simply observe how they *give* love to you and others because they'll use the same 'language' in which they prefer to receive love. You can also straight out *ask them*. The five languages are:

» *Physical touch:* These children crave giving and receiving all kinds of physical contact — not just hugs and kisses, they want to sit on your lap when you read them a story. If your own love language is not physical touch, then you may need to break down your own physical barriers (get out of your 'comfort zone') to be able to initiate touch.

» *Words of affirmation:* These children crave giving and receiving words of affection, appreciation, praise and encouragement (not flattery). This powerfully instils love in them and gives them courage. To quote Gary Chapman, 'Such words are like a gentle, warm rain falling on the soul; they nurture the child's inner sense of worth and security.'

» *Quality time:* These children crave giving and receiving undivided, focused attention. It doesn't have to be a special event, they just need our time, because our presence is the present they seek. It tells their soul, 'I make time for you because you are important to me.' Bedtime can be a particularly perfect opportunity for quality time by having an evening ritual of a conversation sharing the day's thoughts and feelings, with plenty of eye contact.

» *Gifts:* These children crave giving and receiving of gifts, because for them a gift is a powerful symbol — but not gifts that are 'bribes', 'thank yous' or 'paybacks'. It's also not about materialism or vanity, or giving lavishly to impress that counts. It is all about giving a gift sincerely, especially ones given for no reason. It is about giving with grace, as a tangible extension of love.

» *Acts of service:* These children crave giving and receiving physical and emotional acts of loving service (not parental 'slavery'). So they really appreciate you, say, fixing their bicycle tyre or mending their dolly's dress — gifts of service given freely with no strings attached. Having a parental role model for giving acts of service is also extremely empowering for these children, such as the family helping at a charity fundraiser, or Dad coaching the soccer team, or Mom being on the school committee, or Mom and Dad being lovely hosts to visitors — these are all great treasures for this child.

Chapter Nine

PARENTING GOLDEN INSIGHT NO. 10

Identify your child's 'love language' and use it!

BIRTH ORDER

The influence of birth order is one of those 'pop psychology' topics on which experts tend to adamantly disagree. Does being the first born, second born, third born, eldest child, baby of the family or only child have any effect on us? Logically it must. Does it make any difference to our later development? Perhaps not. Does it influence the development of our personality? Probably so. I certainly believe that a child's position in the family structure (hierarchy) does contribute to defining them as an individual.

Birth order is also a topic that can have particularly complex dynamics, such as the familial intricacies of twins, adopted children, all-girl families, all-boy families, divorce, blended families, only boy among girls, only girl among boys, long age gaps between siblings — and rare as it's becoming there's also the family dynamics beyond just *three* children! I believe birth order must have an impact on personality, because every action has a reaction, and every cause creates an effect. This doesn't imply that the impact is necessarily negative.

There is, however, certainly a dominant theme of personality characteristics for each birth-order position that researchers generally agree on, which is interesting to consider. Also interesting to note is that birth-order behaviours tend to operate only within the family setting, and away from home the traits are less noticeable.

ONLY CHILD

» *Natural positives:* Scheduled organiser; confident and self-assured; thorough perfectionist; stable and ambitious; obedient and dependable; considerate and accommodating; busy goal-orientated list-maker; logical straight-thinker; well-read problem-solver; craves ethics and freedom.

» *Potential negatives:* Self-centred if they are the parents' 'centre of the universe'; critical perfectionist; inflexible; worrier, stress-junkie, gets frustrated; anal busy-busy list-maker; self-righteous; too serious; overly emotional.

FIRST CHILD

» *Natural positives:* Take-charge leadership commanding respect; compromising, compliant, cooperative team player; thorough perfectionist; scheduled organiser; ambitious; competitive, goal-orientated list-maker; sensible, logical straight-thinker; well-read problem-solver; craves loving relationships.

» *Potential negatives:* Feels excess guilt; aggressive; can be bullied; critical perfectionist; inflexible; overly stresses; anal busy-busy demanding list-maker; self-righteous; too unemotionally serious.

MIDDLE CHILD

» *Natural positives:* Unspoiled, realistic and practical; emotionally strong; makes and keeps friendships; independent; friendly, pleasing and helpful; can compromise and mediate; intensely sympathetic and compassionate; evaluates and compares; diplomatic peacemaker; gives constructive criticism; trustworthy; self-disciplined determination; craves discipline; devotionally sacrificing.

» *Potential negatives:* Rebellious; cynically suspicious; overly worried about o ending; critically aggressive; feels inadequate or vulnerable; stubborn bullheadedness; deceiving; avoids confrontation for peace at any price; embarrassed to ask for help.

YOUNGEST CHILD

- *Natural positives:* Likeably charming and fun; relate well socially; independent hard-worker; analytical thinker; risk-taker; persistent tenacity; willing, affectionate and giving; caring, understanding and empathetic; loves giving and receiving 'warm fuzzies'; genuine and uncomplicated; funny and entertaining; craves the spiritually mystical.

- *Potential negatives:* Manipulative or flaky; too talkative; pushes people too hard; gullible or impulsive; absentminded airhead; secretively withdrawn; easily angered; self-centred ego.

SCHOLASTIC EDUCATION STYLES

All parents are aware of the impact schooling and education have on children's future prospects and happiness. Some of us have wonderful memories of our school years, others of us look back with anger and resentment. As the theoretical physician Albert Einstein said, 'It is a miracle that curiosity survives formal education'.

As parents, the choices of educational style begin during the early preschool years, with more decisions to be made at primary and again at secondary school levels. Sorting through the labyrinth of educational systems and philosophies is a daunting task for any parent and often it has to start very early when choosing between:

- *Play centres* — managed and run by parents.

- *Community crèches* — not-for-profit centres run by trained staff, providing inexpensive, usually half-day care.

- *Home-based care* — such as Barnados, Amanda's, Porse and Jemma's, with maximum of four children.

- *Daycare* — generally privately owned businesses providing 7am-6pm childcare, from newborns to five-year-olds.

- *Kindergartens* — inexpensive government-run institutions which, depending on local demand, may only be able to accept children from four years of age.

» *Preschools* — generally privately owned operations o ering half-day and full-day education, geared especially to three- to four-year olds in preparation for primary school.

I appreciate, at the end of the day, what all parents want to know is simply: *What is the best education for my child?*

The question sounds simple enough, but in reality it can be a complex question that requires an understanding of the individual child and the education options available, combined with personal parental philosophies. Other more practical considerations also need to be made, with finances playing a big part, as does location. There are also national regulations and examinations to be considered.

Schooling options fall under four main umbrellas, and each of these has many subsets. Your child's success will be influenced not only by the type of school you choose, but also the quality of relationship you have with the school and each individual teacher they have.

With the assistance of my girlfriend, fellow author and Mums On Top website creator Marilynn McLachlan, let us summarise:

GOVERNMENT (STATE) EDUCATION

This form of schooling is the one that is most familiar to most people. In the West all children have a right to free education, and the government provides for this right with state education. Run by the local Ministry of Education, it goes from public kindergarten right through to secondary school.

The government writes the national guidelines for schooling, and these can vary according to where the school is located, such as its decile zone. This is traditional schooling, with a set number of days' attendance per year and qualified teachers.

INDEPENDENT (PRIVATE) EDUCATION

Independent education, alternatively called private, is based on individual groups that have formed a school focused on a particular belief system. Some are state-integrated, so charge reasonable fees and work within government education guidelines, such as Catholic schools. Some are totally independent, so charge expensive fees, and are able to completely dictate the type and quality of teaching, school policies, organisational and educational expectations and implementation.

Independent schools have long had a reputation for providing a superior education for their students. This is generally accurate as they consistently show higher grades in national testing systems than their state school counterparts. With their higher levels of autonomy and competitive philosophies to drive success for their students, these schools are reliant on their successful reputations to charge medium to high fees.

Unlike government schools, there is usually also no traditional area of 'zoning', dictating the students who can attend. This means instead testing and interviews — sometimes rigorous — are often carried out prior to a student's acceptance into the school. While this does encourage elitism, it also means the school can carefully select the quality of students.

Many of these schools provide education from the beginning of primary school right through to the end of high school. Children may enter or leave at various times, but most parents choose to keep their child at the school throughout their learning career.

With a variety of teaching methods, many resources and high expectations, these schools can typically provide some of the best opportunities for educational success. Knowing this, many parents are prepared to pay the financial price. These schools generally work very hard to build a school environment that is challenging, positive, nurturing and supportive.

ALTERNATIVE EDUCATION

Alternative education, as opposed to private but conventional independent education, differs in its overall philosophy, which shapes the environment, curriculum and day-to-day life of its students. There are many, many different forms of alternative education, but we will discuss only two here.

MONTESSORI

The Montessori approach, named after its founder, clinician Maria Montessori, began with the establishment of 'children's houses', or *case dei bambini*, in the slums of Italy in 1907. Montessori later studied anthropology and psychology in order to work with so-called 'normal children', and then published her first book, *The Montessori Method*, which clearly showed her scientific approach to childcare. Her subsequent books made her ideas even more accessible to parents and teachers alike.

In understanding this method, Montessori's achievements must first be appreciated. She sought to understand children, particularly 'poor' children or children who were thought to have less intelligence than others. Because of her success in changing these children into competent, independent and inspired learners, experts from around the world visited her children's houses to see her philosophy in action.

The basic principles synonymous with Montessori are outlined below:

> **The teacher is a skilled observer — a 'non-teacher' or 'directress'**

Montessori believed that too often adults impose their ways and ideas on young children, leading to a suppression of their natural desire for independence. Hence, observation was her teacher's main 'tool'. Being skilled at observation, the teacher detects minute details of individual student needs, and seeks to respond accordingly. Her primary role is to prepare the child to learn according to natural laws — a sequential process, but with time variables. The role of the teacher, then, is to facilitate the organisation of work.

The environment is essential

A visit to a Montessori early childhood centre or primary school reveals a different kind of environment than is found in more traditional schools. Items are in baskets, colored mats are available, and there are a range of activities in maths, language, motor skills and knowledge, such as geography and physical science.

Montessori placed great emphasis on the importance of the environment, maintaining that order, cleanliness and category enable the child to respond to an auto-education, meaning that they rely on their own interests and abilities to learn. Her schools, however, were not to be restricted specifically to her houses, as financial circumstances and opportunities differ between groups and individuals. Basically, she wanted people to do the best they could in their given circumstances.

The activities are not 'toys'

Montessori preschools are not filled with random toys but a series of carefully tested and chosen activities that have associations with practical life. For example, you will not find plastic dolls or tea sets, as these children learn to set proper tables, and to care for their environment using 'real' objects. Montessori did not believe in 'dumbing down' children; she believed that children want to learn and want to become independent, and that adults are merely insulting them by controlling them. The emphasis is on liberty for the child.

Modern Montessori

There are schools of thought that believe the 'exact' Montessori apparatus must be used, while others embrace more modern technologies, such as computers. You will find, on visiting Montessori preschools and primary schools, that the essentials remain consistent: the teacher is the observer and organiser of work; the environment is ordered and clean; and the philosophy for the child is 'teach me to do it myself'.

STEINER–WALDORF

Rudolf Steiner, the founder of anthroposophy, created a system of education which is based on 'universal human values, educational pluralism and meaningful teaching and learning opportunities'. The first school was opened in 1919 in Germany for children of the employees of the Waldorf-Astoria cigarette factory. Steiner himself was a philosopher, sociologist and educationalist, and highly spiritual.

The integration

In a Steiner–Waldorf-style school, each age and stage of a child's development is to be thoroughly enjoyed and experienced, from kindergarten through to secondary school. Each stage consists of academic, artistic and social aspects, otherwise known as 'head, heart and hands'. These areas are integrated into all aspects of learning.

Steiner said, 'The need for imagination, a sense of truth and a feeling of responsibility — these are the three forces which are the very nerve of education.' As such, much emphasis is placed on heritage — folk tales, myths and legends, history, poems, and music and games. It is in this context that the more traditional subjects, such as reading and maths are taught.

The Waldorf teacher

The second concept regards teacher/child interaction which, according to Steiner, is 'That which passes from soul to soul'. As such, relationships are highly regarded in a Steiner–Waldorf school and there is a massive emphasis on filling any learning with feeling.

There are three golden rules for teachers within a Steiner–Waldorf school:

» To receive the child in gratitude from the world they come from

» To educate the child with love

» To lead the child into the true freedom that belongs to man.

Through working closely with other teaching staff, parents and the child, the teacher's aim is to develop in the child a genuine love of learning. There is no rush to push a child into 'adult matters', and reading, for example, does not begin until age seven.

The curriculum

Day-to-day learning and experience is dependent upon the age of the child. Steiner believed that children seven years and under should have their imaginations nurtured, and as such free and creative play is the emphasis for this age group. The environment is carefully chosen using natural items that allow the children to create and play with active imaginations rather than with toys that tell them how to play. All equipment is scaled to the child's size and children experience a wide range of house-and-garden-type activities, such as gardening, cooking, looking after animals and building. Artistic skills and awareness are developed through the use of beeswax, clay and watercolor paints. At all times, rhythm and structure based on the day, week, season and year is paramount.

For seven- to 14-year-olds, the main difference from a traditional school is that the child will stay with the same teacher throughout these years. At all stages, imagination, art and feeling are used to provide depth of experience and learning.

HOME-SCHOOL EDUCATION

Home-schooling, or home education, is when children are educated at home, usually by a parent and is often conducted with the assistance of a Correspondence School, which supplies the curriculum, or the parent might work with an 'umbrella' school.

Home-schooling in many countries is a legal alternative to school, though laws will vary from place to place. In some locations, families must use an approved curriculum to be legally entitled to home-school their children. Home-schooling is becoming increasingly popular, and parents have many and varied reasons for choosing to do so. These include:

- » Higher academic grades
- » Controlled socialisation
- » Dissatisfaction with the public-school environment
- » Religious reasons
- » Children with special learning needs
- » Greater control over character and value development.

Home-schooling, just like traditional school, varies in its approach and materials, depending on finances, parental philosophies and the needs of the child. Approaches include Montessori and Steiner but also:

- » *Unschooling:* A curriculum-free philosophy, based on the idea that children are always learning and learn naturally.

- » *Classical education:* A curriculum founded upon education from Ancient Greece to the Middle Ages. This includes Charlotte Mason (a schooling methodology using 'living' books, narration, poetry, history and nature), Trivium (classical focus on grammar, logic and rhetoric) and Quadrivium (the Four Arts of arithmetic, geometry, music and astronomy).

- » *Theory of multiple intelligences:* This curriculum uses the full spectrum of intelligences as advocated by Howard Gardner (see the introduction to Section Three of this book).

- » *School at Home:* The curriculum is the same as that which the child would receive in a school. It uses a correspondence school or delivered curricula.

- » *Unit studies:* This is when a child works through a topic in an in-depth manner, across all curriculum areas.

- » *Online education:* The internet has opened up numerous opportunities for home-schoolers to access a wide range of resources to plan and implement their own home-school curriculum.

EDUCATION BUZZ WORDS

It is handy for parents to understand some of the popular educational jargon. These include:

- » *Acceleration:* Moving a child up by skipping a class.
- » *Assessment:* A way of evaluating student progress, including teacher-made, national or international tests.
- » *Cooperative learning:* Where students of mixed ability are placed together to complete learning tasks.

- » *Enrichment:* Various programmes to provide extra 'depth and width' to the school curriculum, such as lunchtime classes in dance, drama and art, and school clubs like maths and science.
- » *Gifted and talented education (GATE):* This can offer differentiated, supplemental and/or challenging education for students who have been identified as intellectually gifted or talented.
- » *Inclusion:* The practice of placing students with disabilities in mainstream classrooms — also called 'mainstreaming'.
- » *Individual education plan (IEP):* A written plan for a student's school experience (usually for those with learning, behavioural or physical difficulties) completed by teachers, parents and any other support organisations.
- » *Learning styles:* It is now known that we each have a preferred method of learning (or a combination) that includes kinaesthetic, visual or auditory (see Neuro-linguistic programming modalities, earlier in this chapter).
- » *Personalised learning:* This is simply realising that no two children learn precisely the same way.

Finally, twenty-first-century state education is starting to write syllabuses that take all this into account, such as letting children choose what works for them. This personalised learning is likely, over the next decades, to become the norm of classroom education style. For example, our eldest spent junior college years in experimental independent learning classes (ILC), which cultivated active and creative learning techniques, especially focusing on maths and problem-solving, and our youngest changed at senior high-school from a very traditional old-school college, to a very open-plan and liberally-thinking University-style setting. And our middle child relished seven straight years at a local all-girls Catholic middle-senior high-school. We were blessed to be able to have such choices.

DIVINE DESTINIES

We are all familiar with the fact that most newspapers contain astrological horoscopes, hundreds of weekly magazines contain psychic columns, and that there are many top-rating TV shows featuring spiritual mediums. So, evidently, there is an insatiable desire in ordinary people to learn extraordinary information. In fact, the popularity of reading one's astrological horoscope is so prevalent that even the most conservative and discerning of news publications includes these future forecasts to meet consumer demand.

I get the fact that some people feel they need substantially more evidence to be convinced of anything otherworldly. My aim here is not to consciously teach you the 'right' path towards your own, or your child's, personally fulfilled spirituality. *Man, that's your business!* My task in this book is to give you heaps of basic information, *in a non-judgemental, non-religious, vaguely spiritual* format, so you can continue along your life path with a little more awareness.

Well-documented surveys show that most people do believe in the supernatural, paranormal and occult. Here are the facts in the developed world:

» Four out of five adults believe in God
» Three out of four believe in miracles
» Two out of three believe in heaven, angels and that the soul survives us after death
» Over half believe in haunted houses, UFOs, communicating with the dead, astrology, and that guardian angels protect us
» One in four say they've witnessed a miraculous healing

» One in five say they've heard God speak to them.

So there you go. That's what y'all are saying. Only a minority are studying it, but mystical experiences seem to be very widespread indeed.

I passionately believe everyone is born on this earth to experience a singularly exclusive journey along an individual road (their unique life path, if you will). I also passionately believe that parents have many bright lights illuminating an adjoining pathway to our children's life paths — when we innately know what information to look out for and how to interpret the knowledge. And I believe some of that information can come in the form of divine guidance (or divination) — which remains a hotly contentious and controversial topic.

In the same breath, I must also emphasize that although it may be a soul's destiny to climb certain mountains, and experience particular tragedies and triumphs during an individual lifetime, I do not believe it is entirely predestined. To quote Swedish statesman and former Secretary-General to the United Nations Dag Hammarskjöld, 'We are not permitted to choose the frame of our destiny. But what we put into it is ours.'

However, at the end of the day, I'm not here to debate the viewpoints; I'm just here to contemplate them. Attributable to several wondrous events in my own lifetime, (when the spiritual world has materialised in my own physical world), there is absolutely no convincing me that other realms don't exist beyond the five senses contained within our 3D world. That would be as ridiculous as telling me that I only ever imagined I gave birth to my children.

DIVINATION

Divination is the act of predicting future events, or fortune-telling, through the use of occult knowledge. Anthropology (the study of mankind's physical, behavioural, social and cultural development) has discovered clear evidence of divination since the earliest histories of *Homo sapiens*.

The world's three most popular modalities of receiving foresight from divinely guiding sources are cartomancy (cards, such as Tarot); astrological horoscopes (the influence of stars, planets, the sun and moon); and numerology (the meanings of numbers, primarily birth dates). They are the big three our entire human civilisation has relied upon for umpteen centuries.

Other fairly well-known forms of divination or receiving divine information include palmistry (the palm's lines, marks and patterns); casting (such as using sticks, bones, beans and rune stones); graphology (handwriting); dowsing, using a divining rod or pendulum; tribal inspection of slaughtered animal entrails; I Ching (Chinese hexagrams); scrying (such as crystal ball reading); portents (prophetic omen signs which warn of good or evil); and oracles, which are people, such as priestesses, who can reveal God's answer to questions asked, often in the form of symbolic and enigmatic responses (remember the cookie-baking oracle in the *Matrix* movies).

ASTROLOGY

I have already talked about the popularity of astrology but it's worth thinking about why so many people refer to something so few of them publicly admit to having faith in. Maybe modern society's flippant reading of daily horoscopes is better described as our playful dabbling in divination, or perhaps they are simply another avenue for spirituality to reach the masses . . . then again, maybe not.

Astrology, in a nutshell, is a study that believes the positions and movements of celestial bodies (stars, planets, sun and moon) influence humanity. All ancient civilisations devised prophetic systems of astrology. Today astrological horoscopes remain one of the most popular and oldest forms of divination.

In reality, celestial bodies exert influence over human beings every day, all the time: the moon a ects the tides, and women's ovulation-menstruation cycles are usually 28 days, often in sync with the moon's 28-day cycles. During full moons, many midwives, including myself, comment that more pregnant women's amniotic sacks rupture and more babies are born (especially if the barometer is dropping, predicting a storm!). Considering we human beings are predominantly water molecules and made up of the same molecular material as the rest of the universe, perhaps it's not just within the realm of possibility that the planets influence us, but within the realm of potential logic.

HISTORY

Astrology is the oldest science known to humankind, and is based on mathematical cycles. There are three main forms of astrology: Jyotish Vedic (Indian Hindu), Chinese (East Asian) and Western.

Early European Catholicism eventually outlawed astrology — deeming it sacrilegious heresy, for only the pope could receive divine information. Later, when there was increased interest in astronomy during the Renaissance, astrology made a significant comeback, becoming dominant in the fourteenth and fifteenth centuries when many notable scientists practised it, and astrology and astronomy were almost indistinguishable. But by the eighteenth century, astronomy had separated itself from astrology.

In 1930, celebrating the birth of Princess Margaret, the London *Sunday Express* printed her astrological profile — and so rekindled the public's interest in astrology and resulting current insatiable consumption of newspaper horoscopes. However, today astronomy still views astrology as a pseudo-science, a concoction of synchronous superstition and fluky coincidence.

But globally many, many millions remain staunch believers in astrology's ability to provide a better understanding of themselves and others — I've had multiple clients who wait for their beloved baby's exact birth time before deciding on their ideal name. Surely, if it was all foolishness, then this ridiculed science of divining fate — practised by all the great kingdoms of antiquity, pre-dating nearly all religious sacred writings — would have become historic poppycock! But it hasn't. Instead, its influences continue to be so far-reaching, they impact daily and are felt globally.

THE ZODIAC

The word 'zodiac' is derived from the Greek meaning 'circle of animals'. The 360-degree zodiac is divided into 12 constellations, of 30 degrees each, each represented by a symbol. The sun travels about one degree every day, so travels through one constellation each calendar month and the entire zodiac each year. The zodiac is also divided by the summer and winter equinoxes, and spring and autumn solstices.

Today, Western astrology uses the ancient zodiac names and symbols blended with philosophy originally derived from classical Greece, which in turn was influenced by ancient Egypt.

The signs of the zodiac are divided into four sub-groups:

» *Fire signs:* Aries, Sagittarius and Leo.
» *Water signs:* Cancer, Scorpio and Pisces.
» *Air signs:* Libra, Aquarius and Gemini.
» *Earth signs:* Capricorn, Taurus and Virgo.

Astrology is the study of the position of the celestial bodies and their influence on us, including their relationship to one another, both in the birth chart and when casting a horoscope.

Horoscopes are an astrological forecast of a person's future, based on the position of planets and stars at any given moment, such as at the moment of your birth, or perhaps for the following week, in the case of magazine horoscopes, for example.

Sun signs are the 'star signs' we identify ourselves by, determined by our date of birth. These are said to influence our innermost character and outward demeanour.

Moon signs are said to be equally as important as sun signs, as they represent the outer emotional personality of your 'inner nature'. The moon travels much quicker through the zodiac, transiting each sign in just two-and-a-half days, and completing the entire zodiac every 29 and a half days. A person's moon sign needs to be astrologically calculated in relation to their date of birth. (You can look on the internet to work out your moon sign.) *Rising signs* or *ascendants* relate to the sign rising on the eastern horizon at your moment of birth, and are associated with your appearance, self-image, the way you approach life and the way others see you. As the earth rotates on its axis every 24 hours, it takes just one day for all the signs to ascend over the horizon, and each sign transits for around two hours. Obviously the place and time of birth is critical to calculating this attribute.

Astrology is complex, and includes many other technicalities, particularly the *ruling planets* Mercury, Venus, Mars, Jupiter, Saturn, Uranus, Neptune and Pluto.

You can acquire insight into your own, and your children's, astrological destinies by gaining a little wisdom from the numerous astrological books and websites that are available — and which this book doesn't intend to replicate. Although one could argue that any of the star-sign descriptions could potentially match any child, usually the descriptions are uncanny in their accuracy.

Chapter Nine

BORN ON THE CUSP

If someone is born on the cusp, or border, of an astrological sign their birth date may be listed under two signs. Contrary to the common myth, being born on the cusp isn't a matter of being a mix of two signs. It simply means that without looking at your unique birth chart, it is too close to call which zodiac sign you fall under.

The sun moves into each sign at around the same time every year, with up to 36 hours' difference, depending on where we are in the leap-year cycle. This means that each year the date/time that the sun moves into a sign varies. General horoscopes can't list all the dates for each year, as well as the time zones, so to simplify things they take an average.

In saying that, those born early in a sign are more likely to have at least one of the planets from the sign before, and those born late in the sign are more likely to have planets in the sign after. For clarification, anyone is welcome to email my divine colleague, the astrologer Anne Macnaughtan, at onthecusp@forecasters.co.nz for free verification. And special thanks go to Anne for her assistance and guidance with this chapter.

PARENTING GOLDEN INSIGHT NO. 11

Take time to understand a little of the temperament predicted in your child's astrological birth chart.

ARIES, the Ram (March 20–April 20)

(Children born 18–22 March may have Pisces traits.
Those born 18–22 April may have Taurus traits.)

The Aries child is number one in everything, meaning 'I am', 'I can', 'I will', 'Let me do it' and 'I will do it'. They are strong children, mentally and physically, with bright alert minds. They enjoy climbing, exploring, jumping and touching, and they love action and activity. They seek and need fun and excitement before boredom sets in, which can be demanding on parents and playmates. These on-the-go, active, restless children can border on hyperactive, so they need structured discipline at home.

Aries children have the most fantastic imaginations — which parents can appeal to — because for them life is a big adventure! Don't stifle them by wasting money on expensive toys; instead encourage them to use their imagination. They have a vigorous constitution and an adventurous, impulsive, courageous spirit that will have a go at anything. They are rarely bullied and make good leaders, with others drawn to their confidence and presence.

Aries children can be sensitive, but quickly bounce back. They can be determined and domineering, screaming in rage until a practical solution is found. When you allow the child to cool down by talking out their frustrations, gradually reason will return. Parents may have their patience tested as they justify why they want it, why they will do it, and why they need it. Instead of telling them they can't, it could be better to help them do it. Parents of an Aries child tend to become overprotective, but instead need to train the child to stop, think, then act. It is the wise parent who allows a child to put wood on the fire, under supervision. These noisy, boisterous, self-assertive Aries children like to investigate and need outlets for their energy. Through patient, guiding restrictions (don't send them to their room) they can develop wonderful self-confidence.

TAURUS, the Bull (April 20–May 21)

(Children born 18–22 April may have Aries traits. Those born 19–23 May may have Gemini traits.)

Taurean children can appear to be slow thinkers or learners, but this is a mirage, because once deep-thinking Taurean children learn something, they never forget it. Their greatest gifts are learnt from Mother Nature, and so they generally love nature, including all creatures, visiting parks and zoos, watching plants grow, feeding the ducks and collecting shells. Give them a special place to keep their treasures, and a pet for companionship.

They can appear lazy because they can sit for hours watching a bumblebee, bird or worm — but they love playmates and games that interest their mind and challenge them. Encouraging outdoor activities is important, especially sand and water play, tricycles and bicycles. They enjoy a playhouse or tree-hut because it can be a world of their own for role-playing games, and they can put on a bit of a loud paddy when it's time to pack things up.

A Taurus child has an inner strength that allows them to go on and on, even when they should drop, so it is wise to develop good sleeping habits from a young age. They love food, but at the same time can get into the bad habit of wanting to eat the same thing all the time. It can be a big mistake to allow them to eat whatever they want, and the wise parent will say 'eat your veggies, then you can have a sweet'.

A Taurus child can be passive, loving, giving and compassionate, but they also have a strong stubborn streak that ensures they do things at their own slow, steady speed, and once they've made up their mind, it can be very difficult to alter it. So parents need to earn the respect of their Taurus from the start and clearly explain why they are being punished. A Taurus child has good intentions, even when their actions don't show it.

They can sometimes be possessive and when emotionally upset may cling to a favourite toy or suchlike for comfort. Because they can get a little fixed in their ways, they need to be pre-prepared for changes (such as shifting home, changing school or a new teacher), to give them time to adjust. With communication and loving understanding, they can adapt to change.

When a Taurus child whimpers instead of screams, it's a sign of emotional unhappiness. They have a wonderful warm, affectionate, kissy, cuddly nature, so need lots of hugs and holding. They want to know things in the home are happy, so need to be shown that Mom and Dad love each other. When parents can't demonstrate their love, Taurean children can become introverted, but given love, security and affection, they will respond by giving their all!

GEMINI, the Twins (May 21–June 22)

(Children born 19–23 May may have Taurus traits.
Those born 18– 24 June may have Cancer traits.)

Parents of Gemini children can have difficulty keeping up with them, for they can out-run and out-think most parents! These alert children are easily bored, so Moms especially may need to dish out toys and activities all day long. In extreme cases, Gemini children just want to talk and talk and talk, quickly and loudly . . . it's their greatest discovery when they learn to talk! Set aside some 'chat time' each day.

They are usually happy, bright, full of laughter, cheerful people to have around — and through their changeable moods, parents can discover many interesting sides to their Gemini. They can love 'I Spy' games, storytelling or sing-along sessions. Typically, they can have wiry, fast-moving and slightly built bodies, and at the end of the day they should flop, going out like an exhausted Energizer bunny. But if restless, unhappy or over-stimulated, they can stay awake for hours, so a disciplined routine is important.

Their minds are very quick, so it is a great idea for parents to focus their Gemini children's hands and minds simultaneously. They can work out a puzzle, play a game, read a book and listen to music all at the same time — and still pay attention to conversation on the other side of the room. Boredom can be their biggest challenge, and so parents may need to supply constant interesting action.

The Gemini child can be difficult to control because they can be so changeable — like the wind. So with choices, give them just two, because with too many choices they may not really know what they want. It can be pretty easy from an early age to teach them to share.

For the Gemini to properly pay attention, you need to have their complete attention, such as waiting until no one else is around, putting all their toys aside and saying 'I'm going to talk to you now and I need you to look at me.' And diet wise, to avoid becoming problem eaters, Gemini children do need variety.

Gemini children are often particularly intelligent, and so they can get on especially well with other air signs (Libra and Aquarius) because they are all 'mind' people. They are curious, with a thirst to understand. It is an important milestone when they master the ability to read and write. The Gemini child who is taught not to be cruel or hurtful, and taught to forgive, can be very kind and loving, and will never forget the special things!

CANCER, the Crab (June 22–July 23)

(Children born 18-24 June may have Gemini traits. Those born 21- 25 July may have Leo traits.)

This is the most sensitive sign. When young, Cancerian children are shy, clingy and can withdraw from strangers; it is part of their character to learn to be friendly, open and sociable. Musical interests and fairytales can be a must for them, as they find them soothing. They're not 'clingy', but need lots of cuddles, including a need to occasionally hop into their parents' bed. If there is trouble at home between parents, although they may appear unaffected, Cancer children can feel insecure and can retain vivid memories of such trauma.

Being a water sign, they enjoy water because they find it calming, and can be entertained and amused for hours by playing in the bath, outdoor water-play, washing tea-sets, bathing a dolly or playing with little boats. They have a great a nity with playing outside, and may search out special hiding places.

They can be hoarders with untidy rooms, which can be challenging for fastidious parents. They hate giving up collections of objects, old toys, much-loved clothes, adored dress-up jewellery or other treasures; they can even reject new toys, books or clothes, preferring to stick to their sentimental favourites.

Without kind discipline Cancerians can be critical, bad-tempered or silent when things don't go their way, or they can release a torrent of tears as a weapon to get sympathy. If using 'time-out' discipline, to avoid the crab going into its shell it can be important to discuss the problem with them, or else their negative emotions can build up.

The Cancerian child can become withdrawn. But with a family life that helps them mix with people and encouragement to bring friends home, they can blossom into lovely social people. Cancerian children are able to grow into independent, thoughtful, helpful and a ectionate teens.

LEO, the Lion (July 23–August 23)

(Children born 21–25 July may have Cancer traits.
Those born 21–25 August may have Virgo traits.)

Parents of Leos can find it di cult to accept how strong-willed their child is, but adore their loveable, sunny, warm, outgoing nature, and the courageous way that they'll try anything. Play is essential to Leos, because they need outlets to express their vivid imaginations, such as finger-painting, dress-ups, making up stories and acting them out, or putting on concerts for family.

As they get older, this creative energy and drive to express themselves can be guided into activities such as sports, karate, dancing, singing, cooking, sewing or music. But when expectations seem impossible to attain, Leos can create emotional scenes to recapture the centre of attention. Parents may need to curb their own pride to not push their Leo too far into the limelight.

They can be determined little people who have to have things done the way they want them done, or they roar to demand attention. So parents of Leos need to be aware of their child's potential 'acting', such as using threats like 'You don't love me.' If the actor or actress in the child is allowed to develop into attention-seeking behaviour, then this prince or princess of the limelight can grow into a demanding bully. All that a Leo really needs is to be able to shine and be important in their own adoring family.

Having jobs at school can bring out their leadership qualities and loving, helping and giving nature. Artistic and creative tools, such as paper and crayons, can keep them happy for ages. The Leo child can develop a great following and receive constant invitations.

Never ridicule the Lion's pride as this can create hurt feelings. They need to be respected and learn to respect others, such as learning the lesson of sharing with family and friends. The wise adult gets the Leo child to set an example for other children to follow, because it can be the Leo child's nature to want to assist within the home.

VIRGO, the Virgin (August 23–September 23)

(Children born 21–25 August may have Leo traits.
Those born 21–25 September may have Libra traits.)

The Virgo child can be shy and reserved, too squirmy to cuddle or a cautious little being. However, in reality, they do care and do want to be picked up and made a fuss of, so they can express their loving nature. They like a little giggle and tickles too — but don't overdo it. If you ask them 'How are you?' they may not reply to someone not in their 'inner circle'. But if you ask them 'What did you eat for dinner last night?' or 'What are your favourite toys?' they can reel o the information, because they like to talk.

Privacy is important to them and they can be modest. Living with the stress of nervous tension can bring on bedwetting, tummy upsets, sickness or other 'hypochondriac' tendencies. They need to learn not to fret and worry so much. They can be fussy with their foods, poor at going to sleep and scared of doctors or dentists. They simply need guiding discipline, with a bit of loving pandering, to create positive habits, including eating a balanced diet.

Parents need to develop their Virgo's independence from an early age by making them responsible for certain chores like setting the table or feeding pets. Avoid setting standards too high for them, as it can stress their perfectionist nature. Instead, the parent needs to give coaxing encouragement. Given little tasks, Virgo children are willing and helpful. It is part of their make-up to be neat and tidy, but they can also go through phases where their bedroom is an utter mess – although to the child it isn't disorganised as they know where everything is. Their special toys, clothes, plate or spoon can all be important to them.

The Virgo child can thrive on activity, and loves toys they can manipulate, such as rocking horses, bells, pull-along toys, ride-on toys and push-along carts. Their minds can be busy for hours simply with crayons, paper and shapes (such as biscuit cutters) that they can draw around; a sandbox with measuring cups and jelly moulds for them to make shapes with; or a special interest in insects, bugs, ladybirds or butterflies. They can also especially need to be involved in social activities with other children.

Chapter Nine

LIBRA, the Balance (September 23–October 24)

(Children born 21–25 September may have Virgo traits. Those born 22–26 October may have Scorpio traits.)

Amiable by nature, these children can be thoughtful little people who love to receive special treats and pleasures, and love to give gifts — especially if it's a gift they've made. They can have plenty of playmates and plenty of invitations. It is important for them to be liked, and they should for their whole life have the ability to make friends — they're the 'peacemakers' who can shrink away from criticism or verbal conflict.

Their one trait that shows a lack of confidence is the 'Do you like me?' line. But generally they are an easy-to-deal-with, manageable child, who enjoys smiles from a loving parent or grandparent. Relationships are important to them. The Libra child needs people, especially playmates.

The Libra girl may have a beautifully set out tea party with silent dolly guests, but will also have interesting conversations backwards and forwards across the tea-party table. Key questions from adults during play activities with a Libra child can go along the lines of 'Do you want to . . . ?', 'Shall we do this?' or 'Would you like to try it together?' They can be very sensitive to changes in the parent's voice, and love to please and keep the peace.

Wise parents will also encourage the child's artistic abilities that may lie dormant, because they may need outlets for their creative abilities. This could start with finger-painting, poster-painting or decorating things and move on to interests like drawing patterns, music, dance and perhaps an interest in the heavens, as planets and moons can fascinate them.

The Libra child can leave no doubts about their happiness, sadness, frustrations or joys. When they rebel, their defiant, negative traits can come out, such as cheekiness or temper tantrums, followed by tears. But love and understanding can restore cooperative peace. The Libra child can be a deep-feeling, very sensitive child with a caring personally that ideally is surrounded by an especially loving family.

SCORPIO, the Scorpion (October 24–November 22)

(Children born 22–26 October may have Libra traits.
Those born 20–24 November may have Sagittarius traits.)

Parents can find their intensely loving and inquisitive Scorpio child hard to understand, because their great emotional capacity can be hidden deep within them. They are intense little people who may jump higher on a trampoline, swing higher on a swing or climb the highest tree — they have a zest for living! They have an enormous capacity for understanding because of their sensitivity.

These deeply emotional children can secretively scheme to get what they want. Parents can help their child develop that loving, giving, sharing nature by giving them the responsibility to care for a younger child or pet.

A Scorpio child's docile outward appearance can conceal deep, powerful emotional feelings that eventually come out, such as pent-up stress erupting in anger or tears. They need a happy, carefree childhood, with meaningful interests and important goals to strive for. The key word for a Scorpio's happiness is 'meaning'; they may need to find fulfilment and significance in their hobbies, studies and work.

They can take a while to accept other people, so don't force them; they may tend to have 'love you and hate you' type relationships that are just part of their nature. They can also be a little too quick to gossip.

Scorpio children can find routine good, but can take it to the extreme of demanding the same music, story, food, clothes or playmate over and over again — but this can be overcome with communication. They can become emotionally attached to particular friends, teachers, doctors or other special people.

They enjoy jigsaw puzzles and these can be a great way to teach the discipline of finishing things. They can enjoy books as an avenue for their vivid imagination's wild adventures. They have a natural curiosity about life and death, and they can be fascinated watching the birth of baby animals, such as kittens, rats, mice and butterflies, or the busyness of an ant farm. Give them the most truthful answer possible to their inquisitive questions.

SAGITTARIUS, the Archer (November 22–December 22)

(Children born 20–24 November may have Scorpio traits. Those born 20–24 December may have Capricorn traits.)

The on-the-go, zest-for-life, outgoing, alert and inquisitive nature of the Sagittarius child can amaze their parents, because they are such intensely bright little children with such a lovely, happy disposition. The Sagittarian child needs routine, but also the mental stimulation of varied activities because they do get bored.

They need the freedom to play independently, but also need a watchful eye as they can get over-boisterous, over-excited or over-adventurous. They enjoy dress-ups and their inventive minds love gadgets. They may enjoy the excitement of entertaining, such as having a birthday party, or having a change of scenery by visiting people and places.

At school, boredom should be avoided for these quick-moving, intelligent children. Education should entertain their minds, as they absorb learning quickly. They need a stimulating life, but also need to learn to give and take. They can be naturally gifted as speakers.

They can be born lovers of animals and nature, and willing to give most things a try, as they have an aptitude for games and sports or creative outlets. They can learn well from, and throw themselves into, activities requiring physical exertion because they need to burn o their energy during the day. They can enjoy 'hanging around' adults because older people are like magnets to them and they feel affinities with them — it's almost as if they need the stability and knowledge of adults. They are friendly, but their fresh, cheeky nature of asking or saying almost anything means they can sometimes come across as being a smart alec.

If their need for the freedom to express themselves is restricted, they can become emotionally explosive; they love to express themselves, and frustrating misunderstandings can create outbursts.

They can find it difficult to conform or accept criticism, so using tact, rules of fair play and third-party examples can be particularly effective, such as 'your friend at school wouldn't like that' or 'the little girl down the road wouldn't do that'. The high-spirited, energetic and good-humoured Sagittarian child can be an open, outgoing and assertive born leader, with a flair for the unusual. For them, the world is a fascinating place to live in!

CAPRICORN, the Goat (December 22–January 20)

(Children born 20–24 December may have Sagittarius traits. Those born 18–22 January may have Aquarius traits.)

These are determined children who seem to have enough patience and endurance to achieve what they want to do, even when the going gets hard. They are practical, persevering and constructive in all that they do. The Capricorn child should be given responsibilities from an early age, such as tidying their room, folding clothes or helping with little jobs — but be careful not to let them take on too much because they are so willing.

Capricorn children tend to be quite serious-minded deep thinkers, sometimes loners, and can mature quite early in life. If they are worrying about things in their lives, such as what is going on in the home, they can be prone to depressive moods. They can be insecure around strangers, and may be reluctant to join in with other children and need time to form friendships. They need to be dissuaded against tattling on others, and discouraged from 'parroting' dos and don'ts to others, such as 'wipe your feet' or 'clean up your mess'. Frustration and anger or being teased can bring out the hidden side of their nature, that of hitting out verbally or physically. What they may need is touching and cuddling to bring out their natural responsiveness.

Fantasy and make-believe are not their cup of tea. What they enjoy is animal, adventure and real-life stories. And they enjoy constructive toys, such as a real hammer and nails or a real tea-set or pots and pans or real needles, thread and material — these can amuse them for hours.

The Capricorn child can also particularly enjoy climbing trees, fences, chairs, drawers — whatever. They can find music soothing, and have the ability to become an accomplished player of a musical instrument.

AQUARIUS, the Water Bearer (January 20–February 19)

(Children born 18–22 January may have Capricorn traits. Those born 17–21 February may have Pisces traits.)

You may think you're a well-organised household . . . and then an Aquarian arrives! These unconventional, independent individuals will cutely snuggle up when they need to. The Aquarian child can embarrass their parents as they can have almost no inhibitions — from the stubborn horror of a temper tantrum, to interrupting your conversation for a cuddle, to pointing out to everyone that you're picking your nose, to loudly describing the funny old lady in the shop. On the flipside, they may struggle with a coordinated dress sense, such as constantly having shoes on the wrong feet or T-shirts inside-out or back-to-front.

Don't try to be the heavy parent who harshly disciplines their Aquarian — it only ends in many tears. The best discipline is compromise, such as saying 'Because you have been naughty you cannot play in the sandpit this morning, but if you are good this afternoon, you can play in it later today.' If you need them to agree to something, then simply phrase questions that can't be answered with a 'No'. They may try to hold back their thoughts — but their eyes and facial expressions tell you everything.

Through the discipline of practical chores, they can learn to take on the responsibility of doing things properly. While they may initiate arguments, once they learn to respect the childhood friendships they make, then they can develop long-lasting friendships.

The Aquarian child needs the freedom to be themselves and to 'do their own thing'. The Aquarian child may prefer to play with old 'real' things, rather than toy imitations. They love bits of old clocks or small appliances to invent things with, or bits of old make-up, perfume bottles and old clothes for dress-ups.

Beware: Aquarians love the water — so never leave them unattended near water. They can also be fascinated with and inquisitive about electrical cords, appliances and power points.

An Aquarian is a master of discussion, and will logically present why they should or should not do this or that. If they give the impression of being a scatterbrain — it's all show. They are actually quick on the uptake, and their little eyes and ears never miss anything.

PISCES, the Fish (February 19–March 20)

(Children born 17–21 February may have Aquarius traits. Those born 18–22 March may have Aries traits.)

Like other water signs (Cancer and Scorpio), the Pisces child can be sensitive. They have a loving, caring, sympathetic nature, and like to help when someone is hurt, crying or the underdog. Sometimes when little, they can irritate their parents by being too 'clingy', particularly if they find themselves being forced to participate when they don't want to.

Never label them lazy by saying 'You're not trying', as they will live up to that description. They need to develop positive confidence in their ability to achieve what they want, and gentle, loving guidance can give them the courage to do things.

They enjoy non-rugged outdoor play, and they can love animals of all kinds but may need reminders to feed their pet. Music allows their creative mind to wander, and paper, paints and crayons can keep them creatively amused for hours. The Piscean child enjoys play-acting games, such as dress-ups, and school plays, and acting or singing are a great outlet for them.

When playing, these children live in their own little world. So when they don't hear you, they're not being disobedient, they are just absorbed in their game, a TV show or in a story. They leave behind the physical world for fairytale adventures. Sometimes their own stories can be exaggerated by their imagination. They don't intend to enlarge stories with lies, it is just their dreamy nature.

If they have a disturbing dream, remove them from their room, and even invent a 'good' story to reassure them they are being looked after and don't need to be frightened. These children need a hero or heroine to look up to — a cartoon superhero or clever uncle — who will influence their daydreams.

An angry word can easily bring them to tears, and if another child bullies them, they can be reluctant to retaliate. When frustrated or angry, they may rebel through tears, tantrums or even refusing food. They can find it difficult to find the words to express themselves, and so parents need to be patient.

Being sentimental, the Pisces child can hang on for years to their favourite toy, book or clothing, or hold on to memories of specific happy times. They are the dreamer — the fairy prince or princess — who needs love but also returns it.

NUMEROLOGY

Numerology to mathematics is as astrology to astronomy, and alchemy to chemistry — each was once one indistinguishable half of a complete traditional belief system, and this is still the case in much of the world.

History repeatedly shows mankind has used many and various numerological systems, including the Chaldeans (Semitic people who ruled Babylonia in Mesopotamia, now Iraq), the Phoenician sages (from present-day Syria and Lebanon), the Hellenes (Greek astrological thinkers), the Egyptian priests of Alexandria, the Indian Hindus (Vedic divine knowledge), the Mayans (of Central America), the Chinese (prophetic Book of Changes), the Hebrews (mystical Kabbalah teachings), the early Gnostic Christian mystics; and of course Pythagoras, the 'father' of Western numerology. All these societies had mathematical systems of personal prediction to define man's relationship to the cosmos.

Prior to the Dark Ages, numerology was part of mainstream Christianity too, with the mystical Saint Augustine preaching 'Numbers are the universal language o ered by the deity to humans as confirmation of the truth.' When Catholicism abolished numerology (as it was decreed only the pope could receive divine guidance from God), devout Christian numerologists secretly held on to their knowledge about the sacredness of numbers.

Today in postmodern nations, many Westerners still believe that all divinatory arts are bogus science — yet a growing number are discovering such esoteric knowledge is often uncanny in its accuracy.

Today there are three main recognised formal versions of numerology: the Chaldean (used in this chapter), the Kabbalah (Hebrew mysticism of name interpretation) and the Occidental (Western Pythagorean system). Each provides slightly di erent interpretations because it is understood that no one sacred form of divination can ever provide *all* the answers to understanding ourselves and the world around us.

The Chaldean number system, originally developed in ancient Babylon, is now generally recognised as the most accurate version of numerology known today, with compound numbers (double digits) revealing the 'outer' aspects of a person, and single digits revealing the 'inner' influences — thus enabling a comprehensive blueprint of a soul's destiny.

There are also many, many other intricacies of numerology, such as ruling name numbers, number inter-compatibilities, personal and spiritual year numbers, pyramidal and cyclic numbers of maturity, and birthchart arrows. To be a master of numerology requires much knowledge and can potentially provide much insight.

Of course, as parents, we are never supposed to know every aspect of our children; they are meant to be somewhat of a mystery to us — and to themselves! But as pupils attending this remarkable school called Planet Earth, I believe we always have had, and always will have, access to divine guidance. Personally, I have found numerology to be one of the most easily accessible and accurate forms of divination in assisting parents with illuminating their obscured intuition, and corroborating their niggling instincts.

> NOTE: I must give special thanks to the departed New Zealand psychic-medium Francie Williams for her indirect help with this section. She devoted much of her life to investigating, researching and recording the synchronicities between astrology, numerology, prophecy and many other paranormal topics, and dedicated countless hours to teaching others such profound wisdom, often for nominal financial reward. Thank you Francie and Rex.

Personalities! Personalities! Each so magical and mystical!

MASTER NUMBERS

Master numbers of 11 and 22 denote the person is a highly spiritually developed soul, and 33 represents the avatar (incarnation of god/goddess or embodiment of wisdom) — even though these human master souls can sometimes seem oblivious to their inherent wisdom!

A person *without* an 11, 22 or 33 can also still be a very old wise soul — but these three master numbers point towards an increased responsibility to overcome their lower aspects and live up to their full spiritual potential by recognising and facing up to their unique life journey.

LIFE-PATH NUMBERS

ADDITION OF BIRTH DATE

You can calculate your life-path number by adding together the numbers in your birth date, until you reach a single digit. For example:

23 July 2001 (23/07/2001) = 2 + 3 + 7 + 2 + 0 + 0 + 1 = 15.

15 = 1 + 5 = 6.

Life-Path Number: 15/6

The life-path number governs and symbolises the main spiritual lesson we must learn in this life; that is, our more 'karmic pathway'.

PARENTING GOLDEN INSIGHT NO.12

Compassionately support your child through the karmic life lessons their wise soul has desired to complete learning in this lifetime's Life Path.

---

1 LIFE PATH (10, 19, 28, 37, 46, 55)

Chapter Nine

Individual, adaptability, unity, creation, independence, yang, active and masculine

Confident, bright and happy when positive, 1s are destined to grow through compromising in one-on-one relationships, learning to become a strong, harmonious, aggression-free person. They need a good foundation of childhood discipline and sharing in their first seven years, so they are able to learn to willingly adapt to life's sudden or unexpected changes, and also to help others adjust and harmonise with external circumstance.

MOTTO: Harmony comes from cooperation and compromise!

2 LIFE PATH (20)

Balance, union, receptive, duality, emergence yin, passive and feminine

Reliable, intuitive and compassionate, with a special strength of character, these peacemakers are destined to learn diplomacy and cooperation with other people. For them, life is about seeking out, working with and supporting dynamic leaders who can appreciate the 2s' complementary capabilities.

MOTTO: Desire creates life and other people are the key to learning!

11 MASTER SOUL (11, 29, 38, 47, 56)

Master number, spirituality and metaphysical faculties, intuition, clairvoyance

Sensitive, honest and compassionate, these lovers of refinement have chosen a responsible incarnation to lead mankind in the New Age, but they usually first need to learn to recognise their own potential power for higher purpose.

MOTTO: Listen to intuition and follow creative thoughts!

3 LIFE PATH (12, 21, 30, 39, 48, 57)

Communication, interaction, neutrality, reasoning, power and generative forces

Mentally alert, analytical and purposeful, 3s are destined to grow through their thinking, reasoning and planning capabilities and associations with people (especially family) to gain self-confidence and positive thought attitudes. For them, people are their learning ground.

MOTTO: Stick at it to accomplish your desires!

4 LIFE PATH (4, 13, 31, 40, 49, 58)

Creation, materialism, consistency, solidity, orthodoxy and organising

Orthodox, typically good with their hands, commonly interested in sport and initially materialistic, these 'children of fate' are destined to use their endurance, discipline and practical organisation to face life's confusing, unexpected occurrences. They need to learn adaptability, harmony, patience and love to thus receive awareness, trust, responsibility, recognition and wisdom.

MOTTO: Expect the unexpected — stick at it and keep trying, no matter what!

22/4 MASTER SOUL

Master number, unlimited potential, high spirituality and intense practicality

When aware, the 22 is intuitive and has passion for humanitarian causes, such as welfare. They are the dreamers of good dreams. This highly evolved master soul, with its courage and archetypal emotional restraint, has chosen the highest level of personal responsibility, destined to be the exceptionally gifted teacher, enlightening artistic reformer or outstanding diplomatic leader, because they are capable of achieving the seemingly impossible. 22s need to be guided not by other people's judgements, but by their own feelings and thoughts.

MOTTO: Leave the world a better place by having passed through it!

5 LIFE PATH (5, 14, 23, 32, 41, 50, 59)

Action, pleasure, sensitivity, sensuality and non-confinement

Independent, intuitive, artistic and adventurous, 5s can swing from sullen emotions if suppressed to exuberant emotions if free to sensitively express themselves. They are destined to use their mind's reasoning abilities, life experiences and constructive communication to gain deeper understandings of life, and thus command a positive attitude.

MOTTO: Wisdom comes from stability and moderation in all things!

6 LIFE PATH (6, 15, 24, 42, 51)

Reaction, flux, responsibility, perfection, harmony and balance

Creative and loving, these tolerant, unselfish and fair 6s have brilliant perceptions that feed creative power and are destined to work with and for other people. For them, they need to learn to cheerfully face responsibilities without anxious worrying.

MOTTO: Rewards come from giving love and affection!

33/6 MASTER SOUL

Promise of assistance, positions of authority, true divine love, spiritual protection and healing talents

The 33/6 is a sign of a highly evolved spiritual soul — however, 33s need to learn the lessons of the straight-6 of facing responsibilities and giving service to humanity, in order to be given the use of their wonderful spiritual gifts, for true love is overcoming the physical.

MOTTO: Overcome the physical to find the meaning of love!

7 LIFE PATH (7, 16, 25, 34, 43, 52)

Experience, conscious thought, mysticism, psychic, magic and the teacher

Assertive, philosophical, anti-discipline and the helpful teacher, 7s learn by personal experience, because they are destined to transcend 'normal' life through sacrifice, as their soul experiences remarkable dreams and takes major steps towards spiritual enlightenment.

MOTTO: Happiness comes from giving love and service!

8 LIFE PATH (8, 17, 26, 35, 44, 53)

Independence, complexity, power, justice, sacrifice and material success

Independent, reliable, self-confident, unemotional, business oriented and with great strength of character and empathy for those in need, 8s are destined to work hard, respect authority and earn money, to learn to use their material possessions wisely, and use tolerance to gain respect. This will allow them to transcend any difficulties in expressing appreciation to others, which in turn creates their own personal happiness.

MOTTO: 'Wrong' values, like 'right' values, bring on the Law of Cause and Effect!

9 LIFE PATH (9, 18, 27, 36, 45, 54)

Completion, responsibility, humanitarian concerns, spiritual and mental achievement

Chapter Nine

Responsible, honest, artistic, ambitious and typically with a serious attitude to life, 9s are destined to be humanitarians giving service in the a airs of mankind by guarding our cultural heritage as the reforming philosopher. They grow through misunderstandings — especially with home and family — to learn tolerance, balance, deep compassion and how to translate the idealistic into the practical.

MOTTO: The 'answer' is found through giving compassionately with love and understanding!

DAY-BORN NUMBERS

This is the date of your birth day. For example, if you were born on the sixth day of any month your birthday number is a straight '6', or the thirty-first of any month is a 31/4 (3+1=4)

The Day-Born number indicates the main lesson the soul has chosen to experience in this particular lifetime, it is the spiritual guidance that goes on 'underneath' daily life, and so it is the important wisdom one's soul has come here to learn.

When fulfilling our destiny our role will always somehow incorporate the task of helper, comforter, healer or teacher — for that is *everyone's* ultimate life purpose.

PARENTING GOLDEN INSIGHT NO. 13

Be consciously aware of the Day-Born life experiences your child's wise soul has intentionally chosen for this lifetime — and teach them the necessary skills they'll need.

NO. 1s (born on the 1st, 10th, 19th and 28th)

The stand-up-to-you children

No. 1s can be determined children who don't like being told what to do, for whom frustration turns into a 'paddy' — especially Aries, Capricorn, Scorpio and Sagittarius children — so parents may need to compromise. When unhappy, they may show their need for attention! Talking things out can help them settle their minds. Never put 1s to bed upset, as they will stay upset for hours.

Children born on the 1st may need freedom to express themselves and develop intuition. They can seem aloof or detached, but it's just them enjoying seclusion, as they work best on their own. No. 10s, 19s and 28s can be outgoing, energetic, well liked, easy to please and adaptable — but they can also appear selfish or shallow, so may need to learn not to waste their life.

Breaking point: When they cannot cope anymore mentally, they cry. No. 1s need a comforting attitude, touch and the chance to cry things out and talk about their challenges.

NO. 2s (born on the 2nd, 11th, 20th, 29th)

The sensitive cry-baby children

No. 2s can be sensitive children for whom a quiet reprimand is sufficient, especially Pisces, Cancer and Scorpio. When they are not coping they will grizzle or cry — this simply means they need a cuddle and comforting words. Harsh words easily give them heartache.

No 2s, 20s and 29s can be naturally light-hearted and happy, and want to be around bright, humorous people. No. 20's can be rebellious, even violent, but discipline and the responsibilities of a family pet can teach caring love. Never put 2s to bed upset, as their emotions register deeply in their soul, especially 29s, and then learning forgiveness becomes difficult. No. 11s can be highly intuitive, which is a valuable tool they need to be taught how to master to avoid exhausting emotional upsets.

Breaking point: They crack emotionally and burst into tears from fear, despair or for relief. No. 2s need to be left alone, then given understanding love.

NO. 3s (born on the 3rd, 12th, 21st, 30th)
The in-their-own-world children

No. 3s can be introverted, quiet children, possibly with 'imaginary friends' as they are natural psychics. No. 3s can also be the bright extroverts and humorous part-time entertainers with an active brain and quick reply. These 3s may need to learn how to appreciate people with more serious personalities.

No. 3s can carry childhood emotional hurts into adulthood, so parental communication is particularly important. They can also be worriers, especially 12s, who take criticism to heart, potentially losing self-confidence — but talking things out can help.

Breaking point: They crack from mental stress, for things play on their mind until they scream. Then they withdraw into themselves and into their own world. No. 3s need tolerance and patience to get things across, and giving them responsibility can bring them back from their withdrawn state.

NO. 4s (born on the 4th, 13th, 22nd, 31st)
The back-to-front children

No. 4s can be introverted, sturdy children with a quiet energy and hidden stubbornness that turns your world topsy-turvy. Tell them not to do it, and they will do it, so a little parental reverse-psychology can be useful. If frustrated or angry, 4s will hit out, and all 4s can be outspoken with the truth, so need to learn diplomacy. No. 4s, 13s and 31s can be practical and capable, but if their life-path number is an even number (especially 4, 8 or 10), they need to learn how to avoid materialistic greed.

No. 22s can be susceptible to dynamic influences in their life, particularly if their life-path number is even (especially 2, 4 or 10) so they need to 'stand on their own two feet' by listening to their intuition. No. 22s can make stupid mistakes and do silly things that backfire, so need to be taught the discipline of doing things the right way. To direct their power constructively, 22s need to have their feet firmly planted upon their destined path.

Breaking point: Can unpredictably crack by becoming quiet or withdrawn, or reacting loudly with their voice. Fours need to be kept warm afterwards, as they can have nervous reactions, such as a quivery voice or shaking legs.

NO. 5s (born on the 5th, 14th, 23rd)

The into-everything children

No. 5s may love to express their feelings — they're talkers! Some 5s can refrain from talking due to shyness or fear, so it's important they learn to chill out and act naturally. Their busy minds seek freedom, and their on-the-go bodies want to explore, climb, experience, natter, ask questions and have a go at anything. They are curious about life, and always will be.

For 5s, learning the discipline to obey instructions is very important from an early age. The 14s' mind can enlarge the truth — but they are not lying, simply unintentionally exaggerating.

Breaking point: When their mind can no longer cope, they will push themselves beyond their limits, overtaxing themselves. No. 5s are impulsive, with reactive, expansive minds, and rebound quickly from stress. They need to talk about fears or traumas to get rid of them.

NO. 6s (born on the 6th, 15th, 24th)

The wrap-you-around-their-little-finger children

No. 6s can be very loving, giving children who are willing to help with little jobs, and they can create love and beauty in the home. No. 6s can be attracted to other children, and have a talent for making friends.

Don't try emotional blackmail on 6s, as they will manipulate you and get around the threat by using loving grace to get out of trouble. No. 6s can also over-dramatise problems with fears and whinging. So they need love and affection when being disciplined, such as words of endearment in front of the discipline. Be particular about teaching 6s personal grooming and tidying up after themselves.

Breaking point: They try hard to overcome difficulties and opposition, taking cheerful responsibility and leadership to uplift others by easing their suffering with sympathy and understanding. Later, when they cannot take it anymore emotionally, the 6s release their tension by tears or swearing.

NO. 7s (born on the 7th, 16th, 25th)

The do-it-my-way children

No. 7s can happily spend hours playing outside in a secure backyard, and can become immersed in the roles of what they are playing, often making realistic sounds. No. 7's can be determined to have things their way once they've decided what that is, because they like to be themselves and do things their own way. But when told how to do things properly, they will eventually heed to the right discipline.

The 7's special influence is to provide life lessons that instil deeper values, particularly affecting the heart, the health and especially the pocket. So, the quicker they learn this, the easier it is.

Breaking point: Being independent, they will rise above their own fears and learn what they need to through personal experience, and 7s need the freedom to do so.

NO. 8s (born on the 8th, 17th, 26th)

The foot-in-mouth children

No. 8s can be emotionally sensitive children, and can find it hard to let hurts go. They can get it in their mind to say something outspoken but then it comes out wrong and wasn't what they meant to say. So 8s need to be taught how to speak with diplomacy in a thoughtful way — otherwise as adults they can be sharp-tongued with their criticism. Eights can be misunderstood, and need parents to take the time to talk with them.

No. 8s can also need times of self-directed mental independence to attain higher self-awareness — moments to get away from being part of a group all the time. No. 26s are the butterflies that flit from one interest or friend to another at a time when they need to establish foundation roots. They need wise, understanding parents who encourage them to finish projects, and to avoid emotional stresses and heartaches.

Breaking point: Prone to emotional see-saws and breakdowns when they cannot cope mentally any more, 8s may need understanding and encouragement to help them cope with their emotions.

NO. 9s (born on the 9th, 18th, 27th)

The I-don't-know-why-I-did-it children

No. 9s can be placid, well behaved, loving, a ectionate, giving and helpful. But when they clash with people, especially in bitter family quarrels, their strong nature can feel threatened, so they will be pushed to defend themselves. No. 9s can enjoy developing personally and increasing their level of responsibility when striving towards improvements for humanity — so long as it is not for the selfish gain of personal ambition.

Although they can mean well, 9s can be misjudged as being smart, cheeky and full of attitude. No. 9s need guidance to discipline their cruel streak and face up to struggles.

Breaking point: When unhappy, 9s can do almost anything to get attention, but this cry for help is simply indicating their need for a ection, sympathy, compassion and understanding.

AT THE END OF THE DAY…

How is it best to communicate to these Alpha Gen-Zs? You don't need to use their 'own language' … just need to simply treat them with respect. (And don't complain that they're always on their phone – coz so are their moms and dads.)

#mamacanusehashtagstookids

SUMMARY — THE BIG PICTURE

We are born at a given moment, in a given place and, like vintage years of wine, we have the qualities of the year and of the season of which we are born.

Carl Jung (1875–1961), *Swiss psychiatrist*

Psychology traditionally describes a child's personality as being acted on by five major influences: their sex (and their society's gender roles); their birth order; their collective culture; their belief systems; and their life experiences. And in recent times Western parents have also accepted the influences from 'nature' (genetics/heredity) and 'nurture' (environment).

Anyone reading this book will soon realise that I clearly believe there is a great deal more going on in this universe we are yet to fully comprehend — in fact, the more we learn, the more we begin to realise just how little we know. The purpose of this book is to begin to fill in some of the missing pieces, to begin to understand *holistically* who our children truly are, from the perspective of the *mind*, *body* and *spirit*, and thus enable us to be better equipped to guide our children.

I believe personality is *far* more dynamic, and that the powerful influences are actually three-fold:

1. GENES AND THEMES

» *The influence of heredity:* Genetically from grandparents and parents.

» *The influence of inheritance:* Spiritually from Karma.

2. NURTURE AND NATURE

» *The influence of environmental surroundings:* From life experiences, including birth order; from people such as family, friends and school; and from places such as neighbourhood, country, culture and religion.

» *The influence of the individual's inner self:* From the spirit's innate personality and temperament, the child's birth date (i.e. numerology and astrology), and the child's given name.

3. EVOLUTION AND REVOLUTION

» *The influence of progression:* As explained in Jag Steward and Andi Mac's DVD *Evolution of Consciousness*, we are each part-way along our own pathway to enlightened peace: complainer, to blamer, to guilty obeyer of authority, to pleaser, to self-improver, to sticker-upper-of-rights.

» *The influence of transformation:* How do we finally free our minds of all the inner suffering, conflict and struggle? By finally realising we are each the one we've been waiting for, all our life.

Don't feel you are alone in the parental plight of struggling to come to grips with your child's personality. We could each of us have a degree in psychology and still struggle to keep our own child a happy creature! *Cripes — we struggle to keep our own inner mind at peace!* Our children's personalities are supposed to be infinitely complex — just like our own.

After teaching a child to sleep through the night, usually the next major challenge of parenthood is teaching a child to maintain a *joyful loving outlook*, which can be a task that characteristically goes on for at least the next 15 years — if not more. But this is our job, our *biggest* job.

Chapter Ten

THE FOUR NEW IQS — ENVIRONMENTAL, COSMOPLITAN, OLD AGE-NEW AGE AND STREETWISE IQ

Live so that when your children think of fairness and integrity, they think of you.

H Jackson Brown, Jr, *Life's Little Instruction Book*

In our grandparents' days, children were simply expected to learn the Three Rs: Reading, wRiting and aRithmetic. Life was so much simpler back then — heck, even calling them the 'Three Rs' was a spelling mistake in itself, and no-one gave a hoot!

In our generation, we were expected to get some reasonable levels of pass-marks to get into some reasonable levels of skilled career. But today, it's so different! Today our kids need multiple intelligences for this convoluted and problematic humanity, as 'we live in a postmodern world, where everything is possible and almost nothing is certain' (Vaclav Havel, Czech President).

However, as parents of this Alpha Generation-Zs, we might feel self-assured explaining the grammatical difference between when to use 'I' and when to use 'me' . . . and we might be confident to dig up from the depths of our brain the knowledge of how to perform old-fashioned long-division . . . but oh cripes, how poorly equipped we can feel with some other way more important wisdom. Lest we forget the Greek philosopher Socrates' definition of wisdom: *It's knowing that you don't know.*

So in this chapter I've attempted to hone it down to four IQs in particular, which are 'new intelligences' we as parents must teach our children, yet we can find ourselves stumped and flummoxed on this topic, because when we were growing up it would seem no-one (no parent or teacher) was ever required to teach it to us! But our kids need to be well-equipped, well-appointed and well-resourced on the topics of Environmental IQ, Cosmopolitan IQ, New Age-Old Age IQ and Streetwise IQ.

ENVIRONMENTAL IQ
KNOWLEDGEABLE CHILDREN CARING FOR THEIR PLANET

> *We the human species face a planetary emergency. That phrase still sounds shrill to some ears, but it is deadly accurate as a description of the situation that we now confront.*
>
> Al Gore's address to the
> United Nations Climate Change Conference, 2007

AN INCONVENIENT TRUTH

Modern civilisation's dominating, violent assault on the earth, with a wanton indiscriminate destruction of nature, is ferociously holding our planet's ecological equilibrium under siege, and blind tolerance is collectively perpetrating its continuation through silent complicity. The 'Inconvenient Truth' is that we're drastically running out of time and can no longer muck around chatting about possible solutions to preserve and nurture ecology from these unprecedented threats. Right now, civilisation is capable of destroying itself.

I wish to push past the speechifying and rhetoric to summarise the nitty-gritty environmental concerns we need to be knowledgeable about — both as responsible citizens and informed parents — to enable us to teach our children the *Environmental Intelligence* of why and how they too must do their part in protecting our planet.

There are literally endless environmental issues, but these are the crucial four:

- » Population eruption
- » Mass-species extinction
- » Our throw-away society
- » The planet's atmosphere (ozone depletion and global warming).

1. POPULATION ERUPTION

In the past 50 years a startling surge in human population has occurred! It took 10,000 generations for the planet's population to reach two billion by the baby-boom period. Then, after not even one complete human lifetime, the planet's population more than tripled, and is now at almost seven billion. Every hour our global population grows by around 9000, primarily in the poorest countries where *children* — not the local government — are the means of parental security in old age or ill health. Here in the West our average lifespan is more than 75 years but in much of Africa it is somewhere in the forties. Today, cities consume three-quarters of the world's resources, yet take up just three per cent of land mass. This unparalleled global growth and these societal transformations have created phenomenal food and water demands, and immense burdens on the planet's limited natural resources. We have 800 million people hungry, including 100 million starving, yet half the world's population is involved in farming. Hunger is a political problem, and ignored preventable genocide: *a failure of distribution.*

However, the solution to population stabilisation is very well documented: lowering infant mortality rates, providing access to birth control, and improving literacy and education. But today, stabilising developing countries is only feasible if wealthy nations eliminate their *strangulating* debts and share environmentally benign, sustainable technology to allow these countries to make their own economic progress.

2. MASS SPECIES EXTINCTION

Of the world's diverse plants and animals, it is calculated that around 100 living species are made extinct each day. This seems virtually impossible to comprehend as so much of it goes on unnoticed — but biologists estimate that if humans continue with their current rates of biosphere destruction, then more than a million species will be extinct by 2050, and one-half of *all* species will be extinct within the next hundred years... *our children's lifetimes.*

Rainforests are disappearing through insatiable, exploitive slashing and burning at a rate of one and a half acres a second, often just for the disposable short-term value of the wood. Our deserts are expanding (some by several kilometres annually), soil is eroding, land is being denuded, wetlands are being destroyed, and we are also swiftly contaminating our water resources with pollutants. Of around 10,000 bird species worldwide, in the region of 130 have already disappeared and around 1200 are currently seriously threatened with extinction because of destroyed habitats and the introduction of non-native species. The worldwide fishing catch has increased by a staggering 500 per cent since 1950 and every day 50,000 sharks alone die needlessly in nets. We are in the midst of oceanic 'ecocide'.

And what of crops? Staggeringly, 97 per cent of vegetable varieties grown a hundred years ago in the West are now extinct. The world once had 7000 varieties of apples, 5000 varieties of potatoes and thousands of varieties of rice, but not any more. This agricultural monoculture has created ecological vacuums with increased vulnerability to potential disease, insects and super-weeds.

Across our planet there are 12 genetic 'germplasm homes', where virtually all of our crops derive from 130 original species. For example, all varieties of rice stem from the Indo-Burma centre, all varieties of coffee stem from Ethiopia, and all varieties of potato stem from southern Chile. However, all but one of these centres is located in the developing world, whose impoverished farmers are quickly converting this genetically rich land to growing subsistence, uniform, hybrid crops from elsewhere. Because of this lack of diversity, food crops have become increasingly vulnerable to natural enemies, and the biggest threat to our food is genetic erosion.

3. OUR THROW-AWAY SOCIETY'S WASTE CRISIS

Beyond the ridiculously frivolous tonnes of over-packaging, almost every item we purchase is eventually destined for the wastelands of garbage heaps. There are in fact two prime issues: our crazed, over-packaged, buy-and-replace mentality and its subsequent mass, non-recycled environmental pollution. Let's face it, unless we're already in our old age, we know practically everything we own — except photo albums — will be replaced and updated in the next five to 20 years.

But the problem is there are no guarantees as to the long-term safety of all this waste: fetid substances are disgorged into the earth or incinerated rubbish pollutes the air with highly toxic ash. The volume of hazardous chemical waste is staggering — and no one wants to store it.

Chapter Ten

Then there is our individual share of industrial solid waste produced by commercial manufacturing — around a tonne per week, each. Then there's our individual share of our nation's car pollution waste pumped into the atmosphere — around half a tonne per week, each.

And why the hell is industrial wastewater and municipal e uent *still* being dumped into our coastal waters. *What the?!*

We are in a waste crisis.

4. THE PLANET'S ATMOSPHERE

In reality, the most vulnerable part of our planet's ecological system is its atmosphere, because it is so unbelievably thin! Global air pollution is profoundly changing its make-up and these imbalances are rapidly causing catastrophic consequences.

There are two main parts to the environmental atmospheric crisis:

» The amounts of ozone-depleting gases, reducing the ozone layer that protects us from solar ultraviolet radiation

» The amounts of 'greenhouse' heat-trapping gases, increasing the absorption of solar infrared radiation.

Ozone Depletion

Ozone regulates the amount of solar ultraviolet radiation that reaches the earth's surface, protecting us from the most harmful, but invisible, solar rays. However, in the past 50 years, a massive increase in chlorine ozone-depleting chemicals was observed in our stratosphere, which corresponded to a worldwide thinning of the ozone layer. The main culprits were CFCs (chlorofluorocarbons), which were popularly used in many processes, particularly cooling units (such as fridges and air-conditioners) and as an aerosol spray propellant.

Then in the mid-1980s, worldwide concern mounted with confirmation of the seasonal formation of an 'ozone hole', primarily over Antarctica, three times the size of the mainland United States. The subsequent fall-out was increased rates of skin cancer, especially in Australia, New Zealand, Argentina and Chile. Crops, particularly rice, and plankton were also affected.

In 1987, 43 nations signed the Montreal Protocol to phase out the use of ozone-depleting substances. So long as global warming doesn't spiral out of control, the ozone layer will have recovered by around the year 2050. Well done humankind!!

Global warming (Increased greenhouse gases)

Our planet's 'greenhouse gases' naturally trap the sun's heat, preventing air temperatures from plummeting to freezing extremes every evening. But since the end of World War II, there has been a 25 per cent increase in atmospheric greenhouse gases, primarily carbon dioxide (CO_2). With increased emissions from the burning of fossil fuels, and with fewer trees to absorb the gases, we are now well on the path to rapidly doubling our atmospheric CO_2 which 'thickens' the atmosphere, trapping more infrared heat and thus warming up the planet's surface.

Not only does this mean that the ice caps are melting, but the rate of melting is also accelerating. Greenland's ice sheet is melting, glaciers are retreating, and Arctic and Antarctic ice shelves are rapidly disappearing. And of course all this melting ice increases sea levels, putting coastal populations at risk.

Atmospheric water vapour also increases, consequently altering the patterns of ocean and wind currents that circulate heat and cold around the planet, causing more frequent floods, droughts, heatwaves and wildfires. Warmer waters also increase wind velocity, causing stronger storms, such as the more frequent occurrence in recent years of tornadoes, hurricanes and typhoons.

Who are the biggest contributors to greenhouse gas emissions? An incredible three-quarters comes from industrialised countries in North America, the UK, Europe and Australasia. Before we can realistically insist that economies such as India and China discontinue their use of polluting technologies, the West must lead by example with efficient, non-polluting energy generation, fuel-efficient vehicles, better mass transport, more eco-housing, energy-efficient appliances, waste reduction, pollution taxation and tree-planting programmes.

PARENTING GOLDEN INSIGHT NO. 14

Teach our children to care for their planet!

TAKING ACTION — TEACHING ENVIRONMENTAL IQ

The *insane* reality is that humanity already possesses all the fundamental technical, scientific and industrial knowledge needed to solve the crisis of carbon, climate and other environmental problems — bar political determination to ratify such changes.

We, as citizens concerned for our yet-to-be-born grandchildren, need to support the large shift in public opinion by forcing our governments to reduce ecological impact and heal our global environment.

Continuing research without commencing action is unconscionable, but that is the current policy for many politicians, while they question whether or not the damage to our fragile Mother Earth is bad enough to warrant them giving a crap, during their limited term in office, for it appears only an imminent threat of our own extinction may perhaps be the final straw.

And as parents who care, we must vote for (or become ourselves) decisive outraged environmental leaders, compelled by conscience, who demand enlightened governments who will remedy ecological problems using 'eco-nomics', to decelerate environmental destruction, create environmental stability, and avoid pending ecological catastrophe.

And where are we really, right now? We're at the absolute outer limits of sustainability.

The children of today (our leaders of tomorrow) need parents who have an overtly clear understanding of the major environmental issues facing mankind this century. Environmentalism fundamentally should be a parent-led matter and ideally should be simply a normal part of the average household culture. Fortunately parents en masse are beginning to realise this, as disquiet has surfaced, and the challenge now is simply to accelerate the momentum. Just as Winston Churchill decreed at the commencement of World War II, 'The era of procrastination, of half-measures, of soothing and ba ing expedients, of delays, is coming to its close. In its place we are entering a period of consequences.'

If you think it's di cult telling your kids there's no Santa, try telling your grandkids there used to be a North Pole. *Good planets are hard to find!*

COSMOPOLITAN IQ
INSIGHTFUL CHILDREN UNDERSTANDING THE FAITHS OF OTHERS

> *Because so large a portion of our fellow human beings articulate their own meaning, purpose, and values through their religions, it is essential that our children know as much as possible about those religions: their beliefs and practices, their literatures and traditions, and their meaning to their practitioners. To be fully engaged members of the human society, they must be religiously literate . . . Regardless of whether we call ourselves religious, we are our children's first*

Chapter Ten

and primary religious educators.

Dr Roberta Nelson in Dale McGowan's
Parenting Beyond Belief

Today our children live in a cosmopolitan, multi-ethnic society, where more than 15,000 cultures and four and a half billion people believe in a higher power. Our children need to demonstrate insightful religious tolerance through sophisticated religious intelligence. Unfortunately, our society presently has little broad-based religious education for our children: state schools often focus on the Christian Bible, and private schools teach their own beliefs.

If you are devoutly religious, and unless your parents had a liberal understanding of theology's 237 known holy scriptures, then chances are you know a lot only about your one religion.

If you are not devoutly religious then, commonly, you are the generation once or twice removed from strong religious faith. In those cases, generally you either experienced a childhood enveloped in a religious doctrine where you were not permitted to question it, and now you are; or you are the second (or third) generation of the irreligious, because it was your parents (or grandparents) who were raised with and subsequently rejected strong religion, then went on to raise you without religion.

For the purpose of this book it doesn't matter where you personally stand on the topic of religion: it is irrelevant if you believe God to be the Universal Truth or mass delusion. Even if you don't believe in God, the world is run by people who do. And beliefs about what God wants, legislate morality. Children need to learn Cosmopolitan IQ because the reality is:

- » *Globally:* One in three people are Christian, one in five are Muslim, one in six are Hindu, and only one in every six people is non-religious.
- » *The world's 'big seven' religions are:* Christianity, Islam, Hinduism, Buddhism, Chinese Traditional (Taoism, Confucianism), Judaism and Sikhism. Each religion also has various broad sub-sects.
- » *The biggest religion in the world:* Christianity has over 2.2 billion followers, one third of the whole world's population. Many define Christianity as having three main sects: Catholic, Protestant and Orthodox.
- » *The fastest growing religion in the world:* Islam is second with over 1.6 billion followers, mainly Shiites and Sunnis. The numbers are increasing not just from conversions, but also from births as Muslims generally have larger families than Christians.

WHERE THE BLOODY HELL HAS GOD GONE?

In a secular age of a global humanistic society governed by accelerating change, the past's 'divine revelations' have been replaced by empirical science's acquisition of reliable knowledge, resulting in an information explosion. Religion is no longer concerned with something supernatural that interferes in natural laws; instead, the traditional religions have been adapted into privatised community enterprises.

These days authority is internalised in the individual — *we decide for ourselves* — because we have replaced the historic, absolute authority held by monarchs and priests. Democracy has arisen and spread, human rights have been recognised, slaves have been emancipated, women have been liberated, and we now accept sexual diversity, and condemn racism. We have more personal freedom than ever before!

But are we capable of handling such unconstrained decision-making and unbridled personal responsibility?!

Chapter Ten

What of the future? What are the dangers of this humanistic age?

With the loss of social pressure to conform to stereotypes, and our new freedoms authorised in law, we have almost too much personal responsibility! Subsequently, there is now a potential slide into social chaos.

So where the bloody hell has God gone?

This eclipse of the traditional God has left a God-shaped hole to be filled — and it is being filled, for sure . . . sometimes by the self-assertion of a megalomaniac's own wishes and views, or by reactionary fundamentalists blindly returning to the certainties of past faiths, or by radicals turning to New Age cults professing the one exclusive truth, or by escapists seeking solace and looking for diversion with alcoholism and illicit drugs.

But some, like me and perhaps you, are actually accepting the new, diverse abundance of choice with conscientious responsibility.

TAKING ACTION — TEACHING COSMOPOLITAN IQ

It seems to me that there are two types of people in the world: those who want to believe, and those who want to know.

In the olden days, God created and controlled the species, and they were sacred. But now humans carelessly destroy old species, while carefully creating new species through cloning, genetic modification, planned breeding and in-vitro fertilisation.

We have taken God's place.

In the olden days, God determined our health and the limits of our life, for 'The Lord giveth and the Lord taketh away'. But now humans can, and do, lengthen life with medical science, prevent life by contraception, and determine time of birth and death by caesarean sections and euthanasia.

We have taken God's place.

We as humans can no longer avoid 'playing God' — it has become unavoidable. All we can do is try to keep within considerations governed by nature, with as much wisdom as we can muster, to ensure we are guided by truth, justice and compassion.

PARENTING GOLDEN INSIGHT NO. 15

Teach your children at least a basic understanding of the world's most popular religions.

Regardless of our own upbringings, our millennium children need to be far more broadly religiously educated than we, their parents' generation, ever needed to be. Consequently, raising children who have *Cosmopolitan Intelligence* is solely a parental responsibility: the buck stops with us.

If this topic is of especial interest to you, far more extensive information can be found in my body-mind-spirit literary-award finalist manuscript OH GOD - WHAT THEY HELL DO I TELL THEM?! *The Guide for Vaguely Spiritual Parents* (www.kathyfray.com).

OLD AGE-NEW AGE IQ
DISCERNING CHILDREN APPRECIATING THE BELIEFS OF OTHERS

Across the world today there is an enormous, and escalating, undercurrent of spirituality — what I describe as a sphere of human consciousness beginning to envelop the world, a dissolving veil of long-standing deceptions starting to disintegrate deep-rooted lies, a faction of esoteric New-Agers splintering Western theosophy's fissures. Many of us, as adults parenting adults-to-be, are sensing a very real, very

Chapter Ten

palpable air of change. Globally and personally, something eerie is going on around us. Something unusual is happening in our world; something odd is happening to us internally. We aren't quite sure what it is — but nearly all of us are feeling it. To quote the renowned yoga teacher Sharron Rose, 'It's like a shadow on the wall . . . we're not sure if it's an illusion or not, we just know that it's there.'

It's a transformation . . . no, revolution . . . no, revelation . . . oh, God knows what to call it — let's call it *the something*.

The something, this upheaval of global ambiance, this disruption to nonchalant apathy, this evolution of universal consciousness, is relentlessly evidenced by our insatiable desire for movies, books, and documentaries on topics that are magical, supernatural, paranormal, mystical, miraculous, ethereal, biblical, enigmatic. Collectively mankind now has an appetite for otherworldly fantasies and spiritual mysteries, on a scale so voracious that its intensity is beyond anything ever previously documented in human society!

So this is the environment our children are growing up in.

But the really screwy side of this bizarre postmodern-world phenomenon is that unless parents are devoutly religious, then most — the great majority, in fact — fail to talk directly with their children about human spirituality. We close down, with tight-lipped silence. For like the generations before us who were unable to discuss sexual intercourse, we are a generation unable to discuss spirituality. It's our taboo we-don't-go-there topic. However, that's definitely not true of *all* our generation — me included, obviously — and perhaps you?

In the next breath, as voting adults, we're also very ready to move on from centuries of warfare and bloodshed. And yes, we're so weary of hearing the burdensome, constant tumultuous stream of bad news about genocide, injustice and recession. We all just want a better future for our families, one brimming with hopes of a better tomorrow on a better planet ruled by better governments that have successfully found better ways to provide the basic necessities for all humankind. We're all so, *so* ready for that.

Then we hear more and more words bandied about like 'sacred mysteries', 'Armageddon' or the 'Apocalyptic End-Times'. *What's with that?* we ask. We all, without any doubt — *hear me wail* — live in an era of unprecedented expanding spiritualism. Religious or not, we humans have always, historically focused on our spirituality. To deny to our children the worth of any of it, let alone all of it, is, in my biased opinion, pig-headed idiocy. So among all the nonsense — what the heck is sense?

PARENTING GOLDEN INSIGHT NO. 16

Be clued-up and conversantly au fait with mankind's Old Age-New Age spiritual trends.

TAKING ACTION — TEACHING OLD AGE-NEW AGE IQ

Our job, as parents, is to teach our children about the entire world they live in. We shouldn't just edit out pieces of it — and Old Age-New Age spirituality is very much part of today's global environment, even if it hasn't arrived on your doorstep yet. And if it hasn't yet, well, I bear news: it just did.

Up until now, you may have taken the personal position of 'ignorance is bliss'. You may choose not to inform your children — to protect them from radical drivel and jibber-jabber codswallop. Or you may choose to enlighten your child — to protect them from extremist twaddle and nonsensical hogwash. My point is, it's your call and this requires you to make an intentional, conscious decision as to how you're going to parent on these and similar topics. It requires you and me, as parents, to live our lives consciously, with intent, fully participating in our own development. So, will you be the open-minded freethinker, or the guardian protector? The pioneer, or the shield? Only you can decide, and decide you must — and will — for even failing to make a decision results in a decision being made. Some of the topics and theories you may be interested in looking at are: the hippy beginnings of the New Age movement; apocalyptic Armageddon and the Anti-Christ; dream interpretation; the global-consciousness evolution; the human-potential movement; intuition; karma; the Mayan calendar; Neale Donald Walsh's *Conversations with God*; out-of-body experiences; reincarnation; sacred geometry; soul ascension; UFOs and aliens, and uterosexuals.

Perhaps *all* this 'stu ' is derived from kooks, charlatans, heretics, quacks and swindlers, touting superstitious claptrap, absurd hogwash, fishy baloney, unorthodox profanity or dubious twaddle. At the end of the day, I believe however, it's actually just Humans attempting to answer the meaning-of-life questions: the why-are-we-here, what's-the-meaning-of-it-all, and what's-the-point questions humankind yearns to receive credible answers to.

For me personally, as a parent, it's about teaching looking backwards (and forwards) in time and sifting through the layers of prominent spiritual theories, philosophies, conspiracies and prophecies. For as Betty Shannon Cloyd writes in *Parents and Grandparents as Spiritual Guides*, 'We must realise that our children are going to be formed spiritually, if not by us by someone or some ideology. They will not remain a blank slate until they are old enough to choose. The question is, who do we want to assist them in this formation?'

So what truly are the real answers? God knows, *literally!*

STREETWISE IQ
EMPOWERED CHILDREN SAFE FROM ILLICIT DRUGS

As parents of teenagers we will worry about marijuana and alcohol. We will worry about gangsta music and promiscuity. We will worry about pornography and, sadly, suicide. I could talk more about these ugly topics, but this isn't a book on raising teenagers.

But — a *big* but — I recognise the scariest thing most preteens (and definitely teens) will be exposed to, in various shapes or forms, will be illicit street drugs. From the parenting perspective, there is much understated, and exaggerated, misinformation out there.

Today's parents must be acutely street-smart regarding illicit drugs, because statistically over half our children will experiment with them — just as our generation did. But the big difference these days is the easy access to the lethal Class A, hard-core drug 'P' (crystal meth), the wickedly addictive crack cocaine, and the insanely nuts online-available synthetic party-pills. It's essential that we begin to build the solid concrete foundations of *streetwise intelligence* in our preteens before the hormones of adolescent puberty begin to cloud rational judgement!

Some recreational drugs are fairly harmless — don't shoot the messenger — but other drugs wreck lives permanently. And preteens need to understand the difference, before they ever try any of them. And this is why:

Research shows that more than 17 out of 20 six-year-olds feel positive about themselves, but a decade later, by 16 years of age, only around three of 20 still like themselves. That means at least 85 per cent of our teens are in a precariously vulnerable position, verging on clinical depression, with its telltale loss of interest in stuff they used to enjoy — and illicit drugs can provide the positivity they hunger for.

After alcohol, street-illicit and online-licit drugs remain the world's most sought-after substances on the planet, in order to experience chemically induced joy and contentment. Getting high can make you feel euphorically wonderful, ecstatically happy and exhilaratingly confident — and that's hard to turn down when you're feeling awkwardly insecure, uncomfortably self-conscious and socially pressured.

PARENTING GOLDEN INSIGHT NO.17

When it comes to crystal meth ('P') and legal online party-pills make sure our kids are too terrified to indulge!

TAKING ACTION — TEACHING STREETWISE IQ

I know almost all parents reading this book will be planning to dissuade their children from dabbling in all mind-altering drugs. But let's face it, rebellious teenagers have consistently jolly well tried drugs, marijuana in particular, anyway... just like half of us did. As for my own personal experiences, let's just call it quits by saying: 'You have to be young and stupid before you can be old and wise.' But I was lucky, and for three big reasons.

First, many of my friends from my druggy days didn't have parents sitting at home with the fervent moral values that my parents had. It didn't matter so much the specifics of what it was they stood for — of more importance was that they fervently stood for something. It was this backbone of right and wrong that kept me from spiralling irreversibly. The big difference was that I knew that what I was doing was wrong, whereas some of my hippy friends weren't so lucky, because they never really thought any of it was wrong at all.

Second, I am lucky not to have an addictive genetic disposition. In other words, I don't have the inherent personality type that has an inborn 'addiction gene'. Some of my friends clearly did.

And third, the other reason I came out the other side unscathed (and frankly a more interesting person, I reckon!) is because crystal meth and the party-pill culture didn't even exist. If it did, I guarantee I would have tried it, and P would very likely have been the beginning of my end.

We, as the adults, need to be able to di erentiate between the level of risk certain drugs pose. If you can't, then how the heck do you expect your preteen to be able to appreciate the monumental and life-threatening di erences? We must teach them street-drug savvyness. They need to know we know, that puffing on the occasional joint of marijuana is highly unlikely to completely ruin their life. But puffing just once on a pipe of crystal meth, has a significant chance of impacting their entire life.

Parenting LOVE IT! moment

While attending the local Catholic primary school, our eldest Rick's class was viewing a DVD on various cultural dancers.

As they watched a Hindu woman putting on her make-up, some in the class were mumbling "What's she doing?"

Nonchalantly, our 9-year-old yawns "She's just putting a bindi on her third-eye chakra".

Dah!

SUMMARY

Becoming responsible adults is no longer a matter of whether children hang up their pajamas or put dirty towels in the hamper, but whether they care about themselves and others — and whether they see everyday chores as related to how we treat this planet.

Eda LeShan (1922–2002), *author and celebrity*

There is no doubt we now live in a multi-cultural, multi-ethnic and multi-religious world, rich in contrasting values woven into a whole gamut of human social fabric. We are poised on a cornucopia of knowing! I could describe such societal intelligences as wisdom, creative uncertainty and openness — but then hey, that's simply the ideological foundations of democracy. No, it's deeper and broader than that.

Some may describe this chapter's four IQs as essential, collaborative, moral, or multi-model — but whatever you want to term them, it's about possessing IQ at a societal level far beyond anything ever required of human beings before — it's a higher self-conscious social intelligence.

It's about tolerating differences, by respecting other voices of mind, while honouring our own way of life; and it's about protecting our home, by defending Gaia our planet earth, while shielding our own spirit's body and mind.

It's really all about an ultimate holistic *Universal Intelligence*.

Section Four

CHILDREN'S SPIRITS

Parenting using Soulful IQ

Section Four Introduction

TEACHING SOUL

You are both embarked on the journey of soul-making. The only difference is the roles you have chosen . . . The most good you can do for yourself spiritually is to play your role as parent with total love, conviction, and purpose . . . As an all-knowing, immortal spirit, your child has decided to be a weak, vulnerable infant, totally dependent upon your help . . . As parents, then, what we teach our children is no different from what we must keep teaching ourselves.

Deepak Chopra,
The Seven Spiritual Laws of Success for Parents

Question: Why do we as parents typically dedicate several hours a week to our children's soccer practice or music lessons or suchlike, when we probably have minimal expectation of them becoming a professional sports ace or musical diva? Yet, often, we may spend zero hours a week consciously teaching them about love and joy, when more than anything we hope they will grow into joyful, loving people. *What's with that, I have to ask? Do we hope it all happens by accident, by default, by osmosis?*

In this final section of *Oh Grow Up* my aim is to provide practical suggestions on how to parent with *soul*, without needing to be devotedly spiritual. This chapter is designed to assist everyone, regardless of where on the spectrum of faith you dwell.

For parents who are already devoutly religious; Mother Earth homeschoolers; positive, peaceful parenters; or any other deliberate type of parent, then *parenting with soul* will probably already be an automatic place in which you reside . . . and so for you these final chapters will hopefully provide simply an even broader depth of universal wisdom to accompany your existing strong convictions.

But on the flipside, for the escalating numbers of secular, humanistic, vaguely spiritual parents, who don't necessarily feel comfortable identifying themselves with a specific parenting ideology, then being able to *parent with soul* may be a place you yearn to exist in. So, for you, in the next chapters, a meaning-of-life supermarket is open! It's ready for you to consider some options, and select the magical secrets and universal laws that seem appetising to you at the moment. It's open 24/7, so you can always pop back any time you like to try something new — or exchange items that didn't work for your family.

Once you've found an item that really works for you, your family, your philosophies and your lifestyle, then you will have *adopted a policy*, which is yours for the keeping for however long you decide it's still working for you. So buckle up and get ready, highlighter pen in hand, to choose some life philosophies to impart to your children. As the saying goes: 'Your decisions are important — they add up to be your life'. However in this book, there is no 'right' or 'wrong'.

God almighty and God forbid, you could instead do what I've done, and honest to God read what feels like almost every Goddamn, Godawful, God-fearing, Godless, Godforsaken, Godly, God-given, God-sent, Godlike and Goddess book ever written about religion, spirituality and parenting! Or alternatively you can stroll leisurely up and down the aisles of the next chapters, reading it all, analysing ingredients, noticing different brand packaging, figuring out the best quality, considering your many options, listening to your intuition, observing your gut reactions, taste-testing ... Just don't spend *too* long before putting something into your trolley.

Later down the track your kids may be back for seconds ... and you'll probably be back to these chapters for seconds, too. Then, as the kids get older, hopefully they'll also become more discerning, more questioning, more astutely judicious, and they'll expect you to have an even sharper and more discriminating, wise opinion — because that's what children do: seek insight.

And so you probably have only the next 10 years to formulate big chunks of your own wisdom, while considering author Angela Schwindt's famous adage, 'While we try to teach our children all about life, our children teach us what life is all about.'

This book absolutely, categorically, is *not* about me telling you how to parent, or what you should believe in. But this book absolutely, categorically, *is* about shoving you in a few directions, and encouraging you to make a few decisions. It's about getting grounded, getting centred and balanced — while appreciating we're all a little wonky.

At the end of the day I believe *parenting with soul* is a non-negotiable necessity. It's about recognising that although the brain gives the heart its sight, it is the heart that gives the brain its vision.

Chapter Eleven

PARENTING WITH SOUL

At first our inadequacy at being a spiritual guide to our children can threaten to overwhelm us. How can I possibly guide my child, we wonder; because to be a guide means to show the way by leading, or by directing, or by advising . . . This sometimes sends a shudder of fear through us. We know ourselves as parents to be so imperfect.

Betty Shannon Cloyd
Parents and Grandparents as Spiritual Guides

For many of us, prior to parenthood, we found existing as an adult in the spiritual vacuum or no-man's-land between the two extremes of devout religion and devoted spirituality can be a reasonably comfortable place to reside. It is very possible indeed to be one of these people-in-limbo, living a successful, accomplished and respected life. Even the current Dalai Lama himself wrote in *Ancient Wisdom, Modern World*, 'It is doubtful whether, globally, even a billion are what I would call dedicated religious practitioners . . . [so] we can also conclude that we humans can live quite well without recourse to religious faith'.

Chapter Eleven

But then...

PARENTS OF THE VOID

Through the explosive transformation of childbirth, we all as parents move up a rung in our genealogy: the female instantly metamorphoses from daughter to mother, as she discovers motherhood's bonding is accompanied by maternal bondage. And in new fatherhood, the male slowly tranforms from son into father, as he eventually gets to grip with the overwhelming pressure of his new paternal responsibilities. Meanwhile, they both stare in awe at their little precious, miraculous cherub as it peacefully sleeps, looking so innocent, virtuous, holy and angelic.

Then, as we begin to grow as new parents, we also begin to fathom — especially mothers — that we are not just ultimately responsible for our child's well-being physically, mentally, emotionally, socially and academically, but also spiritually, because possessing philosophies becomes a parental duty. In fact, at the birth of every couple's first child, there are really three births: the birth of a brand-new baby (the student), and the birth of a mother and father (two brand-new teachers).

The reality is, in our modern developed world, with all its labor-saving appliances, electronic gadgets, endless varieties of takeaway, and infinite TV channels all simultaneously screening 'nothing worth watching', somehow we've collectively lost a big chunk of our soul. For these days, along with the atheist, the agnostic, the cynic, the indi erent, the devout, and the fanatical, the West has become a place that also harbours the vaguely spiritual *parents of the void*, who can go on unintentionally continuing the cycle by raising another generation of 'spiritual orphans with a gnawing spiritual homesickness', as Kent Ira Gro describes them.

However, if piety to orthodox religion is already a large part of your life, you probably feel very well equipped, trusting in God's will. Or, if devotion to New Age spirituality is already a large part of your life, you too probably feel very well equipped, trusting in the Universe. Or maybe you're like Albert Einstein, who described himself as 'a deeply religious unbeliever'. Or maybe you're like Eddie in Mitch Albom's *The Five People You Meet In Heaven:* 'Eddie admitted that some of his life he'd spent hiding from God, and the rest of the time he thought he went unnoticed.'

Often we dream the common pipe dream that our children will be so special and wise, they won't even need to be taught 'life laws', because they will inherently behave with such immense love and deep wisdom. *Ha! Ha! Ha! Ha! Ha! Ha! Ha! Ha! Ha! Ha! Ha! Ha! Ha! Ha! Ha!*

Or you could use the go-with-the-flow and take-it-as-it-comes methodology with its strategy of *I'll leave it for my child to make up his own mind when he's old enough.* Crikey, that doesn't really make proper sense, especially if we don't provide them with any useful information with which to make informed decisions. We don't generally do this with less important things like allowing a child to make up his own bedtimes, or make up his own food menus, or make up his own rules about acceptable manners. Yet, with perhaps the most consequential decisions of *life*, it's somehow okay to o er the child no structured guidance? That doesn't sound logical — and it isn't. It denies their soul the opportunity to live a spiritually endowed *childhood,* missing opportunities of mystical awe. That is equivalent to saying, 'We won't give our son the opportunity to play any sport when he's a child — instead when he's an adult he can choose what sport he wants to play.' Or, 'I won't give my daughter the opportunity to try di erent styles of dance while she's growing up — she can decide when she's older if she prefers jazz, tap or ballet.' *Ridiculous!*

A possibility is that you could, personally, somehow become 'spiritually awoken', but that typically demands letting go, releasing uncertainties and liberating fears — yet parenting children requires holding on, structure, nurturing and dependability! (This is partially why traditionally, for many indigenous cultures, true spiritual awakening often doesn't happen until family life is complete, or it is the vocation of those not drawn to having a family.)

There is the one extreme of structured Religions, which for some can seem antiquated or evangelical, and there is the other extreme of New Age spirituality, which for some people can seem asphyxiating with its supermarket-syndrome of unlimited choices. Between those two extremes you can feel at times bewildered, without even knowing where to start to understand spiritual truths, let alone how to manage to pass such wisdom down to your children.

If you believe in something, but nothing in particular, and you have no intention of signing up to any particular doctrine — well, that's got to be one of the toughest life quests of all. Surely it would be easier to have a specific faith one believes strongly in: 'Just follow this Rule Book and you'll get into Heaven' !

Yet *many* of us just can't abide doing that — not because we believe it is necessarily wrong, but more because we have been born with a quest to find our own path. We feel like Copernicus, the Renaissance scientist, saying 'But hold on, maybe the sun doesn't go around the earth'.

In our minds we're not anti-establishment, but we are anti-doctrine. We're not anti-religion, but we are anti some churches. We're very pro-freedom, and very anti-war. We live in a world where heads of state use war to enforce peace, and where the developed world's supplies of excess food could easily eradicate starvation in the entire developing world — yet selfish politics and monetary greed are stronger than compassionate common sense. And many of those same politicians, businessmen and religious leaders are devout followers of orthodox faith.

So yes, oh yes, we question. Yet, we all know, when shit hits the fan of life, it is always the strength of our *spirit* — far more than our body or our mind or our emotions — that gets us through our darkest trials and tribulations. It's the Who-We-Are and What-We-Stand-For that keeps us strong, and that's our *spirit*.

But wherever we each dwell along the spectrum of spirituality, and whether it's our conscious choice to teach, or not teach, our child to develop their spirit; either way we're all sure as heck responsible for our children's spiritual wisdom or lack thereof.

EMACIATED CHILDREN

We are able to nourish our children's bodies when we have some food; and we are able to nourish our children's minds when we have some knowledge; then too we are able to nourish our children's spirit when we have some spirituality — that is, 'our own tangible soul, relating to its own intangible faith'. *(Well, that's my definition — feel free to discover your own.)* Without food, our body becomes emaciated. Without stimulation our mind atrophies. These are scientific facts. And without wisdom, our spirit can feel malnourished (a hunger easily sated by the temporary highs of recreational drugs and excessive alcohol). Humans can survive a friggin' long time relying on just the body and mind — but eventually an undernourished spiritual anaemia results in lingering emptiness.

Right now we have almost an entire generation of Western children who I believe are really, really *hungry* for spiritual wisdom. They just want us, as their parents, to pick something, anything, we think is palatable, and finally feed it to them.

EMANCIPATED CHILDREN

Our spirit is the essence of our soul . . . our inner self . . . our life force — whatever you wish to call it. And as parents our own spiritual essence is also the guiding light for our children to follow. In fact, I believe our spirit is fundamentally the most important aspect of our entire humanity! 'We are not human beings having a spiritual experience; we are spiritual beings having a human experience' (Dr Wayne W Dyer, self-empowerment motivator).

So *Oh Grow Up* is about 'parenting with soul'. But you must also feel free to decide whatever spirit it is that hits your 'on' button ... gutsy, courageous strength of character or *Star Wars*-like life-force; religious piety or ethereal soul; devout faith or oriental inner-self chi ... It doesn't matter to me how you prefer to define *spirit*. Just so long as you define it!

OH GOD ... WHAT THE HELL DO WE TELL THEM?!

STEP 1: Know your own spirit

Assisting a child's spirituality to bud gives meaning to their whole life! But to do this, ideally a parent will possess their own spiritual foundation with which a child can clearly identify. And as Michael Shermer writes in Dale McGowan's *Parenting Beyond Belief*, 'It matters less to me what your specific beliefs are than that you have carefully arrived at your beliefs through reason and evidence and thoughtful reflection.'

As parents it's now time to decide *who you are* and *what you stand for* at this moment in time. This is not to say that later in life you can't change your mind, or to say that you know it all right now, or to imply that you've got all the answers already, but just to say, 'This is who I am right now — I stand for these beliefs' — whatever those beliefs may be.

It's about being able to parent from a position of empowerment, derived from the knowledge that our parenting philosophies are intentional — and not a random, hit-and-miss, winging-it, haphazard jumble of incidental values and inherited beliefs.

Our kids may not always accept and incorporate all our ideals and core values into their lives — but they still need us to have them. As Neale Donald Walsch says in *Conversations with God*: 'Life may more than once call upon you to prove Who You Are by demonstrating an aspect of Who You Are Not.' And so these next chapters are simply about empowering you to know more, so you can define *who you are*, and *who you are not*.

Step 1 is about coming to terms with where your own spirit is at right now, and learning to pay attention to your own spiritual life. Underpinning our everyday life should be a constant craving to be a kind, grateful and caring person, because we need to lead by example as much as we possibly can.

This can mean making concrete efforts to eradicate our own arrogance and self-centred self-absorption, excessive greed, cynicism and scepticism, impatience and helplessness, and cold aloofness. This can also mean making concrete efforts to work past any personal fears of expressing closeness, empathy, compassion, joy and love. (And if baggage from your past history is in your way, then clear it up — so your children can move on.)

This also means patiently accepting that everything is not going to instantly change overnight, because we take a lifetime to perfect, (maybe even several lifetimes) and that's totally normal. It is simply critical for our kids' sake that we have at least *consciously begun* our individual journey.

So do whatever you personally must to strengthen your own vital force with activities that nourish your spirit: say a rosary, bow to the east, chant a mantra, do hatha yoga, go on a guided meditation, visit a retreat, go fishing, learn belly-dancing, attend synagogue, swing on a hammock, have your aura cleansed, get your chakras tuned, read beautiful poetry in a bubble bath, learn reiki, practise tai chi, bash bongo drums to baroque music, practise qigong — whatever suits you. And read uplifting books; autobiographies can

be especially inspiring. Also, if you can't work at a creative job, at least get a creative hobby, because creativity helps us all find meaning.

As Steve Biddulph writes in *More Secrets of Happy Children*, 'You can't give love if you don't have a clear sense of self. And a sense of self only comes when you give yourself space to be.' So somehow, in some way, frequently connect with your spiritual side! Get nourished, get grounded, get centred, get balanced — so you can regularly find your own equilibrium. It's about connecting with your own spirit.

STEP 2: Know your children are gifts

Step 2 is about consciously remembering, every day, that our children are gifts from the universe, for we have been given no greater responsibility than our children! And know their Spirits have chosen us as their Parents to learn from (good and bad).

I know your children are more important to you than your work, which of course they are supposed to be. But do we fail to make them aware of this as an overt, clearly understood fact?

The two most rudimentary human needs are to feel *welcome* and *worthy*. This can be summed up as the deepest and most important desire we all as individuals crave: *to be appreciated*. We can't assume what our kids know. We mustn't presume our children know we want them, or that they're worthy of our love. We must *tell* them. None of us ever outgrow our need to be appreciated.

One of my favourite parenting philosophies comes from Paul Faulkner's *Raising Faithful Kids* when he talks about the positive-negative comment ratio. Theories vary, but in general, our kids' self-esteem requires about 10 appreciative, encouraging remarks to counter one critical, negative remark.

STEP 3: Know love is not enough

Contrary to many philosophies, I don't believe that simply loving our children is necessarily enough. As author Dr John Gray says in *Children Are from Heaven*, 'Without an understanding of their children's needs, parents cannot effectively support their children.'

Gray goes on to explain: the deep 'n' serious 'sensitive' children need listening and understanding; the strong-willed centre-of-attention 'active' children need preparation and structure; the bright 'n' breezy stimulation-seeking 'responsive' children need distraction, variety and direction; and the well-mannered and cooperative 'receptive' children need ritual, rhythm and routine. And that's what this whole book has been about too, because love is not enough!

From extensive research, Professor Phil Silva explains in *The Listener*, 'Some absolutes have emerged: love is necessary, but not sufficient — children also need luck ... the more experiences a parent gives a child, the better.' You see, some children may need a lot of help accessing their emotions to identify their feelings. I love Brandon Bays' line in *The Journey for Kids*, 'I know you don't know what you're feeling, but if *you did* know, I wonder what that might be?'

The bottom line is, our kids must experience the knowledge that their family members are their friends, who give them courage and self-confidence. It's about being parents who have an obvious, effervescent and overflowing love for each child, equally.

On the flipside, to cite John Lennon, love *is* all you need! Because love ensures we search for better ways to understand our children.

So there is a paradox within these statements: love in exclusion is not enough, but love in inclusion is all we ever need.

STEP 4: Know you already know everything you need to know

In general terms, parents can be quite accepting of the fact they can adequately feed their children, even when they aren't qualified nutritionists. Parents can also be quite accepting of the fact they can adequately access academic learning for their children, even on topics outside their own knowledge.

But the crazy, frustrating thing about parents passing the baton of spirit on to their children is that unless parents are devoutly religious or deeply spiritual, they can often find themselves overwhelmed by a debilitating sensation of inadequacy. Subsequently, they customarily just avoid the topic altogether.

From my perspective, I have no agenda except to instil in you, the parent, the need for you to have an agenda. It doesn't matter to me *what* you believe in, so long as you find something to believe in, stand for something, have a viewpoint, hold an opinion, even if that opinion is that you don't yet have enough knowledge to form a firm outlook. But please have your own perspective, based on sound information, never on ignorance. Our children *need* us to stand for *something*!

However, this is what I firmly believe is the *real key* to parenting our children's spirits, which hardly any 'expert' ever points out, so let me give it to you loudly and boldly:

We *don't* need to feel spiritually *complete* ourselves to impart important wisdom to a child's spirit!

We *don't* need to have finished our own 'spiritual journeys' and feel we know it all before we can begin to assist our children along their spiritual journeys.

We weren't supposed to know it all before having kids, and in fact the act of becoming a parent increases our spirituality at a deep foundational level. Remember, our spirit's journey in this body, with this mind, doesn't actually end until this body dies.

The next learning curve is always just around the corner.

PARENTING GOLDEN INSIGHT NO. 18

Decide *who you are*, and *what your spirit stands for* ... and make sure your children know it.

SUMMARY

Now more than ever, in this age of violence and confusion, there is an urgent need for parents to take on the role of spiritual teachers to their children... The deepest nurturing you can give your child is spiritual nurturing... The birth of a baby launches us as teachers of spirit.

Deepak Chopra,
The Seven Spiritual Laws of Success for Parents

Parenting with soul isn't about middle-of-the-road parenting — it's much more than that: it's about middle-path parenting! Historically, the 'middle path' is a Buddhist term somewhat equivalent to the Western world's 'middle-of-the-road', but actually infinitely more philosophically complex, and simple. The famous Japanese author DT Suzuki (1870–1966) sums it up astutely in *An Introduction to Zen Buddhism*: 'The middle way is where there is neither middle nor two sides. When you are fettered by the objective world, you have one side; when you are disturbed in your own mind, you have the other side. When neither of these exists, there is no middle part, and this is the middle way.'

This section is all about parenting with strength of character, which takes courage and determination, instead of a wishy-washy, permissive, spineless parenting style.

It's about parenting with power of mind, which takes guts and fortitude, instead of being drained by others' judgemental expectations, or reverting to an authoritarian, domineering style requiring unquestioning obedience.

It's about parenting with the life-force of soul, which takes a divine heart, pure love and authoritative guiding knowledge; instead of being left forever frustrated by a permissive, indifferent and unexceptionally mediocre parenting technique.

Parenting is not just about raising well-adjusted, self-controlled and socially responsible children, or about raising children who respect and love who they are. It's also about raising well-adjusted, self-controlled and socially responsible *parents*, who respect and love who they are, so they can respect and love who *all other people* are.

Chapter Twelve

PARENTING'S 21 MAGICAL SECRETS

> *It is the fortunate but rare parent who feels clear and strong and ready to be the religious educator of his children . . . [instead], they bring to this dimension of their parenting only a fuzzy, undefined sense . . . but no coherent, grounded, articulated sense . . . Now that it is their watch . . . the centre doesn't hold. What language they have feels archaic and disconnected. They may know that they are believers but aren't quite sure just what it is they believe.*
>
> Jeanne Harrison Nieuwejaar, *The Gift of Faith*

With babies, we know we need to show love, affection and attention. With toddlers we need to show freedom, restriction, encouragement and respect. But from preschoolers onwards our role gets more complex: we need to teach giving, sharing, truth, insight, discrimination, self-awareness, responsibility and ultimately independence.

As Generation Xs and Generation Ys, we know in our gut that we must do this for our Alpha-Z cyber-generation children. Yes, our *job* as parents is to make our children self-sufficiently independent, imbuing them with the gifts of driving passion and a zest for life!

Scattered throughout this book have been my *Parenting 21 Golden Insights* (not 'golden rules', as I'm not here to tell you what to do), which are what I, as the investigative writer, have concluded to be many of the crucial activities of holistic parenting — that is; the foundations of who we are, and what we stand for as unique family units.

Contained within this chapter are my *Parenting 21 Magical Secrets*, which are what I, as the investigative writer, have concluded to be many of the key actions of holistic parenting; that is the thoughts, words and deeds of how our individual family deals with the everyday practicalities of life.

In the same breath, it's important to appreciate that this chapter's secrets aren't secrets at all — but they can have some rather miraculously magical results.

These Magical Secrets are a culmination of philosophies from many of the greatest parenting thinkers and spiritual sages. They strongly o er some of the most important means to allow our children to live lives that are charming, delightful and enchanting — while still providing reliably solid foundations for them to mature into adulthood and support their individual life quests.

PARENTING GOLDEN INSIGHT NO. 19

Embrace parenting's magical secrets!

Chapter Twelve

PARENTING MAGICAL SECRET NO. 1

PARENTS NEED TO PARENT, NOT BEFRIEND

Kids can make plenty of friends — but they can't make parents

Perhaps in reaction to society's historical strictness — the children-should- be-seen-and-not-heard generation — is the opposing postmodern, child-focused generation that wishes to be a *friend* to their centre-of-attention children. This can be a misguided philosophy because it can create selfish, egotistical, the-world-must-revolve-around-me children, whose parents seem to have forgotten how to *parent*. The tail is wagging the dog, the parents have become manipulated by the child, and children in control are out of control.

Great parents recognise their power and assume it — they'd never cede or delegate it to others. 'Essential to a child's sense of security are parents who are authoritative, decisive and trustworthy — in a word, powerful!' says John Rosemond in his *Six-Point Plan for Raising Happy, Healthy Children.*

Our job as guiding protector is to be a *parent*. We must honour our children by stepping up to the plate and taking on the role of Boss. It's not about haphazard parenting, it is about parenting with purpose, with conscious intentions. When kids look at another family and think 'I want a family like that', they are nearly always admiring families with some kind of solid foundation defined by a unique set of values — families who know who they are and what they stand for — and that comes from the parents. Paul Faulkner says, 'Our children need structure and guidelines for ethics and morals, not just laws that tell them what is *legal*.'

As the renowned Italian educator Maria Montessori wrote in *The Secret of Childhood,* 'We must indeed realize that the child wants to obey us and loves us. The child loves the grown-up beyond anything, but people speak only of the grown-up's love for the child.'

Eventually, when our children finally come of age into adulthood, we will need to stop parenting them, and we should become one of their most loyal friends. Our parenting goal is: When they're old enough to vote, they're old enough to cope.

This Magical Secret is to teach our children they have guiding parents who lead the way, and while they are still children they must play the game of Follow the Leader.

PARENTING MAGICAL SECRET NO. 2
COUPLEDOM COMES BEFORE FAMILYDOM

One of the best things parents can do for their children is to love each other

If you as a couple jointly and wholeheartedly agree upon a child-centred parenting philosophy, then of course it can work very well indeed, so long as both parents are 110 per cent on board. The difficulty occurs when you become so caught up in parenting that you lose your coupledom and your relationship devolves into a passionless, detached PCU ('Parental Childrearing Unit'), to cite John and Linda Friel in *The Seven Worst Things Parents Do*. Our partner should come first.

Now don't misinterpret this Magical Secret to the extreme, such as feeding your husband dinner before feeding a hungry baby, or buying your wife flowers when your child needs new shoes — use common sense, please. But the crux of the point is our children eventually grow up and leave home, and when they do we should be left with a partner who is still our best friend.

However, it always takes two to tango. When one person in the relationship is not willing to make their partner the priority — such as a mom who since the birth of her first baby is utterly child-centred, or a father who puts the pub ahead of being home on time for the family dinner — then the writing can be on the wall. The couple's partnership is at risk of breaking down, regardless of how hard the other partner is trying to make things work.

An easy way to demonstrate this Magical Secret to children is to habitually put aside a quarter-hour before dinner, perhaps over a wine or beer on the deck, as adult-only, child-free couple time to catch up on each other's day — a Do Not Disturb moment that the children learn is impolite to interrupt. Other great habits are regular date nights; periodic weekends away without the kids and adult-only dinner parties, when the kids are not expecting to stay up late. This book is *not* pretending to imitate a relationship guide, but in the depths of their souls, children love to have loving parents, and this means parents who care more for each other than almost anyone else on the planet. Children adore seeing adoration!

Teach your children that their parents have powerful, respectful love for each other — even if you're divorced — can more than anything or anyone else demonstrate the power of love.

PARENTING MAGICAL SECRET NO. 3
CLEAR BOUNDARIES EQUAL PERSONAL FREEDOM

Yes sir, no sir, three bags full, sir

When a preschooler's backyard doesn't have adequate fencing, the parent needs to constantly limit their child's activities, whereas a preschooler who has a securely fenced backyard can enjoy wonderful freedom because they can safely play anywhere they want *within the boundaries*.

The same principle applies for parents who set strict black-and-white rules of acceptable behaviour for their children. Unambiguous, unmistakable limits give a child incredible freedom to do whatever they choose *within crystal-clear boundaries*. Research shows that laxly controlled toddlers often grow up to be impulsive, unreliable and antisocial; and permissive and inconsistent discipline during childhood is linked with higher levels of mental illness including teenage depression. 'Some things are clear: children need affection, boundaries and affirmation,' says esteemed researcher Richie Poulton.

This insight is also famously illustrated by Bobbie Pingaro in *The Meanest Mother in the World*: 'When others had Cokes and candy for lunch, I had to eat a sandwich . . . She had to know who our friends were and where we were going . . . She made us work. We had to wash dishes, make beds, learn to cook and all sorts of cruel things . . . I thank God, He gave me the meanest mother in the whole world.' I know this sounds tough, and it is tough — flippin' tough — on the parents. Setting limitations requires immense effort, dogged commitment and a bottomless pit of energy — and some days we may just want to be lazy, giving-in parents for a change. But the dividends are priceless: children of lovely character whom people describe as *good as gold*. Kids want to be liked, and joyful cheerful manners make them happy, and therefore likeable.

When they have explicit boundaries, children *know* when they're crossing the line, and when they do then at that moment they're prepared to pay the price — so be it. Good on them, for that takes strength of character and they will have earned the price they'll pay: consequences.

This Magical Secret is about setting clear boundaries — for boundaries provide incredible freedom of choice. So don't be afraid to make your kids unhappy by saying *'No'*. 'It defines their world, and makes it a safe place to live,' says Karen Sullivan in *How to Say 'No' and Mean It*.

Chapter Twelve

PARENTING MAGICAL SECRET NO. 4
WE ARE INTRINSICALLY INNOCENT, NOT INHERENTLY SINFUL

Doing bad things doesn't mean children are bad

Parenting with *innocence* simply means knowing our role is to guide our children, not to control them — to lead them, and not own them.

We all need to remember our children are born innocent, good, gifted and with their own set of unique challenges — but we also cannot take responsibility for all their problems and naughtiness. So we must teach our children they have permission to stuff up and make mistakes, so they can learn to self-correct — heck, that's what we adults are still doing.

It's about our kids really understanding that *doing something bad* doesn't mean *they're bad*. It is about them realizing we don't expect them to be perfect, because no one gets things right all the time.

It is also us knowing that our children are not supposed to measure up to our preconceived notions — they are supposed to go in directions we can't predict and do things we'd never do.

It is us knowing that the best thing we can do for our children is to love them totally, with utter conviction — with them knowing absolutely that our love is deeper than their most difficult and wayward behaviour.

Whatever our value system, we must have an antidote for sin.

This Magical Secret is to teach our children we are all inherently innocent.

It's about teaching them that although we don't always like what they do, we'll always love them, because we are all works in progress.

It is about them and us knowing there are no perfect children, or perfect parents, or perfect families — that is a societal mirage.

PARENTING MAGICAL SECRET NO. 5
CHILDREN MUST BE ALLOWED TO BE CHILDISH

Life is about living not learning — we learn to see as we learn to live

Among the chaos of modern life, we need to not only ensure our children are fulfilling their academic, artistic and sporting potentials, but also fulfilling their potential for childish play, by getting up to mischievous monkey business and *laughing*.

Vegging and blobbing are childhood skills that should be encouraged. It is only within the realms of needing to do nothing in particular that our children can be their most childish, as roguish imps and rascally urchins, with the excitement of being immature, irresponsible scallywags, and the delight of giggling with your accomplices.

Oh, the captivated smiles in our children's eyes as my husband would regale them with sometimes embellished (and sometimes understated) glorious tale of the tomfoolery he and his brothers got up to in childhood. In contrast, what will some of our generation of children tell their own kids they got up to in childhood? 'Well, we just went to lessons and classes and practices, really.' *(Cripes, how is it realistically possible they won't end up rebelling as teenagers?)* We mustn't let them get caught up in the vortex of over-organised activities.

Let us return to a middle path that enables our children to be childish during that brief, innocent period in their lives called childhood. And the window of time is briefer than you think: it's true peak only about three years long, from around seven years old (when they've been at school for a while so have learned a few cheeky street-smarts) to around 10 years old (before hormones can begin the transformation into a pubescent preteen).

So I giggle when we realise it was the Greek philosopher Socrates who said, 'Children today are tyrants. They contradict their parents, gobble their food, and tyrannise their teachers.' Almost 2500 years later, do we really think we should attempt to stop such tradition?

PARENTING MAGICAL SECRET NO. 6
SINCERE PRAISE FOR EFFORT AND INTELLIGENCE
Children should enjoy praise, but not need it

Research shows that when children are constantly praised for their work with the 'Gosh, you're smart at this' style of compliment, rather than the 'Gosh, you must have worked really hard at this' style of compliment, then they tend over time to opt for the cop-out, easy choices. The child learns to divide their world into Things I'm Naturally Good At so will happily do and Things I'm Not Naturally Good At so will refuse to try, or stop doing. We need to offer true, heartfelt praise for sincere effort, and unabashed praise and adoration for genuine endeavour. It's about taking a moment to be *really present* with your child, and highlighting something particularly praiseworthy to point out. As psychologist Carol Dweck from Columbia University explains, 'Emphasising effort gives a child a variable they can control. They come to see themselves as in control of their success.' Consistently praising intelligence can teach children not to risk making mistakes and that innate intelligence is the key to success — not effort or initiative. This can culminate in a look-smart image and avoid-embarrassment philosophy. This we know from research, and many a parenting guru. *But, but, but* — when our children are genuinely clever at something — and most are above average at *something* — then we should let it be known. Kids aren't stupid (most aren't, really) and they soon work out for themselves in the classroom what they're good at and what they're not good at. For example, all our kids are naturally pretty good at maths, primarily because all four of their grandparents are great at maths, including one who has IQ-qualified membership of Mensa. So yes, of course we must praise their maths brainpower — heck, much of the world is based on intellectual aptitude.

But the key to this Magical Secret is teaching our children true praise is only received for true effort and true acumen; this is to avoid turning our children into 'praise junkies'. Otherwise we can inadvertently create children who need to be told through constant glowing praise of their over-the-top fabulosity, just so they have the confidence to function.

So genuinely praise the triumphs and celebrate the accomplishments of work well done, a goal achieved, a certificate received, a medal awarded, an act of kindness. Extraordinary outcomes require extraordinary effort and deserve extraordinary praise.

PARENTING MAGICAL SECRET NO. 7
DINE TOGETHER AND WHINE TOGETHER

The family that eats together stays together

It doesn't matter if it's breakfast or dinner, but as my parenting author colleague Ian Grant, founder of Parents Inc., teaches, 'Shared mealtimes are the cornerstone for families who want to stay connected. Research shows that children who achieve invariably come from homes where families sit down once a day and eat a meal together.' My personal philosophy is that as soon as they can sit up in a highchair, they're joining us at the family dinner table . . . or breakfast table if that suits your family's routine better.

So hold the kids over with a banana or sandwich if you have to, and eat dinner as a family once Dad gets home. Research backs the fact that by just age four or five, being exposed to mealtime conversation raises a child's IQ by an average of eight points.

Sadly, the reality is that every night 30 to 50 per cent of Western children eat their dinner watching TV.

'Breaking bread' at a dining table, *with the TV turned off (!)*, is a vital link to smoothly functioning family communication. For just as the keel stabilises a boat, dining together stabilises family relationships. As respected sociologist John R Kelley states, 'Dinner together is one of the absolute, critical symbols in the cohesion of the family.' And as parents we need to make mealtimes as enjoyable as reasonably possible, while still enforcing polite manners.

Sometimes (often) when young children are tired and cranky at the end of the day, it can be pretty hard work for parents to stay upbeat enough to ensure dinnertime is enjoyable — but hey, that's our job. Dinnertime is also the opportunity for *discussions*. Oh man, we've had some doozy philosophical discussions around our dinner table. Sometimes dinner conversation has gone on way past bedtime — magic! Another idea is to celebrate anything, and have a 'You Are Special' plate that makes a lot of appearances.

This magical secret is about teaching our children dinner is a family meal — because eating together as a family is simply what loving families do. The best recipes always combine family with food!

PARENTING MAGICAL SECRET NO. 8
CHERISH FAMILY AND FRIENDS

Having a social life helps us find meaning in life

Stephen Covey writes in *The 7 Habits of Highly Effective Families*, 'The way you treat any relationship in the family will eventually a ect every relationship in the family.' I'm not going to tell you that you must honour all your family and adore all your friends — but if they're honourable, then adore them, as this teaches our children loyalty.

However, sometimes our families can be far from ideal, and this can also apply to historical friends. Continuing or discontinuing to mix with negative influences becomes an important judgement call parents need to make.

This magical secret is about cherishing family because it teaches our children the important value of their heritage and their belonging; that there is history to their existence (their 'tribe'). This can be demonstrated simply by committing time to visit relatives, having family photos around the home and generally talking about the importance of family.

Cherishing friends is about teaching our children the importance of social interactions, for being human extends beyond the people living in one's home. None of us is meant to live in isolation, no matter how naturally shy — we are social beings. And having a social life helps us to find meaning in our lives.

So become the 'hostess with the mostest'!

This is not about money or belongings that impress others. This is about conversations, sharing meals and laughter; mixing, mingling and meeting people; getting out, entertaining in and making new friends.

It's about *life*. It's about *living*.

Dinner parties, barbecues, playing cards, inviting over the parents of your children's friends — whatever you can imagine. Demonstrate to your children how to be a social being who knows family and friends are a vital, essential link to being a complete and contented, loving, sharing and interesting human being.

Teach your children to socialise by socialising, because no one, no matter how shy, needs to be lonely and isolated.

PARENTING MAGICAL SECRET NO. 9
OUR HOME IS OUR SANCTUARY

Tranquil ambiance is sweet nectar to the soul

Chapter Twelve

We all know children — and parents — need a warm, caring, supportive and encouraging environment; a place of peace, beauty, order, simplicity, joy, and love — a refuge or a safe haven. As parents in charge, we are responsible for our home's atmosphere. If it's ghastly, it's our fault. It's not about money. It's about vibe.

This Magical Secret is about creating *ambiance*. It's about paying attention to the household environment, sensorially. But this magical secret is not so much about creating a verbally non-abusive home environment (which is a given) than it is about using the home to create enlightening inner peace. Decorating a dressing table with family photos, a framed inspirational poem or a little golden Buddha, or using simple feng shui to balance the yin and yang to create chi harmony. It's also about music, scents and flames.

All religions light flames of some kind, be it candles or fires, as a guiding light for spirits. It is no coincidence the most romantic restaurants include candlelight, all priests light candles and all indigenous peoples dance around fires. So, please light candles — it brings us all closer to the universe's soul. And teach children how to light candles, safely and reverently.

Smell too impacts on atmosphere enormously. A whiff of body odour, or the stench of a full rubbish bin, or the perfume of roses, or the scent of incense, or the aroma of coffee — every smell can almost instantly create an ambiance. Our olfactory sense (smell) is the sense most rapidly picked up by the brain.

'Without music, life would be a mistake!' said the German philosopher Friedrich Nietzsche. I so agree! Melody is about cadence, and rhythm is about sensation, which makes divine music exquisitely nourishing to the soul. So let us teach our kids to have a love of music, and many kinds of music — acoustic guitar, classical harp, a symphonic orchestra, Celtic rhythm, shamanic drumming, melodious flute, Gregorian chants, the Beatles, Queen or the Black Eyed Peas — but *please* don't continuously expose your child to the same one genre of music, year in, year out.

Let us teach children they live in Home Sweet Home, for we all need our sanctuary to retreat to.

PARENTING MAGICAL SECRET NO. 10
LIVING FULLY IS BEING IN THE NOW

All that exists, exists only in the now

We mustn't lose our power to the endless what-ifs of life. The past is history and the future unforeseen; the only thing we have is right now. Eckhart Tolle writes in *Stillness Speaks*, 'This one moment — Now — is the only thing you can never escape from, the one constant factor in your life. No matter what happens, no matter how much your life changes, one thing is certain: it's always Now . . . The present moment is as it is. Always. Can you let it be?'

Being fully present is actually *so* important it could have been in the next chapter as the Law of the Present Moment. These days we focus on, talk about and act upon so much that is based on past occurrences and future plans. We spend so much of our 'now' reviewing what was, and planning what will be. We do it all the time, without hesitation — talking about the better times ahead, while dismissing the blessings of right now. Is there truly anything sadder than hearing a parent say, 'It'll be so much better once he starts walking' or 'I'm so looking forward to her going to school' or 'He was so much nicer before puberty set in'?

Then, too often, we hear of a life tragedy that causes a person to completely re-evaluate their priorities, to finally begin *living in the now*. Don't become yet another victim by discovering contentment only through catastrophe. This Magical Secret is about teaching our children not to worry so much about the future or past, but to be in the now with sharp consciousness and untarnished openness, so he or she doesn't miss the mini-moments of euphoria that are constantly occurring.

We also need to teach our children (and remind ourselves) to be completely happy in the now even when we aren't getting what we think we want right now. It's the conundrum of learning to desire more, at the same time as being happy with what we have. By nurturing the now, we can enjoy the journey, because experiencing desires that have been fulfilled only ever occurs in the present.

So be in the now, knowing that every moment is just as it is supposed to be.

PARENTING MAGICAL SECRET NO. 11
THE SPIRIT NEEDS THE TRANSCENDENTAL
Intuitive creativity is soul food

In the Dhammapada teachings, it is written the Buddha preached, 'From meditation comes wisdom, and from lack of it wisdom decays.' This philosophy has resounded repeatedly throughout teachings by prophets and sages for eons. Such guidance also resonates within our souls, rhythmically: *'I think that's true, I think that's true, I think that's true . . .'* But for many of us in this postmodern Western culture, meditation has become so outside our comfort zone that we just don't go there, so of course neither do our children. It took me 50 years to finally come to the full appreciation my Soul needs 15-20 minutes every day to meditate - don't take half a century like I did to learn this lesson.

In *What Do You Say to a Child When You Meet a Flower?*, David O'Neill writes so insightfully: 'Skeptics can easily persuade us that the poets and the artists and the prophets do not live in the real world — that they live in a world that is not as real and practical and useful as the world of the economist and the geologist and the statistician. I think it is the other way around.' *I so agree.*

As parents concerned with our child's development, we already exercise their body with sports and fitness, and we already exercise their mind with learning and homework. However, as parents concerned with our child's developing core essence, we also need to instigate activities that exercise their intuition, because all souls need to feel the spiritual creativity imparted by transcendental activities — that is, activities that transcend our everyday, 3D, five-sense, earthly world.

There are endless options — dancing, martial arts, playing instruments, singing, drama, writing, reading poetry or magical stories. There are painting, sculpture, pottery, sewing, knitting, crochet and handicrafts. There are chess, Scrabble, learning languages, attending concerts or cultural events, listening to a large variety of music. There's stargazing.

Let's teach our children to enjoy their intuitive creativity!

PARENTING MAGICAL SECRET NO. 12
REALISE SILENCE IS GOLDEN

Peace & quiet in the brain brings peace & quiet to the soul

In my midwifery role I have been *stunned*, during postnatal in-home visits, by how often the widescreen TV is droning away in the background — it seems most households have their TV on all day long. *Aaarrrgggghhh!*

It is no surprise our brain these days is so bombarded with a smothering overload of data: the glorious world wide web spews out statistics, facts, figures and opinions; instant communication is obligatory or you risk leaving people on tenterhooks . . . the noise of busyness is non-stop!

It's little wonder that we scream at our children 'Oh, for a bit of peace and quiet!', for we can be as guilty as the kids at suppressing silence.

How many parents walk in the front door and turn the news on straight away?

Today silence has become so rare, our soul spends much of its lifetime yearning for and craving it. It is well overdue that we all remind ourselves of those beautiful words by the thirteenth-century German mystical theologian Meister Eckhart: 'Nothing is so like God as silence'!

This Magical Secret is about teaching our children to enjoy their own quiet company; it's about being able to be content in your own skin, and being quite satisfied with quiet simplicity.

As guardians focused on holistic parenting, let us revive the calm, renew the stillness and encourage the peaceful. The tranquillity of silence is like a drink of cold, sweet spring water to the spirit. Should life really have to be better than lying in a hammock reading a great book on a quiet sunny day? We must teach such simple joys to our children, by doing simple joyful things.

Let us teach ourselves and our children how to wallow in the peace of silence . . . because for the mind to be still, it needs stillness.

PARENTING MAGICAL SECRET NO. 13
NATURE IS ONE OF OUR BEST NURTURERS

We must constantly return to commune with Gaia

For the past 200,000 years, *Homo sapiens* has been required to befriend nature because it was utterly reliant on her. But somehow, often in today's hectic modern life, we seem to have really lost touch with Mother Nature. We are ignoring her needs at our great peril.

As the famous German-Jewish diarist Anne Frank wrote, 'The best remedy for those who are afraid, lonely or unhappy is to go outside, somewhere where they can be quiet, alone with the heavens, nature and

God. Because only then does one feel that all is as it should be and that God wishes to see people happy, amidst the simple beauty of nature.'

So if there's any one thing in which we should utterly overindulge our children, it's their hours spent in the outdoors with their other mother: Nature, because Gaia is a feast for the heart. We must teach our children (and perhaps remind ourselves) how to commune with nature to ensure our kids don't grow into adults who mumble ludicrous statements like 'I don't like the beach, it's too sandy' or 'I don't enjoy the snow, it's too cold'. Let us instead bathe our children in Gaia's grace, immersing them in her glory, infusing them in her beauty and making sure they feel completely at home in her presence.

Demonstrate to your children a love of gardening, such as admiring beans growing. Encourage your kids to hunger for the wind blowing in their face on a bike ride, or yearn for the forest smell on a hiking trek, or bubble up with anticipation of the next wave as they frolic in the surf. It's so important children learn to play outdoor sports, go fishing, feed animals and build sandcastles. This is the stu our magnificently wonderful and exquisitely delightful planet Earth is all about.

PARENTING MAGICAL SECRET NO. 14
DEMONSTRATE CONSERVATION OF OUR PLANET

For our children's children's children

These days we are repeatedly experiencing the hottest, driest, wettest, coldest and stormiest weather in recorded history. Gaia is in trouble and we know now, beyond any shadow of a doubt, that the writing is on the wall.

Clearly it is up to us. We must lead the way. As the native American proverb says: 'We do not inherit the earth from our ancestors — rather, we borrow it from our children.'

Chapter Twelve

Because of pollutionary changes in the air, revolutionary changes are in the air!

This Magical Secret is simply about us demonstrating to our children, through our daily lifestyle and moral code, how we, and they, must care for their Earth Mother, Gaia.

But how? Here's some of what Climate Crisis recommend:

» Use less power at home by replacing regular incandescent lightbulbs with energy-e cient compact-fluorescent lightbulbs, using energy- e cient appliances, and turning o electrical appliances and lights when not in use.

» Drive less — walk, cycle or use mass transport.

» Reduce household waste by recycling and avoiding products with lots of packaging.

» Reduce the amount of petrol you use by running your car e ciently, or, if you can, buy a hybrid car.

» Lower the temperature of your hot-water thermostat and insulate the cylinder.

» Use renewable sources of energy and materials.

» Become carbon neutral by planting lots of trees.

» Spread the word by learning about climate change and speaking up.

» Vote for political leaders who pledge to act boldly, decisively, comprehensively and quickly to solve the crisis.

» Buy products only from companies that have a green environmental policy, backed up by credentials , eg EcoStore household products.

» Get actively involved. There are so many wonderful websites. To name just a few: www.EarthHour.org, www.PeaceTeam.org.nz, www.ArtofLiving.org, www.kidsrgreen.org, www.KidsforSavingEarth.org

PARENTING MAGICAL SECRET NO. 15
WE ALL NEED TO BE THE HELPER, COMFORTER, HEALER AND TEACHER

It is the ultimate fulfilment of human destiny for us all

It was the author Neale Donald Walsch in the *New York Times* bestselling phenomenon *Conversations with God* who summarised each of our destinies in this extraordinary and simple way: the helper, comforter, healer or teacher. Always and only through those roles are we able to become our highest vision.

It does not matter if we are a reclusive Buddhist monk, a New Age organic-farming hippy, a quintessential knitting and baking stay-at-home mother, or a wildly wealthy business tycoon — so long as we are in a role that enables us to help, comfort, heal and teach other people, then we are on the road to becoming our best Self. As the saying goes 'You being yourself helps others be themselves.'

That is one of the biggest reasons why new parents can so often fall in love with their role because for the first time in their life they are suddenly an incredibly essential helper, comforter, healer and teacher - and that feels SO fulfilling: They are needed.

For that reason, learning to be the helper, comforter, healer and teacher is also what we need to actively cheer on our children to become confident at, by encouraging them to feel at ease with assisting, caring, fixing and showing. Maria Montessori described it gorgeously in *The Secret of Childhood* when she wrote, 'The children themselves found a sentence that expressed this inner need. "Help me to do it by myself!" How eloquent is this paradoxical request!'

In reality, probably the most influential part of our children's learning, is them witnessing their parents in our daily interaction with each other, our friends, our family, and other children. So do e ectively demonstrate support, consoling, alleviating hurt, and educational coaching — and also clearly emulate your own role models and mentors.

Teach our children how to help, comfort, heal and teach, because through those roles we all become the best person we can be.

PARENTING MAGICAL SECRET NO. 16
SELFLESS SERVICE GIVES OUR SPIRIT MEANING

Charity begins at home

In general, we can pretty much draw a line down the middle and categorise all people as either natural *givers* or natural *takers*. Personally, I know I'm a giver and all of the close friends I attract are givers too. Givers are people who do things for no particular reason, except to make another person's day brighter.

Then there are the takers. Most of you reading this book will be a giver, because you're searching to enhance what you give as a parent to your child. But there may be a few stray takers reading this too, whose gut instincts are telling them they have a deep-down hunger to become a giver. They yearn to treat everyone with courtesy, kindness and humanity, all the time, instead of selectively discriminating who they show their nice self to. Typically, because of upbringing, snobbery, shyness or another debilitation, they may be just a tad unsure of quite where or how to begin. So this Magical Secret is a great start. As missionary Amy Carmichael points out: 'You can give without loving but you cannot love without giving.'

Teaching our children the meaning of life through acts of selfless service is the 'servant leadership' role, leading from the foot of the table. Teaching our kids about selfless service can only be accomplished by involving our kids in projects where they can contribute to the welfare of others. It's about doing something that's not your responsibility, just because you have a service mentality.

Over time, performing modest, non-dramatic charitable works of service brings an incredibly fulfilling sense of meaning to one's life. This is not the charity of donations, but the charity of giving before it is asked for... paying it forward. In fact, the most virtuous kind of charity is the pure intention of giving anonymously so that the benefactor is unaware of who the giver is and is thus unbeholden.

As Buddha taught his followers, we must teach our children the triple truth: a generous heart, kind speech, and a life of service and compassion — these are the things that renew us.

We cannot get the richness of loving until we fully love the richness of giving.

PARENTING MAGICAL SECRET NO. 17
OWNING PETS HAS MANY POSITIVE BENEFITS

Teaching unconditional love and responsibilities

Some children naturally love caring for all animals, some children are naturally scared of many animals, but all children can potentially benefit from owning pets.

Pets are about learning kindness to animals, understanding responsibility to others and experiencing the loyalty of companionship.

Pets also die, which of course can be a tremendously sad event, but it teaches children to appreciate how fragile life can be, and to develop the capacity to deal with loss from death — all in all, it's about experiencing the circle of life.

According to research by Dr Marty Becker, author of *The Healing Power of Pets*, around 99 per cent of children want to experience a pet's unconditional love and constant companionship. Other research into the benefits of childhood pet ownership also reveals some unforeseen returns, such as better school attendance rates (because they know responsibility); higher self-confidence and self-esteem; a reduced likelihood to criminally o end in later life; deeper capacity to feel empathy and interpret body language; a higher likelihood of involvement in outdoor sports; plus improved general overall health, including reduced allergies and a more robust immune system.

I know kids promise to take care of the pet forever, but most times they don't — it's a learning curve, and pet responsibilities need to be age-appropriate.

If you are in a situation where it's not possible to own the traditional top-pick pets (a dog or a cat), then I can personally recommend a pair of female rats. Their intelligence falls somewhere between a cat and a mouse, they have distinctive personalities, can be trained to do tricks and use a litter tray, and stink less than male rats, and much less than mice.

As Tessa Livingstone points out in *Child of Our Time*, 90 per cent of children with pets put their pet in their top-five relationships, and sometimes pets can be singularly the most important relationship a shy child can have to prevent demoralising loneliness.

Teach our children the responsibility of caring for pets, because all creatures deserve our kindness.

PARENTING MAGICAL SECRET NO. 18
CEREMONIES AND RITUALS ARE CRUCIAL LANDMARKS
It's vital to celebrate rites of passage and milestones

It's interesting to reflect that the word 'spiritual' combines the words 'spirit' and 'ritual' — the spirit needs ritual to make it complete. As Dale McGowan writes in *Parenting Beyond Belief*, 'Imagine life without cycles or landmarks of any kind — just birth, followed by a long, gray line of 27,941 days, then death.'

Ceremonies mark special occasions of importance, such as birth (naming or baptism), marriage and death. These cultivate a family's memories. *Celebrations* are parties that observe something, such as a special birthday, academic achievement and sporting awards. Societal *rituals* are the repetitious, familiar framework of events that occur annually, which can be holy days that have become holidays, such as Jewish Hanukkah, Christian Easter and Christmas, Chinese New Year, American Thanksgiving — even 23 December's 'Festivus for the rest of us' as popularised by *Seinfeld*.

Initiating *family rituals* is about creating unique events in your household, such as Friday evening fish 'n' chips; Saturday breakfast of Dad's special pancakes; kids lighting candles at Sunday night dinners; family DVD movie nights with popcorn, duvets and beanbags; fondue dinners on the last day of school term; or an annual visit to the local big fun park on the last Sunday of the summer holidays — the list is endless. It really doesn't matter what the rituals are, so long as they're enjoyable mini-celebrations that are predictable, reliable and consistently adhered to.

Many indigenous cultures and religious faiths include a puberty coming-of-age or rite-of-passage ritual, such as Judaism's bar mitzvah or Catholicism's confirmation. Sadly, our secular society has seemingly wiped these out, so if you are a humanistic parent, a coming-of-age or rite-of- passage ritual is one I ask you to seriously consider reinstating. It would be a milestone you create as your own family's unique ritual, specifically recognising the entry to early adulthood. As a suggestion, perhaps it could be held on the first 'teen' birthday.

We must teach our children the importance of rituals in the home, because they provide us with a sense of tradition, a sense of belonging, a rmation of milestones and a confirmation of maturation. Plus research shows if you grow up in a family with strong rituals, you're more likely to be resilient as an adult.

Chapter Twelve

PARENTING MAGICAL SECRET NO. 19
PARENTS LEADING THROUGH VERBAL EXAMPLE
It's about talking the talk as you're walking the walk

This magical secret can be one of the toughest and most challenging of them all, because it can take us a lifetime to feel completely competent with an I-no-longer-worry-what-others-think level of personal confidence. This magical secret is posessing the coolness to say *who you are*, at your *core essence*. To quote Buddha, 'When words are both true and kind, they can change our world.' Having fundamental principles provides children with incredibly solid stability, and lets them know their life is predictable, dependable and reliable.

When we as parents stand for little in particular, then probably so too will our children. In the book *Buddha Mom*, Jacqueline Kramer elucidates: 'Becoming a parent has provided me with the opportunity to see the family blueprint that has been passed down through the generations. It has taught me that I can choose to make changes that affect future generations . . . I act out of habit and it takes a great deal of courage, insight, and work to change even the simplest habits, let alone habits that have been ingrained in me since I was born!'

Let's get overtly clear here! This book is not telling you *what* it is you should declare you stand for or believe in. But this book *is* saying you need to *make some decisions*, at this point in time, about what it is you stand for and what it is you believe in. Not in an arrogant, pompous, righteous, condescending, overbearing or opinionated way, but in a gutsy display of backbone, fortitude and strength of character. In the beginning this takes courage, then after a while it will become as easy and natural as brushing your teeth.

In a very real way, this Magical Secret is the ultimate key to all the magical secrets before it. So when you're ready, and have begun to work out some philosophies for living and meanings of life that run true to you, then I encourage you to start to *talk the talk* — not for the purpose of converting anyone to the same beliefs but simply for the sake of demonstrating to yourself and your children and the world who you are and what you stand for. This parenting Magical Secret is about teaching our children how to avoid the emptiness of having no convictions, and instead to walk proud and talk proud too.

PARENTING MAGICAL SECRET NO. 20
OUR JOB IS TO BECOME REDUNDANT PARENTS

Don't fail your kids by ingraining within them they can't do without you.

If our *adult* child 'can't do without us' we have failed them. Some parents seem to forget that raising independent, self-reliant, autonomous individuals is one of their main parenting purposes — it's one of the key job descriptions. Sadly, in reality, for some parents raising a child becomes their whole existence. Hence there are parents who are addicted to being needed by their children and who create adult-age 'children' who won't leave home because it has altogether become just a tad too jolly comfortable and over-welcoming.

Conversely, consciously accountable parents understand it is one of their core responsibilities to successfully raise children to become adults who don't keep 'running home to Mom and Dad' when things turn to custard. For our fundamental task is to instil in our children the resilience, fortitude, stamina and strength of character required to get on with doing whatever needs to be done, most of the time.

Our job is to strategically prepare our kids for life! Our duty is to eventually create young adults who are both networked — that is, they recognise we all need other people's help — and autonomous — that is, self-sufficient, self-determined, self-disciplined, self-reliant and self-motivated . . . and the task begins in childhood.

This magical secret is about looking for opportunities to instil independence in our children, instead of proliferating the rampant number of mollycoddled six to 12+ year-olds. It's about our children unpacking and carrying their own schoolbags; showering themselves and brushing their own hair; doing most of their homework unsupervised; walking, cycling or bussing home from school instead of being picked up; and being responsible for their own present-buying budget. You see, having responsibility and independence is having freedom of choice, and experiencing the personal growth that goes with it.

This magical secret is ultimately about raising our children to be independent little people who are responsible for their choices, *and* the subsequent outcomes — when we choose the behaviour, we choose the consequences. Children discouraged from making individual choices are unable *to learn accountability.*

We have to give them roots by holding them tight, and give them wings by turning them loose.

PARENTING MAGICAL SECRET NO. 21
THE SOUL IS REAL

We are spiritual beings having earthly experiences

I have no doubt our core essence lives on eternally after this physical body dies. But for some parents, this may be *the* most outside-one's-comfort-zone suggestion contained within this entire book, especially if you're still grappling with an agnostic mindset, waiting for proof. But perhaps the only real proof one can receive comes after dying, though obviously that isn't conducive to hands-on parenting! So this may be a leap of faith — and if I'm wrong, you've got nothing to lose!

At the same time, there is nothing wrong with explaining to your child that you don't have all the answers, because frankly no one can ever have all the answers.

Perhaps you have heard the Buddhist proverb 'When the student is ready the teacher will appear', but it also works in reverse: 'When the teacher is ready, the student will appear'. As parents, we do have immense wisdom to teach! And when our children are ready to formulate the questions, then they are ready to receive the answers.

This Magical Secret is to teach our kids to understand they are a triadic being: that is, we have a physical body and cognisant mind that interconnect with our spiritual core essence. We can admire a person's body, or not. We can respect a person's mind, or not. But it is only ever a person's spiritual core essence we truly love ... from one soul, to another.

Chapter Twelve

SUMMARY

When young people ask me for advice today, I generally say, 'Decide what is sacred to you, and put your best life energies at its service. Make that the focus of your studies, your work, the test for your pleasures and your relationships.'

Starhawk (Miriam Simos), *The Spiral Dance*

'There are only three ways to teach a child: the first is by example, the second is by example, and the third is by example.' Albert Schweitzer, theologian, philosopher and physician, was on to something.

All those who know me well, and some who know me a little, would confidently describe me as 'vaguely religious and deeply spiritual'. Other people you know may confidently describe themselves as, say, fanatically Christian, piously Buddhist, radically New Age, zealously Muslim, staunchly Jewish, ardently Atheistic, and so on. The point is, you know where they stand . . . and their children know where they stand. This enables these children to experience the self-assurance and self-confidence of a strong character. To quote the black American writer and civil-rights activist James Baldwin (1924–1987), 'Children have never been very good at listening to their elders, but they have never failed to imitate them.' And there is also the lovely adage: 'Children seldom misquote you. In fact, they usually repeat word for word what you shouldn't have said.'

In *How to Really Love Your Angry Child*, Ross Campbell explains, 'Many parents speak as if their power as parents is limited and they're already doing all they can. But in truth, we have a great deal of power and our children have almost none.' You see, until the age of twelve, most children generally believe what their parents believe — later it becomes their turn to redefine their own beliefs.

At the end of the day, the purpose of our parenting role is to prepare our children for life on their own, without us, because our job description is to make ourselves redundant . . . and that's all about parenting with grace and truth.

Can we parent them honestly?

Heavens, yeah!

Can we parent them perfectly?

Hell, no!

> *The best things in life are not things.*
>
> Amish Proverb

Chapter Thirteen

PARENTING'S
21 UNIVERSAL PRINCIPLES

Children try to understand not only what is happening to them, but why; and in doing that, they call upon . . . the spiritual values they have received.

Robert Coles, *The Spiritual Life of Children*

Around the globe, from ancient religious canons and scriptures to modern New Age spiritualist creeds, the same basic life tenets and beliefs are repeated, over and over, which parents have been passing down to their children for time immemorial — but not so much, lately, in the West.

When we study history's great prophets and philosophers, such as Buddha, Lao-tzu, Confucius, Jesus, and Mohammad (and many other illuminated teachers), there is a very distinct theme of synchronistic teachings. It is perhaps the most profound example in human history of 'great minds thinking alike'.

So from these numerous parallel sources this chapter is extracted. Nothing in it is new. Nothing in it is revolutionary. None of this chapter is radical, ground-breaking stu . These 'laws' are simply teachings nearly all the great messiahs, knowledgeable prophets, astute sages, erudite gurus, learned philosophers and perceptive mystics have unanimously, mysteriously, and synchronistically, agreed upon.

These Natural Laws, Cosmic Rules, Laws of Spirit — whatever the heck you want to call them — are without much doubt our 'Earth School Rules' that strongly govern all our lives. Whether we are religious, spiritual, secular, humanistic, agnostic or atheistic, these are the inexplicable truths we all end up learning, and the sooner the easier, it seems. As a protagonist parent and a proletarian writer, I have summarised these wise teachings as the *21 Universal Principles*.

When I began university study for the first time in my life in my late thirties, I remember my university-savvy adult niece and nephew revealing a 'lightbulb' moment to me, and it was: as an undergraduate student, I know *nothing*. Meaning, as undergraduates we are *not* expected to come up with any original ideas, because all the thoughts that could ever be thought on the subjects we are studying have already been thought by astute intellectuals and expert authorities long before us.

You see, as an undergraduate earning a degree, we are simply there to learn what is already known — to be brought up to date with what everyone else skilled in that knowledge already knows. Later, during a postgraduate master's or doctorate, is the time in academia when you are expected to think a genuinely original new thought.

That is what this chapter is about too. Simply you (and me) learning what is already known by the wise, because when we have such wisdom, we can feel immensely better equipped to teach our kids how the 'Earth School Rules' actually work.

If you thought I cited a lot of quotations before that was *nothing* on this chapter, dear friend! Here, I endlessly quote others' wisdom. Why?

Chapter Thirteen

Because I can't possibly do this by myself! This is the really *big stuff* of *life*: it's the gargantuan, world-shatteringness of the What It's All About and Why Are We Here questions. Of course I can't do this on my own! This chapter is unavoidably, inescapably and necessarily philosophical, theoretical, spiritual, mystical, ethereal and numinous.

However, if you decide to do nothing else after reading this book, except to teach your child these 21 primary tenets — in whatever way it works in your family to do so — then know for sure you will have given your child some of the most empowering gifts of their entire lifetime: the specific knowledge of how life actually works!

As parents, we're just giving them the keys, so they can open their own doors.

PARENTING GOLDEN INSIGHT NO. 20

Teach your children the Universe's principles, 'cause they're the game-rules of Earth School.

---

1. LAW OF POTENTIAL

Only those who risk going too far can possibly find out how far one can go.

TS Eliot (1888–1965), English poet

Anything is possible, no matter what. *Everything* is possible, no matter what! There is virtually nothing that could never possibly be.

This is the never-say-never and never-say-can't law; the 'a forest is contained inside every acorn' law; the 'on earth so it is in Heaven' law.

The Law of Potential means teaching our children we can all be, do or have whatever we can imagine, for there are *no* limitations to our potential. Our children are born as boundless potential! As Glinda, the Good Witch of the North, said in *The Wizard of Oz*: 'You've always had the power.'

The Law of Potential is directly affected, like everything, by the Law of Karma (cause and effect), for potential possibilities of course can feel positive or negative. So we mustn't not care, or take no responsibility, or ignore others' feelings or needs, or just look out for ourselves. But we do need to cultivate our willingness to step into the unknown, which enables us to walk in fields of all possibilities, because, as English writer John Heywood said, 'Nothing is impossible to a willing heart.'

The Law of Potential is also directly affected, like everything, by the Law of Attraction, for realising everything is possible requires believing anything is possible — we can't realise something without believing it. When we realise (understand) it, we realise it (make it real) then 'Success comes from any and all directions,' as Deepak Chopra says in *The Seven Spiritual Laws of Success*.

We need to teach our children they can be, do or have whatever they can imagine, and then some, because they possess hidden possibilities of pure potential to change or create almost anything they want in their life. We are all pure potential, and the purpose of our lives is simply to give birth to and create the best, most accepting, grateful and blessed person we can be.

Teach your children: Everything is possible, no matter what!

2. LAW OF GIVING AND RECEIVING

Giving is better than receiving because giving starts the receiving process.

Jim Rohn (1930–), *business philosopher*

This is the 'we get what we give' and 'give and you shall receive' law. But these days virtually all Western children may su er interminably from the 'ingrate syndrome' of wanting the greener grass on the other side of the Jones' fence. To paraphrase *Conversations with God*, the universe's flow of energy operates through dynamic exchange — and our willingness to give that which we seek keeps abundance flowing into our lives, because giving circulates the universe's abundance of gifts.

Sometimes we can think ourselves to be very good at the *giving*, but know ourselves to be pretty hopeless at the *receiving* — yet this is the key! We *can't* be the best giver we can be unless we are receptively open to receiving! It is through the receiving that we become our best at giving — because the more receptively (openly) we receive, the more receptively (alertly) we give.

Then, we can take this Law of Giving and Receiving to the next level of understanding: the more we *give* then the more we *get*. Then, we can take this law to an even higher level of understanding: whatever we feel we most need is what we most need to give. Then, finally, we can take it to its highest level: happiness is wanting what you have.

Teaching our children the Law of Giving and Receiving is primarily about ensuring they understand societal rituals of showing gratitude and thanking with sincerity, including kind manners and cooperative sharing; and ensuring they learn most of this through witnessing us, their parents, giving generously and receiving graciously.

Teaching our children the Law of Giving and Receiving includes showing them that their innate gifts can truly change other people's lives, because they have the power to give a good day to someone else, and the power to change someone's bad day into a good day. Could there be anything more awesomely powerful than that?

Teaching our children the Law of Giving and Receiving is also about teaching the compassion of empathy and sympathy. For when we always practise (try) compassion, we'll always practise (do) compassion, and then compassion becomes our practice (way).

Teach your children: Receiving is the echo of giving!

3. LAW OF FAITH: ASKING AND ASSUMING

When you put faith, hope and love together, you can raise positive kids in a negative world.

Zig Ziglar (1929–), *motivational author*

The Law of Faith (or 'Law of Hope') has two distinct sides.

First is the Law of Asking — you could call it the 'don't ask, don't get' law, or the 'ask and it shall be given to you' law. It is also the 'God helps those who help themselves' law. (Interestingly, this is not actually written in the Bible. The King James Bible contains the famous phrase, 'Ask and ye shall receive' — but somehow in the tremendous liberties of translation the original text has been morphed. The closest translation is: 'So ask without hidden motive and be surrounded by your answer. Be enveloped by what you desire.')

Second is the Law of Assuming, which is committing to an attitude of confident belief and patience that everything always works out just as it's supposed to — the God-moves-in-mysterious-ways conviction. You could also say it's the living-by-the-seat-of-one's-pants law, but the reality is we're all actually living that way anyway, every day, consciously or unconsciously. We just *think* we're in control, but actually we're in control of squat — because life can change in a millisecond. This Law is not a lazy way out, not at all. It's actually perhaps the ultimate demonstration of faith and hope!

Faith is like a direct link to the wisdom of the universe. It's committing to only living your life in the way that meets up to what you know in your heart and soul to be the right way to live.

Hope is having a desired wish with an optimistic expectation, because as Mark Eddy Smith writes in *Tolkein's Ordinary Virtues,* 'Hope is not a feeling, it is a choice; and even in the midst of despair we can still choose to carry on. There is no greater hope than that.'

When our children learn to have enriched hope in their self-purpose, this provides them with the fortitude of faith and assured conviction of life's big picture. They will feel the power from assuming everything they ever ask for they will always get, as if they were supposed to have it.

Teach your children: Ask life for anything, with faith, then allow life to unfold its great gifts — often more wonderful then we could ever have hoped for.

4. LAW OF DESIRE

Children need permission to ask for more;
otherwise they will never know how much they can get.

John Gray, *Children Are from Heaven*

Desire is not wrong or negative, it is human and it is immensely powerful! Desire is godly; it's what drives a crawling baby to walk, and a walking toddler to talk. 'Everyone in the world has desires. Children need to know, from the beginning, that desire is the most basic drive in human nature,' writes Deepak Chopra in *The Seven Spiritual Laws of Success for Parents.*

In 1943 American psychologist Abraham Maslow (1908–70) proposed the Hierarchy of Needs, which has become a benchmark for understanding human motivations. Humans first seek to meet their physiological needs, such as air, food, water, sleep; then they will seek to meet their safety and security needs; then their need for love and belonging; then their need for self-esteem, such as respect, confidence, achievement; and finally the self-actualisation of creativity, spontaneity and morality.

Greed is a negative desire, for *greed* is wanting more at the same time as being dissatisfied with what you have. Whereas positive desires have the virtues of perfection, passion, assertiveness and intention: It is *perfection* that inspires us to realise, fulfil and achieve our dreams and accomplish our desires, with flawless, faultless excellence. And desire fuels our *passions* because we are supposed to follow our dreams. It is *assertive intention* that imbues us with its bold force to see things through, for although desire drives us, *intention* is its engine. Without asserted intention, desire goes nowhere.

Then — and this is the vital key — we must teach our children (and ourselves) to step back, handing our desires over to the universe for safe-keeping, so they can be fulfilled when the time is right. Once desire's power of intention is harnessed, we must let go of the reins and stop trying to determine all outcomes.

Teach your children: The law of desire is about teaching our child that *desire* is our spirit's energy, and *will* is its product. Every time they wish or want, they plant a seed. We must teach our children the paradox of putting their goals in concrete, but their plans in sand, because often *how* the end goal finally eventuates is so different, and so much better, than any of us can ever imagine. We have to teach our children that *healthy desire* is wanting more at the same time as being satisfied with what we have.

Chapter Thirteen

5. LAW OF GRATITUDE

Gratitude is the most exquisite form of courtesy.

Jacques Maritain (1882–1973), French philosopher

Because Western children rarely experience life-threatening needs, it can feel near impossible to teach them to comprehend deep gratitude. But *gratitude* is the adhesive that allows us to balance perfectly on top of the fence and not fall off into either the 'want-want' or 'give-up' backyards.

Gratitude is truly, deeply appreciating that 'if you have food in the refrigerator, clothes on your back, a roof overhead, and a bed to sleep in — you are richer than 75 per cent of this world'.

Gratitude is about discovering your authentic self by sometimes looking away from problems instead of directly at them, for by looking from another perspective, we can eventually discover there is no problem.

Emphatically, this Law of Gratitude unconditionally requires the virtues of gratefulness, thankfulness for, and appreciation of, the beautiful and excellent blessings in our life — some could even rename it the Law of Grace. However, grace can never be *attained*, but with charity, kindness and mercy amazing grace can be *received*. You see, the point of our journey of giving *gratitude* is so we can eventually receive *grace* and know its wonderful tranquillising effects on the soul.

We must teach our children that if we wallow in the 'bummers', or worse, harp on about them to anyone who will listen, then the nasty thing is people will tire of our company, and we will tire of our life, because when we are ungrateful, no amount of kindness can assist us.

We need to show our children that when we live our life with genuine daily gratitude it enables us to get over negative experiences so much quicker, because they can usually be instantly dwarfed by our abundant blessings, with the consequential spin-o being *happy contentment*. The Gospel of Thomas (discovered in 1945) puts it like this: 'Recognise what is in your sight, and that which is hidden from you will become plain to you.'

Teach your children: It's not about having what you want, it's about wanting what you have.

6. LAW OF ENDEAVOUR

Put every effort into organising your life, but remember that the ultimate organiser is Nature.

Deepak Chopra (1946–), Indian doctor and writer

Also referred to as the Law of E ort, Law of Exertion, Law of Discipline, Law of Action or Law of Struggle, this law is about starting the engine, for only action brings plans to life! Or as Christian minister Vance Havner says, 'Vision isn't enough unless combined with venture. It's not enough to stare up the steps unless we also step up the stairs.'

Maria Montessori in *The Secret of Childhood* explains, 'Thus, through the indefatigable activity, made up of e orts, experiments, conquests and griefs, through harsh trials and wearisome struggles, he, step by step, fulfils his di cult and glorious task, adding always a new form of perfection.'

This principle can also be titled the Law of Perfection, which is actually its own paradox: conventionally, perfection never exists because excellence is the best we can achieve. Yet transcendentally everyone and everything is already unconditionally perfect.

Such a tenet then conflicts with the Western work ethic we have inherited, which says 'the harder we work the better the rewards', while at the same time we have many children struggling to learn *patience,* because their parents have ensured everything instantly comes their way, when and how the kid wants it.

So like many laws, this one also has two sides that require balance: the ambitious I-make-my-own-luck self-motivation, and the tranquil being-in-the-now inner peace. Perhaps this law could more accurately be named the Law of Flexibility, because to find happiness, we also need to possess the chilled-out 'don't say "no", just go with the flow' attitude that allows things to unfold, by embracing living without a need for expected specific results.

Ultimately, this law requires middle-path balance to maintain a personal symmetry between trying too hard and not trying hard enough, because anything we do, we can overdo and under-do. We all need to demonstrate to our children our own equilibrium between career endeavours and carefree harmony, so we can guide our children to do the same in their lives.

Teach your children: Success comes from effort, but true success comes from balanced harmony, and is measured by our level of wisdom, courage and peace.

7. LAW OF FREE WILL

We cannot always control our circumstances, but we can and do choose our response to whatever arises.

Dan Millman, *The Laws of Spirit*

The Law of Free Will could also be named the Law of Choices, and cosmically it is perhaps the most important of all universal principles. In many ways it epitomises the entire experience of being human: free will (having the ability to choose), is what being human is all about.

Free will is also the basis of democratic life, but those concepts can directly conflict with much religious doctrine – the Ten Commandments, Buddhism's Noble Eightfold Path, Islam's Five Pillars . . . the list of rules is virtually endless. This incongruency was inadvertently summed up by American president Ronald Reagan's speech at an evangelical convention in 1983 when he said contradictorily, 'Freedom prospers when religion is vibrant and the rule of law under God is acknowledged.'

So on one hand we have free will and on the other hand we have religious doctrines dictating to us the right choices. Therefore, a fundamental paradox of humankind exists: how can we declare ourselves to have God-given free will when we must follow 'His will'? *Does our free will only amount to a right to get it wrong?*

It is at this point the disparaging cynic can really rear its ugly head. 'Man is born free, and everywhere he is in chains,' said Swiss-French philosopher Jean-Jacques Rousseau. But what about English critic John Ruskin, who said, 'No human being, however great, or powerful, was ever so free as a fish.' And then there's writer George Orwell, who said, 'Freedom is the freedom to say that two plus two make four.'

The true universal Law of Free Will is about the power to choose our truest response, and that challenge is all about finding a middle path within the mind-boggling bazaar of competing thoughts and overlapping feelings, to paraphrase William Marbach.

We need our children to learn that although we are not always responsible for every situation, we are all responsible for our emotional responses, both reactive and proactive, both reactionary and actionary.

Teach your children: We must each take personal responsibility for how we outwardly express our thoughts, feelings, actions and intentions.

8. LAW OF KARMA

Results are what you expect,
and consequences are what you get.

Schoolgirl's definition, *Ladies Home Journal*, 1942

This is the moral cause-and-effect law and the reap-what-we-sow law, because it is the combination of both a person's past actions and present-day conduct that determines our future. Karma is the long-term, big-picture consequences of all our conduct. Traditionally, the Law of Karma states that all living creatures are responsible for their karma — that is, their actions and the effects of their actions.

Teaching our children about karma is teaching them to understand that repercussions are not always immediately visible. Outcomes are cumulative, and are not always about what we do today — it can be about what we did today, yesterday, last week or last month, or do tomorrow, next week, next month and next year. The Law of Karma is about the mushrooming, snowballing and escalating effects of our actions. Teaching our children about karma is teaching them that every action affects the future — even if it appears to have no consequence at the time.

In practical terms, teaching our children to respect one's karma means teaching them to choose the actions that bring happiness and success to others, and thus bring happiness and success to themselves, not in a selfish way of course (which would be 'bad karma') — but always in a loving way. Respecting the Law of Karma is about comprehending the errors of our ways when, as Polly Berrien Berends states in *Whole Child/Whole Parent*, 'We act on assumptions and motives we aren't aware of and reap consequences we don't expect.'

However — and this is a *big* however, in conflict with much of the current New Age spiritual doctrine — it is *essential* we *all* understand that karma may have *nothing* to do with the misfortune (or fortune) you experience in this lifetime. Hear me *roar*: we do *not* make all our good luck, just as we do *not* make all our bad luck! Sometimes, really great things happen to bloody awful people, and sometimes bloody awful things happen to really great people — and these are not necessarily outcomes they have 'attracted'! It is simply their Journey.

Nevertheless, what is *very much* within our control is our reactions to events — that is, the free will, which accumulates as our karma.

Teach your children: Every choice we make affects our future.

9. LAW OF YIN AND YANG

The reverse side also has a reverse side.

Japanese proverb

Life is dualistic and works in the polarity of opposites: black-white, positive-negative, north-south, left-right, up-down, day-night, light-dark, sweet-sour, hot-cold, fast-slow, big-small, young-old, attraction-repulsion, pleasure-pain, fire-water, motion-stillness, land-sky, earth-heaven, truth-lie, love-hate, heaven-hell and good-evil. So this could also be called the Law of Balance, for as Dan Millman writes in *The Life You Were Born to Live*, 'If gravity is the glue that holds the universe together, balance is the key that unlocks its secrets . . . between the polarities rests a balance point, a center.' The Chinese philosophy of yin and yang is about the virtues of balance, cleanliness and peacefulness; it's about the middle path between contraries. The dichotomy of yin and yang represent the fundamental underlying cosmic nature of 'unity in duality' or the harmony of opposites.

To paraphrase *Conversations with God*, how can we understand happiness if we've never understood sadness? How can we appreciate independence if we haven't experienced dependence? How can we know success, unless we've stood on the doorstep of failure?

Opposites are simply how the world functions, and how we learn to comprehend our own weakness, so we can recognise our own greatness! We need to teach our children that life is *supposed* to work in opposites, because it is our goal to cultivate balance.

Michael J Gelb in *Da Vinci Decoded* discusses the artist Leonardo's philosophy of balancing left- and right-brain thinking, culminating in whole-brain thinking. For Gelb, da Vinci's persona and work conveyed more than just a balance between logic and imagination, science and art, masculine or feminine — they symbolised the crucial principle: duality.

The Chinese proverb 'The gem cannot be polished without friction, no man perfected without trials' is of course very true indeed. But please let us put aside the archaic philosophy that we learn harsh lessons through life's trials and tribulations. Instead, let us teach our children to realise such incidents simply provide us with the necessary opposite experiences to enable us to truly comprehend joy and love!

Teach your children: Without experiencing true happiness, it isn't possible to experience true happiness.

10. LAW OF TRINITY

We are truly indefatigable in providing for the needs of the body, but we starve the soul.

Mrs Henry Wood (1813–87), *English novelist*

The Law of Trinity is the law of body, mind and spirit, and finding equilibrium so that there is no dominance. This law is about appreciating that although the world is dualistic (the yin and the yang), people are triadic beings — physical, non-physical and meta-physical; thought, word and deed; the conscious, subconscious and super-conscious.

This law is about respecting we each have three distinct aspects of our whole being, each with its own needs, and each deserving *equal* attention. For example, in India they talk of ayurveda for the body, yoga for the mind and meditation for the spirit — which holistically brings about well-being . . . *oh to be a blissed-out visitor for a few months in an Indian ashram!*

But back in our day-to-day world of mundane domesticity, the Law of Trinity is about teaching our children (and ourselves) to respect our triadic nature by paying equal attention to the body, mind and spirit.

Nourishing the body is about establishing stability between the joy of indulgence and the fitness of healthiness, by feeding our body healthy food and treating treats as treats. Nourishing the mind is about crafting symmetry between humility's modesty and satisfaction's pride, by feeding our minds with both academic knowledge and insightful wisdom, while still being capable of revelling in the comedy of humour. Nourishing the spirit is about creating transcendence between blameless innocence and individual self-awareness, by feeding our soul with divine spirituality and heeding our potent intuition. 'Our souls belong to our bodies, not our bodies to our souls,' said author Herman Melville (1819–91).

That is the goal of living one's life respecting the Law of Trinity. Nonetheless, as the illustrious Swiss psychiatrist Carl Jung wrote in the foreword to Suzuki's *An Introduction to Zen Buddhism*, 'It is a cosmic life and a cosmic spirit, and at the same time an individual life and an individual spirit.' At the end of the day, it's simply about teaching our children to revere their own threefold nature. And as parents we need to lead by example, by caring for our body, mind *and* spirit.

Teach your children: Nurturing the spirit and nourishing the mind are as important as feeding the body.

11. LAW OF JUDGEMENT

Whoever undertakes to set himself up as a Judge of Truth and Knowledge is shipwrecked by the laughter of the gods.

Albert Einstein (1879–1955), *physicist and philosopher*

This could also be called the Law of Perspective, but perhaps it would be more aptly called the Law of Eat Your Words, Take-It-All-Back or Best Bite Your Tongue! When we use judgement for negative, critical or disapproving condemnation . . . it *will* bite us in the bum. It *always* does. On the other hand, when we use judgement for positive, intelligent and discriminating wisdom, we are rarely wrong.

At the same time, it can be rightly argued that changes for good and improvements to society have usually only come about through people having attacked, denounced and rebuked what they feel is deeply wrong. So . . . it is a rickety fence we straddle once again, almost always based on individual perspectives.

We need to teach our 'tall poppies' to be proud of their innate ability to lead, and teach our 'sheep' to be proud of their innate ability to support our leaders — for leaders need followers, and followers need leaders. We must all respect and appreciate that our forthright and outspoken 'tall poppies' are our leaders of revolutions — the dissidents who transform change. Plus we must all respect and appreciate that our cautious and diplomatic 'sheep' are our followers of reform — the supporters who en masse force change.

Then there are the fundamentalists — often judged as radical. Cripes, human history (and the present) is teeming with warped, twisted and distorted ethical codes leading to unbridled hypocrisy, doled out in the name of morality! *Me being judgemental? Cynical? Valid?* You be the judge, or not.

In reality the deepest core essence of possessing *great* judgement is the saintly ability to rise above the human behaviour of judging altogether. The most profound principle of this tenet is simply teaching our children that when others hold different values to them, they need to realise those people have had different experiences. We need to remember goodness, mercy, patience, understanding, compassion and forgiveness.

Teach your children: 'Good judgement comes from experience, and experience comes from bad judgement.' So when our child has been judgemental, and life has kicked back, then our job is to pick them up, dust them off and remind them of this law. No universal law judges us — it just bestows lessons and consequences.

12. LAW OF ATTRACTION

As a man thinketh in his heart, so is he.

Proverbs 23:7

The crux of this law is that like-attracts-like: what you fear you attract; what you resist persists; when you live with great expectations then great things will happen; what you think is not because of who you are, but who you are is because of what you think. 'Attitude determines altitude' and 'As within, so without'. 'You are what you say, no matter what way,' our eldest, Rick, began saying at nine years of age. 'We too are the victims of our own contemplation,' wrote John Jay Chapman in *Practical Agitation*.

It is written in Buddha's Dhammapada teachings, 'All that we are is the result of our thoughts; it is founded on our thoughts and made up of our thoughts . . . If a man speaks or acts with a harmful thought, trouble follows him, as the wheel follows the ox that draws the cart . . . If a man speaks or acts with harmonious thought, happiness follows him as his own shadow, never leaving him.' You see, when we say 'I wish', 'I want' and 'I need' a particular something, then that is exactly what we will get: tomorrow we will still *wish, want* and *need* that something.

Anger, sadness, sorrow, frustration, disappointment, worry, embarrassment, jealousy, hurt, insecurity and shame are all normal human emotions of fear or suffering. So we must teach our children it is okay to experience these negative emotions, for it is part of learning to become cooperative, compassionate and confident. From a child's perspective, learning the Law of Attraction can primarily be about learning to avoid pessimism, and to release doubts and reject fears.

We need to teach our children that for everyone beliefs affect success, and that love, kindness, delight and generosity attract love, kindness, delight and generosity — so it's back to the get-what-you-give tenet. The essence of the Law of Attraction is to teach our children that it is *okay* to have negative internal thoughts because emotional feelings can be difficult for anyone to control. *However*, we all must try to only *react* positively through our outward actions, words and deeds.

Teach your children: Say only what you want to believe as true, for your mind will believe everything you say as the truth.

13. LAW OF FORGIVENESS

Children cannot learn to accept their own imperfections if everyone around them is perfect.

John Gray, *Children Are from Heaven*

This universal law is perhaps better titled the *Art* of Forgiveness, and it has three distinct sides: giving an apology, accepting an apology and forgiving oneself.

Since the fifteenth century, the proverb 'Children should be seen and not heard' has been extremely dominant in the Western childrearing psyche. Until only very recently, the idea of apologising to one's child was a fanciful and unnecessary notion. Regardless of their behaviour, parents, as the penultimate authorities (second only to priests and God), were not accustomed to asking their children for forgiveness, as doing so was believed to undermine their authority. 'An apology? Bah! Disgusting! Cowardly! Beneath the dignity of any gentleman, however wrong he might be,' as so descriptively put by Baroness Emma Orczy, author of *The Scarlet Pimpernel*. And so, the intergenerational cycle of bolshie, obstinate, humbug and mulish adults persistently continued.

Without any doubt the only true way to teach forgiveness to our children is to realise this graceful social art can only be taught by demonstration.

Let's face it, the polite, well-mannered 'good' kids can find themselves constantly saying sorry for various little transgressions. Subsequently the frequent, and sincere, adult response of 'I forgive you', and the less frequent but heartfelt adult 'I'm sorry' do serve as highly effective character-building warm fuzzies — because they directly demonstrate that Mom or Dad know we all blow it sometimes.

It's not about being perfect, it's about intention. The art of forgiveness is about being noble, generous and magnanimous: 'To err is human, to forgive divine.'

It is also important, so *invaluably* important, that first-hand — by receiving our apology — children witness their parents releasing any guilt we carry, by us forgiving ourselves! Oh my God, that's *so* powerful! Ross Campbell writes in *How to Really Love Your Child*, 'A child must be taught by example how to forgive and how to find forgiveness . . . I cannot overstress how important this is. So many people today have problems with guilt. They cannot forgive or they cannot feel forgiven. What can be more miserable?'

Teach your children: forgiveness is something we do for ourselves.

Chapter Thirteen

14. LAW OF SYNCHRONICITY

I am open to the guidance of synchronicity,
and do not let expectations hinder my path.

Tenzin Gyatso, Dalai Lama (1935–)

Synchronicity is the connected meaning of seemingly random unrelated events. The Law of Synchronicity is all to do with our personal level of openness towards, and happiness with, the awareness that nothing ever truly happens by chance. It's us embracing the meant-to-be philosophy in our daily lives.

Our culture certainly is rich with words that attempt to explain synchronistic events: happenstance, concomitance, concurrence, coincidence, simultaneous, chance, luck, fortune, fluke, windfall, serendipity, Godsend, blessing and boon *(which, coincidentally, is my maiden name)*. But even with all that vocabulary, we can still find ourselves searching for words to describe extraordinarily synchronistic events in our life, just as we can find ourselves searching for their meanings, especially when we sceptically or cynically refuse to accept the potential of the universe having a plan beyond our own wish lists.

What is the alternative to living without awareness of synchronicity? Simple: *chaos*. When everything is random, haphazard, arbitrary — a hit-and-miss life — this is almost guaranteed to lead to confusion, bedlam and pandemonium and the resulting internal turmoil. 'Why did this happen to me?' 'Why does this keep happening to me?' 'Why do I have such horrible luck?' 'Life's so unfair'.

Following the Law of Synchronicity is simply about working hand-in-hand with all this universal wisdom, which shows us instinctively the 'best way'.

As children it's all about realising things do happen for a reason, and life's not a series of random events that just happen to us, because there is order in the universe. As adults it's about waking up, as singer Madonna explains: 'When you start tuning in to that frequency, you do have a tendency to look back and go, "Oh God, what was I thinking" — and that's a healthy response.'

Teach your children: Be open to the guidance of coincidences, for as philosopher Friedrich Schiller says, 'There is no such thing as chance; and what seem to us merest accident springs from the deepest source of destiny.'

15. LAW OF INTUITION

Common sense is instinct. Enough of it is genius.

George Bernard Shaw (1856–1950), *Irish writer*

Intuition can be called 'common sense', but that is grounded in the practical; or it can be called 'sixth sense', but that is eerily in the ethereal; or it can be called 'insight', but that is adroitly in the intellectual; or it can be called 'instinct', but that is characterised in personality. No, the best word for intuition is *intuition* — though in parenting it's good for us to embrace all the other terms too, so they become a natural part of everyday conversation.

At its core essence the Law of Intuition is about being sensitive to foresight. Fortunately, all children are born with strong intuition, so it is not something we as parents need to teach our children to possess. It is simply a resource we need to remind them to listen to ongoingly to prevent it from shriveling into insignificance, by explaining that intuition is their most infallible life-tool, and best resource for making right decisions.

Our intuition's language is our emotional *feelings,* such as warm fuzzies, prickly aches or feel-good reactions. So when our children ask for advice, we can simply reply 'What does your gut instinct say?' 'Do you feel comfortable or uncomfortable about the idea?' 'What choice is your heart telling you to make?'

Children taught to trust and heed their intuition have a huge advantage with making 'right' and 'wrong' decisions as they grow up. If 'all his friends' are going to daringly jump off the cliff into the sea below, but your son gets an unpleasant ache in the pit of his tummy at the idea *(and he is used to heeding his intuition because he knows how accurate it is)*, then there is no way he will risk going against his gut instinct for he knows better . . . and he'll stay safe. If your shy-ish daughter is invited to take a lead role in a school play, and she is nervous about going on stage, but every time she thinks about the idea she feels delightful bubbles of excitement, then there is no way she will turn down the opportunity *(if she is used to heeding her intuition because she knows how accurate it is)*, and she will have a wonderful time performing in front of an audience.

Teach your children: The emotional skill of hearing — and heeding — their innate intuition.

16. LAW OF FATE AND DETACHMENT

That which we do not bring to consciousness appears in our lives as fate.

Carl Jung (1875–1961), *Swiss psychiatrist*

The Law of Fate teaches us that in reality we have little or no control over many outcomes that can seem good, bad, fortunate or unfortunate.

The Law of Detachment teaches us that to acquire true wisdom (and true freedom), we all need to let go of the reins and embrace uncertainty, by simply stepping out of our own way. Often the more precisely we plan, the harder destiny can hit. In moments of sadness, of course it's okay to shed tears, but detachment is relinquishing resistance and maintaining the serenity of inner peace. As Eckhart Tolle writes in *The*

Power of Now, 'Too o er no resistance to life is to be in a state of grace, ease, and lightness.'

It is detrimental to our child's eventual adulthood to take fate and detachment lessons away from them, by trying to solve all their problems and protect them from every 'bad day'. Remember, experiencing bad days is how we each learn to recognise good days.

We need to teach our children that everyone has to cope with their own set of problems — so it's vital we all know how to expect the unexpected, to go with the flow, to trust the journey, and to anticipate the blessings in disguise.

We need to teach our children to be willing to embrace ambiguity, paradox and vagueness, for there can be such great wisdom in fresh, new and ever-moving uncertainty. Anyhow, we each kid ourselves if we think we know what is 'normal', or what is 'around the corner', for none of us ever really knows! Any control we think we have is simply a charade, all our lives can be turned upside down in a millisecond!

We need to teach our children there are many optimal paths in our lifetime, and each fork in the road creates new choices, one of which is optimal.

We need to teach our children su ering makes us vulnerable, struggle makes us adaptable, and together they make us gracious. We were all made to be heroic.

Teach your children: Life is like a roller-coaster — so sit back and enjoy the ups and downs of the ride!

17. LAW OF PASSION

There is no greatness without a passion to be great.

Tony Robbins (1960–), *self-help guru*

Of all universal principles, this is surely *the* most vital key to accomplish personal fulfilment, because only through realising our passions can we realise our selves! Dan Millman, in *The Life You Were Born To Live*, says it's about 'recognizing, accepting, and expressing our authentic interior reality'.

When we are enthusiastic, obsessed, infatuated or full of zeal, we experience feelings of excitement and delight, and usually a generous spoonful of audacious courage. For all of us, our passion is the key to life becoming more joyful, because it unlocks a door into true personal freedom.

The Law of Passion is black and white — there is no grey middle ground. To paraphrase *Conversations with God*, life exists as opportunities, and why we do *anything* is a statement of *who we are*. Also, to prove who we are, we will also find ourselves forced to reveal *who we are not*. But the load gets easier, because we are living our chosen life. 'When you serve your passion, when you are willing to risk yourself for something, your greatest creative energies are released. Hard work is required, but nothing is more joyful than work infused by love,' says Starhawk in *The Spiral Dance*. 'If we resist our passions, it is more because of their weakness than because of our strength . . . The passions are the only orators which always persuade,' wrote French author François de La Rochefoucauld (1613–80).

Some children dwell in households that reek of impassionate indi erence, so as insightful adults we also have a responsibility to imbue all children whose lives we touch with as much inspiration as possible. Because, for all of us, *passion* fuels the creation of who we are and who we truly want to be. We must educate and elucidate, so our kids can demonstrate and illuminate.

'What is passion? It is surely the becoming of a person . . . In passion, the body and the spirit seek expression outside of self . . . The more extreme and the more expressed that passion is, the more unbearable does life seem without it,' says English filmmaker John Boorman.

Teach your children: Passion is the key to loving their lives, and enthusiasm is the key to loving themselves.

18. LAW OF DHARMA
A life of purpose reveals the purpose of life.

Deepak Chopra
The Seven Spiritual Laws of Success for Parents

The Law of Dharma (a term first coined by bestselling author Deepak Chopra) is another name for the Law of Purpose. It is appreciating that every single person has a unique special talent to give others, and a unique special purpose in life. To paraphrase *Conversations with God*, our true destiny, our only purpose in life, is simply to grow our talents through opportunities for self-development, excellence, optimism and effort; to create the best, most accepting, grateful and blessed you that you can be. The best you has strong courage, great peace, deep wisdom and self-fulfilment. Self-fulfilment is becoming master of your own destiny, and mastering your true destiny is being all you can be.

Powerful stuff! But how do we take this down to a child's level?

First, we need to tell our children that everyone's life has a purpose, and discovering that purpose fills us with happiness. Knowing they're here for an important reason fills a child with pride and security.

Second, we need to tell our children that none of us knows when or how our purpose will be revealed; sometimes it's slowly over time, sometimes it's all of a sudden on one pivotal day, and sometimes it's as if we've known it all our lives. This knowledge can help to protect and insulate our children from the disappointments, discouragements and frustrations they will face on their journeys, as no path is without obstacles.

Finally, we need to emphasize that although attaining success is about creating their future with ambition and courage, it is not just about conventional accomplishment — performing acts of service and helping others to feel good is the best place they can begin to discover their higher purpose.

Teach your children: It's about us saying to our children — to all children — 'Hey you! You over there! You're here for a reason!'

PARENTING GOLDEN INSIGHT NO. 21

Tell your child we are each here for a reason, and finding our purpose fills us with happiness.

---

19. LAW OF TRUTH

What we need is not the will to believe,
but the wish to find out.

William Wordsworth (1770–1850), *British poet*

This universal law of Truth is all about discovering wisdom. It's about having an open-minded thirst to find wisdom's truths. Philosopher Søren Kierkegaard (1813–55) put it like this: 'There are two ways to be fooled. One is to believe what isn't true; the other is to refuse to believe what is true.' And the *parental* Law of Truth is simple: we must demonstrate our own pursuit of and receptivity towards *truth*, and pass this addiction on to our children, because nothing inhibits imagination or closes the mind tighter than ignorance. Wisdom is always found by those who seek it.

So how do we teach our children truths, yet teach them to seek their own truths? The answer is overt: we coach our infant's voracious craving for knowledge into a childhood ravenous hunger for knowledge into a teenager's insatiable eagerness for knowledge ... then we let them fly solo ... Tell them about the Seven Natural Wonders of the World: the Grand Canyon, Great Barrier Reef, Rio de Janeiro harbour, Mount Everest, the Northern Lights Aurora Borealis, Parícutin volcano, and Victoria Falls.

Tell them about the Seven Wonders of the Ancient World: the Great Pyramid of Giza, Hanging Gardens of Babylon, Statue of Zeus at Olympia, Temple of Artemis at Ephesus, Mausoleum at Halicarnassus, Colossus of Rhodes, and the Lighthouse of Alexandria.

Tell them about the Seven Wonders of the Middle Ages: Stonehenge, Rome's Colosseum, Catacombs of Kom el Shoqafa, the Great Wall of China, the Porcelain Tower of Nanjing, the Hagia Sophia, and the Leaning Tower of Pisa.

Tell them about the seven deadly sins: lust, gluttony, greed, sloth, wrath, envy and pride. Tell them about the seven holy virtues: chastity, abstinence, temperance, diligence, patience, kindness and humility. Tell them about the seven laws of Noah: just laws, no idolatry, no murder, no theft, no sexual promiscuity, no blasphemy and no cruelty to animals.

Tell them about Buddhism's seven factors of enlightenment: mindfulness, investigation, energy, rapturous joy, relaxed tranquillity, concentration and equanimity. Tell them about the seven blunders of the world that Mahatma Gandhi explained to his grandson: wealth without work, pleasure without conscience, knowledge without character, commerce without morality, science without humanity, worship without sacrificem and politics without principle.

Tell them about the seven days of the week, the seven notes in an octave, the seven seas, the seven archangels, the seven colors of the rainbow, the body's seven chakra energy centres, the seven branches of Kabbalah's Tree of Life, Lawrence of Arabia's seven pillars of wisdom, NASA's Mercury Seven, Enid Blyton's Secret Seven, Snow White's seven dwarfs, Star Trek's Seven-of-Nine, poker's seven-card stud, Rugby Union's Rugby Sevens!

Teach your children: To have an insatiably curious and unrelenting quest for knowledge. 'Know the truth, and the truth shall set you free.' (Bible's New Testament, John 8:32) Enlighten, inform, delight!

20. LAW OF JOY

Pain is inevitable but misery is optional so stick a geranium in your hat and be happy.

Barbara Johnson, *author*

The Law of Joy is not actually a law. It's an end result.

'Nothing can give you joy. Joy is uncaused and arises from within,' Eckhart Tolle writes in *The Power of Now*. The Law of Joy simply says: the purpose of our life is joy.

It's about being *free* — free of every nightmare, problem, worry, concern, anxiety, trouble, fear, apprehension or nervous discomfort... it's the realisation of pure joy creating the actualisation of true freedom. Tolle again: 'Beyond happiness, and unhappiness, there is peace.'

As Anne Wilson Schaef writes in *Meditations From Women Who Do Too Much*, 'We are the wellspring of our own happiness. Our happiness resides within us... We think success, recognition, respect, money and prestige will do it for us. They're nice for a while, and the feeling lingers that something is missing... Happiness is ethereal.'

For all of us, the 'earth school' journey is meant to be about becoming a liberated, emancipated and limitless person with the aspired end goal of having the freedom of knowing true joy.

Although we each have different passions, vocations, sacred tasks and destinies, we all have an identical purpose: to be joyful. So don't worry, be happy!

We need to teach our children to adore their unique and awesome individual talents as gifts, for such strengths help lead us towards discovering our potential. Passion creates who we are and who we want to be, and when we find the joy of being our happy, peaceful, whole self, we then also find *true freedom*.

We need to show our children there is no reason not to be joyous from this moment on, most of the time regardless of past sadness, tragedies and regrets. Let us all try to consciously become, what Neale Donald Walsch calls, the Ambassadors of Joy: by *looking* at each other, for we all want to be seen; *smiling* at each other, for a smile can heal a person's whole day; and *touching* each other, for some people haven't been gently lovingly touched in a long time.

Teach your children: We must all be emissaries of joy!

21. LAW OF LOVE

All of the laws described in this book are secondary to the Law of Love. I don't say this merely as poetry or metaphor; I mean it literally ... If we love, then nothing else is necessary.

       Dan Millman, *The Life You Were Born to Live*

Love. The ultimate of ultimates, the final, crucial, definitive part of the human journey.

In reverence to *love*, this small section of one chapter of one book cannot begin to pay adequate homage to how important *love* is. *Love* is everything! Sadly, extolling conditional love has perhaps become both the trademark of many orthodox religions and the greatest crime of fundamentalism.

On top of that, most of the time, especially publicly, we're all lovely. Then privately, alone with our kids or our partner, occasionally, we can be such cranky people — we can disgust ourselves! Because we're human, and we make mistakes. So how can this writer do justice to the power of *love*? It is impossible. These few papers can only ever be but a feeble human attempt to pay homage to *love*. I will get French writer Roland Barthes (1915–80) to explain on my behalf: 'To try to write love is to confront the *muck* of language: that region of hysteria where language is both *too much* and *too little*, excessive . . . and impoverished.'

After pensive soul searching, for ease, I have divided the Law of Love into 10 parenting tenets. *How crazy to try when you think about the enormity of it all, but here goes*:

FIRST TENET OF LOVE — love is all there is

The only true emotion is *love* — all the rest are man-made feelings. Eternal thanks to John Lennon and the Beatles for making the information public: Love is all you need!

SECOND TENET OF LOVE — love has no limits

Often when a couple are expecting their second child, they find themselves wondering how it will be possible to have enough love in them to love a second child as much as they love their first — we can find ourselves worrying if the second child will get the leftovers of love. Then, after the birth, we usually realise, really realise, in genuine amazement (!), that we contain an infinite, limitless ability to love . . . and that's a most wonderful sensation. Parenting is pretty much the world's most intensive course in love.

THIRD TENET OF LOVE — kids think our love does have limits

The fact that we love our children *no matter what they do* is something we need to repetitively drum into their little subconscious minds, so they can't, even in their wildest imagination, ever consider that we don't love them. Kids need to be told 'I don't always like the things you do, but I'll always love you.' Say it clearly, say it often; it will sink in. But when you've been slack for a while you might hear your child say, quite genuinely, 'I don't think you love me any more!' — and one of our heartstrings snaps in pain. Kids fundamentally yearn to be accepted, to feel precious, regardless of how quirky or different they are. But when children have a deep-rooted belief they are not loved, it can manifest as tremendous anger. So never verbally attach conditions to your love, even frivolous, superficial remarks such as 'I'll love you if you bring me the remote'. *Aaarrrgggghhh!* As Jewish-German American psychologist Erich Fromm (1900–80) said, 'Immature love says: "I love you because I need you." Mature love says: "I need you because I love you".'

FOURTH TENET OF LOVE — vanity is insanity

Living with conceited, self-important vanity is ultimately hollow futility because arrogance is not conducive to experiencing the sensation of pure joy, authentic freedom and divine love (heck, pride is one of the seven deadly sins). Yet egotism is strong in my heart, like it is in the king of the lion herd — just as it may be strong in your heart. As Mark Twain said, 'Man will do many things to get himself loved; he will do all things to get himself envied.' Or maybe you have a lack of pride in who you are, due to some complex heavy yoke you wear around your neck that slumps your shoulders; or perhaps your image of yourself, for whatever causes, is in the gutter. Maybe you're sick and tired of being sick and tired — in that case a little more pride (lot more!) in your soul's uniqueness could be a well-deserved thing. Whatever the case, this tenet of love is about finding the balanced 'middle path' of possessing both delighted pride and dignified modesty in one's true self.

FIFTH TENET OF LOVE — children cannot receive 'too much' love

It is certainly possible for children to be 'smother-loved', which is a horrid thing we all witness from time to time in mothers (primarily), whose energy spent on her child, concern over her child, and pride in her child is stifling. She (or he) is suffocating. What are the odds of such a child eventually rebelling? Or worse, as I have seen too often, yadults (young adults) who are still incapable of being even as self-sufficient and independent as our own were as very young teenagers. But smother love aside, know that it is fundamentally not possible for children to receive *too* much parental love. As David P O'Neill writes in *What Do You Say To A Child When You Meet a Flower?*, 'It is something strange about our Western culture — we are a little scared about loving children too much. People say they are afraid to spoil their children with too much love. It is not too much love that spoils children . . . it is a mixture of too little love and a kind of permissive indulgence that treats the children as pretty toys.'

SIXTH TENET OF LOVE — only hurting people hurt people

All our children will get bullied and let down by friends while they're growing up (and occasionally let down by ignoramus adults too). When your kids are not the type to intentionally hurt their friends, it's helpful to have an explanation as to why so many other people feel compelled to behave that way. And I use my wise big sis Helen's 'line' a lot with our kids: 'Only hurting people hurt people.' For when a person loves who they are and loves their life, it's impossible for them to hurt other people. So when people hurt us, we need to understand, they're obviously in deep pain.

SEVENTH TENET OF LOVE — love is goodness, practise it

This is back to the basics of leading by example, and demonstrating to our child in day-to-day life the art of exuding goodness. You, as a reader of this book, already know this. I adore the words of the Body Shop founder Anita Roddick, who said, 'Kindness doesn't have to be insipid or random to be e ective. Far from it. Deliberate kindness can be fierce, tenacious, unexpected, unconditional and sometimes positively revolutionary.'

EIGHTH TENET OF LOVE — everything connects to everything else

The innate interconnectedness of the universe is an enormous topic on its own, but if you've read this book from cover to cover you've probably already come to the conclusion that everything connects to everything else. So including this statement almost becomes as superfluous as having a last instruction on a cake recipe that says, 'You have now baked a cake'. *Duh!* Yes, everything connects with everything, which is the reason why we must all practise love, in everything we do, because we recognise and appreciate the interconnectedness of what we do with who we are, what we stand for, and the life we experience.

NINTH TENET OF LOVE — educate that making love is sacred

When it comes time to educate your child about sex (see also Chapters Four and Five), *please, please, please* treat it with reverence! Obviously I'm biased because I'm a midwife. I think conception, ovum, sperm, ovaries, the uterus, the cervix, the vagina, the placenta, even the penis and the scrotum, for goodness sake, are all glorious! I don't expect you to be quite so OTT, but *please, please, please* don't put any of your own warped sexual hang-ups on your children, such as sex is dirty or rude; or that menstruation is an unpleasant pain in the neck; or that ovulation must be suppressed at all times by contraceptive hormones; or that men's testosterone is insidious. Can we please teach our children that sexual intercourse is not just physically pleasurable and emotionally gratifying, but fundamentally and profoundly spiritually sacred.

TENTH TENET OF LOVE — feel and action only unconditional love

To paraphrase *Conversations with God*, when we're not sure how to react or what action to take, we simply need to ask ourselves, 'What would love do?' Would love put a little ding in a stranger's car and ignore it? Would love send a business a nasty, complaining letter? Would love argue bitterly with a shopkeeper to prove a point? Would love berate itself for being an imperfect human who, like all of us, makes mistakes? Would love routinely act elitist, aloof and snobbishly?

Teach your children: Love is like sunshine, there's no shortage and enough for everyone.

> "Love is the emblem of eternity; it confounds all notion of time; effaces all memory of a beginning, all fear of an end."
>
> Madame Germaine de Staël (1766-1817)
> French revolutionist

SUMMARY

Ultimately, all spiritual laws reveal themselves as needed — not necessarily in words, but rather through our deepest feelings, through the intuitive wisdom in our hearts . . . which are communicated through our instincts and subtle intuitive feelings. All we have to do is pay attention and trust our inner knower.

Dan Millman, *The Life You Were Born to Live*

This chapter is just a snippet of all the cosmic, universal, spiritual laws — others not mentioned (or barely mentioned) include the Laws of Abundance, Acceleration, Accumulation, Action, Attention, Balance, Cause and Effect, Choices, Commitment, Compassion, Compensation, Correspondence, Courage, Creativity, Cycles, Discipline, Divine Oneness, Empathy, Enrichment, Exchange, Expectation, Finality, Flexibility, Gender, Habit, Higher Will, Honesty, Ignorance, Innocence, Integrity, Optimism, Patterns, Perfection, Perpetual Transmutation, Persistence, Perspective, Persuasion, Polarity, Power, Preparation, Presence, Present Moment, Probability, Process, Reciprocity, Relativity, Responsibility, Rhythm, Risk-taking, Sacrifice, Self-reliance, Service, Subconscious Activity, Timing, Unity, Value, Vanity, Vibration, Visualisation . . . there are *hundreds!* For beyond concepts of morality, spiritual laws are the paths of daily life.

Whether you personally take on board all the laws contained in this chapter as 'gospel truth' is for your mind (intellectual rationale), body (gut instinct) and spirit (highest wisdom) to decide. Let's face it, these are simply one writer's interpretation of the rules of 'Earth School'. 'Play your part in life, but never forget it is only a role.' (Author unknown)

Chapter Thirteen

> Without any doubt whatsoever, the writing of this chapter (and the entire ten-year odyssey of this book) has been done with empathy, faith, vitality, thankfulness, perseverance, honesty, idealism, balance, self-awareness, discernment, belief, openness, sensitivity, patience, enthusiasm, purposefulness, humour, tolerance and a love of learning — at least one virtue from every law.

Life isn't like a book. Life isn't logical or sensible or orderly. Life is a mess most of the time. And theology must be lived in the midst of that mess."

Charles Caleb Colton (1780-1832)
Clergyman, sportsman & author

Conclusion

The world is wonderful and beautiful and good beyond one's wildest imagination. Never, never, never could one conceive what love is, beforehand, never.

Life can be great — quite god-like.

DH Lawrence (1885–1930), *English writer*

You have reached the end of this book, and my hope is that it was a deeply worthwhile read for you! I have written it with love, and immense respect and admiration for you and your role as a parent.

Oh Grow Up is about 'wholistic' triadic parenting — caring for your child's body, mind and spirit, and it is written for all parents; from the pristine spanking-new first-time parent, to the gnarled well-honed old-hand guru grandparent; from the advocator of modern medicine to the campaigner of naturopathic therapies; from the devoutly religious to the doubting atheist. Because *Oh Grow Up* is all about abundant diversity.

As we mature along our parenting journey, we begin to truly comprehend that we can never be the perfect parent, and sometimes it takes parenting more than one child to fully realise it... to comprehend our limitations, to experience our thresholds, and to feel the searing burn of our most private shortcomings. That's what parenting teaches us... that sometimes we suck, and sometimes we're magnificent! And what's wrong with that? Nothing!

But maybe more than anything else, parenting teaches us that love has no limitations, and our ability to love is like a bottomless well of pure, sweet spring water. Often the water in our well tastes so thirst-quenching and health-giving; then again sometimes we just want to hide in the darkness of our well, digging out our own little cave, where everything and everyone will just piss off; and sometimes we feel like we're drowning in viscous glueyness of our own sea of liquid love. And that's okay. Welcome to Real Life! It's okay. It's all normal.

Every author on every subject always imbues their writing with their own biases — even when specifically intending not to. It becomes somewhat farcical not to acknowledge the reality that this entire book is skewed to the partiality of my opinions, that's inevitable... 'cause I'm the one sitting here doing the writing. *Sorry about that — unavoidable.* So do please set aside the parts of this book that you feel aren't for you. *Kewl.*

Let's face it, as parents we are all so marvellously different, and you, my dear reader, are of course free to have attitudes and viewpoints that differ greatly from my own, and from those of every other person on the planet! For you are utterly unique. So please, take from this book only that which you felt was of genuine benefit to you. Please, only ever do what you believe is right for you, right for your children and right for your family. (Whether or not it is the same as what was right for our family is irrelevant.) I honour the fact that every child, every parent and every family is unique — I celebrate nonconformity!

Listen attentively to your own intuition, so you can gain total respect for and trust in your own inherent parental wisdom.

My honest wish for you is utter elation, complete rapture and fantastic delight in your immeasurably valuable role — being a parent. For we are all-encompassingly what Life is all about!

For me personally, as the author, *Oh Grow Up* is ultimately about parenting with Soul, which begs the question: What is my personal definition of spirituality? Well, I publicly describe myself as vaguely religious and deeply spiritual, if that helps to define me. I believe Spirituality, it is the tangible soul relating to its intangible faith. I appreciate that description is a bit of a converse back-to-front version from most perspectives, which are usually traditionally based on having a tangible faith for an intangible soul. But for me, right here right now, I disagree with such convention — and I'm allowed to . . . I believe Life's all about our very *tangible* spirit relating to its very *intangible* beliefs.

What do you believe?

Love and light,

Namaste

Kathy Fray

xxx

God remained for me the unknowable mystery of life; he could be neither contained in, nor explained by, any creed . . . rather, the mysterious process of an evolving universe is itself God.

Emeritus Prof Lloyd Geering, *Wrestling With God*

With grateful thanks

And, ultimately, the real co-author is Grace itself. With all my being I thank Grace. May every breath be breathed, every moment be lived as a never-ending prayer of gratitude in service to Truth.

Brandon Bays, *The Journey for Kids*

To the 'Professional Support Crew' — I couldn't have done this anywhere near as well without all your wisdom, expertise and encouragement. Many, many people have given their support to this project, and to them I gratefully say *thank you*! And I must extend my particular thanks to:

The distinguished, professing and faithful Lloyd Geering, such a dignified gentleman — it is my humble honour you got to know me.

An amazing ensemble of natural health experts — too many to list — but especially Damian Kristof of TV's *Downsize Me*; Lani Lopez of TV's *About Health*; America's charismatic wholefood pharmacist Don Tolman; Pennsylvania's irrepressible Dr Eric Miller; Tauranga's renowned Dr Mike Godfrey; WellPark College head honcho of naturopathy Philip Dowling; microbiologist, nutritional biochemist and naturopathic physician David Holden; Annaliese Jones of Natural Health Check-Up; Sheena Hendon of Elementa; the irrepressible *Feed Me Right* mother-daughter team of Dee and Tamarin Pignéguy; and Albany Yoga's beautiful yogi Sue Grbic. *Thanks guys!*

A terrific troupe of persona experts, especially Personality Plus' award-winning speaker-author Allie Mooney; Personality Dynamic's expert Sue Blair; Forecaster's astrological scholar Anne Macnaughtan; Chicken Soup happiness guru Talia Mana; motherhood author and women's magazine journalist the irrepressible and divine Marilynn McLachlan; and Indigo Children experts South Africa's Kate Spreckley and Germany's Hawaiian-Easter Islander Carolina Hehenkamp. *Go girls!*

All the environmental and complementary health activists on this planet earth, especially Green politician Sue Kedgley; world-class marathoner Allison Roe; and GreenPlanetFM's mobiliser of consciousness Tim Lynch.

All the revolutionary New Agers awakening mankind, especially hummus queen Lisa Er, the noble soultman Tony Knight, and the courtier sage Tony Minervino, for all being such revolutionary forums on your sacred quests.

My first literary agent, the renowned and highly regarded Ray Richards — an officer and a gentleman, always - who has passed over and has hopefully been sipping some Gewürztraminer with me Dad. Thank you Ray for believing in me at a time when I'd lost touch with feeling lucky.

Oh my father Ron, thank you for your innate judicious wisdom, which this book so unconsciously emanates. Thank you for being there, in my yesterdays, and my todays – and especially for quietly watching over me for years during the night, as most others sleep, energising me through the sacred arrival of each new human being at hundreds of overnight births.

My mother Colleen, for a lifetime of countless acts of service, you truly are an extraordinary person, as everyone who gets to know you soon finds out. Kind, giving, serving, sparkling. It's an honour to be your daughter.

And two extraordinary souls, Heather Bridgford and Jeanette Cahill, who together went completely out of their way to support me during a time of intense powerlessness. Describing them as 'pillars of strength' understates just how much the generosity of their compassionate hearts will always mean to me.

My sister Helen, and her husband Clive, for having had our backs for decades (also always appreciated is their connoisseurs' ability to select a fabulous red).

My brother Phil, as the endless email recipient of partially written chapters of this manuscript, while I paranoically ensured a current manuscript copy was always offsite (before the days of iCloud), and for you just having always been such a bloody good guy. Also to his wife Pam, for her camaraderie in being as insane as I was to attain a university degree in our forties.

Mark's family, for being such a wonderful bunch of genuinely lovely people.

The gorgeous girlfriends, particularly Lisa, Rose, Tanya, Ali, Jane, Jude, Talei, Tanz, Heather, Petra, Anna, Maree, Laurene, Melissa, Michaela, Jody and Adele. OMG, don't we always know how to have a great night! You're all so incredibly special to me, and know me so, so well – greatest of times, saddest of times, for me, and for you. I am so blessed.

All their men too, but especially Shane, Brett, Glenn, Richard, Phil, Bradie, Warwick and Bryce — all such good guys since forever.

And deep, deep luv to the guys and gals who so bloody well should still be on this planet - especially Jim, Mike, Rob, Jacky, Becs - OMG we all miss you so much it aches.

Demons to Darlings super-granny Diane Levy — a writing mentor and friend.

The divine 'Somen-Kusum' Prana Retreat team whose Ohui Lodge construction stirred the energetic life-force of this literary vocation. Tom, you are missed by hundreds of souls you inspired.

The kind, gentle and caring Judith Bone — a midwifery mentor and friend who held my hand when it felt like no-one else would.

To an old girlfriend called Gail Swift, who in her Woodstock-like way, taught me at 15 how to discover who I was, and to like what I found. A true gift that stayed with me forever. I think you know now have much you impacted who I am and what I stand for. If not, I'm just telling you again.

Of course, of course I give *eternal* thanks to the Universe for my darlings, my sweet precious children. Without them in our lives, this book definitely would never have been written — but much more importantly to me, I would have missed out on the most enriching transformations of my life. You're only on loan to us as children, until you spread your wings and fly on your own adventurous journeys — and I'm honoured to be a guide during your odysseys, and even more honoured that you chose us as your parents. Thank you. Thank you. You are the reason I do what I do, and you've made me a much better me.

Richard, with your self-taught dangerous weapons busker's permit for machete twirling, judo nationals silver medal, leadership in the transgender community, and University at only 17 years of age ... deeply intuitive, inherently caring and fervently passionate. You teach the world: you can be anyone you want to be.

Candyce, with your effervescent attitude, who saved $10,000 in 18 months (by working weekends at the local supermarket and fundraising) to travel (aged only 15yrs) to Nicaragua and Costa Rica for a month of jungle treks and humanitarian work ... a dancer and a visionary. You teach the world: you can do anything you want to do.

Angelo, with your academic prowess, sharp *mise en place* knife skills, brilliant dance talent, suave dress sense and charismatic charming of the ladies ... noble, honourable, magnetic. You teach the world: to truly be a manly-man is actually to be a gentle-man.

I remember once reading a book acknowledgement where the author (to whom I sincerely apologise, since I can't recall who it was) thanked her husband for "indulging her endless ideas and flights of fancy". She called him her 'equilibrium'. For me, it is such a brilliant description that I have to say ditto! Thank you, Mark, for being my Equilibrium, for being such a cool and caring dad, for being such a hard working provider, for being such a talented lover, and for being my best friend for over 30 years. I am so blessed!

We absolutely have had our fair share of crap dumped into our lives over the past decades, enough to stretch any marriage to snapping point, but you, my true Rock of Gibraltar, have just kept going, through the sleet and hail. And thank God for that. I truly don't know how I would have got through it all, still sane, without you.

Twenty years ago we 'had it all'. We'd built a beautiful home on a picturesque acreage, our property portfolio was increasing, we had good businesses and a prosperous future. But at that time, we weren't content. Of course not. We planned for more, we longed for more, for the next millisecond of euphoria, always looking ahead, rarely living in the now. At that time, we also well and truly believed we deserved everything we had, because we were a hard-working couple, and none of it had been 'handed to us on a platter'. We completely believed we had created all our own 'good fortune', with barely a shred of 'good luck' involved. We were thirtysomething self-made successes.

Ha! What a fucking joke.

Then it came, what felt like an unfathomable and countless series of inexplicable and unforeseeable incidences of 'bad luck', which went on for many years. A relentless, innumerable succession of unfortunate events — mostly financial, some occupational — which at times appeared to teem down upon us. And guess what — in the early days, we didn't believe we deserved any of it! *'Why is this happening to us?'* I'd plead to the Universe! (And from my 'personal development' phase, I'd recall Norman Vincent Peale's adage 'Whenever God wants to send you a gift, he wraps it up in a problem' and I'd just want to vomit!)

So these were our first big life lessons, *huge* life lessons. 'You don't know what you got until it's gone' was just one of them. Please reader, friend, don't, whatever you do, ever place me on some pedestal of success. Behind every person is their story, the 'thing' they deal with day in day out. We are twenty years down the track later, and still recovering financially. Ours is absolutely nowhere near as difficult as many others journeys that's for sure, and I thank God for that! But it is the living color of our journey. To quote author Barbara Coloroso, 'the seemingly incompatible expressions that are three parts of the whole of living: life is unfair, life hurts, and life is good'.

These days my motto is well known by everyone that knows me well: 'Happiness isn't having what you want, it's wanting what you have'. But man, sometimes, it is tough not to wonder how much easier it could all be, if 'this' was different, or 'that' would change. So I find myself constantly reminding myself that you have to go through ups and downs and highs and lows to arrive at a place where you're finally comfortable with what you have.

These days I try real hard every day, to appreciate every thing that does go well; and I try, real hard every day, to ensure that nothing but goodness goes from me. I'm not perfect at that, for sure. But the difference these days is that I am continuously making conscious, concerted efforts to be a joyful, grateful and gracious person.

These days I try, real hard every day, to remember to thank the Universe for all the wondrous things in my life. My amazing husband, my healthy inspiring children, my caring family, my loyal friends, the safe roof over our heads, the carefree neighbourhood in which we reside, the peaceful country in which we live, my freedom, my health, my family's well-being, my work, my everything. I truly do possess infinite blessings. How is it possible, only two decades ago, that I lived my life so blind to so much goodness?

These days I realise Mark and I deserve all our blessings, just as much as a Sudanese mother deserves to raise her children in a Darfur tent; or as much as abandoned children deserve to be institutionalised as Romanian orphans; or as much as the several dear friends of ours who have lost a child or spouse to diseases and accidents.

These days I truly understand a lot can happen — anything can happen — in a decade or in a moment. 'The more lessons we learn the more business we finish, and the more fully we live, really live life. And no matter when we die, we can say, "God, I have lived!" (Elisabeth Kübler-Ross, *Life Lessons*).

These days I now know, at a soul level, that all my blessings, are only with me in the Now, because any one of them — or even all of them, God help me — could vanish in a moment. 'We are not here to be punished — we are here to be educated' (author Andrew Matthews).

Thus today, I am just beginning to learn not to crave for quite so much any more, to just be more content, to just be Me . . . a work-in-progress.

Love and light,

Namaskar,

Kathy Fray

Bibliography

It is what you read when you don't have to that determines what you will be when you can't help it.

Oscar Wilde (1854–1900), *Irish writer*

Addison, Elaine (2005). *Miss Poppy's Guide to Raising Perfectly Happy Children.* HarperCollins: London.

Allen, K Eileen and Marotz, Lynn R (2000). *By the Ages: Behaviour and development of children pre-birth through eight.* Delmar Thomson Learning: New York.

Arguelles, José (1987). *The Mayan Factor: Path beyond technology.* Traditions- Bear: USA.

Bartlett, Jane (2004). *Parenting With Spirit: 30 ways to nurture your child's spirit and enrich your family's life.*

Marlowe: New York.

Bays, Brandon (2003). *The Journey for Kids: Liberating your child's shining potential.* Element HarperCollins: London.

Beaver, Marion, Brewster, Jo, Jones, Pauline, Keene, Anne, Neaum, Sally and Tallack, Jill (1999). *Babies and Young Children: Book 1 Early years development.* Stanley Thornes: Cheltenham.

Behari, Bepin (2002). *Fundamentals of Vedic Astrology.* Lotus Press: Wisconsin.

Berk, Laura E (2002). *Infants, Children and Adolescents.* Pearson Education: Boston.

Berman, Jenn (2007). *The A to Z Guide to Raising Happy, Confident Kids.* New World Library: Novato, CA.

Biddulph, Steve (1984). *The Secret of Happy Children.* HarperCollins: Australia.

—— (1988). *The Secret of Happy Parents.* Thorsons HarperCollins: London.

—— (1994). *More Secrets of Happy Children.* HarperCollins: Australia.

—— (1997). *Raising Boys: Why boys are different — and how to help them become happy and well-balanced men.* Finch Publishing: Sydney.

Borba, Michele (1999). *Parents Do Make a Difference: How to raise kids with solid character, strong minds, and caring hearts.* Jossey-Bass: San Francisco.

Braden, Gregg (2007). *The Divine Matrix: Bridging time, space, miracles, and belief.* Hay House: London.

—— (2009). *Fractal Time: The secret of 2012 and a new world age.*

Hay House: London.

Burt, Kathleen (2002). *Archetypes of*

the Zodiac. Llewellyn Publications: St Paul.

Butler, Hilary and Peter (2006). *Just a Little Prick.* Robert Reisinger Memorial Trust: New Zealand.

—— (2008). *From One Prick to Another.* Robert Reisinger Memorial Trust: New Zealand.

Byron, Tanya. (2007). *Your Child, Your Way: Create a positive parenting pattern for life.* Michael Joseph: London

Byrne, Lorna (2008). *Angels in My Hair.*

Century Random: London.

Byron, Katie; and Mitchell, Stephen (2002). *Loving What Is: Four questions that can change your life*. Rider: London.

Byron, Tanya (2007). *Your Child, Your Way: Create a positive parenting pattern for life*. Michael Joseph: London.

Byron, Tanya and Baveystock, Sacha (2005). *Little Angels: The essential guide to transforming your family life and having more*. BBC: London.

Calleman, Carl (2001). *Solving the Greatest Mystery of our Time: The Mayan Calendar*. Garev Pub: London.

—— (2004). *The Mayan Calendar and the Transformation of Consciousness*. Bear and Co: Rochester, VT.

Campbell, Don (2000). *The Mozart Effect for Children*. HarperCollins: New York.

Carroll, Lee and Tober, Han (1999) *The Indigo Children: The new kids have arrived*. Hay House: Carlsbad, CA.

Charlesworth, Rosalind (2000).

Understanding Child Development. Delmar Thomson: New York.

Clark, Ron (2004). *The Excellent 11: Qualities teachers and parents use to motivate, inspire and educate children*. Hyperion: New York.

Cloud, Henry and Townsend, John (1999). *Raising Great Kids: Parenting with grace and truth*. Zondervan Pub: Grand Rapids, MI.

Coloroso, Barbara (1994). *Kids Are Worth It! Giving your child the gift of inner discipline*. Avon Books: New York.

Colquhoun, James and ten Bosch, Laurentine. *Food Matters: You are what you eat*. Permacology Productions DVD.

Compain, Glenn (2008). *Street Wise Parenting*. HarperCollins: Auckland.

Cooper, Carol, Halsey, Claire, Laurent, Su and Sullivan, Karen (2008). *Your Child Year By Year: Everything you need to know to raise happy, healthy kids*

— *What to expect from 3 to 14 years.* Dorling Kindersley: London.

Cosby, Bill (1986). *Fatherhood.* Bantam: New York.

—— (1991). *Childhood.* G P Putnam's Sons: New York.

Cox, Robert (1996). *The Pillar of Celestial Fire: The lost science of the ancient seers rediscovered.* 1st World Library: USA.

Crain, William (2003). *Reclaiming Childhood: Letting children be children in our achievement-orientated society.* Owl Henry Holt: New York.

De Botton, Alain (2004). *Status Anxiety.*

Pantheon: New York.

Doherty, William (2003). *Confident Parenting: How to set limits, be considerate and stay in charge.* Finch Pub: Sydney.

Dougan, Abdullah (1987). *Mirrors.*

Ghostic Press: London.

Eadie, Betty J (1992). *Embraced by the Light.* Element HarperCollins: London.

Emoto, Masaru (2004). *The Hidden Messages in Water.* Beyond Words: Hillsboro, OR.

Faulkner, Paul (1995). *Raising Faithful Kids in a Fast-paced World.* Howard Publishing: West Monroe, LA.

Foundation for Inner Peace (1996). *A Course in Miracles.* Viking: New York.

Friel, John and Linda (1999). *The Seven Worst Things Parents Do.* Health Communications: Deerfield Beach, FL.

Fray, Kathy (2005). *Oh Baby . . . Birth, babies and motherhood uncensored*. Random House: Auckland.

—— (2010). *Oh God — What the Hell do I Tell Them?! The guide for vaguely spiritual parents*. Triple-X: Auckland. Gelb, Michael (2004). *Da Vinci Decoded:*

Discovering the spiritual secrets of Leonardo's seven principles. Delacorte Press: New York.

Gottman, John and DeClaire, Joan (1997). *The Heart of Parenting: Raising an emotionally intelligent child*. Simon and Schuster: New York.

Grabhorn, Lynn (2000). *Excuse Me, Your Life is Waiting: The astonishing power of feelings*. Hampton Roads: Charlottesville, VA.

Grant, Ian (2006). *Growing Great Boys: 100s of practical strategies for bringing out the best in your son*. Random House: Auckland.

Grant, Ian and Mary (2008). *Growing Great Girls: 100s of practical strategies for bringing out the best in your daughter*. Random House: Auckland.

Grille, Robin (2005). *Parenting for a Peaceful World*. Longueville Media: Alexandria, NSW.

Gurian, Michael (2002). *The Wonder of Girls: Understanding the hidden nature of our daughters*. Pocket: New York.

—— (2004). *The Wonder of Children: Nurturing the souls of our sons and daughters*. Atria: New York.

—— (2007). *Nurture the Nature: Understanding and supporting your child's unique core personality*. Jossey- Bass: San Francisco.

Gurian, Michael and Stevens, Kathy (2005). *The Minds of Boys: Saving our sons from falling behind in school and life*. Jossey-Bass: San Francisco.

Hall, Judy (2003). *The Crystal Bible: A definitive guide to crystals*. Walking Stick Press: Cincinnati.

Harrison, Harry (2003). *Father to Daughter: Life lessons on raising a girl*. Workman Publishing: New York.

Harrison, Harry and Harrison, Melissa (2005). *Mother to Daughter: Shared wisdom from the heart*. Workman Publishing: New York.

Haslam, David (1995). *Food Fights: A practical guide for parents worried about their children's eating habits*. Cedar: London.

Hicks, Esther and Jerry (Abraham — Spirit) (2002). *Ask and It Is Given: Learning to manifest your desires*. Hay House: Carlsbad, CA.

—— (2007). *The Law of Attraction: The basics of the teachings of Abraham*. Hay House: Carlsbad, CA.

Hochschild, Adam (2005). *Bury the Chains: Prophets and rebels in the fight to free an empire's slaves*. Houghton Miflin: Boston, MA.

Hogue, John (1997). *Nostradamus: The complete prophecies*. Element: Shaftesbury, Dorset.

Hogue, John. (1998). *The Last Pope: The decline and fall of the Church of Rome: The prophecies of Saint Malachy for the new millennium*. Element: Shaftesbury, Dorset.

—— (1999). *Messiahs: The visions and prophecies for the Second Coming*. Element: Shaftesbury, Dorset.

Hurtak, JJ (2004). *The Book of Knowledge: The keys to Enoch*. The Academy for Future Science: USA.

Isaacs, Susan (1932). *The Children We Teach: Seven to eleven years*. London University Press.

—— (1968). *Children and Parents: Their problems and difficulties*. Routledge and Kegan Paul: London.

Jenkins, John Major and McKenna, Terence (1998). *Maya Cosmogenesis 2012: The true meaning of the Maya Calendar end date*. Inner Tradition's Bear & Company: Rochester, VT.

Kabat-Zinn, Myla and Jon (1997). *Everyday Blessings: The inner work of mindful parenting.* Hyperion: New York.

Karp, Harvey (2004). *The Happiest Toddler on the Block: The new ways to stop the daily battle of wills and raise a secure and well-behaved one- to four-year-old.* Bantam Random: New York.

Katie, Byron (2002). *Loving What Is: Four questions that can change your life.* Rider Ebury Random: London.

Kedgley, Susan (1998). *Eating Safely in a Toxic World: What really is in the food we eat.* Penguin: Auckland.

Kitzinger, Sheila and Celia (2000). *Talking With Children about Things that Matter.* Pandora: London.

Klein, Mavis. *Understanding Your Child: A–Z for parents.* Piatkus: London.

Kübler-Ross, Elisabeth (2000). *Life Lessons: How our mortality can teach us about life and living.* Simon and Schuster: London.

LaHaye, Tim and Jenkins, Jerry (1995). *Left Behind: A novel of the earth's last days.* Tyndale House: Wheaton, IL.

Lashlie, Celia (2005). *He'll Be OK: Growing gorgeous boys into good men.* HarperCollins: Auckland.

Latta, Nigel (2006). *Before Your Kids Drive you Crazy, Read This! Battlefield wisdom for stressed out parents.* HarperCollins: Auckland.

—— (2008). *Before Your Teenagers Drive You Crazy, Read This! Battlefield wisdom for stressed out parents.* HarperCollins: Auckland.

Leigh, Richard, Baigent, Michael and Lincoln, Henry (1996). *The Holy Blood and the Holy Grail.* Arrow: London.

Leman, Kevin and Bell, Kathy Flores (2004). *A Chicken's Guide to Talking Turkey with Your Kids about Sex.* Zondervan: USA.

Levy, Diane (2002). *Of Course I Love You . . . NOW GO TO YOUR ROOM!*

Strategies for raising toddlers to teens in New Zealand. Random House: Auckland.

Lindsey, Hal (1989). *The Road to Holocaust.* Bantam: New York.

Littauer, Florence (1988). *Raising Christians — Not Just Children.* Word Publishing: Dallas.

Littauer, Marita (1991). *Home-made Memories: Making memories that matter.* Harvest House: Oregon.

Livingstone, Tessa (2005). *Child of Our Time: How to achieve the best for your child from conception to 5 years.* Transworld Bantam: London.

Loomans, Diana and Godoy, Julia (2005). *What All Children Want Their Parents to Know: 12 keys to raising a happy child.* Kramer New World: California.

Lopez, Lani (2004). *Natural Health: A New Zealand A to Z guide.* David Bateman: Auckland.

MacDonald, Glynn (1998). *The Complete Illustrated Guide to the Alexander Technique.* Element Books: Shaftesbury, Dorset.

Macfie, Rebecca (2008). 'Show Me The Child: The shaping of personality.' *NZ Listener*, Jan 19–25, 2008, pp 16–22.

Martin, Andrew. (2005). *How to Help Your Child Fly through Life: The 20 big issues.* Bantam: Sydney.

Melody (1995). *Love Is in the Earth: A kaleidoscope of crystals.* Earth-Love: Wheat Ridge, CO.

Millman, Dan (1980). *Way of the Peaceful Warrior: A book that changes lives.* H J Kramer: Tiburon CA.

—— (1993). *The Life You Were Born to Live: A guide to finding your life purpose.* Kramer New World Library: Tiburon, CA.

—— (1995). *The Laws of Spirit: A tale of transformation: powerful truths for making life work*. H J Kramer New World Library: California.

Moody, Raymond (1975). *Life After Life*. HarperCollins: San Francisco.

Murrin, Kristina and Martin, Paul (2004). *What Worries Parents: The most common concerns of parents explored and explained*. Vermillion: London.

Myss, Caroline (1996). *Anatomy of the Spirit: The seven stages of power and healing*. Harmony: New York.

—— (2001). *Sacred Contracts: Awakening your divine potential*. Bantam: Sydney.

Northrup, Christine (2005). *Mother- Daughter Wisdom: Creating a legacy of physical and emotional health*. BantamDell Random: New York.

Pert, Candace (1997). *Molecules of Emotion: Why you feel the way you feel*. Scribner: New York.

Phillips, David (1992). *Secrets of the Inner Self: The complete book of numerology*. Pythagorean Press: Australia.

Pignéguy, Dee and Tamarin (2007). *Feed Me Right: Nutritional know-how and body science*. Papawai Press: Auckland.

Pollack, William and Shuster, Todd (2001). *Real Boys' Voices*. Random House: New York.

Pratt, Steven and Matthews, Kathy (2004). *SuperFoods: Fourteen foods that will change your life*. William Morrow HarperCollins: New York.

Renard, Gary (2004). *The Disappearance of the Universe: Straight talk about illusions, past Lives, religions, sex, politics, and the miracles of forgiveness*. Hay House: Carlsbad, CA.

Rinpoche, Sogyal (1992). *The Tibetan Book of Living and Dying*. Harper: San Francisco.

Roizen, Michael and Mehmet, C Oz (2006). *You the Smart Patient: An insider's handbook for getting the best treatment.* Free Press: New York.

Rose, Sharron (2003). *The Path of the Priestess.* Sacred Mysteries Books: USA.

Rosemond, John (1989). *Six-Point Plan for Raising Happy, Healthy Children.* Andrews and McMeel: Kansas City.

Rosenfeld, Alvin and Wise, Nicole (2000). *The Over-scheduled Child: Avoiding the hyper-parenting trap.* St Martin's Gri n: New York.

Ruiz, Miguel (1997). *The Four Agreements: A practical guide to personal freedom.* Amber-Allen: San Rafael, CA.

Salikhova, Eva-Maria (2007). *You Shut Up! Re-defining Teenager.* Axas: Wellington.

Sasse, Margaret (2009). *Smart Start: How exercise can transform your child's life.* Exisle: Wolombi, NSW.

Sax, Leonard (2007). *Boys Adrift: The five factors driving the growing epidemic of unmotivated boys and underachieving young men.* Basic Perseus Books: New York.

Schaefer, Dr Charles E and DiGeronimo, Theresa Foy (2000). *Ages and Stages: A Parent's guide to normal childhood development.* John Wiley and Sons: New York.

Schlessinger, Laura (2001). *Stupid Things Parents Do to Mess up Their Kids.* Cli Street Books: USA.

Scroufe, L Alan, Egeland, Byron, Carlson Elizabeth A and Collins, W Andrew (2005). *The Development of the Person: The Minnesota study of risk and adaptation from birth to adulthood.* Guilford Press: New York.

Scroufe, L. Alan, Cooper, Robert G and DeHart, Ganie B (1992). *Child Development: Its nature and course.* McGraw-Hill: New York.

Sears, William and Martha (2005). *The Good Behaviour Book: How* to have a better-behaved child from birth to age ten. Thorsons: London.

Shapiro, Lawrence E (1997). *How to Raise a Child with a High EQ (Emotional Quotient): A parents' guide to emotional intelligence.* HarperCollins: New York.

—— (2003). *The Secret Language of Children: How to understand what your kids are really saying.* Sourcebooks: Naperville, IL.

Siegel, Daniel and Hartzell, Mary (2004). *Parenting from the Inside Out: How a deeper self-understanding can help you raise children who thrive.* JP Tarcher Putnam: New York.

Simmons, Rachel (2004). *Odd Girl Speaks Out: Girls write about bullies, cliques, popularity, and jealousy.* Schwartz Pub: Melbourne.

Singer, Peter and Mason, Jim (2006). *The Ethics of What We Eat.* Text Publishing: Melbourne.

Solter, Aletha (2006). *Raising Drug-free Kids: 100 tips for parents.* Da Capa Perseus: Cambridge, MA.

Spiller, Jan and McCoy, Karen (1985). *Spiritual Astrology.* Simon and Schuster: New York.

Stefanino, Olivia (2007). Be Your *Own Guru: Personal and business enlightenment in just 3 days.* Blackwell-Wiley: Australia.

Stray, Geo and Jenkins, John Major (2009). *Beyond 2012: Catastrophe or awakening: A complete guide to end-of- time predictions.* Tradition-Bear: VT.

Sullivan, Karen (2003). *How to Say 'No' and Mean It: Survival skills for parents.* Thorsons: London.

—— (2007). *You Want To Do What? Instant answers to your parenting dilemmas.* HarperCollins: London.

Sullivan, Karen and Shealy, C Norman (1997). *The Complete Family Guide to Natural Home Remedies: Safe and effective treatments for common ailments*. Element: Shaftesbury, UK.

Sunderland, Margot (2006). *What Every Parent Needs to Know: The remarkable effects of love, nurture and play on your child's development.* Dorling Kindersley: London.

Taylor, Jim (2005). *Your Children are Under Attack: How popular culture is destroying your kids' values and how you can protect them.* Sourcebooks: Naperville, IL.

Timms, Moira (1996). *Beyond Prophecies and Predictions.* Random Ballantine: New York.

Tolle, Eckhart (2001). *The Power of Now.* New World Library: Novato, CA.

—— (2003). *Stillness Speaks.* New World Library (California) and Nameste Publishing (Vancouver).

Tolman, Don (2005). *Farmacist Desk Reference: Encyclopedia of whole food medicine.* Benacquista: USA.

Tynan, Bernadette (2008). *Make Your Child Brilliant: Uncovering your child's hidden talents.* Quadrille Electric Sky: London.

Villoldo, Alberto (2006). *The Four Insights: Wisdom, power and grace of the EarthKeepers.* Hay House: Carlsbad, CA.

Virtue, Doreen (2003). *The Crystal Children: A guide to the newest generation of psychic and sensitive children.* Hay House: Carlsbad, CA.

—— (2004). *Angel Medicine: How to heal the body and mind with the help of the angels.* Hay House: Carlsbad, CA.

—— (2006). *Angels 101: An introduction to connection, working, and healing with angels.* Hay House: Carlsbad, CA.

Wallis, Glenn (2004). *The Dhammapada: Verses on The Way: A new translation of the teachings of the Buddha, with a guide to reading the text.* Modern Library: New York.

Walsch, Neale Donald (2001). *Conversations with God for Teens.* Hampton Roads: Charlottesville, VA.

—— (2002). *The New Revelations: A conversation with God.* Atria Simon and Schuster: New York.

Walsh, David (2004). *Why Do They Act That Way? A survival guide to the adolescent brain for you and your teen.* Free Press Simon and Schuster: New York.

Williamson, Marianne (1995). *Illuminata: Thoughts, prayers, rites of passage.* Rider: London.

—— (2004). *The Gift of Change: Spiritual guidance for a radically new life.* Harper: San Francisco.

Winston, Robert (2003). *The Human Mind: And how to make the most of it.* Transworld Random: London.

—— (2004). *What makes me me?* Dorling Kindersley: London.

Winston, Robert (ed.) (2004). *Human: The definitive visual guide.* Penguin Dorling Kindersley: London.

Wolfe, Sidney M, Sasich, Larry D Lurie, Peter, Hope, Rose-Ellen, Barbehenn, Elizabeth et al., Public Citizens' Health Resource Group (2005). *Worst Pills, Best Pills: A consumer's guide to avoiding drug-induced death or illness.* Pocket Simon and Schuster: New York.

Zukav, Gary (1990). *The Seat of the Soul.* Fireside Simon and Schuster: New York.

Read not to contradict and confute; nor to believe and take for granted; nor to find talk and discourse, but to weigh and consider.

Sir Francis Bacon (1562–1626),
English philosopher and writer

Also by Kathy Fray:

www.ingramcontent.com/pod-product-compliance
Lightning Source LLC
Chambersburg PA
CBHW071951290426
44109CB00018B/1988